Deleting "elect" in the Bible

A reasonable historical case for removal of the word "elect" in the English Bible

Also by Jacques More

Will there be Non-Christians in heaven?
Leadership is Male?
So you think you're chosen?
Revival – The Battleplan
Serious Mistranslations of the Bible

Deleting “elect” in the Bible

A reasonable historical case for removal of the word “elect” in the English Bible

By Jacques More

JAROM BOOKS

First published in Great Britain 2015

ISBN 978 1 898158 25 7

See adjoining page for copyrights of other bible versions

Cover design by
Grange Graphics Ltd

Printed and bound in UK

www.jarom.net

All quotes and direct English translation from
The Septuagint – LXX are taken from
THE SEPTUAGINT WITH APOCRYPHA: GREEK AND ENGLISH
by Sir Lancelot C.L. Brenton and published by Hendrikson
Originally published in1851

Word searches in the LXX were taken from
A CONCORDANCE OF THE SEPTUAGINT
compiled by George Morrish and published by Zondervan
First published in 1887

To David Pawson

David is a bible teacher and author of many books

CONTENTS

PASSAGES AFFECTED

Ref.[1]	OT Heb.	KJV
2 Samuel 21:6	BACHIR	choose
1 Chronicles 16:13	BACHIR	chosen
Psalm 89:3	BACHIR	chosen
Psalm 105:6	BACHIR	chosen
Psalm 105:43	BACHIR	chosen
Psalm 106:5	BACHIR	chosen
Psalm 106:23	BACHIR	chosen
Isaiah 42:1	BACHIR	elect
Isaiah 43:20	BACHIR	chosen
Isaiah 45:4	BACHIR	elect
Isaiah 65:9	BACHIR	elect
Isaiah 65:15	BACHIR	chosen
Isaiah 65:22	BACHIR	elect
	NT Gk.	
Matthew 20:16[2]	*EKLEKTOS*	chosen
Matthew 22:14	*EKLEKTOS*	chosen
Matthew 24:22	*EKLEKTOS*	elect
Matthew 24:24	*EKLEKTOS*	elect
Matthew 24:31	*EKLEKTOS*	elect
Mark 13:20	*EKLEKTOS*	elect
Mark 13:22	*EKLEKTOS*	elect
Mark 13:27	*EKLEKTOS*	elect
Luke 18:7	*EKLEKTOS*	elect
Luke 23:35	*EKLEKTOS*	chosen
Romans 8:33	*EKLEKTOS*	elect
Romans 16:13	*EKLEKTOS*	chosen
Colossians 3:12	*EKLEKTOS*	elect
1 Timothy 5:21	*EKLEKTOS*	elect
2 Timothy 2:10	*EKLEKTOS*	elect
Titus 1:1	*EKLEKTOS*	elect
1 Peter 1:2 (Gk. 1:1)	*EKLEKTOS*	elect
1 Peter 2:4	*EKLEKTOS*	chosen
1 Peter 2:6	*EKLEKTOS*	elect
1 Peter 2:9	*EKLEKTOS*	chosen
2 John 1	*EKLEKTOS*	elect
2 John 13	*EKLEKTOS*	elect
Revelation 17:14	*EKLEKTOS*	chosen

[1]For a full list of abbreviations see the end folio
[2]KJV, YLT, NKJV

Deleting "elect" in the Bible

A reasonable historical case for removal of the word "elect" in the English Bible

The word "elect" is perhaps the foremost word in the bible identified with the teaching of Calvinism. Calvinism is the name commonly used to identify the doctrine of unconditional predestination to salvation of individuals: the "elect" are said to have been picked by God before their existence, to be saved, and all others lost. This whole work is about the word "elect" in the English bible.

Etymology is the study of words. Since history is central to that study, the case for "elect" to be removed as a word is an etymological case.

Hebrew (Heb.[1]) and Greek (Gk.) are the two main languages in which the bible is found. Aramaic was used for some portions, mainly of Daniel and Ezra, but as a whole, what we now call the Old Testament (OT) was first written in Heb. All of the New Testament (NT) was written in Gk. You will read that during the first centuries of Christianity there was another meaning for the Heb. and the Gk. words from which "elect" has been lately translated.

It is a reasonable case.

Step by step reasonable claims are made from the evidence of the exhaustive study out of the Septuagint (LXX): the first bible of the early Church. To the LXX was added the letters and gospels which then made up the NT: together the LXX and the NT documents were recognised as the Christian's Scripture.

The main historical source for this work is the LXX.

Now, the word "chosen" (77 in OT) and "choose" (also 77 in OT) is found plentifully from the Heb. word BACHAR[2] (total 172) in the OT and equally so from the Gk. words *EKLEGÓ*[2] (113 in LXX; 21 in NT),

---

1 For a full list of abbreviations see the end pages

2 All Heb. and Gk. words are Anglicised and in capitals with the added variation of italics to identify Gk. Words from Heb. words (cf. format information below)

and *HAIRETIZÓ* (12 in LXX; 1 in NT). So that the verb "to choose" is present and it's derivative "chosen", both from the Heb. and the Gk. irrespective of this work on the source words for "elect". The concept of "selected" however, was not read at that time – for about the first 300 years of the Church - in the passages where today we find "elect" (20), "chosen" (15) or, "choose" (1) translated from the Heb. word BACHIR (13) in the OT and from the Gk. word *EKLEKTOS* (23) in the NT. And, since the word "elect" is only translated from BACHIR (4) or *EKLEKTOS* (16) in English (Eng.) bibles, it is these two source words that are in the spotlight.

[20 + 15 + 1 = 13 + 23]

This is about the word "elect" then, and the word "chosen": It is about the idea of a selection, a choosing having occurred as the meaning coming from the two source words: BACHIR in the Heb. and *EKLEKTOS* in the Gk. But, since the word "chosen", is itself legitimately present from the source words BACHAR and *EKLEGÓ*, for the sake of bringing the matter to the attention of the Saints - the Church, and the word "elect" only translated from BACHIR and *EKLEKTOS*, as well as "elect" being an integral part of a doctrine still extant in the Church, it is of prime interest and value to introduce and conclude this matter by a focus on the word "elect".

The study

This study (or "work") uses as its primary source the first bible used by the early Christians, commonly named as the Septuagint (LXX): The name we give to the translation of the Hebrew OT into the Gk. of the day. Alongside the LXX is used a number of Eng. translations of the Heb. OT. These together make up the source documents. To help dig into these there are concordances which help search these sources.

Before the letters and gospels by the followers of Jesus became part of the NT and then added to the OT, to thus fully complete the Christian Scripture, the LXX was their sole bible. The NT was composed in the same language that the LXX was written in. It is thereby reasonable to expect that the meaning of Gk. words in the LXX is the way they are used in the NT. So this study, in identifying what *EKLEKTOS* meant to the LXX translators, informs us what the word means in the NT.

The LXX text is compared in this work with how the Heb. was translated into Eng. in the KJV and frequently the YLT. Other versions are also checked occasionally, and most of them if not all, as a reasonable cross section of most versions, where it is needful for the analysis. This cross section of Eng. versions is made up of the NKJV, the NASB, the NIV and the NLT and added to the KJV and YLT. The looking at the way the Heb. is translated into Eng. thus provides an independent means by which to observe what *EKLEKTOS* meant to the LXX translator. Since, as is shown, BACHIR is the only Heb. word translated as "elect" and every occasion (13) that it occurs, it is found translated by *EKLEKTOS* in the LXX, these two words are unequivocally tied to each other. The look at *EKLEKTOS* therefore, by the independent reasonable observations of the translation of the Heb. connected words, is the means whereby we can learn what the LXX translators used *EKLEKTOS* for and thus also BACHIR, and thereby fully identify if "elect" – a "chosen" emphasis - is a valid representation: this identification is thus relevant in any part of the bible. *EKLEKTOS* thus informs us on the meaning of BACHIR as far as the LXX translators were concerned.

As an additional testimony to how *EKLEKTOS* was used in the early church: as an affirmation of the study's outcome, I also quote the 1st century letter written by Clement (known as his first) to the Corinthian church.

How did I get here?

In the Nineties [in 1994 or 1995] I first read *God's Strategy in Human History* by Roger T. Forster and V. Paul Marston (published by Highland Books 1989). I read (pages 130 and 143) that *EKLEKTOS* was used in the LXX where the Heb. was rendered as "**choice silver**" (Proverbs 8:19). Now, since *EKLEKTOS* was only (presently) translated as "**chosen**" or "**elect**" in the NT, I thought this could be significant and wanted to check this out for myself. I called my friend Dave Lock who managed *Manna Christian Centre* in Streatham, London, and I asked whether he could get me a copy of the LXX. He mentioned that he had a copy that had been ordered, but was never paid for or collected. And, would I like a concordance to go with that?!

It just "happened" that he had a LXX as well as a concordance of Gk. words to be found in the LXX. Terrific!

My first study of this made me see that this rendering of *EKLEKTOS* in Proverbs 8:19 was accurate. It indeed stood there for quality silver. I also quickly found by using the concordance of the LXX that this high quality idea was the most common use for *EKLEKTOS* and identified it as such for an undisputed 52 times[3].

Publishing this information as a booklet in 2002 I took care to openly show every place where the word was found in the LXX and compare it with how the Hebrew word, from which it came, was equally given in the KJV. The Bible Society purchased a number of copies. The booklet is out of print, but in 2009 I reproduced all the contents of the booklet as an appendix in my book *So you think you're chosen?* - a comprehensive response to Calvinism. Since all this work covered all the places where *EKLEKTOS* was in the LXX and how its Heb. counterpart was translated by the KJV, it thereby included all the other renderings different from a high quality idea (as at 1st glance): i.e. The 52 undisputed connection with "quality" as well as the 23 connected with the KJV "chosen" type: all out of the 75[3] directly translated from the Heb. words.

To address the apparent "chosen" idea within the next study of this, in my book *SERIOUS* (see end pages abbreviation list), I highlighted the different Gk. words for "chosen" and the verb "to choose" and also added a further analysis to help show *EKLEKTOS* should not also be represented by "chosen". This further analysis was not however, also backed up and thus demonstrated fully, by a comprehensive body of source work to help show all the reality of the disconnection from "chosen" or "to choose". This current work does. Here is an exhaustive look at all places of every Heb. word, which was identified as translated by *EKLEKTOS* in the LXX.

So that, this assembly of words is 85% reference material and only 15% of introduction, analysis and arguments. The 85% taken up by the reference section, as I call it, is over half commentary and literal word for

3 As you read on you will see 52 out of 75 is now corrected to 51 out of a 74 total cf. The Analysis

word translation work of the LXX Gk. text. That means overall the book is less than 50% a direct quoting of various bible versions as follows: the LXX text in Gk, a full translation of that and the Heb. rendered by up to 6 Eng. bible versions with the KJV and the YLT the main versions and these sometimes joined by the NKJV, NASB, NIV and NLT.

The Eng. bible versions serve as an independent verification element and is necessary to validate the discovery and observation of meaning sought out of the LXX.

The current work

This is a pre look at some of what you will find from the analysis.

What this current work does is establish reasonable ground for seeing there is no valid case to use "**chosen**" for *EKLEKTOS* and thereby "**elect**". It goes further in analysis than in *SERIOUS* as it is exhaustive in looking at the LXX. It is not just the places where *EKLEKTOS* is found that are looked at, but every place where any of the Heb. words rendered by *EKLEKTOS* are found everywhere else.

That *EKLEKTOS* cannot be used for "**chosen**" – a "selected" idea - is as clear as that for *NEANIAS* "**young man**" having nothing to do with being "selected". And yet *NEANIAS* (young man, youth - 4), *NEANISKOS* (young man, boy - 1) and *DUNATOS* (strong, mighty - 4) are used, like *EKLEKTOS* (8), to translate the Hebrew word BACHAR (to choose) and "**chosen**". If there were a place where *EKLEKTOS* could be seen to mean "chosen" it would be with BACHAR, but instead, it is shown identical in use to *NEANIAS, NEANISKOS* and *DUNATOS*.

Then, in view of the Hebrew word BACHIR only translated by *EKLEKTOS* in the LXX and with the meaning of "**chosen**" for *EKLEKTOS* removed everywhere else, a reasonable view arises of the LXX translators of the Hebrew Scripture not seeing "**chosen**" at all in BACHIR, but instead with a meaning of "high quality: to be chosen: preferred: excellent".

The 1st century Christian then, in only using the LXX in Gk. as his bible, with the added gospels and letters from the apostles and partners also in Gk., he could not read "**elect**" – a selected idea - since in only reading Greek, *EKLEKTOS* would be seen in all the current places where we now have "**elect**".

This work thereby, by the exhaustive look at the way all the Heb. words connected with *EKLEKTOS* are given: both in the way the Hebrew words are rendered in Eng. and, by all the Gk. words employed in the LXX for the same Heb. words: effectively closes the door shut to "**chosen**" (selected) as a valid meaning for both *EKLEKTOS* and BACHIR: thus showing the word "**elect**" should not be in the bible.

An exceptional example

It is of note in the history of bible translation that there is a significant exception in regards to the modern rendering of *EKLEKTOS*. Robert Young (Ys) who, in producing both his *Analytical Concordance* (Conc. - 1879) and his *Young's Literal Translation of the Holy Bible* (YLT - 1862) is recognised as having done much study of word meanings. For "**elect**" the recommendation he gives, is to think (*read*) "**choice one**" – he gives this in an *Explanation of Bible Terms*: a list of 100 bible terms in the introduction to the NT - and indeed, he goes further by translating it that way also in a number of places.

For example his good rendering of 1 Peter 1:1

"Peter, an apostle of Jesus Christ, to the choice [*EKLEKTOS*] **sojourners of the dispersion of Pontus, Galatia, Cappadocia, Asia, and Bithynia, according to a foreknowledge of God the Father, in sanctification of the Spirit, to obedience and sprinkling of the blood of Jesus Christ: Grace to you and peace be multiplied!"** ***1 Peter 1:1-2 YLT***

This is a world apart from:

"Peter, an apostle of Jesus Christ, to the strangers scattered throughout Pontus, Galatia, Cappadocia, Asia, and Bithynia, Elect [*EKLEKTOS*] **according to the foreknowledge of God the Father, through sanctification of the Spirit, unto obedience and sprinkling of the blood of Jesus Christ: Grace unto you, and peace, be multiplied."** ***1 Peter 1:1-2 KJV***

Also note the re-arrangement of the words in the KJV to give an emphasis not seen in the Greek: A re-arrangement which has been repeated in other versions like the NKJV and the NASB. It is good to see the arrangement is correct in the NIV and the NLT.

Here is a rough interlinear with the same Greek text as the KJV, NKJV and YLT showing the YLT follows the arrangement well.

1 Peter 1:1-2 Gk. RT

PETROS APOSTOLOS IÉSOU CHRISTOU EKLEKTOIS PAREPIDÉMOIS
Peter apostle of Jesus Christ to choice sojourners

DIASPORAS PONTOU GALATIAS
of dispersion of Pontus Galatia

KAPPADOKIAS ASIAS KAI BITHUNIAS KATA PROGNÓSIN THEOU
Cappadocia Asia and Bithynia according to foreknowledge of God

PATROS EN HAGIASMÓ PNEUMATOS
Father in holy-ing of Spirit

EIS HUPAKOÉN KAI RANTISMON HAIMATOS IÉSOU CHRISTOU
into obedience and sprinkling of blood of Jesus Christ

CHARIS HUMIN KAI EIRÉNÉ PLÉTHUNTHEIÉ
Grace to you and peace be multiplied

THE SEPTUAGINT

So what is the Septuagint?

The first language the bible was written in is Hebrew. Then Greek came along.

As was shown prophetically to Daniel c534BC a number of things would happen. A king would arise, as represented by bronze as part of a statue in a dream (Dan. 2:39). This king would take over the kingdom that had overrun king Nebuchadnezzar whom Daniel knew. Nebuchadnezzar was represented by the head of gold in the statue. Then there was the chest and arms made of silver, a 2nd kingdom. Then its belly and thighs made of bronze, a 3rd new kingdom.

The succeeding revelations given Daniel inform him a little more about each character in the first prophecy. A little later this new 3rd kingdom was then shown Daniel as represented as a leopard with four wings and four heads (Dan. 7:6). The next representation of this kingdom given Daniel was as a male goat coming from the West with a large horn that was then superseded by four smaller ones (Dan. 8:5-8). Daniel was told "**And the male goat *is* the kingdom of Greece. The large horn that *is* between its eyes *is* the first king. As for the broken *horn* and the four that stood up in its place, four kingdoms shall arise out of that nation, but not with its power.**" (Dan. 8:21-22 NKJV).

In 334BC Alexander the Great was the large horn, the great king from Greece. In that year he first invaded the Persian Empire that had indeed overrun the Babylonian one which Daniel knew for himself. Alexander conquered the known world. Then following his demise, Alexander's rule was divided into four. Just as per the prophecy over two hundred years earlier. The then stable ongoing government in these four regions meant that Greek became the dominant language, not just for administration of civil government, but also all commerce and trade. This led to the need being seen for a translation of the Hebrew scripture into Greek. And this task is understood to have been completed in the middle of the 3rd century BC. Josephus (37-100AD) the Jewish historian who worked under Titus (39-81AD) relates the story that 72 scholars did the job of translating and it appears to be from this idea that the name Septuagint arose for this translation of the OT Heb. scripture.

The significance of the Septuagint

The New Testament is what gives the most authority to the Septuagint for Christians. It is now readily recognised that the translation of the Hebrew Scripture in the LXX is not inspired like the original authorship of the Hebrew text. A cursory look at the contents of this current work shows many direct translated sections in the LXX, but equally many divergent sections. The passages quoted in the NT however, indicate by that inclusion in the sacred text, their very real value, let alone the reality of its existence. A testified existence predating the Christian era is also seen with manuscripts of the LXX found in the Dead Sea Scrolls. But, for the Christian the LXX quoted by Jesus and the apostles indicates not just their familiarity with its text, but that their own use of the same words elsewhere in the NT, as found in the LXX, gives weight to those very words meaning the same. Moreover the first centuries of the Christian Church saw believers only read the LXX and the NT gospels and epistles in the one Greek language. At that early time there was no need for a translation as all the world of the day spoke Greek. This was so for the first centuries of the Church as can be seen with the first universal Church Council of Nicea in 325AD which saw all the proceedings in Greek. So we can see this was how they read the NT: with the Gk. words there meaning the same as those read in the LXX. This is the prime use of the LXX here. In identifying the meaning given or understood by a word used in the LXX this is how it should be read in the NT. Equally in seeing this use beyond reasonable doubt for *EKLEKTOS*, then with the use of BACHIR firmly grounded in that appreciation, we are bound to recognise both words as having been mistranslated in recent times, indeed since those first centuries.

Jesus and the apostles' use of the LXX

I've largely borrowed this portion from my earlier work in *SERIOUS*.

Matthew 4:10

Jesus said to the Devil in the wilderness:

> **Away with you, Satan! For it is written, '*You shall worship the LORD your God, and Him only you shall serve.*'**
>
> ***Matthew 4:10 NKJV***

The LXX contains the words *KAI AUTÓ MONÓ* in Eng. "***and Him only***", and this "***only***" translated from Deuteronomy 6:13 is not found in the Heb.

Because our OT is translated from the original Heb. the word "***only***" cannot be read in the OT passage of our modern bible.

As we can see:

> **You shall fear the LORD your God and serve Him, and shall take oaths in His name.** ***Deuteronomy 6:13 NKJV***

The word "***only***" is not there. This vouches therefore for Matthew and Jesus' use of the LXX. It vouches for Luke too, who quotes Jesus saying the same thing against the Devil "**and Him only you shall you serve**" (Luke 4:8 NKJV).

Matthew 15:8-9

> ***'These people draw near to Me with their mouth, and honor Me with their lips, but their heart is far from Me. And in vain they worship Me, teaching as doctrines the commandments of men.'*** ***Matthew 15:8-9 NKJV***

Here is a quote by Jesus primarily of Isaiah 29:13. Similar sentiments are found in Psalm 78:36-37 and Ezekiel 33:31. The Heb. does not contain "***in vain they worship Me***" whilst it is there in the Septuagint: *MATÉN DE DEBONTAI ME*

John

John quotes Isaiah 53:1 like this:

> ***'Lord, who has believed our report? And to whom has the arm of the Lord been revealed?'*** ***John 12:38 NKJV***

The translated Hebrew version in our bibles has:

> **Who has believed our report? And to whom has the arm of the Lord been revealed?** ***Isaiah 53:1 NKJV***

The passage begins without "***Lord***" in the Heb.; it is there in the LXX which John is quoting.

Paul

A good example of Paul's use of the LXX:

> **Beloved, do not avenge yourselves, but *rather* give place to wrath; for it is written, '*Vengeance is Mine, I will repay,*' says the Lord. '*Therefore if your enemy hungers, feed him; if he thirsts, give him a drink; for in so doing you will heap coals of fire on his head.*'** ***Romans 12:19-20 NKJV***

This latter OT quote is direct from Proverbs 25:21-22. The Gk. is exactly the same in the LXX as the NT text whilst in the Heb. text and our Bibles Proverbs 25:21-22 reads,

> **If your enemy is hungry, give him bread to eat; and if he is thirsty, give him water to drink; for *so* you will heap coals of fire on his head . . .** ***Proverbs 25:21-22 NKJV***

Paul makes no mention of "**bread**" or "**water**" but it is clearly there in the Heb. Equally he mentions "***in so doing***" which is in the LXX and nowhere in the Heb. This common use of the LXX by the NT writers makes it a valuable resource for appreciating the meaning of words in the language of the NT.

Peter

A good example of Peter's use of the LXX:

> ***All flesh is as grass, and all the glory of man as the flower of the grass. The grass withers, and its flower falls away, but the word of the LORD endures forever.*** ***1 Peter 1:24-25 NKJV***

This is a quote of Isaiah 40:6-8. In our bibles translated from the Heb. this reads,

> **All flesh *is* grass, and all its loveliness *is* like the flower of the field. The grass withers, the flower fades, because the breath of the LORD blows upon it; surely the people *are* grass. The grass withers, the flower fades, but the word of our God stands forever.** ***Isaiah 40:6-8 NKJV***

Peter's quoting is not as accurate as Paul's was, but the main sections are identical to the LXX. The LXX translation of Isaiah and Peter's quote make no mention of "**the breath of the Lord blows upon it**". Equally the LXX and Peter mention "**the glory of man**" which is not in the Heb. Interestingly Peter ends with "**the word of the Lord**" - I did say his quoting was not so accurate – whereas both the LXX and the Heb. have "**the word of our God**".

The LXX proof of use in Nazareth

[This is not in *SERIOUS*]

Finally, Luke 4:18 can be seen in Isaiah 61:1 of LXX in particular the three Gk. words I highlight:

KAI TUPHLOIS ANABLEPSIN = Luke 4:18 Gk. exactly as per LXX, but not in Heb. at all, as you can see in full for yourself here:

Isa. 61:1 The Spirit of the Lord GOD *is* upon me; because the LORD hath anointed me to preach good tidings unto the meek; he hath sent me to bind up the brokenhearted, to proclaim liberty to the captives, and the opening of the prison to *them that are* bound;

YLT The Spirit of the Lord Jehovah *is* on me, because Jehovah did anoint me to proclaim tidings to the humble, He sent me to bind the broken of heart, to proclaim to captives liberty, and to bound ones an opening of bands.

LXX ***PNEUMA KURIOU EP EME HOU HEINEKEN ECHRISE ME EUAGGELISASTHAI***
spirit of Lord upon me where for cause anoint me to proclaim
PTÓCHOIS APESTALKE ME IASASTHAI TOUS SUNTETRIMMENOUS TÉN KARDIAN
to poor sent me to heal the broken with the heart
KÉRUXAI AICHMALÓTOIS APHESIN KAI TUPHLOIS ANABLEPSIN
to proclaim to captives release and to blind seeing

engLXX The Spirit of the Lord is upon me, because he has anointed me; he has sent me to preach glad tidings to the poor, to heal the broken in heart, to proclaim liberty to the captives, and recovery of sight to the blind;

Luke 4:17-18 And there was delivered unto him the book of the prophet Esaias. And when he had opened the book, he found the place where it was written, 18 The Spirit of the Lord *is* upon me, because he hath anointed me to preach the gospel to the poor; he hath sent me to heal the brokenhearted, to preach deliverance to the captives, **and recovering of sight to the blind**, to set at liberty them that are bruised,

YLT and there was given over to him a roll of Isaiah the prophet, and having unfolded the roll, he found the place where it hath been written: 18 'The Spirit of the Lord *is* upon me, because He did anoint me; to proclaim good news to the poor, sent me to heal the broken of heart, to proclaim to captives deliverance, **and to blind receiving of sight**, to send away the bruised with deliverance,

Luke 4:18 NT Gk. RT *PNEUMA KURIOU EP EME HOU HENEKEN ECHRISEN ME EUAGGELIZESTHAI*
spirit of Lord upon me where for cause anoint me to proclaim

PTÓCHOIS APESTALKEN ME IASASTHAI TOUS SUNTETRIMMENOUS TÉN
to poor sent me to heal the broken with the

KARDIAN KÉRUXAI AICHMALÓTOIS APHESIN ***KAI TUPHLOIS ANABLEPSIN***
heart to proclaim to captives release and to blind seeing

APOSTEILAI TETHRAUSMENOUS EN APHESEI
to send ones oppressed in release

Here is the LXX again

Isa. 61:1 LXX *PNEUMA KURIOU EP EME HOU HEINEKEN ECHRISE ME EUAGGELISASTHAI*
spirit of Lord upon me where for cause anoint me to proclaim

PTÓCHOIS APESTALKE ME IASASTHAI TOUS SUNTETRIMMENOUS TÉN KARDIAN
to poor sent me to heal the broken with the heart

KÉRUXAI AICHMALÓTOIS APHESIN ***KAI TUPHLOIS ANABLEPSIN***
to proclaim to captives release and to blind seeing

Here is the Heb. translated by the YLT again

YLT The Spirit of the Lord Jehovah *is* on me, because Jehovah did anoint me to proclaim tidings to the humble, He sent me to bind the broken of heart, to proclaim to captives liberty, and to bound ones an opening of bands.

There is no "**and recovering of sight to the blind**" in the Heb.

This means Matthew, Jesus, the scroll of Isaiah in the synagogue in Nazareth, all, had the LXX in use.

Other use of the LXX

Relevant to our reading of the NT

In a number of places NT writers were making reference to the LXX by saying things readers of it would appreciate.

For example Paul says:

> **Nevertheless the solid foundation of God stands, having this seal: "The Lord knows those who are His," and, "Let everyone who names the name of Christ depart from iniquity."**
> *2 Timothy 2:19 NKJV*

The quote "**The Lord knows those who are His**" whilst substituting the word "Lord" for "God" is in Numbers 16:5 in the LXX where the event of Korah and those with him is narrated.

The Gk. of the NT (RT) has:

2 Timothy 2:19

	NT Gk.	*EGNÓ KURIOS TOUS ONTAS AUTOU* knows Lord the being of him
Num. 16:5	LXX	*EGNÓ HO THEOS TOUS ONTAS AUTOU* knows the God the being of him
Num. 16:5	NKJV	and he spoke to Korah and all his company, saying, "Tomorrow morning **the LORD will show who *is* His** and *who is* holy, and will cause *him* to come near to Him; that one whom He chooses. He will cause to come near to Him.
	YLT	and he speaketh unto Korah, and unto all his company, saying, 'Morning!-and **Jehovah is knowing those who are his**, and him who is holy, and hath brought near unto Him; even him whom He doth fix on He bringeth near unto Him.

The KJV, NKJV, NASB, NIV and NLT render the Heb. word YADA as "show" who is His; the YLT is like the LXX and the NT quoting "know" who is His.

The early church LXX reader hearing the words written to Timothy would make the connection.

Jerome (347-420)

As Latin became the more used language of Western Europe and North Africa, translations of the LXX and the NT into Latin arose. Jerome was commissioned by the bishop of Rome to do the same. He began translating the OT into Latin from the LXX. Then, on reflection, decided to translate the OT into Latin directly from the Heb. Text. In view of the high view of the LXX in his day this was a courageous move, but one we are now much indebted to him for doing. In this work not a few passages can be seen as having been well translated in the LXX as "direct" from the Heb. But also we can see that not a few passages in the LXX are "divergent" with word additions, or removals, or complete different meanings rendered in contrast to the Heb. To return closer to the inspired text of the Heb. Scripture was the right thing to do. But the LXX as shown by this study remains a valuable resource to help us have a clear view of the meaning of individual words used in the original writing of the NT. This work has focused on *EKLEKTOS* and BACHIR. For other words the LXX helps throw light on, I refer the reader to my previous book *SERIOUS*.

LXX Inspired?

As Jerome led the way to move away from the LXX as the primary source for reading the OT, a return to the inspired text was in play. A return to a more accurate read of the OT was obtained. But, there is a balance to be regained.

The rejection of the LXX has led to a move away from accurate translation itself of the NT. This is seen by this work as the meaning of some words has altered, and that divergence been repeated, ad infinitum, or so it feels, as it is taken for granted when lexicons are quoted and saying: "this is what this word means".

But, the move away from the LXX was needful. The LXX very divergent elements are there. They tell us, though the LXX is a helpful work, as highlighted above, it is nevertheless not inspired like the original which it translates.

Examples of LXX divergence:

When we read in the LXX king David gathered 70,000 young men, when the Heb. tells us 30,000 (2Sa. 6:1)

When the LXX gives 23,000 warriors and the Heb. 26,000 (Jud. 20:15)

LXX: 700 ambidextrous men, well able to use either hand to cast stones with a sling, whilst the Heb. has 700 left handed (Jud. 20:15-16)

The LXX gives David as saying that he will look after someone's son and "**will do to him what is good in my sight**", whilst the Heb. has "**I do to him that which *is* good in thine eyes**" (YLT – 2Sa. 19:38).

Just a glimpse of errors in the midst of a multitude of directly rendered passages throughout the LXX and the resource offered by the interlinear of the LXX Gk. text and the comment sections in the reference work provides the reader with much more material of both directly translated and divergence to observe.

What this study consists of – what you will find

There are 74 places in the LXX where *EKLEKTOS* is rendered from a Heb. word.

24 separate Heb. words are involved and in total these Heb. words are found in the OT 594 times.

Every place these Heb. words are found in the OT is quoted in the Eng. translation and in the LXX.

This then helps us identify all the Gk. words used to translate each Heb. word.

With such an exhaustive study the following can then be seen from the analysis:

> The main meaning of *EKLEKTOS* is clearly that of "high quality" and well rendered by the English "excellent" or similar words like "good" e.g. "good angels" in contrast to the fallen…
>
> There is no reasonable pattern for *EKLEKTOS* having a secondary or alternative meaning. To suggest it does from the minimal renderings is to infer that Gk. words like *NEANIAS* have equally such secondary meanings: i.e. it is as preposterous as that.
>
> Instead, these different Heb. words are well represented in Gk. with other characteristic words: e.g. the Heb. BACHAR "to choose" is well represented by the Gk. *EKLEGÓ*.
>
> Since *EKLEKTOS* is seen as in a different category of meaning than *EKLEGÓ*, then these two are not related: they do not form part of the same family: *EKLEGÓ* is in the same family as *EPILEGÓ* whilst *EKLEKTOS* is in the same family as *EPILEKTOS* aNT.[4]

The Heb. word BACHIR is only rendered by *EKLEKTOS* in the LXX.

> The meaning of *EKLEKTOS* fully testified to, BACHIR is thus fully seen as meaning of high quality – the best - to the LXX translators.
>
> Since the Gk. *EKLEKTOS* and the Heb. BACHIR are the only words translated by the Eng. word "elect" in English bibles, the word "elect" should be removed from the bible. There are a number of appropriate words to render "high quality" like "excellent" or, where "chosen" has been placed, a good example is "*have* mettle" instead of "*are* chosen" as in, "many are called, but few *have* mettle" (Mat. 22:14). See also *SERIOUS*.
>
> Finally quotes of sections of a 1st century letter, from one church to another, shows well how *EKLEKTOS* was understood as "high quality": a further testimony to the above.

4 aNT = word not found in the NT

FORMAT INFORMATION

Hebrew words

These are to be found anglicised in the same manner as Young's Concordance end section: all in capitals: e.g. Heb. BACHAR "to choose"

Greek words

These are to be found anglicised in the same manner as Young's Concordance, in capitals, but also in italics thus differentiating from Hebrew words: e.g. *KALLOS* aNT "beauty" is a Gk. word. For a full representation of each letter of the Gk. alphabet, please see end pages chart alongside the abbreviations list.

Format for each passage of a Hebrew word in the Reference chapters

How each passage is formatted - An example

Heb. Word in view: PERI

Please NOTE:

The reference section of this book involves multiple lines of information from different sources. This provides the reader with material that can be compared. To assist with visibility and presentation of the great mass of comparative material, all the reference sections have been placed at right angles: providing maximum access to comparative information for the reader. It is a work of resource; not a work of easy reading.

Deu. 26:10 And now, behold, I have brought the **firstfruits** of the land, which thou, O LORD, hast given me. And thou shalt set it before the LORD thy God, and worship before the LORD thy God:

YLT And now, lo, I have brought in the first of the **fruits** of the ground which thou hast given to me, O Jehovah; - and thou hast placed it before Jehovah thy God, and bowed thyself before Jehovah thy God,

GENNÉMA – produce - A divergent translation with the added "flowing with milk and honey" – produce of the land

LXX *KAI NUN IDOU ENÉNOCHA TÉN APARCHÉN TÓN* ***GENNÉMATÓN*** *TÉS GÉS HÉS*
and now look I have brought the first(-fruit) of the produce of the land which

EDÓKAS MOI KURIE GÉN REOUSAN GALA KAI MELI KAI APHÉSEIS AUTO
gave to me Lord land flowing milk and honey and shall leave it

APENANTI KURIOU TOU THEOU SOU KAI PROSKUNÉSEIS ENANTI KURIOU TOU
before Lord the God of you and shall worship before Lord the

THEOU SOU
God of you

engLXX And now, behold, I have brought the first of the fruits of the land, which thou gavest me, O Lord, a land flowing with milk and honey: and thou shalt leave it before the Lord thy God, and thou shalt worship before the Lord thy God;

The KJV quote:

First the reference (ref.) is given for the text.

Where *EKLEKTOS* is found in the corresponding section of the LXX the **ref.** is also placed in bold.

The initial full verse is as found in the KJV rendering where the Hebrew word was found translated. The KJV is used due to its use as the source for both Young's Analytical concordance and Strong's. Remember this section is the English translated from the Hebrew text.

Other Version quote:

The reference shared is not repeated. Letters then introduce the version e.g. "YLT".

This section is optional and added, in particular the YLT version, due to its more literal translation of the Hebrew. This then provides an easier gauge to see how loose the translation of the Hebrew by the LXX was: Sometimes the KJV is not as accurate a translation and the LXX is closer which can be seen by placing the YLT there: it thus helps show no divergence or loose translation is occurring, but a direct rendering instead. It is also added occasionally, or another version, to gather more on the flavour of the Hebrew word in question or, to help provide comprehension of the particular passage.

Remember this section is also the English translated from the Hebrew text.

The comment section – this is placed immediately before the LXX Greek portion. It consists of:

1 - Greek word in the LXX that translates the Hebrew word: then, often a brief word or words that translate that Greek word into English. Where *EKLEKTOS* is found the word is placed in bold and no eng. equivalent given as that is the task of the analysis. The same is done for *EPILEKTOS* in its own chapter.

Or, where the Heb. is not translated "NOT in the LXX" is put: followed by an explanation or description of what is missing

2 - The style of translation found in the LXX is then given in one of three categories:

Direct – well following the meaning and themes in the original, but not necessarily literal

Loose – paraphrased, but still readable in the original: one or occasionally more examples given to demonstrate: often just one example given in the expansion

Divergent – missing words, added words using different concepts that can not be read reasonably in the original: added or missed concepts in contrast to the original: one or more examples given to demonstrate: often just one example given in the expansion

3 - A short expansion of the style observed and why or, a comment on the passage itself

4 - Finally, what the Greek word tends to emphasise or portray - with simpler words or, just the basic representation

The Septuagint section

This is the Greek of the LXX translating the Hebrew text in three sections preceded by the ref. LXX

1 - The Reference is given whenever it differs from today's OT accounting. For example: in the Psalms and Jeremiah many of the same passages are in different numbered places or, the 1st book of Samuel is known as 1 Kings in the LXX.

2 - The word for word Greek text of the LXX. Every letter is in a capital and in Anglicised characters for each letter in the Greek word. All accents and punctuations have been removed from the Greek text of the passage. This format helps give the reader a taste, a small idea, of what the first written versions of the LXX looked like, and felt like to read; just like the New Testament first manuscripts. These first manuscripts are only found in Uncial form; there were no Miniscules: i.e.

everything was written in capitals. Miniscules took over from Uncials in the 8th century onwards. There is a difference from an Uncial manuscript here in that a space is retained (added) between the words to differentiate them from each other: there are no spaces in the Uncial manuscripts: no spacing, no punctuations, no accents, no new paragraphs: So, the reader by this presentation gets a taste, but only a small taste, as I still wish to enable the reader an easier means to see which English word or words corresponds with the Greek word (above).

3 - The line below each line of Greek text contains an interlinear word or words which represent the meaning of the Greek words in the preceding line. This English section word for word, or words for word, are a rough literal translation only; they are not claimed or aimed at being a full translation of the Greek word or set of words, though they often are. The primary purpose is to observe that the Greek text present is truly that of the verse or passage in question: no more. However, in this literal, but rough form, often a flavour is observed that provides more out of the passage than an interpretation as given in a full translation; sometimes less.

I am responsible for any composition errors in this section.

The full LXX translation

The final part of the presentation of each passage is a full translation of the LXX into English by Sir Lancelot. See Tools used (below).

It is of note that the KJV, the YLT, the NKJV and the engLXX sections occasionally are found with *words in italic*. This common practice is to identify the words in the Eng. which are added by the translator and means these words in italics do not correspond to a word in the passage being translated. In the NT this practice also represents words quoted from the OT as seen under the heading "**Jesus and the apostles' use of the LXX**" above.

TOOLS USED

SEPTUAGINT (LXX)

Samuel Bagster's (1772–1851) edition of the Greek text which includes

Sir Lancelot Charles Lee Brenton's (1807-1862) full English Translation

First published 1851

Both copiously borrowed and proofed from throughout this study

This is the most common available text of the LXX from the British Library Service

It is also online in photographic page by page form here:

http://www.ccel.org/ccel/brenton/lxx/Page_Index.html

CONCORDANCES

For words in Gk. in the LXX

George Morrish's (1814-1911) Conc.

For words in Eng. in the KJV

Robert Young's (1822-1888) Analytical Conc.

James Strong's (1822-1894) Conc.

LEXICON

For words in Gk. in the LXX

Analytical Lexicon to the Septuagint Expanded Edition

By Bernard A. Taylor

With Word Definitions by J. Lust, E. Eynikel, and K. Hauspie

© 2009 by Hendrickson Publishers Marketing, LLC

It is of note that Morrish's source version of the LXX differed in arrangement to the one translated by Sir Lancelot. This will show up in about 6 places.

BIBLES USED are as per Title pages

ANALYSIS

List of *EKLEKTOS*

From the Conc. of the LXX inc. Heb. word connection

The first list of importance is to identify where *EKLEKTOS* is found and to what Hebrew word, if any, each corresponds: i.e. which Heb. word/s does *EKLEKTOS* translate?

The Concordance of the LXX by George Morrish (1814-1911) mentions "**As the modern** [written late 19th century] **printed editions of the Septuagint are not quite uniform, and vary a great deal in marking the chapters and verses, it was necessary to follow some *one* Edition: that of Tischendorf (in two vols. 8vo. Leipsic) has been adopted. The Sixth Edition, 1880, has been used.**" Tischendorf (1815-1874) did a lot of work on textual criticism: the study of source texts. His version of the LXX differs in arrangement from the version translated by Sir Lancelot in 6 places as regards to this analysis: these are shown in the 3rd column in chart below by "a*EKLEKTOS*" to say the word *EKLEKTOS* is not in that section of the LXX used as a source in this study: the version used to examine the text throughout is the one Sir Lancelot translates from, since it is a commonly accessible version from the British Library system and from bookshops: e.g. from Hendrickson Publishers (reproducing Samuel Bagster) A scan of the page from Morrish is in the end pages giving his Conc. list for *EKLEKTOS*

Format

1st column - represents every place mentioned in Morrish's conc. of the LXX plus two lines identified in (parentheses) or [square brackets]:

The refs. In this column are those of the LXX text (see end pages for Jeremiah differences).

2nd column - is the ref. as found in most of today's bibles and the Heb.

3rd column - identifies the Hebrew word which was rendered by *EKLEKTOS*; "NOT from Heb." i.e. *EKLEKTOS* was added by the LXX translator with no Heb. word to translate it from; "a*EKLEKTOS*": where *EKLEKTOS* is not present (see above); "*EPILEKTOS*" = 1 occasion where the wrong word identified in the Conc.

4th column - identifies the word in the KJV that translates the Hebrew word. [N.B. 1Sa. in LXX is 1Ki. - 2Sa. is 2Ki. - 1Ki. is 3Ki. - 2Ki. is 4Ki. - See separate chapters]

Ref. LXX		Ref. bible	Heb.	KJV
Gen.	23:6	=	MIBCHAR	choice
	41:2	=	BARI	fat*fleshed*
	4	=	BARI	fat
	5	=	BARI	rank
	7	=	BARI	rank
	18	=	BARI	fat*fleshed*
	20	=	BARI	fat
Exo.	14:7	=	BACHAR	chosen
	30:23	=	DEROR	pure
Num.	11:28	=	BECHURIM/ BECHUROTH	young men
Deu.	12:11	=	MIBCHAR	choice
Jud.	20:15	=	BACHAR	chosen
	34	=	BACHAR	chosen
1Sa.	24:3	24:2	BACHAR	chosen
	26:2	=	BACHAR	chosen
2Sa.	8:8	=	NOT from Heb.	N/A
	21:6	=	BACHIR	choose [*margin*: chosen]
	22:27 (a)	=	BARAR	pure
	27 (b)	=	BARAR	pure
1Ki.	3:46 (a)	N/A	NOT from Heb.	N/A
(1Ki.	3:46 (b)	N/A	NOT from Heb.	N/A)
	4:23 (a)	=	BARI	fat
	23 (b)	=	NOT from Heb.	N/A
	23 (c)	=	a*EKLEKTOS*.	N/A

2Ki.	3:19	=	a*EKLEKTOS*	N/A
	8:12	=	BACHUR	young men
	19:23	=	MIBCHOR	choice
1Ch.	7:40	=	BARAR	choice
	9:22	=	BARAR	chosen
	16:13	=	BACHIR	chosen ones
	18:8	=	NOT from Heb.	N/A
Ezr.	5:8	=	GELAL	great
Neh.	5:18	=	BARAR	choice
Job	37:10	37:11	NOT from Heb.	N/A
Psa.	17:26 (a)	18:26	BARAR	pure
	26 (b)	26	BARAR	pure
	77:31	78:31	BACHUR	chosen
	88:4 (a)	89:3	BACHIR	chosen
	4 (b)	89:3	a*EKLEKTOS*	N/A
	20	89:19	BACHAR	chosen
	104:6	105:6	BACHIR	chosen
	43	105:43	BACHIR	chosen
	105:5	106:5	BACHIR	chosen
	23	106:23	BACHIR	chosen
	140:4	141:4	MANAMMIM	dainties
Pro.	8:19	=	BACHAR	choice
	12:24	=	CHARUTS	diligent
	17:3	=	NOT from Heb.	N/A
Sng.	5:15	=	BACHAR	excellent
	6:8	6:9	BAR	choice
	9	6:10	BAR	clear
Isa.	22:7	=	MIBCHAR	choicest
	8	=	NESHEQ	armour
	28:16	=	BOCHAN	tried
	40:30	=	NOT from Heb.	N/A
	42:1	=	BACHIR	elect
	43:20	=	BACHIR	chosen
	45:4	=	BACHIR	elect
	49:2	=	BARAR	polished

	54:12	=	CHEPHETS	pleasant
	65:9	=	BACHIR	elect
	15	=	BACHIR	chosen
	23	65:22	BACHIR	elect
Jer.	3:19	=	CHEMDAH/ CHAMUDOTH	pleasant
	10:17	=	MATSOR	fortress
	22:7	=	MIBCHAR	choice
	26:15	46:15	NOT from Heb.	N/A
	31:15	48:15	MIBCHAR	chosen
	32:20	25:20	a*EKLEKTOS*	N/A
	[32:34	25:34	CHEMDAH/ CHAMUDOTH	pleasant]
	38:39	31:39	NOT from Heb.	N/A
Lam.	1:15	=	BACHUR	young men
	5:13	=	BACHUR	young men
	14	=	BACHUR	young men
Eze.	7:20	=	TSEBI	beauty
	17:3	=	*EPILEKTOS*	N/A
	22	=	TSAMMERETH	highest
	19:12	=	PERI	fruit
	14	=	PERI	fruit
	25:9	=	TSEBI	glory
	27:20	=	CHOPHESH	precious
	22	=	a*EKLEKTOS*	N/A
	24	=	BEROMIM	rich
	31:16	=	MIBCHAR	choice
Dan.	11:15	=	MIBCHAR	chosen
Amo.	5:11	=	MASETH	burdens
Hab.	1:16	=	BARI	plenteous
Hag.	2:7	=	CHEMDAH/ CHAMUDOTH	desire
	2:22	=	a*EKLEKTOS*	N/A
Zec.	7:14	=	CHEMDAH/ CHAMUDOTH	pleasant
	11:16	=	BARI	fat

There are 91 lines above.

Morrish's Conc. gives a total of 89 occasions.

I found the word twice in 1 Ki. 3:46 in the LXX: The extra line for the 2nd occasion is in (parentheses)

I found an occasion in Jer. 32:34 not mentioned in Morrish, but it corresponds to Morrish's text at Jer. 32:20: I have placed this extra line in [square brackets].

6 are a*EKLEKTOS*: 1Ki. 4:23; 2Ki. 3:19; Psa. 88:4; Jer. 32:20; Eze. 27:22; Hag. 2:22

These 6 from the Conc. LXX do not show *EKLEKTOS* in the LXX text used in this study for quoting and checking – See separate chapter for the a*EKLEKTOS* with each passage quoted in full

These 6 were not shown in the list of *SERIOUS*

91 – 6 = 85

1 is not a ref. giving *EKLEKTOS* but *EPILEKTOS*

This was not shown in the list of *SERIOUS*

See separate chapter on all the places for *EPILEKTOS* in the LXX with each passage quoted in full A useful addition as part of the family of *EKLEKTOS* with a similar meaning

85 – 1 = 84

10 have no corresponding Heb. word: they are just added by the LXX translator

See separate chapter on non Heb. word related passages with each passage quoted in full

84 – 10 = 74

This leaves a total of 74 places of *EKLEKTOS* found rendering a Hebrew word that can be verified and independently examined with reference to the Heb. word in question: the means of this exercise to obtain a more original understanding of *EKLEKTOS*.

This is 1 less than in *SERIOUS* as 1 of the 2 occasions in 1 Ki.4:23 is re-classified as NOT from Heb.

Also 1 was added and another removed cf. with *SERIOUS*:

(-1) Isa. 40:30 removed & added to "NOT from Heb." (+1) Jer. 32:34 [See above: 1st Set of paragraphs below table]

24 Hebrew words rendered by 74 *EKLEKTOS* are now identified

Here is a list of how much each of these Hebrew words were represented by *EKLEKTOS*

Summary List of Heb. words

	Heb. Word	Total times in Heb. OT		Translated by *EKLEKTOS* in LXX
1	BACHAR	172		8
2	BACHIR	13	=	13
3	BACHUR	45		5
4	BAR	7		2
5	BARAR	18		8
6	BARI	13		9
7	BECHURIM/ BECHUROTH	3		1
8	BEROMIM	1	=	1
9	BOCHAN	1	=	1
10	CHARUTS	18		1
11	CHEMDAH/ CHAMUDOTH	25		4
12	CHEPHETS	39		1
13	CHOPHESH	1	=	1
14	DEROR	10		1
15	GELAL	2		1
16	MANAMMIM	1	=	1
17	MASETH	15		1
18	MATSOR	30		1
19	MIBCHAR	12		7
20	MIBCHOR	2		1
21	NESHEQ	10		1
22	PERI	119		2
23	TSAMMERETH	5		1
24	TSEBI	32		2
		594		74

Here we can see that the Hebrew words appear a total of 594 times and are represented by *EKLEKTOS* 74 times.

5 Heb. words are only translated by *EKLEKTOS*:

4 of these occur only once each:

BEROMIM "rich apparel"

BOCHAN "tried"

CHOPHESH "precious"

MANAMMIM "dainties"

BARI "fat" (full) is more translated by *EKLEKTOS* than by any other Gk. word

BARAR "pure, clear" is about half translated by *EKLEKTOS* (8 out of 18)

The same could be said for MIBCHOR "choice" and GELAL "great".

Each of those occurs twice:

So, MIBCHOR is translated by *EKLEKTOS* × 1 & by *OCHUROS* aNT (secure, strong) × 1

And GELAL is translated by *EKLEKTOS* × 1 & by *KRATAIOS* (mighty, great, strong) × 1

MIBCHAR "the best" is more translated by *EKLEKTOS* than by any other Gk. word: MIBCHAR is 7 × *EKLEKTOS* out of 12

2 of those *EKLEKTOS* are "chosen" in KJV

Jer. 48:15 (LXX 31:15), also "chosen" in NKJV, & Dan.11:15

But in other versions MIBCHAR at these two passages are:

Jer. 48:15 (LXX 31:15): "choice" YLT; "choicest" NASB; "finest" NIV; "most promising" NLT

Dan. 11:15: "choice" YLT, NKJV; """choicest" NASB; "best" NIV, NLT

Rough pattern for *EKLEKTOS*

A pattern is already present:

"fat" (full)	most
"the best"	5 out of 12 [see other versions above for 2 more]
"pure, clear"	as much
"choice"	as much
"great"	as much

As 1 alone

"dainties"	incidental
"tried"	incidental
"precious"	incidental
"rich apparel"	incidental

The main rough view is here.

These give us the idea that something of high quality is understood in the mind of the LXX translator when using *EKLEKTOS* to render these Heb. words.

Let's have a fuller look at how each of the Heb. words are rendered in English.

The full account – where every passage in full is given - is in each chapter allocated to that Hebrew word.

Here is a summary look of the Eng. words (KJV) for all the places the Heb. words are found.

English words that translate the Heb.

A summary look (KJV)

In **bold** the **Eng.** words associated with *EKLEKTOS*

[Placed in reference like format to observe information better and differentiate it from analysis content]

Heb. Word		× in Heb.	Eng. Words for the Heb.	Translated in the LXX as *EKLEKTOS*
1 **BACHAR**	to choose	172	choose (77) chosen (78) choice (6) choose out (5) acceptable; appoint; excellent; rather; require; (1 each) not translated (1)	**8**

to choose [many] (in various conjugations: chose, chose out, choose, chooseth, choosest, **chosen**) – choice *men* – the king shall appoint – thou shalt require – rather be a doorkeeper – **choice** silver – more acceptable to the LORD – not translated Ecc.9:4 – **excellent** as the cedars

2 **BACHIR**		13	chosen (8) elect (4) chose (1)	**13**

Saul, whom the LORD **did choose** - Jacob, **his chosen ones** - covenant **with my chosen** - Jacob **his chosen** - brought forth his people with joy, ***and*** **his chosen** with gladness - That I may see the good of **thy chosen** - Moses **his chosen** - my servant, whom I uphold; **mine elect**, *in whom* my soul delighteth - to my people, **my chosen** – Israel **mine elect** - **and mine elect** shall inherit it - shall leave your name for a curse **unto my chosen** - my people, **and mine elect** shall long enjoy the work of their hands

3 **BACHUR**		45	young man (42) the chosen (1) young (1) not translated (1)	**5**

the young man/men and/or the/their maid/virgin/maidens (6) – used the young men to do – followedst not young men – your goodliest young men – a choice/chosen young man/men (2) – their **young men** be/wilt/have I/thou slay/slain (3) – slew/consumed their young men (2) – the **chosen** *men* of Israel – glory of young men – young man, in thy youth – no joy in their young men – nourish up young men – (her/his) young men shall (be) (utterly) fall/discomfited (4) – not translated - a young man marrieth a virgin - assembly of young men – young men from the streets – young men shall die/are fallen by the sword (2) – mother of the young men – young men and old together – spare not her young men – to crush my **young men** – my young men are gone into captivity – the **young men** to grind – the **young men** from their musick – slay utterly old *and* young – desirable young men (3) – young men of Aven – your young men shall see visions – your young men for Nazarites – make the younger men cheerful

4 **BAR** 7 clean (3) pure (2) choice (1) clear (1) **2**

clean in thy eyes – commandment of the Lord is pure – a pure heart – a clean heart – crib is clean – she is the **choice** one of her – **clear** as the sun

5 **BARAR** 18 pure (5) choice (2) clean (2) chosen (2) clearly (1) purge (1) manifest (1) bright (1) purge out (1) polished (1) purified (1) **8**

with the **pure** thou wilt – shew thyself **pure – choice** and mighty men of valour – **chosen** to be porters -

6 **BARI** fat (full) 13 fat (5) fatfleshed (2) rank (2) fatter (1) plenteous (1) firm (1) fed (1) Rank: Eng. In the sense of complete **9**

favoured kine and **fatfleshed** – **fat** kine – stalk, **rank** and good – **rank** and full ears – kine, **fatfleshed** – **fat** kine – **fat** man - **fat** oxen – strength is firm – them that are fed – fairer and fatter in flesh – meat **plenteous** (food fat YLT) – flesh of the **fat**

7 **BECHURIM/ BECHUROTH** 3 youth (2) young men (1) **1**

one of his **young men** – in the days of thy youth (2)

8 **BEROMIM** 1 rich apparel (1) **1**

chests of **rich apparel**

9 **BOCHAN** 1 tried (1) **1**

a **tried** stone

10 **CHARUTS** [1] & [2] 18 [1]: gold (6);
[2]: diligent (5) decision (2) threshing instrument (1) sharp (1) sharp things (1) wall (1) **1**

sharp pointed things upon mire – feathers with yellow gold – fine gold (2) – rather than choice gold – better than gold - hand of the **diligent** shall bear rule, maketh rich – substance of the diligent man is precious – soul of the diligent shall be made fat – better to get wisdom than gold – thoughts of diligent tend only to plenteousness – threshed with a threshing instrument – sharp threshing instrument – the wall – valley of decision (2) – threshing instruments of iron

11 **CHEMDAH/ CHAMUDOTH**	25	pleasant (12) desire (4) precious (4) beloved (3) goodly (2)	**4**

goodly raiment – the desire of Israel – precious jewels, as gold, vessels, things – without being desired (praised) – **pleasant** jewels, vessel/s, pictures, houses, land, portion (of land), bread, things, furniture – goodly vessels – greatly beloved – desire of women – **desire** of all nations

12 **CHEPHETS**	39	pleasure (16) desire (12) delight (3) purpose (3) acceptable (1) delightsome (1) matter (1) pleasant (1) willingly (1)	**1**

delight in burnt offerings - king desireth not any dowry – all my salvation, and all *my* desire – I will do/accomplish all thy/my desire (2) – *according to* all his desire (2) – all her desire (2) – what pleasure *hath he* in – *is it* any pleasure to the Almighty – withheld the poor from *their* desire – his delight *is* in the law – in whom *is* all my delight – their desired haven – that have pleasure therein – all the things thou canst/that may be desire/d (2) – worketh willingly with her hands – every purpose under the heaven – for/to every purpose (2) – no pleasure in (3) – marvel not at the matter – find out acceptable words – shall perform/will do all my pleasure (2) – he will do his pleasure on – the pleasure of the LORD – borders of **pleasant** stones – in the day of your fast ye find pleasure – thy pleasure on my holy day – finding thine own pleasure – a vessel wherein *is* no pleasure (3) – delightsome land

13 **CHOPHESH**	1	precious (1)	**1**

precious clothes for chariots

14 **DEROR** 10 liberty (7) swallow (2) pure (1) **1**

pure myrrh – proclaim(-ing) liberty (6) – the swallow a nest – the swallow by flying - the year of liberty

15 **GELAL** 2 great (2) **1**

builded with **great** stones – three rows of great stones

16 **MANAMMIM** 1 dainties (1) **1**

eat of their **dainties**

17 **MASETH** 15 burden (3) mess (3) collection (2) flame (2) gifts (1) oblations (1) reward (1) sign (1) lifting up (1) **1**

sent messes – Benjamin's mess was five times – a great flame with smoke – the flame began to arise – mess of meat from the king – out of Jerusalem the collection – to bring in . . . the collection – and gave gifts – the lifting up of my hands as the evening sacrifice – set up a sign of fire – gave him victuals and a reward – false burdens – firstfruits of your oblations – **burdens** of wheat – bearing for her sake reproach

18 **MATSOR** 30 siege (13) besieged (4) besieged place (2) strong (2) defence (2) fortress (2) bulwarks (1) fenced (1) hold (1) tower (1) fortified (1) **1**

in/for the siege (8) – build bulwarks against the city – rivers of besieged places (2) – city was besieged (2) – fenced/fortified cities (2) – cities for defence – strong city (2) – brooks of defence – the **fortress** (2) – lay/laid siege against it/us (2) – shall be besieged – the siege of Jerusalem – days of thy/the siege (2) – upon the tower – a strong hold

19 **MIBCHAR** the best 12 choice (7) choicest (1) chosen (4) **7**

choice of our sepulchres – his chosen captains (choice of his captains YLT) - **choice** vows – **choicest** valleys – choice fir trees – **choice** cedars - **chosen** young men (choice of its young men YLT) – the chosen men of Assyria (choice of the sons of Asshur YLT) – choice bones – choice of the flock - the **choice** and best of Lebanon – his **chosen** people (the people of His choice YLT)

20 **MIBCHOR** 2 choice (2) **1**
every choice city – **choice** fir trees

21 **NESHEQ** 10 armour (3) weapons (3) battler (1) armed (1) harness (1) armoury (1) **1**

and garments, and armour - a fenced city also, and armour - and raiment, harness, and spices - going up to the armoury - the iron weapon – armed men - the **armour** of the house - burn the weapons (2)

22 **PERI** fruit 119 fruit (114) fruitful (2) firstfruit (1) reward (1) Bough (1) **2**
fruit [many] (of trees, of the earth, of land, of womb, of life, of wisdom, of the heart)

23 **TSAMMERETH** 5 top (3) highest branch (2) **1**
highest branch of the cedar, high cedar - his top among the thick boughs (2), was among the thick boughs

24 **TSEBI** 32 roe (9) glory (8) glorious (6) roebuck (5) beautiful (1) beauty (1) goodly (1) pleasant (1) **2**

the roebuck and the (fallow-)deer, hart [many] – beauty of Israel – a wild roe – roes upon the mountains – by the/like a roe – the branch of the LORD be beautiful and glorious – chased roe – glory of the kingdoms – pride of all glory – glory to the righteous – glorious beauty (2) – crown of glory – goodly heritage – **beauty** of his ornaments – **glory** of all lands (2), of the country – glory in the land of the living – the pleasant land – the glorious land (2) – glorious holy mountain

Table of all Gk. words translating the Heb. words

Heb. words rendered by non bold Eng. words (above) are given in the LXX by non bold Gk. words as follows:

LIST of Greek words

That translate the 24 Hebrew words as connected with *EKLEKTOS*

1 – **BACHAR**

EKLEGÓ (to choose, pick - 113); *HAIRETIZÓ* (to choose - 12); ***EKLEKTOS*** (**8**)
EPILEGÓ (pick out, select - 6); *DUNATOS* (strong, mighty, able - 4)
NEANIAS (young man, youth - 4); *HAIREÓ* (to choose, prefer - 3)
DIAKRINÓ (judge, decide - 2); *EPHISTÉMI* (set up, establish - 2)
EXAIREÓ (to choose, select out - 2); *HAIRETOS* aNT (to be chosen, elected - 2)
PROAIREÓ (to choose, prefer - 2); *APALLASSÓ* (set free - 1)
ARESKÓ (to do what pleases - 1); *ARESTOS* (acceptable, pleasing - 1)
DOKIMAZÓ (to approve, assay - 1); *EPITHUMEÓ* (desired, coveted - 1)
METOCHOS (partaking - 1); *NEANISKOS* (young man, boy - 1)
PUROÓ (to burn with fire, purge - 1); *ZÉLOÓ* (to esteem, emulate - 1)
NOT in LXX (3)

2 – **BACHIR**

EKLEKTOS (**13**)

3 – **BACHUR**

NEANISKOS (young man, boy - 34); ***EKLEKTOS*** (**5**)
NEANIAS (young man, youth - 2); *ANÉR* (man, husband - 1); NOT in LXX (3)

4 – **BAR**

KATHAROS (clean, pure - 2); ***EKLEKTOS*** (**2**); *AMEMPTOS* (blameless - 1)
EUTHUS (straight, direct – 1); *TÉLAUGÉS* aNT (far shining – 1)

5 – **BARAR**

EKLEKTOS (**8**) - *EKLEGÓ* (to pick, choose - 2); *KATHAROS* (clean, pure - 2)
PUROÓ (burn up, purify - 2); *APHORIZÓ* (to define, determine - 1)
DIAKRINÓ (to decide, judge - 1); *PARASKEUAZÓ* (make ready - 1)
NOT in LXX (1)

6 – **BARI**

EKLEKTOS (**9**); *ASTEIOS* (handsome - 1); *ISCHUROS* (strong, mighty - 1)
PACHUS aNT (stout - 1); *STEREÓMA* (firm - 1)

7 – **BECHURIM/BECHUROTH**

NEOTÉS (youth - 2); ***EKLEKTOS*** (**1**)

8 – **BEROMIM**

EKLEKTOS (**1**)

9 - **BOCHAN**

EKLEKTOS (**1**)

10 – **CHARUTS**

CHRUSION (gold - 6); *ANDREIOS* aNT (manly, vigorous - 2)
DIKÉ (judgment, vengeance - 2); ***EKLEKTOS*** (**1**); *CHRUSOS* (gold - 1) *KATHAROS* (pure, honest - 1); *PRIÓN* aNT (saw - 1)
SKLÉROTÉS (hard, rigid - 1); *TEICHOS* (wall - 1); *TROCHOS* (wheel -1)
NOT in LXX (1)

11 – **CHEMDAH/CHAMUDOTH**

EPITHUMÉTOS aNT (desirable - 11); *EPITHUMIA* (desire, yearning - 5)
EKLEKTOS (**4**); *EPAINOS* (praise - 1); *EPITHUMÉMA* aNT (object of desire - 1)
HÓRAIOS (beautiful - 1); *KALOS* (good - 1); *KALLOS* aNT (beauty - 1)

12 – **CHEPHETS**

THELÉMA (desire, will - 19); *PRAGMA* (deed, act - 4); *CHREIA* (need - 3)
AXIOS (worthy - 2); *THELÉTOS* aNT (wished for, desired - 2)
ACHRÉSTOS (unprofitable, useless - 1); *BOULOMAI* (to will, wish - 1)
BOULEU-Ó/OMAI (take counsel - 1); ***EKLEKTOS*** (**1**); *ERGON* (work - 1)
EUCHRÉSTOS (useful, serviceable - 1); *MELÓ* (to care - 1)
THELÓ (to be willing - 1); NOT in LXX

13 – **CHOPHESH**

EKLEKTOS (**1**)

14 – **DEROR**

APHESIS (release - 7); ***EKLEKTOS*** (**1**); *STROUTHOS* aNT (sparrow - 1)
TRUGÓN (turtle-dove - 1)

15 – **GELAL**

EKLEKTOS (**1**) - *KRATAIOS* (mighty, great, strong – 1)

16 - **MANAMMIM**

EKLEKTOS (**1**)

17 – **MASETH**

MERIS (part, portion - 2); *SUSSÉMON* (signal - 2)
APHORISMOS aNT (offering - 1); *ARSIS* aNT (distilled, portion - 1)
DÓRON (gift, present - 1); ***EKLEKTOS*** (**1**); *EPARSIS* aNT (rising, swelling - 1)
KRINÓ (distinguish, judge - 1); *LAMBANÓ* (to take, receive - 1)
LÉMMA aNT (argument - 1); *SÉMEION* (mark, sign - 1)
NOT translated in LXX (2)

18 – **MATSOR**

PERIOCHÉ (surrounding, siege - 10); *SUGKLEISMOS* aNT (siege - 3)
THLIPSIS (pressure, affliction - 3); *OCHUROS* aNT (strong - 2)
SUNOCHÉ (besiege - 2); *CHARAKÓSIS* aNT (siege - 1)
CHARAX (siege stake -1); *DIÓRUX* aNT (canal, defence trench - 1)
EKLEKTOS (**1**); *OCHURÓMA* (fortress - 1); *petra* (rock - 1)
SUGKLEIÓ (shut, closed - 1); *SUNAGÓGÉ* (gathered together - 1)
TEICHÉRÉS aNT (walled in - 1); *TUROS* (Tyre - 1)

19 – **MIBCHAR**

EKLEKTOS (7); *EPILEKTOS* aNT (3); *KALLOS* aNT (beauty - 1)
NOT translated in LXX (1)

20 – **MIBCHOR**

EKLEKTOS (**1**) - *OCHUROS* aNT (secure, strong - 1)

21 – **NESHEQ**

HOPLON (arm, weapon - 3); ***EKLEKTOS*** (**1**); *ISCHUS* (strength - 1)
POLEMOS (war, battle - 1); *PURGOS* (tower - 1)
SIDÉROS (iron - 1) - NOT in LXX (2)

22 – **PERI**

KARPOS (fruit - 82); *gennéma* (produce - 10); *EKGONOS* (born of – 10)
EKLEKTOS (**2**); *EKPHORION* aNT (increase of land - 2)
KARPOPHOROS (fruitful - 2); *BOUKOLION* aNT (herd - 1)
EULOGIA (blessing - 1); *KARPIZ-Ó/-OMAI* aNT (enjoy fruit of - 1)
KARPIMOS aNT (fruit bearing - 1); *SPERMA* (seed - 1)
TEKNON (child - 1); NOT in LXX (5)

23 - **TSAMMERETH**

ARCHÉ (top, first - 3); ***EKLEKTOS*** (**1**); *EPILEKTOS* aNT (1)

24 – **TSEBI**

DORKAS aNT (doe, type of deer - 10); *DUNAMIS* (power, might -3)
EKLEKTOS (**2**); *DOXA* (glory - 2); *ELPIS* (hope, expectation - 2)
ENDOXOS (honoured, gloried - 2); *KÉRION* (honeycomb - 2)
DORKADION aNT (fawn, little gazelle - 1); *DORKÓN* aNT (roe, buck - 1)
EPILAMPÓ aNT (to shine upon - 1); *STÉLOÓ* aNT (stand still, set up stone - 1)
SABAEIM aNT (beauty, glory - 1); *SABAEIN* aNT (beauty, glory - 1)
SABEI aNT (beauty, glory - 1); NOT in LXX (2)

REASONABLE ARGUMENT 1

Expanded View

The rough view then, can be expanded somewhat.

The fat [*EKLEKTOS*] cows that came up out of the Nile in Pharaoh's dream which Joseph interpreted; the fat [*EKLEKTOS*] kernels of wheat in the same dream; young men [*EKLEKTOS*] i.e. guys in their prime; to the pure [*EKLEKTOS*] You will show Yourself pure [*EKLEKTOS*]; pleasant [*EKLEKTOS*] land; pleasant [*EKLEKTOS*] jewels; desire [*EKLEKTOS*] of all nations; tried [*EKLEKTOS*] stone; precious [*EKLEKTOS*] clothes; choice [*EKLEKTOS*] silver; highest [*EKLEKTOS*] branch of the cedar; and many more.

A total of 51 undisputed [in the KJV] out of the total 74 have an overall idea of:

"best, top quality, excellent"

This then is the main meaning for *EKLEKTOS* in the LXX

Here they are:

EKLEKTOS as "best, top quality, excellent"

Eng KJV	Qty	Heb	Refs (LXX)
Choice (the best)	9	BACHAR	Pro. 8:19
		BAR	Sng. 6:8
		BARAR	1Ch. 7:40; Neh. 5:18
		MIBCHAR	Gen. 23:6; Deu. 12:11; Jer. 22:7; Eze. 31:16
		MIBCHOR	2 Ki. 19:23
Fat	6	BARI	Gen. 41:2, 4, 18, 20; 1Ki. 4:23; Zec. 11:16
Pure	5	BARAR	2Sa. 22:27, 27; Psa. 17:26, 26
		DEROR	Exo. 30:23
Young men	5	BACHUR	2Ki. 8:12; Lam. 1:15; 5:13, 14
(Guys in their prime)		BECHURIM/ BECHUROTH	Num. 11:28

Eng KJV	Qty	Heb	Refs (LXX)
Pleasant	4	CHEMDAH/	Jer. 3:19; 32:34
		CHAMUDOTH	Zec. 7:14
		CHEPHETS	Isa. 54:12
Fruit	2	PERI	Eze. 19:12, 14
Rank (old Eng. complete)	2	BARI	Gen. 41:5, 7
Armour of the house	1	NESHEQ	Isa. 22:8
Beauty of his ornaments	1	TSEBI	Eze. 7:20
Burdens of wheat	1	MASETH	Amo. 5:11
Choicest valley	1	MIBCHAR	Isa. 22:7
Clear as the sun	1	BAR	Sng. 6:9
Dainties	1	MANAMMIM	Psa. 140:4
Desire of all nations	1	CHEMDAH	Hag. 2:7
Diligent	1	CHARUTS	Pro. 12:24
Excellent as the cedars	1	BACHAR	Sng. 5:15
Fortress	1	MATSOR	Jer. 10:17
Glory	1	TSEBI	Eze. 25:9
Great stones	1	GELAL	Ezr. 5:8
Highest branch	1	TSAMMERETH	Eze. 17:22
Plenteous (or, dainty) meat	1	BARI	Hab. 1:16
Polished shaft (of an arrow)	1	BARAR	Isa. 49:2
Precious clothes	1	CHOPHESH	Eze. 27:20
Rich apparel	1	BEROMIM	Eze. 27:24
Tried stone	1	BOCHAN	Isa. 28:16

= 51 as "best, top quality, excellent"

It is evident from these 51 occasions the most regular and common use of *EKLEKTOS* in the LXX is as a word of description that emphasizes the best, the excellent, of people or things.

This leaves 23 in an apparent **"chosen"** category

Here they are:

***EKLEKTOS* as "chosen" at 1st glance**

Eng KJV	**Qty**	**Heb**	**Refs (LXX)**
Chosen	18	BACHAR (6)	Exo. 14:7; Jud. 20:15, 34; 1Sa. 24:3, 26:2 Psa. 88:20
		BACHUR (1)	Psa. 77:31
		BARAR (1)	1Ch. 9:22
		MIBCHAR (2)	Jer. 31:15; Dan.11:15
Chosen		BACHIR (8)	1Ch. 16:13; Psa. 88:3; 104:6, 43, 105:5, 23 Isa. 43:20, 65:15
Elect	4	BACHIR	Isa. 42:1, 45:4, 65:9, 65:23
Choose	1	BACHIR	2Sa. 21:6

= 23 as "chosen" type

2 reasonable truths from above

51 as "best, top quality, excellent"

23 as "chosen" type

Total 74

REASONABLE ARGUMENT 2 BACHIR postponed

The word "elect" comes from one of two words in the bible, either the Heb. word BACHIR in the OT or, the Gk. word *EKLEKTOS* in the NT.

Now, the OT in Gk. – the LXX – reveals that BACHIR is only translated by *EKLEKTOS*.

It is reasonable then to say the 13 occasions where these appear, are not able in themselves, to inform us on the validity of "chosen" or "elect" as a meaning from the LXX.

As far as the LXX is concerned, the meaning of BACHIR is tied to the meaning of *EKLEKTOS* and until the completion of the analysis of all the other places where *EKLEKTOS* is found, as translated from a Heb. word in the LXX, BACHIR is unknowable.

It is reasonable then, to remove the 13 from the above accounting and return to BACHIR after a look at:

BACHAR	(6 "chosen" – 2 "best, top quality, excellent")
MIBCHAR	(2 "chosen" – 5 "best, top quality, excellent")
BACHUR	(1 "chosen" – 4 "best, top quality, excellent")
BARAR	(1 "chosen" – 7 "best, top quality, excellent")

3 reasonable truths from above

51 as "best, top quality, excellent"

10 as "chosen" type

13 pending from BACHIR

Total 74

REASONABLE ARGUMENT 3 BACHAR

The Heb. word BACHAR is the most used word in the Heb. bible for the verb "to choose" and its derivative "chosen".

Here are all the BACHAR renderings in the KJV

Ys Conc.	Count	Ss Conc. No. H 977	Count
appoint	1	choose	77
be rather	1	chosen	77
choose	152	choice	6
choose out	5	choose out	5
require	1	acceptable	1
choice	2	appoint	1
excellent	1	excellent	1
be chosen	3	chosen men	1
acceptable	1	rather	1
choice	3 +1[5]	require	1
+1 not translated in Ecc. 9:4 See "joined" from CHABAR next to it			
TOTAL	172	TOTAL	172

5 See p.164 Ys Conc.

BACHAR is rendered in the LXX as *EKLEKTOS* 8 times out of 172

The Heb. BACHAR rendered in Eng. - as regards the 2 categories in the above reasonable arguments – compares with *EKLEKTOS* as 6 "chosen" and 2 "best, top quality, excellent"

But, BACHAR is far more represented in Gk. by other Gk. words than *EKLEKTOS*.

Here is the list again:

BACHAR *EKLEGÓ* (to choose, pick - 113)
HAIRETIZÓ (to choose - 12)
EKLEKTOS (**8**)
EPILEGÓ (pick out, select - 6)
DUNATOS (strong, mighty, able - 4)
NEANIAS (young man, youth - 4)
HAIREÓ (to choose, prefer - 3)
DIAKRINÓ (judge, decide - 2)
EPHISTÉMI (set up, establish - 2)
EXAIREÓ (to choose, select out - 2)
HAIRETOS aNT (to be chosen, elected - 2)
PROAIREÓ (to choose, prefer - 2)
APALLASSÓ (set free - 1)
ARESKÓ (to do what pleases - 1)
ARESTOS (acceptable, pleasing - 1)
DOKIMAZÓ (to approve, assay - 1)
EPITHUMEÓ (desired, coveted - 1)
METOCHOS (partaking - 1)
NEANISKOS (young man, boy - 1)
PUROÓ (to burn with fire, purge - 1)
ZÉLOÓ (to esteem, emulate - 1)
NOT in LXX (3)

REASONABLE ARGUMENT 3 (a)

Now, if *EKLEKTOS* has a secondary or dual meaning at all, so that one of its meanings is as something which involves a selection at all: someone being "chosen", then with BACHAR "to choose" as the most prominent Heb. word for the meaning of "chosen" (Ss 77), here then is the most reasonable place to observe *EKLEKTOS* could possibly mean that.

With the LXX as our source historical text, we are looking here at the perception of the LXX translator in regards to *EKLEKTOS*. This is what we want to discover. And this perception would be similar to that of modern translators when translating a word with two meanings from the Heb.

We saw that many Gk. words translate BACHAR

That *EKLEKTOS* translates BACHAR only 8 times.

And two of those eight are immediately seen as being about select items: ones of high quality:

"Choice silver" (Pro. 8:19)

"excellent as the cedars" (Sng. 5:15)

BACHAR is well seen to have more than 1 meaning. This is attested by various lexicons.

The LXX gives us good examples that illustrate this well.

Here follows two passages that show us both the Heb. writer and the LXX translator seeing in BACHAR 2 different meanings – 2 different emphases – by the fact of the near proximity of the same word with the 2 differences in the very same text.

I offer 2Sa. 10:9 and 1Ch. 19:10

2Sa. 10:9a When Joab saw that the front of the battle was against him before and behind, he **chose** of all…

1st and most regular main meaning for BACHAR

Given elsewhere as "chooseth" YLT; "chose" NKJV; "selected" NASB; "selected" NIV; "chose" NLT

The LXX uses the Gk. word *EPILEGÓ* – pick out, select, remove

It is a direct translation

Basic meaning of Verse: Joab chose quality soldiers in the midst of seeing a strong attack on two fronts

LXX **2Ki.10:9a** *KAI EIDEN IÓAB HOTI EGENÉTHÉ PROS AUTON ANTIPROSÓPON TOU POLEMOU*
and saw Joab since it be to him facing the war
EK TOU KATA PROSÓPON EXENANTIAS KAI EK TOU OPISTHEN KAI ***EPELEXATO***
out of the against face right opposite and out of the rear and chose
EK PANTÓN…
out of all

engLXX And Joab saw that the front of the battle was against him from that which was opposed in front and from behind, and he chose out *some* of all…

The 2nd and not as regular meaning for BACHAR is,

2Sa. 10:9b . . . the **choice** *men* of Israel, and put *them* in array against the Syrians:

Given elsewhere as (the) "chosen" (in Israel) YLT; (the) "choice" (*men* of Israel) NKJV; (the) "choice men" (of Israel) NASB; (the) "best troops" (in Israel) NIV; (Israel's) "elite troops" NLT

The LXX uses the Gk. word *NEANIAS* – young man

A direct translation

The second meaning of BACHAR "to be chosen: preferred: excellent": here, soldiers in view, at their best, this being when they are fittest in prime of life: the young men

LXX **2Ki.10:9b** …*TÓN* ***NEANIÓN*** *ISRAÉL KAI PARETAXANTO EX ENANTIAS SURIAS*
the young men of Israel and deployed out of opposite Syria

engLXX …the young men of Israel, and they set themselves in array against Syria.

Having already provided the explanations in the 2Sa. 10:9 example above, instead of repeating these, here is the 1Ch. 19:10 example exactly as it is to be found in the BACHAR reference chapter. It can be readily observed with BACHAR twice in the same verse, but with two distinct separate meanings:

1Ch. 19:10a — Now when Joab saw that the battle was set against him before and behind, he **chose out** of all…

YLT — And Joab seeth that the front of the battle hath been unto him, before and behind, and he **chooseth out** of all . . .

NKJV — When Joab saw that the battle line was set against him before and behind, he **chose** some of . . .

NASB — Now when Joab saw that the battle was set against him in front and in the rear, he **selected** from all . . .

NIV — Joab saw that there were battle lines in front of him and behind him; so he **selected** some of . . .

NLT — When Joab saw that he would have to fight on both the front and the rear, he **chose** some of . . .

EKLEGÓ – to pick, choose, elect - a direct translation – Joab chose quality soldiers as a response to the threat before and behind him

LXX — ***KAI EIDEN IÓAB HOTI GEGONASIN ANTIPROSÓPOI TOU POLEMEIN PROS AUTON***
and saw Joab since it be face off the war to him

KATA PROSÓPON KAI EXOPISTHE KAI* EXELEXATO *EK PANTOS…
according to front and behind and chose out of all

engLXX — And Joab saw that they were fronting *him* to fight against him before and behind, and he chose *some* out of all…

1Ch. 19:10b	. . . the **choice** of Israel, and put *them* in array against the Syrians.
YLT	. . . the **choice** in Israel, and setteth in array to meet Aram,
NKJV	. . . the **choice men** of Israel and put *them* in battle array against the Syrians.
NASB	. . . the **choice men** of Israel and they arrayed themselves against the Arameans.
NIV	. . . the **best troops** in Israel and deployed them against the Arameans.
NLT	. . . Israel's **elite troops** and placed them under his personal command to fight the Arameans in the fields.

NEANIAS – young man – a direct translation - the secondary meaning of BACHAR of "to be chosen: preferred: excellent": the best troops, those in their prime: young men

LXX ...***NEANIOU*** *EX ISRAÉL KAI PARETAXANTO ENANTION TOU SUROU*
young men out of Israel and set before the Syrian

engLXX ...the young men of Israel, and they set themselves in array against the Syrian.

So, BACHAR has the main emphasis of **"to choose", "chosen"**

i.e. make a decision, to consider, wish, judge

This fits with our "**chosen**" category

And another meaning of **"choice", "excellent"**

i.e. (something or someone) *to be chosen*: preferred: excellent

This fits with our "**best, top quality, excellent**" category

Note the difference between "**chosen**" i.e. selected, in contrast with: "**to be chosen**" [in the "best, top quality, excellent" category]

This then requires a division of the Greek words which render BACHAR

What will decide here, which category each Gk. word fits, is how BACHAR is perceived in the Eng. rendering.

How is that method appropriate?

The choice of meaning for a word with two possible meanings is dependent on the immediate context: it is governed by the word or words either side.

It is like the Eng. words "table" or "chair" with more than one meaning.

Here is an example of two meanings for each of the Eng. words "table" and "chair":

> **The Chair of the committee sat on a wooden chair and, on the table in front of him was a book which contained on the first page a table of contents.**

The immediate words in the context inform us how to read and understand the two separate meanings of "chair" and of "table".

This is the same for translators of BACHAR into modern languages.

So, to assist here, how is BACHAR translated in relation to where the Gk. words appear in the LXX?

To this end the KJV, the YLT, the NKJV, the NASB, the NIV, and the NLT are all used to glean the Eng.

So for *EKLEGÓ* (to choose, pick – 113), the most used Gk. word to translate BACHAR, we find:

EKLEGÓ (113) I quote the first 7 out of the 113 [for all the full verses, at minimum as found in KJV, see the chapter on BACHAR]

With 113 *EKLEGÓ* and 12 *HAIRETIZÓ* I have only used the 7 first examples for each of those two

All other Gk words have the Eng. rendering of BACHAR quoted in full (they are less than 7 except for *EKLEKTOS* which has 8).

Gen. 6:2 "they chose"; "they have chosen" YLT; "they chose" NKJV; "they chose" NASB; "they chose" NIV; "they wanted" NLT

Gen. 13:11 "chose"; "chooseth" YLT; "chose" NKJV; "chose" NASB; "chose" NIV; "chose" NLT

Num. 16:5 "chosen"; "He doth fix on" YLT; "He chooses" NKJV; "He will choose" NASB; "he chooses" NIV; "he selects" NLT

Num. 16:7 "doth choose"; "chooseth" YLT; "chooses" NKJV; "chooses" NASB; "chooses" NIV; "chooses" NLT

Num. 17:5 "I shall choose"; "I fix" YLT; "I choose" NKJV; "I choose" NASB; "I choose" NIV; "I choose" NLT

Deu. 4:37 "he chose"; "I doth" (also) "fix" YLT; "He chose" NKJV; "He chose" NASB; "chose" NIV; "he chose" NLT

Deu. 7:7 "choose"; "fixeth" YLT; "choose" NKJV; "He choose" NASB; "choose" NIV; "he choose" NLT

Without exception then, the perception of the translators of BACHAR into Eng. by means of the words in the vicinity, shows *EKLEGÓ* means "to choose" in one form or another.

Note the YLT's use of "fix" i.e. "to fix on to do…" is in the sense of mentally decided: chose to

So, with this unambiguous rendering the Gk. word *EKLEGÓ* is only used for "to choose"

And since "to choose" is in the "chosen" category that is where *EKLEGÓ* goes

REASONABLE ARGUMENT 3 (b)

Using this reasonable and independent means then, all the Gk. words for BACHAR can be fitted into either category: The "**chosen**" category or the "**best, top quality, excellent**" category

Remember this is according to the Heb. translated into English in the places where each Gk. word renders BACHAR in the LXX:

"to choose", "chosen" Category

EKLEGÓ	(to choose, pick - 113)	as per above
HAIRETIZÓ	(to choose - 12)	as per below

HAIRETIZÓ (12) I quote the first 7 – all following words are given in full

> 1Ch. 28:4b "he hath chosen"; "He hath fixed" YLT; "He hath chosen" NKJV; "He hath chosen" NASB; "He chose" NIV; "he has chosen" NLT
>
> 1Ch. 28:6 "I have chosen"; "I have fixed" YLT; "I have chosen" NKJV; "I have chosen" NASB; "I have chosen" NIV; "I have chosen" NLT
>
> 1Ch. 28:10 "hath chosen"; "hath fixed on" YLT; "has chosen" NKJV; "has chosen" NASB; "has chosen" NIV; "has chosen" NLT
>
> 1Ch. 29:1 "hath chosen"; "hath fixed" YLT; "has chosen" NKJV; "has chosen" NASB; "has chosen" NIV; "has" (clearly) "chosen" NLT
>
> 2Ch. 29:11 "hath chosen"; "hath" (Jehovah) "fixed" YLT; "has chosen" NKJV; "has chosen" NASB; "has chosen" NIV; "has chosen" NLT
>
> Psa. 25:12 "shall choose"; "doth choose" YLT; "chooses" NKJV; "should choose" NASB; "should choose" NIV; "should choose" NLT
>
> Psa. 119:30 "have chosen"; "have chosen" YLT; "have chosen" NKJV; "have chosen" NASB; "have chosen" NIV; "have chosen" NLT

"to choose", "chosen" Category

EKLEGÓ	(to choose, pick - 113)	as per above
HAIRETIZÓ	(to choose - 12)	as per above
EPILEGÓ	(pick out, select - 6)	as per below

EPILEGÓ (6)

Exo. 17:9 "choose"; "choose" YLT; "choose" NKJV; "choose" NASB; "choose" NIV; "choose" NLT

Exo. 18:25 "chose"; "chooseth" YLT; "chose" NKJV; "chose" NASB; "chose" NIV; "chose" NLT

Deu. 21:5 "hath chosen"; "fixed" YLT; "has chosen" NKJV; "has chosen" NASB; "has chosen" NIV; "has chosen" NLT

Jos. 8:3 "chose out"; "chooseth" YLT; "chose" NKJV; "chose" NASB; "chose" NIV; "chose" NLT

2Sa. 10:9 "chose"; "chooseth" YLT; "chose" NKJV; "selected" NASB; "selected" NIV; "chose" NLT

2Sa. 17:1 "choose out"; "choose" YLT; "choose" NKJV; "choose" NASB; "choose" NIV; "choose" NLT

"to choose", "chosen" Category

EKLEGÓ	(to choose, pick - 113)	as per above
HAIRETIZÓ	(to choose - 12)	as per above
EPILEGÓ	(pick out, select - 6)	as per above
HAIREÓ	(to choose, prefer - 3)	as per below

HAIREÓ (3)

2Sa. 15:15 "shall appoint"; "chooseth" YLT; "commands" NKJV; "chooses" NASB; "chooses" NIV; "think is best" NLT

Job 34:4 "let us choose"; "let us choose" YLT; "let us choose" NKJV; "let us choose" NASB; "let us discern" NIV; "let us discern" NLT

Jer. 8:3 "shall be chosen"; "chosen is" YLT; "shall be chosen" NKJV; "will be chosen" NASB; "will prefer" NIV; "will wish" NLT

"to choose", "chosen" Category

EKLEGÓ	(to choose, pick - 113)	as per above
HAIRETIZÓ	(to choose - 12)	as per above
EPILEGÓ	(pick out, select - 6)	as per above
HAIREÓ	(to choose, prefer - 3)	as per above
DIAKRINÓ	(judge, decide - 2)	as per below

DIAKRINÓ (2)

Job 9:14 "choose out"; "choose out" YLT; "choose" NKJV; "choose" NASB; "how can I find" (words) "to argue" NIV; "I should try to - reason" NLT

Job 15:5 "choosest"; "choosest" YLT; "choose" NKJV; "choose" NASB; "adopt" NIV; "are based on" NLT

"to choose", "chosen" Category

EKLEGÓ	(to choose, pick - 113)	as per above
HAIRETIZÓ	(to choose - 12)	as per above
EPILEGÓ	(pick out, select - 6)	as per above
HAIREÓ	(to choose, prefer - 3)	as per above
DIAKRINÓ	(judge, decide - 2)	as per above
PROAIREÓ	(to choose, prefer - 2)	as per below

PROAIREÓ (2)

Deu. 7:6 "hath chosen"; "fixed" YLT; "has chosen" NKJV; "has chosen" NASB; "has chosen" NIV; "has chosen" NLT

Pro. 1:29 "choose"; "have" (not) "chosen" YLT; "did" (not) "choose" NKJV; "did" (not) "choose" NASB; "did" (not) "choose" NIV; "chose" (not) NLT

"to choose", "chosen" Category

EKLEGÓ	(to choose, pick - 113)	as per above
HAIRETIZÓ	(to choose - 12)	as per above
EPILEGÓ	(pick out, select - 6)	as per above
HAIREÓ	(to choose, prefer - 3)	as per above
DIAKRINÓ	(judge, decide - 2)	as per above
PROAIREÓ	(to choose, prefer - 2)	as per above
APALLASSÓ	(set free - 1)	as per below

APALLASSÓ (1)

Job 7:15 "chooseth"; "chooseth" YLT; "chooses" NKJV; "would choose" NASB; "I prefer" NIV; "I would rather be" NLT

"to choose", "chosen" Category

EKLEGÓ	(to choose, pick - 113)	as per above
HAIRETIZÓ	(to choose - 12)	as per above
EPILEGÓ	(pick out, select - 6)	as per above
HAIREÓ	(to choose, prefer - 3)	as per above
DIAKRINÓ	(judge, decide - 2)	as per above
PROAIREÓ	(to choose, prefer - 2)	as per above
APALLASSÓ	(set free - 1)	as per above
ARESKÓ	(to do what pleases - 1)	as per below

ARESKÓ (1)

Deu. 23:16 "choose"; "he chooseth" YLT; "he chooses" NKJV; "he shall choose" NASB; "they choose" NIV; "they choose" NLT

"to choose", "chosen" Category

EKLEGÓ	(to choose, pick - 113)	as per above
HAIRETIZÓ	(to choose - 12)	as per above
EPILEGÓ	(pick out, select - 6)	as per above
HAIREÓ	(to choose, prefer - 3)	as per above
DIAKRINÓ	(judge, decide - 2)	as per above
PROAIREÓ	(to choose, prefer - 2)	as per above
APALLASSÓ	(set free - 1)	as per above
ARESKÓ	(to do what pleases - 1)	as per above
EPITHUMEÓ	(desired, coveted - 1)	as per below

EPITHUMEÓ (1)

Isa. 1:29 "have chosen"; "have chosen" YLT; "have chosen" NKJV; "have chosen" NASB; "have chosen" NIV; NOT translated NLT

"to choose", "chosen" Category

EKLEGÓ	(to choose, pick - 113)	as per above
HAIRETIZÓ	(to choose - 12)	as per above
EPILEGÓ	(pick out, select - 6)	as per above
HAIREÓ	(to choose, prefer - 3)	as per above
DIAKRINÓ	(judge, decide - 2)	as per above

PROAIREÓ	(to choose, prefer - 2)	as per above
APALLASSÓ	(set free - 1)	as per above
ARESKÓ	(to do what pleases - 1)	as per above
EPITHUMEÓ	(desired, coveted - 1)	as per above
ZÉLOÓ	(to esteem, emulate - 1)	as per below

ZÉLOÓ (1)

Pro. 3:31 "choose"; "fix" (thou on any of his ways) YLT; "choose" NKJV; "do" (not) "choose" NASB; "choose" NIV; "copy" (their ways) NLT

So, the **"to choose", "chosen" Category** of Gk. words rendered from BACHAR are

EKLEGÓ	(to choose, pick - 113)
HAIRETIZÓ	(to choose - 12)
EPILEGÓ	(pick out, select - 6)
HAIREÓ	(to choose, prefer - 3)
DIAKRINÓ	(judge, decide - 2)
PROAIREÓ	(to choose, prefer - 2)
APALLASSÓ	(set free - 1)
ARESKÓ	(to do what pleases - 1)
EPITHUMEÓ	(desired, coveted - 1)
ZÉLOÓ	(to esteem, emulate - 1)

All the above involved an unambiguous rendering of "to choose" type in Eng. from BACHAR

Bearing in mind that "to be chosen" is in the "**best, top quality, excellent**" category i.e. (something or someone) *to be chosen*: preferred: excellent

The remaining words – leaving *EKLEKTOS* till last – then fit in with the "**best, top quality, excellent**" category or I place in an indeterminate section: the latter do not contain enough examples to be accurate in determining the category by this method

"best, top quality, excellent" Category

DUNATOS	(strong, mighty, able - 4)	as per below

DUNATOS (4)

2Ch. 13:3a (400,000) "chosen" (men); (400,000) "chosen" (men) YLT; (400,000) "choice" (men) NKJV; (400,000) "chosen" (men) NASB; (400,000) "able" (fighting men) NIV; (400,000) "select" (warriors) NLT

2Ch. 13:3b (800,000) "chosen" (men - mighty men of valour); (800,000) "chosen" (men - mighty of valour) YLT; (800,000) "choice" (men - mighty men of valor) NKJV; (800,000) "chosen" (men – valiant warriors) NASB; (800,000) "able" (troops) NIV; (800,000) "select" (troops) NLT

2Ch. 13:17 (500,000) "chosen" (men); (500,000) "chosen" (men) YLT; (500,000) "choice" (men) NKJV; (500,000) "chosen" (men) NASB; (500,000 – Israel's) "able" (men) NIV; (500,000 – Israel's) "select" (troops) YLT

2Ch. 25:5 (300,000) "choice" (*men, able* – to war); (300,000) "chosen ones" (holding spear and target) YLT; (300,000) "choice" (*men, able* – to war) NKJV; (300,000) "choice men" (*able* – to war) NASB; (300,000) "men fit" (for military service) NIV; (300,000) "select troops" (trained) NLT

"best, top quality, excellent" Category

DUNATOS	(strong, mighty, able - 4)	as per above
NEANIAS	(young man, youth - 4)	as per below

NEANIAS (4)

2Sa. 6:1 (*the*) "chosen" (*men* of Israel - 30,000); (every) "chosen one" (in Israel - 30,000) YLT; (*the*) "choice" (*men* of Israel - 30,000) NKJV; (the) "chosen" (men of Israel - 30,000) NASB; (the) "able young men" (of Israel – 30,000) NIV; "the elite troops" (in Israel - 30,000) NLT

2Sa. 10:9 (the) "choice" (*men* of Israel); (the) "chosen" (in Israel) YLT; (Israel's) "choice" (*men* of Israel) NKJV; (the) "choice men" (of Israel) NASB; (the) "best troops" (in Israel) NIV; (Israel's) "elite troops" NLT

1Ki. 12:21 (180,000) "chosen men" (which were warriors); (180,000) "chosen" (warriors) YLT; (180,000) "chosen men" (who were warriors) NKJV; (180,000) "chosen men" (who were warriors) NASB; (180,000) "able young men" (to go to war) NIV; (180,000) "select troops" (to fight) NLT

1Ch. 19:10 (the) "choice" (of Israel); (the) "choice" (in Israel) YLT; (Israel's) "best" NKJV; (the) "choice men" (of Israel) NASB; (the) "best troops" (in Israel) NIV; (Israel's) "elite troops" NLT

"best, top quality, excellent" Category

DUNATOS	(strong, mighty, able - 4)	as per above
NEANIAS	(young man, youth - 4)	as per above
EPHISTÉMI	(set up, establish - 2)	as per below

EPHISTÉMI (2)

Jer. 49:19 "chosen"; "chosen" YLT; "chosen" NKJV; "chosen" NASB; "chosen one" NIV; "choice" NLT

Jer. 50:44 "chosen" (*man*); "chosen" YLT; "chosen" (*man*) NKJV; "chosen" NASB; "chosen one" NIV; "choice" NLT

"best, top quality, excellent" Category

DUNATOS	(strong, mighty, able - 4)	as per above
NEANIAS	(young man, youth - 4)	as per above
EPHISTÉMI	(set up, establish - 2)	as per above
DOKIMAZÓ	(to approve, assay - 1)	as per below

DOKIMAZÓ (1)

Pro. 8:10 "choice" (gold); "choice" (gold) YLT; "choice" (gold) NKJV; "choicest" (gold) NASB; "choice" (gold) NIV; "pure" (gold) NLT

"best, top quality, excellent" Category

DUNATOS	(strong, mighty, able - 4)	as per above
NEANIAS	(young man, youth - 4)	as per above
EPHISTÉMI	(set up, establish - 2)	as per above
DOKIMAZÓ	(to approve, assay - 1)	as per above
NEANISKOS	(young man, boy - 1)	as per below

NEANISKOS (1)

2Ch. 11:1 (180,000) "chosen" (*men*, which were warriors); (180,000) "chosen" (warriors) YLT; (180,000) "chosen" (*men*, who were warriors) NKJV; (180,000) "chosen men" (who were warriors) NASB; (180,000) "able young men" (to go to war) NIV; (180,000) "select troops" (to fight) NLT

"best, top quality, excellent" Category

DUNATOS	(strong, mighty, able - 4)	as per above
NEANIAS	(young man, youth - 4)	as per above
EPHISTÉMI	(set up, establish - 2)	as per above
DOKIMAZÓ	(to approve, assay - 1)	as per above
NEANISKOS	(young man, boy - 1)	as per above
PUROÓ	(to burn with fire, purge - 1)	as per below

PUROÓ (1)

Pro. 10:20 "choice" (silver); "chosen" (silver) YLT; "choice" (silver) NKJV; "choice" (silver) NASB; "choice" (silver) NIV; "sterling" (silver) NLT

Indeterminate

There are four Gk words in this overall list of LXX renderings of BACHAR that could be argued for either category using the current ID criteria so I place them here:

EXAIREÓ	(to choose, select out - 2)	as per below

EXAIREÓ (2)

Job 36:21 "hast thou chosen"; "thou hast fixed" YLT; "you have chosen" NKJV; "you have preferred" NASB; "you seem to prefer" NIV; NOT translated NLT

Isa. 48:10 "have chosen"; "have chosen" YLT; "have tested" NKJV; "have tested" NASB; "have tested" NIV; "have refined" NLT

HAIRETOS aNT (to be chosen, elected - 2) as per below

HAIRETOS aNT (2)

Pro. 16:16 "be chosen"; "be chosen" YLT; "be chosen" NKJV; "be chosen" NASB; "to get" (understanding) NIV; NOT translated NLT

Pro. 22:1 "to be chosen"; "is chosen" YLT; "is to be chosen" NKJV; "is to be" (more) "desired" NASB; "is" (more) "desirable" NIV; "choose" NLT

ARESTOS (acceptable, pleasing - 1) as per below

ARESTOS (1)

Pro. 21:3 (*is*) "more acceptable"; "is chosen" YLT; (*is*) "more acceptable" NKJV; "is desired" NASB; "is more acceptable" NIV; "is more pleased" NLT

METOCHOS (partaking - 1) as per below

METOCHOS (1)

1Sa. 20:30 "hast chosen"; "art fixing" YLT; "have chosen" NKJV; "are choosing" NASB; "have sided" NIV; "want" (him to be) NLT

Where does *EKLEKTOS* fit in?

Let's see:

EKLEKTOS (8)

Exo. 14:7 "chosen chariots"; "chosen chariots" YLT; "choice chariots" NKJV; "select chariots" NASB; "the best chariots" NIV; "best chariots" NLT

Jud. 20:15 (700) "chosen men"; (700) "chosen men" YLT; (700) "select men" NKJV; (700) "able young men" NIV; (700) "elite troops" NLT

Jud. 20:34 (10,000) "chosen men"; (10,000) "chosen men" YLT; (10,000) "select men" NKJV; (10,000) "choice men" NASB; (10,000) "able young men" NIV; (10,000) "elite" (Israelite) "troops" NLT

1Sa. 24:2 (3,000) "chosen men"; (3,000) "chosen men" YLT; (3,000) "chosen men" NKJV; (3,000) "chosen men" NASB; (3,000) "able young men" UK; (3,000) "elite troops" NLT

1Sa. 26:2 (3,000) "chosen men" (of Israel); (3,000 men) "chosen ones" (of Israel) YLT; (3,000) "chosen men" (of Israel) NKJV; (3,000) "chosen men" (of Israel) NASB; (3,000) "select" (Israelite) "troops" NIV; (3,000 of Israel's) "elite troops" NLT

Psa. 89:19 (holy - mighty) "chosen"; (saint – mighty one) "a chosen one" YLT; (holy one - mighty) "one chosen" NKJV; (godly ones - mighty) "one chosen" NASB; (faithful people - warrior) "a young man" NIV; (faithful people - warrior) "selected" NLT

Pro. 8:19 "choice" (silver); "choice" (silver) YLT; "choice" (silver) NKJV; "choicest" (silver) NASB; "choice" (silver) NIV; "sterling" (silver) YLT

Sng. 5:15 "excellent" (as the cedars); "choice" (as the cedars) YLT; "excellent" (as the cedars) NKJV; "choice" (as the cedars) NASB; "choice" (as its cedars) NIV; "noble" (cedars of Lebanon) NLT

So, the "**best, top quality, excellent**" **Category** of Gk. words rendered from BACHAR are

EKLEKTOS (8)

DUNATOS (strong, mighty, able - 4)

NEANIAS (young man, youth - 4)

EPHISTÉMI (set up, establish - 2)

DOKIMAZÓ (to approve, assay - 1)

NEANISKOS (young man, boy - 1)

PUROÓ (to burn with fire, purge - 1)

The **"to choose", "chosen" Category** of Gk. words rendered from BACHAR (from above) are

EKLEGÓ (to choose, pick - 113)

HAIRETIZÓ (to choose - 12)

EPILEGÓ (pick out, select - 6)

HAIREÓ	(to choose, prefer - 3)
DIAKRINÓ	(judge, decide - 2)
PROAIREÓ	(to choose, prefer - 2)
APALLASSÓ	(set free - 1)
ARESKÓ	(to do what pleases - 1)
EPITHUMEÓ	(desired, coveted - 1)
ZÉLOÓ	(to esteem, emulate - 1)

And not as clear within criteria are:

EXAIREÓ (to choose, select out - 2)

HAIRETOS aNT (to be chosen, elected - 2)

ARESTOS (acceptable, pleasing - 1)

METOCHOS (partaking - 1)

We know which category *EKLEKTOS* falls into by the same means used for *DUNATOS* (strong, mighty), *NEANIAS* (youth, young man), or *NEANISKOS* (young man). As we shall see with the Heb. BACHUR "young man" in the Reasonable argument 5 below, *EKLEKTOS* is seen used 5 times to represent "young man". So it is then natural to observe that within the mind of the LXX translator *EKLEKTOS* has an affinity with "young man": as someone to be chosen: preferred: excellent – for a time in history when a nation was dependent on the most fit as soldiers, a young man is the most fit for purpose: *EKLEKTOS*: A word firmly within the "**best, top quality, excellent**" Category.

Remember, BACHAR was the most likely Heb. word to reveal whether *EKLEKTOS* had a "selective" emphasis.

At the end of reasonable argument 2 we had:

BACHAR	(6 "chosen" – 2 "best, top quality, excellent")
MIBCHAR	(2 "chosen" – 5 "best, top quality, excellent")
BACHUR	(1 "chosen" – 4 "best, top quality, excellent")
BARAR	(1 "chosen" – 6 "best, top quality, excellent")

We can now reasonably see all 8 from BACHAR are in the same category

3 reasonable truths from above

57 as "best, top quality, excellent"

4 as "chosen" type

13 pending from BACHIR

Total 74

REASONABLE ARGUMENT 4 MIBCHAR

We now have 3 Heb. words left before BACHIR:

MIBCHAR	(2 "chosen" – 5 "best, top quality, excellent")
BACHUR	(1 "chosen" – 4 "best, top quality, excellent")
BARAR	(1 "chosen" – 6 "best, top quality, excellent")

MIBCHAR "the best" is more translated by ***EKLEKTOS*** than by any other Gk. word:

MIBCHAR is 7 × *EKLEKTOS* out of 12

2 of those *EKLEKTOS* are "chosen" in KJV
Jer. 48:15 (LXX 31:15), also "chosen" in NKJV, & Dan.11:15

But in other versions MIBCHAR at these 2 passages are given as:

Jer. 48:15 (LXX 31:15): "choice" YLT; "choicest" NASB; "finest" NIV; "most promising" NLT

Dan. 11:15: "choice" YLT, NKJV; ""choicest" NASB; "best" NIV, NLT

That is, 2 out of the 4, from the total 12 MIBCHAR which are rendered as "chosen" in KJV

The other 2 MIBCHAR that are rendered as "chosen" in KJV are:

Exo. 15:4 (also NKJV) and Eze. 23:7 both rendered by *EPILEKTOS* aNT in the LXX

But in other English versions these two are rendered:

Exo. 15:4 - "choice" YLT; "choicest" NASB; "best" NIV; "finest" NLT

Eze. 23:7 - "choice" YLT, NKJV; "choicest" NASB; "elite" NIV; "most desirable" NLT

See separate chapter produced for *EPILEKTOS* aNT which is of value as it is in the same family as *EKLEKTOS*.

So, the 4 times "chosen" in the KJV MIBCHAR is rendered, it is elsewhere more often seen with a high quality meaning.

With all the LXX rendering of MIBCHAR we had:

EKLEKTOS 7; *EPILEKTOS* aNT "choice" 3; *KALLOS* aNT "beauty" 1

The 5 non "chosen" for *EKLEKTOS* are:

"choice of our sepulchres" (Gen. 23:6)

"choice vows" (Deu. 12:11)

"choicest valleys" (Isa. 22:7)

"choice cedars" (Jer. 22:7)

"trees . . . the choice and best" (Eze. 31:16);

So, with all occasions of MIBCHAR reasonably visible with a meaning of high quality from the above observations:

It is reasonable then to include all of MIBCHAR in the "best, top quality, excellent" category

3 reasonable truths from above

59 as "best, top quality, excellent"

2 as "chosen" type

13 pending from BACHIR

Total 74

REASONABLE ARGUMENT 5 BACHUR

We now have 2 Heb. words left before BACHIR:

BACHUR (1 "chosen" – 4 "best, top quality, excellent")

BARAR (1 "chosen" – 6 "best, top quality, excellent")

From the discovery of the different Greek words in the LXX for Heb. words

For BACHUR we have

BACHUR *NEANISKOS* (young man, boy - 34)
EKLEKTOS **(5)**
NEANIAS (young man, youth - 2)
ANÉR (man, husband - 1)
NOT in LXX (3)

Now, BACHUR is found only translated as "chosen" (KJV) once (at all)

It is at Psa. 78:31 as below.

This was rendered in the Gk. by *EKLEKTOS*

The other 4 times BACHUR is translated by *EKLEKTOS* are:

2Ki. 8:12 "young men"; "sucklings" YLT; "young men" NKJV, NASB, NIV, NLT
Lam. 1:15 "young men"; "young men" YLT, NKJV, NASB, NIV; "young warriors" NLT
Lam. 5:13 "young men"; "young men" YLT, NKJV, NASB, NIV, NLT
Lam. 5:14 "young men"; "young men" YLT, NKJV, NASB, NIV, NLT

Here is BACHUR in Ys and Ss:

Ys Conc.	Count	Ss Conc. No. H 970	Count
choice young man	1	young man	42
chosen	1	the chosen	1
young	1	young	1
young man	42	not translated	1
TOTAL	45	TOTAL	45

This one time as "chosen" is in LXX at Psalm 77:31

Psa. 78:31 The wrath of God came upon them, and slew the fattest of them, and smote down **the chosen** *men* of Israel.

YLT And the anger of God hath gone up against them, and He slayeth among their fat ones, and **youths** of Israel He caused to bend.

NKJV The wrath of God came against them, and slew the stoutest of them, and struck down the **choice** *men* of Israel.

NASB The anger of God rose against them and killed some of their stoutest ones, and subdued the **choice men** of Israel.

NIV God's anger rose against them; he put to death the sturdiest among them, cutting down the **young men** of Israel.

NLT the anger of God rose against them, and he killed their strongest men. He struck down the **finest** of Israel's **young men**.

This makes this occasion of BACHUR as "chosen" by the KJV as the sole exception and can reasonably be said to be out of character for BACHUR. Only the KJV renders it so. The word as seen in all other places in KJV is: "young man" (42), "young" (1) or not rendered (1).

It is basically in meaning like the Gk. *NEANIAS* and *NEANISKOS* meaning "young man".

It is reasonable then to understand "young man" here too. And as this singles out men that are at their physical best: in the prime of life, they are thereby seen as "the excellent" among men: physically best able to use hand to hand weapons of war.

It is of note now to see *EKLEKTOS* renders "young man" from BACHUR 5 times:

A young man is understood as a guy in his prime: at his physical best

3 reasonable truths from above

60 as "best, top quality, excellent"

1 as "chosen" type

13 pending from BACHIR

Total 74

REASONABLE ARGUMENT 6 BARAR

Just as BACHUR was only once given as "chosen" (Reasonable Argument 5), we see BARAR also only once given as "chosen" in connection with *EKLEKTOS* in the LXX

BARAR (1 "chosen" + 7 "best, top quality, excellent" = 8× *EKLEKTOS*)

Now, BARAR is found translated as "chosen" (KJV) twice:

The once at 1Ch. 9:22 with *EKLEKTOS* in the LXX

And also at 1Ch. 16:41 with *EKLEGÓ* in the LXX

The 7 other times BARAR is rendered by *EKLEKTOS* are given as:

2Sam. 22:27a "pure"; "pure" YLT, NKJV, NASB, NIV, NLT

2Sam. 22:27b "pure"; "pure" YLT, NKJV, NASB, NIV, NLT

1Ch. 7:40 "choice"; "chosen ones" YLT; "choice men" NKJV; "choice" NASB; "Choice men" NIV; "select men" NLT

Neh. 5:18 "choice"; "fat" YLT; "choice" NKJV, NASB, NIV, NLT

Psa. 18:26a "pure"; "pure" YLT, NKJV, NASB, NIV, NLT

Psa. 18:26b "pure"; "pure" YLT, NKJV, NASB, NIV, NLT

Isa. 49:2 "polished" (shaft); "clear" (arrow) YLT; "polished" (shaft) NKJV; "select" (arrow) NASB; "polished" (arrow) NIV; "sharp" (arrow) NLT

From the discovery of the different Greek words in the LXX for Heb. words

For BARAR we have

BARAR ***EKLEKTOS* (8)**
EKLEGÓ (to pick, choose - 2)
KATHAROS (clean, pure - 2)
PUROÓ (burn up, purify - 2)
APHORIZÓ (to define, determine - 1)
DIAKRINÓ (to decide, judge - 1)
PARASKEUAZÓ (make ready - 1)
NOT in LXX (1)

Here is BARAR in Ys and Ss:

	Ys Conc.	Count	Ss Conc.	Count
= to purify (P.165)			No. H 1305	
	manifest	1	pure	5
	purge out	1	choice	2
	choice	2	chosen	2
	chosen	2	clean	2
	polished	1	clearly	1
	pure	1	manifest	1
	clearly	1	bright	1
	be clean	1	purge out	1
Partic.	pure	2	polished	1
	purge	1	purge	1
	cleanse	1	purified	1
	make bright	1		
	be purified	1		
	shew self pure	2		
	TOTAL	18	TOTAL	18

The one time as "chosen" and in LXX as *EKLEKTOS* - taken whole from the chapter on BARAR

1Ch. 9:22 All these *which were* **chosen** to be porters in the gates *were* two hundred and twelve. These were reckoned by their genealogy in their villages, whom David and Samuel the seer did ordain in their set office.

YLT All of those who are **chosen** for gatekeepers at the thresholds *are* two hundred and twelve; they *are* in their villages, by their genealogy; they whom David and Samuel the seer appointed in their office.

NKJV All those **chosen** as gatekeepers *were* two hundred and twelve. They were recorded by their genealogy, in their villages. David and Samuel the seer had appointed them to their trusted office.

NASB All these who were **chosen** to be gatekeepers at the thresholds were 212. These were enrolled by genealogy in their villages, whom David and Samuel the seer appointed in their office of trust.

NIV Altogether, those **chosen** to be gatekeepers at the thresholds numbered 212. They were registered by genealogy in their villages. The gatekeepers had been assigned to their positions of trust by David and Samuel the seer.

NLT In all, there were 212 gatekeepers in those days, and they were **listed** according to the genealogies in their villages. David and Samuel the seer had appointed their ancestors because they were reliable men.

EKLEKTOS – a divergent translation with "in their villages" (KJV) rendered as "in their courts" (engLXX) – Ys in his Conc. places the "chosen" and that of 1Ch. 16:41 (see below) under the header "*to purify*" BARAR P. 165: The use of BARAR here as opposed to BACHAR means purification was involved: the translator two chapters earlier is clearly following the pattern of the LXX of quality for the word *EKLEKTOS* [see 7:40 in quality list of 7 above] and uses a well used word for "chosen" seven chapters later [see 16:41 below]: with a preparation involved due to the root "to purify" from BARAR the "choosing" here is not independent of quality: they are clean

LXX *PANTES HOI* ***EKLEKTOI*** *EPI TÉS PULÉS EN TAIS PULAIS DIAKOSIOI KAI*
all the choice upon the gate in the gates two-hundred and

DEKADUO HOUTOI EN TAIS AULAIS AUTÓN HO KATALOCHISMOS AUTÓN
twelve these in the courts of them the distribution of them

TOUTOUS ESTÉSE DAUID KAI SAMOUÉL HO BLEPÓN TÉ PISTEI AUTÓN
these established David and Samuel the seer the trust of them

engLXX All the chosen porters in the gates *were* two hundred and twelve, these *were* in their courts, *this was* their distribution: these David and Samuel the seer established in their charge.

The one time as "chosen" and in LXX as *EKLEGÓ* is at 1Ch. 16:41

1Ch. 16:41 And with them Heman and Jeduthun, and the rest that were **chosen**, who were expressed by name, to give thanks to the LORD, because his mercy *endureth* for ever;

YLT And with them *are* Heman and Jeduthun, and the rest of those **chosen**, who were defined by name, to give thanks to Jehovah, for to the age *is* His kindness,

NKJV and with them Heman and Jeduthun and the rest who were **chosen**, who were designated by name, to give thanks to the LORD, because His mercy *endures* forever;

NASB With them *were* Heman and Jeduthun, and the rest who were **chosen**, who were designated by name, to give thanks to the LORD, because His lovingkindness is everlasting.

NIV With them were Heman and Jeduthun and the rest of those **chosen** and designated by name to give thanks to the LORD, 'for his love endures for ever.'

NLT David also **appointed** Heman, Jeduthun, and the others chosen by name to give thanks to the LORD, for "his faithful love endures forever."

EKLEGÓ - to pick, choose, elect – a direct translation – the chosen by name to the job of praising God

LXX *KAI MET AUTOU AIMAN KAI IDITHOUN KAI HOI LOIPOI* ***EKLEGENTES*** *EP*
and with of him Aiman and idithon and the rest chosen out upon

ONOMATOS TOU AINEIN TON KURION HOTI EIS TON AIÓNA TO ELEOS AUTOU
name of the to praise the Lord since into the ages the mercy of him

engLXX And with him *were* Aeman and Idithun, and the rest chosen out by name to praise the Lord, for his mercy *endures* for ever.

Now, we saw from BACHAR "to choose" above how *EKLEGÓ* was the most used word to translate it and clearly *EKLEGÓ* is a word fully in the "chosen" and "to select" category. So, why is *EKLEGÓ* found twice rendering BARAR and only 1 is found with BARAR as "chosen"? The 2 different renderings related to *EKLEGÓ* show how loose the LXX translation can be.

Here is the other occasion:

Eze. 20:38 And I **will purge out** from among you the rebels, and them that transgress against me: I will bring them forth out of the country where they sojourn, and they shall not enter into the land of Israel: and ye shall know that I *am* the LORD.

YLT And **cleared out** from you the rebels, and them transgressing against Me, from the land of their sojournings I bring them out, and unto the land of Israel they come not, and ye have known that I *am* Jehovah.

NKJV I **will purge** the rebels from among you, and those who transgress against Me; I will bring them out of the country where they dwell, but they shall not enter the land of Israel. Then you will know that I *am* the LORD.

NASB and I **will purge** from you the rebels and those who transgress against Me; I will bring them out of the land where they sojourn, but they will not enter the land of Israel. Thus you will know that I am the LORD.

NIV I **will purge** you of those who revolt and rebel against me. Although I will bring them out of the land where they are living, yet they will not enter the land of Israel. Then you will know that I am the LORD.

NLT I **will purge** you of all those who rebel and revolt against me. I will bring them out of the countries where they are in exile, but they will never enter the land of Israel. Then you will know that I am the LORD.

EKLEGÓ - to pick, choose, elect – a divergent translation with an added "Lord" – to clean, purge out, pick out the wicked from the land of Israel

LXX *KAI **EKLEXÓ** EX HUMÓN TOUS ASEBEIS KAI TOUS APHESTÉKOTAS DIOTI EK*
and I shall choose out of you the impious and the revolters because out of

TÉS PAROIKESIAS AUTÓN EXAXÓ AUTOUS KAI EIS TÉN GÉN TOU ISRAÉL OUK
the sojourning of them I will lead them and into the land of the Israel not

EISELEUSONTAI KAI EPIGNÓSESTHE DIOTI EGÓ KURIOS KURIOS
shall enter and shall know because I Lord Lord

engLXX And I will separate from among you the ungodly and the revolters; for I will lead them forth out of their place of sojourning, and they shall not enter into the land of Israel: and ye shall know that I am the Lord, *even* the Lord.

The thing is, BARAR, unlike BACHAR does not have two clear meanings, and in the use of *EKLEKTOS* and *EKLEGÓ* with BARAR, if we use the same method and criteria as with BACHAR to identify which Gk. word was in which category, both *EKLEKTOS* and *EKLEGÓ* would be in both categories:

EKLEKTOS 7 × in "best, top quality, excellent" category and 1 × in "chosen" category

EKLEGÓ 1 × in "best, top quality, excellent" category and 1 × in "chosen" category

So that if we claim *EKLEKTOS* involves a decision, a selection based on 1 occasion in the LXX and the comparison of how the Heb. is independently translated, then we must do the same for 1 occasion that *EKLEGÓ* occurs and claim that involves someone or something of excellence, when in fact it is just about choosing either of anything, whether good or not: of high value or not. Not a reasonable proposition.

The essential to remember is that the Heb. original of the OT is the Scripture and the inspired text, just as the Gk. original of the NT is the Scripture and the inspired text. The LXX is not inspired like the Heb. but is a valuable historical pointer to the use of Gk. words in the NT as this work shows, but it is not comprehensive and here could be seen as an exception but to use an exception as the rule is deception and certainly not reasonable.

The LXX is not itself inspired as can be well seen in the very passage with the "chosen" being divergent. The comment I wrote for it says:

EKLEKTOS – a divergent translation with "in their villages" (KJV) rendered as "in their courts" (engLXX) – Ys in his Conc. places the "chosen" and that of 1Ch. 16:41 (see below) under the header "*to purify*" BARAR P. 165: The use of BARAR here as opposed to BACHAR means purification was involved: the translator two chapters earlier is clearly following the pattern of the LXX of quality for the word *EKLEKTOS* [see 7:40 above] and uses a well used word for "chosen" seven chapters later [see 16:41 below]: with a preparation involved due to the root "to purify" from BARAR the "choosing" here is not independent of quality: they are clean

Leaving out the references in the [square brackets] which are for the reader's use in the chapter on BARAR, the divergence from the inspired text is evident.

But the real use for any Gk. word to render BARAR is as an expression of a root meaning of cleaning and purifying. This is well seen where it is rendered "manifest" in the KJV, "cleanse" in the YLT and the LXX has the Gk word *DIAKRINÓ* - to decide, judge, distinguish. Any decision as indicated, just as with "chosen" being discussed, is only due to the person or item in question in some cleansing or purifying involvement.

Ecc. 3:18 I said in mine heart concerning the estate of the sons of men, that God might **manifest** them, and that they might see that they themselves are beasts.

YLT I said in my heart concerning the matter of the sons of man that God might **cleanse** them, so as to see that they themselves *are* beasts.

NKJV I said in my heart, "Concerning the condition of the sons of men, God **tests** them, that they may see that they themselves are *like* animals."

NASB I said to myself concerning the sons of men, "God has surely **tested** them in order for them to see that they are but beasts."

NIV I also said to myself, 'As for humans, God **tests** them so that they may see that they are like the animals.

NLT I also thought about the human condition—how God **proves** to people that they are like animals.

DIAKRINÓ - to decide, judge, distinguish – a divergent translation with "the estate of the sons of men" (KJV or "the matter of the sons of men" (YLT), rendered as "the speech of the sons of men" (engLXX) – God's examination of the life of someone reveals things, as they are brought to His light, and thereby cleansed in recognising they are "beasts": the Gk. has it as judge, but the manifestation itself is a form of judgment by enabling the sight for men to see themselves

LXX *EIPA EGÓ EN KARDIA MOU PERI LALIAS HUIÓN TOU ANTHRÓPOU HOTI*
said I in heart of me about talk of sons of the man since
DIAKRINEI *AUTOUS HO THEOS KAI TOU DEIXAI HOTI AUTOI KTÉNÉ EISI*
judge them the God and the to show since they beasts are

engLXX I said in my heart, concerning the speech of the sons of man, God will judge them, and that to shew that they are beasts.

So, with BARAR 7 × times given as *EKLEKTOS* well seen in the "best, top quality, excellent" category:

2Sa. 22:27a	With the **pure** . . .
2Sa. 22:27b	. . . thou wilt shew thyself **pure**
1Ch. 7:40	**choice** *and* mighty men of valour
1Ch. 9:22 (as above)	
Neh. 5:18	six **choice** sheep
Psa. 18:26a	With the **pure** . . .
Psa.18:26b	. . . thou wilt shew thyself **pure**
Isa. 49:2	a **polished** shaft; in his quiver (of an arrow)

So 1 × in "chosen" category, this "chosen" example involving the "porters in the gates" or "gatekeepers" which had involved a cleaning and preparation for this task by BARAR's use as well seen in the "manifest" rendering in English, given as *DIAKRINÓ* in the LXX: With such contexts, the decision is not a pointer to a choosing irrespective of item or person being of high or low quality; it is a decision involving a high quality: having been already cleansed with BARAR "to purify" (Ys Conc. P. 165).

This then reasonably removes this *EKLEKTOS* from the "chosen" category.

3 reasonable truths from above

61 as "best, top quality, excellent"

0 as "chosen" type

13 pending from BACHIR

Total 74

REASONABLE ARGUMENT 7 BACHIR

We are now left with the 13 pending from BACHIR

We saw that every place BACHIR occurs this is rendered in the LXX by *EKLEKTOS*

EKLEKTOS

We saw above how a Gk. reader – and that was all Christians to begin with: when Peter spoke to the crowd in Acts 2 it was in Greek as it was the unifying language of the day, in spite of each also having their own peculiar tongue which they had witnessed listening to, when the disciples' first practiced speaking in tongues at Pentecost – these Gk. readers would only have the LXX as their OT text through the first 3-400 years of the Church's existence. In it they read of,

The fat [*EKLEKTOS*] cows that came up out of the Nile in Pharaoh's dream which Joseph interpreted; the fat [*EKLEKTOS*] kernels of wheat in the same dream; young men [*EKLEKTOS*] i.e. guys in their prime; to the pure [*EKLEKTOS*] You will show Yourself pure [*EKLEKTOS*]; pleasant [*EKLEKTOS*] land; pleasant [*EKLEKTOS*] jewels; desire [*EKLEKTOS*] of all nations; tried [*EKLEKTOS*] stone; precious [*EKLEKTOS*] clothes; choice [*EKLEKTOS*] silver; highest [*EKLEKTOS*] branch of the cedar; and many more.

We also saw above that there is no reasonable case for *EKLEKTOS* reflecting the main meaning of BACHAR as "chosen", a derivative of "to choose", but instead its other meaning "to be chosen: preferred: excellent" and is in equal standing in this manner as the Gk. words *NEANIAS* (young man, youth), *NEANISKOS* (young man, boy) and *DUNATOS* (strong, mighty, able). No one reads these with a "chosen", "selected" emphasis in translation work now. If there were any hint of *EKLEKTOS* having a "chosen" (selected) emphasis, in its association with BACHAR is the best place where this could have been seen: it is completely lacking.

We saw the word BACHUR which is best translated as "young man", someone in their prime of life, fit for purpose, is several times rendered by *EKLEKTOS* (5) instead of its usual *NEANISKOS* (young man, boy - 34): *EKLEKTOS* is the second most used word to translate "young man".

The separate chapter about *EPILEKTOS*, a word in the same family as *EKLEKTOS* shows us that the meaning difference with *EKLEKTOS* is negligible. Both *EK* and *EPI* being prepositional additions to the same root word meaning. And thereby wholly unlike and unconnected to the other family of words which *EKLEGÓ* and *EPILEGÓ* belong to: something fully attested to by the BACHAR examination.

We saw there is reasonable ground for every place where the Heb. rendered as "chosen" in Eng. and the LXX translator used *EKLEKTOS* as that Heb. word, to be about an excellent or high quality type emphasis/ meaning.

With all these things in mind, is it reasonable thereby to consider BACHIR which is only translated by *EKLEKTOS* to be read by a Greek reader of the LXX as anything other than to be about a high quality, excellent appreciation?

No, it is not reasonable.

Clement of Rome

At the end of the 1st century, Clement is seen as one of the first senior bishops of Rome. He wrote a letter on behalf of the Rome leadership to the Church at Corinth. We find this letter in the Gk. of the NT. In this letter it is reasonable to see his use of the word *EKLEKTOS* just like the New Testament and also just like the LXX.

It is of note: Clement wrote his letter, not on his own authority, but that of the team for whom he spoke and indeed for the whole church at Rome. This can be seen from his use of the plural pronouns "**we**" and "**us**", at the beginning,

> **By reason of the sudden and repeated calamities and reverses which are befalling us, brethren, we consider that we have been somewhat tardy in giving heed to the matters of dispute that have arisen among you, dearly beloved** ***C1:1***

At the end,

> **For ye will give us great joy and gladness, if ye render obedience unto the things written by us through the Holy Spirit, and root out the unrighteous anger of your jealousy, according to the entreaty which we have made for peace and concord in this letter** ***C63:2***

And, at the middle, in saying new leaders should be appointed by Corinth in the following manner, it testifies well that this is the process already in place at Rome too:

> **with the consent of the whole Church** *C44:2*

This was not a letter with authority over another, but a letter of support and entreaty from brothers to brothers.

Clement quotes a portion of Samuel – I quote here a translation from the Heb. into Eng.

> **With the merciful You will show Yourself merciful; With a blameless man You will show Yourself blameless; with the pure You will show Yourself pure; And with the devious You will show Yourself shrewd.** *2 Samuel 22:26-27 NKJV*

The LXX equivalent section is 2 Kings – 1 and 2 Kings in the LXX are "our" 1 and 2 Samuel and 3 and 4 Kings in the LXX are the Heb. 1 and 2 Kings.

The portion of Scripture Clement quotes is word for word identical to the LXX:

> *KAI META EKLEKTOU EKLEKTOS ESÉ KAI META STEBLOU*
> ***C46:3 element***

This has been translated directly (note the word "**elect**" assumed by the later translator) as:

> **. . . and with the elect thou shalt be elect, and with the crooked . . .** ***C46:3 a translation***

We saw how BARAR where the word "**pure**" in the Heb. "**with the pure You will show Yourself pure**" is in the LXX by *EKLEKTOS*. Quality is the emphasis here for this Greek word. We can see this is also Clement's reading and use for the Greek word *EKLEKTOS* because of the progression of thought readable in his letter:

> **But they that endured patiently in confidence inherited glory and honor; they were exalted, and had their names recorded by God in their memorial for ever and ever. Amen.** *C45:8*

> **To such examples as these therefore, brethren, we also ought to cleave.** *C46:1*

> **For it is written; Cleave unto the saints, for they that cleave unto them shall be sanctified.** ***C46:2***

> **And again He saith in another place; With the guiltless man thou shalt be guiltless, and with the *EKLEKTOU* thou shalt be *EKLEKTOS*, and with the crooked thou shalt deal crookedly.** ***C46:3***

Clement shares in 45:8 about saints who "**endured patiently**". In 46:1 he mentions these guys are an example to stick to. In 46:2 he says that to those who stick to this example for themselves, there is a reward of sanctification. Then in 46:3 he quotes the Scripture to prove his point that those who act as saints are treated as saints by God and, conversely, those who do wickedly are treated as sinners.

So, Clement's use of this passage is to emphasise quality: righteous living in contrast to wickedness. The flow of meaning involves being good, as per the preceding example and, in doing so, there is a corresponding reward from God. There is no implication of a selection involved: "elect" in its "selected or chosen by God" meaning is excluded from the flow of thought portrayed to us by Clement in the letter. Clement then seals off the quality emphasis with:

> **Let us therefore cleave to the guiltless and righteous: and these are the *EKLEKTOI* of God.** ***C46:4***

Following in his flow about quality, here Clement is explicit in describing the EKLEKTOS: it is all those who equally exemplify the guiltless and righteous: no inference of a decision of God in the process, but only of the individual living righteously.

It is reasonable to see then that - with the Ecumenical Council of Nicea in 325AD which was conducted and recorded in Greek - we know the whole Christian world, for the first full three centuries, read EKLEKTOS with the idea of "best, top quality, excellent" in their OT bible and in their NT letters and gospels.

CONCLUSION

The word "elect" (20) in the bible comes from either of 2 words: The Heb. word BACHIR (13) in the OT and the Gk. word *EKLEKTOS* (23) in the NT. Other English words from these two in the KJV are "chosen" (15) and "choose" (1). [20 + 15 + 1 = 13 + 23]

The LXX gives us a different picture for *EKLEKTOS* and BACHIR.

The LXX only translates BACHIR by *EKLEKTOS* so the meaning of BACHIR according to the LXX translators is totally related to the meaning of *EKLEKTOS*.

The LXX shows 24 Heb. words (occurring 594 times) which are translated by *EKLEKTOS* on 74 occasions, and a majority at first glance (51), are fully seen as about "excellence": something of high quality.

The fat [*EKLEKTOS*] cows that came up out of the Nile in Pharaoh's dream which Joseph interpreted; the fat [*EKLEKTOS*] kernels of wheat in the same dream; young men [*EKLEKTOS*] i.e. guys in their prime; to the pure [*EKLEKTOS*] You will show Yourself pure [*EKLEKTOS*]; pleasant [*EKLEKTOS*] land; pleasant [*EKLEKTOS*] jewels; desire [*EKLEKTOS*] of all nations; tried [*EKLEKTOS*] stone; precious [*EKLEKTOS*] clothes; choice [*EKLEKTOS*] silver; highest [*EKLEKTOS*] branch of the cedar; and many more.

It is understandable then for a 1st century Christian reading "**For many are called, but few *EKLEKTOS***" not to see,

For many are called, but few *are* chosen. ***Matthew 22:14***

But, instead it was natural to read,

For many are called, but few *have* mettle.
Matthew 22:14 JM **[taken from** SERIOUS**]**

Take away the 13 for BACHIR since *EKLEKTOS* is its only translation in the LXX we get 51 out of 61.

[74 – 13 = 61]

This leaves us with 10 places where the Heb. rendered as *EKLEKTOS* in the LXX, is given as "chosen" in the Eng. [61 – 51 = 10]

A closer look at these 10 remaining by each of the four Heb. words, BACHAR (6), MIBCHAR (2), BACHUR (1) and BARAR (1), then shows us these are reasonably seen as also about high quality, not a "selected" idea.

BACHAR (172) is particularly revealing since it is the most used word in Heb. for "to choose, choosing, chosen". If *EKLEKTOS* has any reasonable secondary meaning of "chosen, elect", then it is reasonable to see it with that emphasis in rendering BACHAR. We see the primary use of BACHAR as "to choose, choosing, chosen" well rendered by such Gk. words as *EKLEGÓ* (to choose, pick - 113), and *HAIRETIZÓ* (to choose - 12). But, in its secondary use as "to be chosen: preferred: excellent" BACHAR is rendered by such Gk. words as *NEANIAS* (young man, youth - 4), *NEANISKOS* (young man, boy - 1) and *DUNATOS* (strong, mighty, able - 4): The use of *EKLEKTOS* (8) in rendering BACHAR is identical to these.

BACHUR (young man - 45) is also revealing in that *EKLEKTOS* (5) is the second most used word to translate it after *NEANISKOS* (young man, boy - 34).

So, with all 61 occasions of *EKLEKTOS* as within the category of "best, top quality, excellent", a reasonable view can be seen that the LXX translators saw *EKLEKTOS* and thus BACHIR as about excellence: an indicator of high quality. As a result of the above observations there is no reasonable pointer to any occasion of *EKLEKTOS* in the LXX as meaning other than excellence. [61 + 13 = 74: 100%]

And, since we know the early Church all spoke Greek and read the LXX as their OT Scripture, let alone the Gk. NT documents for the first three centuries of its existence – the Nicea Ecumenical Council of 325AD being all recorded in Gk. an excellent pointer to that - then, we can reasonably see that the idea of (let alone the word) "elect" was never in their view, in any of the passages where it is found today in the English bibles: The "excellent" were in view.

1 - BACHAR

Translated into Greek in the LXX

EKLEKTOS		**8**		***EKLEKTOS*:**
EKLEGÓ	(to choose, pick)	113		**Exodus 14:7; Judges 20:15**
HAIRETIZÓ	(to choose)	12		**Judges 20:34; 1 Samuel 24:2**
EPILEGÓ	(pick out, select)	6		**1 Samuel 26:2; Psalm 89:19**
DUNATOS	(strong, mighty, able)	4		**Proverbs 8:19; Song of Songs 5:15**
NEANIAS	(young man, youth)	4		
HAIREÓ	(to choose, prefer)	3		
DIAKRINÓ	(judge, decide)	2		
EPHISTÉMI	(set up, establish)	2		
EXAIREÓ	(to choose, select out)	2		
HAIRETOS	(to be chosen, elected)	2	aNT	
PROAIREÓ	(to choose, prefer)	2		
APALLASSÓ	(set free)	1		
ARESKÓ	(to do what pleases)	1		
ARESTOS	(acceptable, pleasing)	1		
DOKIMAZÓ	(to approve, assay)	1		
EPITHUMEÓ	(desired, coveted)	1		
METOCHOS	(partaking)	1		

NEANISKOS	(young man, boy)	1
PUROÓ	(to burn with fire, purge)	1
ZÉLOÓ	(to esteem, emulate)	1
NOT in LXX		3
	TOTAL	172

Translated into English - Both KJV related

Ys Conc.	Count	Ss Conc. No. H 977	Count
appoint	1	choose	77
be rather	1	chosen	77
choose	152	choice	6
choose out	5	choose out	5
require	1	acceptable	1
choice	2	appoint	1
excellent	1	excellent	1
be chosen	3	chosen men	1
acceptable	1	rather	1
choice	3 +1[1]	require	1
+1 not translated in Ecclesiates 9:4 See "joined" from CHABAR next to it			
TOTAL	172	TOTAL	172

1 See p.164 Ys Conc.

Refs		Text quotes KJV unless otherwise stated
Gen. 6:2		That the sons of God saw the daughters of men that they *were* fair; and they took them wives of all which **they chose**.
	YLT[2]	and sons of God see the daughters of men that they *are* fair, and they take to themselves women of all whom **they have chosen**.
	NKJV	that the sons of God saw the daughters of men, that they *were* beautiful; and they took wives for themselves of all whom **they chose**.
	NASB	that the sons of God saw that the daughters of men were beautiful; and they took wives for themselves, whomever **they chose**.
	NIV	the sons of God saw that the daughters of humans were beautiful, and they married any of them **they chose**.
	NLT	The sons of God saw the beautiful women and took any **they wanted** as their wives.

EKLEGÓ - to pick, choose, elect - a direct translation – chose wives from among the daughters of men

LXX **6:3** *IDONTES DE HUIOI TOU THEOU TAS THUGATERAS TÓN ANTHRÓPÓN HOTI*
saw and sons of the God the daughters of the men since

KALAI EISIN ELABON HEAUTOIS GUNAIKAS APO PASÓN HÓN ***EXELEXANTO***
good they are they took to themselves wives from all of whom they chose

engLXX that the sons of God having seen the daughters of men that they were beautiful, took to themselves wives of all whom they chose.

Gen. 13:11	Then Lot **chose** him all the plain of Jordan; and Lot journeyed east: and they separated themselves the one from the other.

2 For the sake of the analysis the first 7 of *EKLEGÓ* and of *HAIRETIZÓ* are looked at in all 6 Eng. versions utilised in this study (all of them for the other Gk. words since they are less than 7)

YLT and Lot **chooseth** for himself the whole circuit of the Jordan; and Lot journeyeth from the east, and they are parted - a man from his companion;

NKJV Then Lot **chose** for himself all the plain of Jordan, and Lot journeyed east. And they separated from each other.

NASB So Lot **chose** for himself all the valley of the Jordan, and Lot journeyed eastward. Thus they separated from each other.

NIV So Lot **chose** for himself the whole plain of the Jordan and set out towards the east. The two men parted company:

NLT Lot **chose** for himself the whole Jordan Valley to the east of them. He went there with his flocks and servants and parted company with his uncle Abram.

EKLEGÓ – to pick, choose, elect - a direct translation – Lot chose the plain of Jordan

LXX *KAI* ***EXELEXATO*** *HEAUTÓ LÓT PASAN TÉN PERICHÓRON TOU IORDANOU KAI APÉRE LÓT APO*
and he chose for himself Lot all the around place of the Jordan and departed Lot from

ANATOLÓN KAI DIECHÓRISTHÉSAN HEKASTOS APO TOU ADELPHOU AUTOU
east and they were parted each from the brother of him

engLXX And Lot chose for himself all the country round Jordan, and Lot went from the east, and they were separated each from his brother.

Exo. 14:7 And he took six hundred **chosen** chariots, and all the chariots of Egypt, and captains over every one of them.

YLT and he taketh six hundred **chosen** chariots, even all the chariots of Egypt, and captains over them all;

NKJV Also, he took six hundred **choice** chariots, and all the chariots of Egypt with captains over every one of them.

NASB and he took six hundred **select** chariots, and all the *other* chariots of Egypt with officers over all of them.

NIV He took six hundred of the **best** chariots, along with all the other chariots of Egypt, with officers over all of them.

NLT He took with him 600 of Egypt's **best** chariots, along with the rest of the chariots of Egypt, each with its commander.

EKLEKTOS – a divergent translation with "all the chariots" (KJV) rendered as "all the cavalry" (engLXX) – the secondary meaning of BACHAR given: the choice: i.e. the best chariots

LXX *KAI LABÓN EXAKOSIA HARMATA* ***EKLEKTA*** *KAI PASAN TÉN HIPPON*
and he took six hundred chariots choice and all the horse

TÓN AIGUPTIÓN KAI TRISTATAS EPI PANTÓN
of the Egyptians and tribunes over all

engLXX having also taken six hundred chosen chariots, and all the cavalry of the Egyptians, and rulers over all.

Exo. 17:9 And Moses said unto Joshua, **Choose** us out men, and go out, fight with Amalek: tomorrow I will stand on the top of the hill with the rod of God in mine hand.

YLT and Moses saith unto Joshua, '**Choose** for us men, and go out, fight with Amalek: to-morrow I am standing on the top of the hill, and the rod of God in my hand'

NKJV And Moses said to Joshua, "**Choose** us some men and go out, fight with Amalek. Tomorrow I will stand on the top of the hill with the rod of God in my hand."

NASB So Moses said to Joshua, "**Choose** men for us and go out, fight against Amalek. Tomorrow I will station myself on the top of the hill with the staff of God in my hand."

NIV Moses said to Joshua, "**Choose** some of our men and go out to fight the Amalekites. Tomorrow I will stand on top of the hill with the staff of God in my hands."

NLT Moses commanded Joshua, "**Choose** some men to go out and fight the army of Amalek for us. Tomorrow, I will stand at the top of the hill, holding the staff of God in my hand."

EPILEGÓ – pick out, select, remove - a loose to divergent translation with "mighty" men added – Joshua is asked to choose men to fight

LXX *EIPE DE MÓUSÉS TÓ IÉSOI* ***EPILEXON*** *SEAUTÓ ANDRAS DUNATOUS KAI*
said but Moses to the Jesu choose for yourself men mighty and

EXELTHÓN PARATAXAI TÓ AMALÉK AURION KAI IDOU EGÓ ESTÉKA EPI TÉS
going forth parade against the Amalek tomorrow and look I stand upon the

KORUPHÉS TOU BOUNOU KAI HÉ RHABDOS TOU THEOU EN TÉ CHEIRI MOU
top of the hill and the rod of the God in the hand of me

engLXX And Moses said to Joshua, Choose out for thyself mighty men, and go forth and set the army in array against Amalec to-morrow; and, behold, I *shall* stand on the top of the hill, and the rod of God *will be* in my hand.

Exo. 18:25 And Moses **chose** able men out of all Israel, and made them heads over the people, rulers of thousands, rulers of hundreds, rulers of fifties, and rulers of tens.

YLT and Moses **chooseth** men of ability out of all Israel, and maketh them chiefs over the people, heads of thousands, heads of hundreds, heads of fifties, and heads of tens,

NKJV And Moses **chose** able men out of all Israel, and made them heads over the people: rulers of thousands, rulers of hundreds, rulers of fifties, and rulers of tens.

NASB Moses **chose** able men out of all Israel and made them heads over the people, leaders of thousands, of hundreds, of fifties and of tens.

NIV He **chose** capable men from all Israel and made them leaders of the people, officials over thousands, hundreds, fifties and tens.

NLT He **chose** capable men from all over Israel and appointed them as leaders over the people. He put them in charge of groups of one thousand, one hundred, fifty, and ten.

EPILEGÓ – pick out, select, remove - a direct translation – Moses chooses able men

LXX *KAI* ***EPELEXE*** *MÓUSÉS ANDRAS DUNATOUS APO PANTOS ISRAÉL KAI EPOIÉSEN AUTOUS EP*
and chose Moses men mighty from all of Israel and made them over

AUTÓN CHILIARCHOUS KAI EKATONTARCHOUS KAI PENTÉKONTARCHOUS KAI DEKADARCHOUS
them officers of thousands and officers of hundreds and officers of fifties and officers of tens

engLXX And Moses chose out able men out of all Israel, and he made them captains of thousands and captains of hundreds, and captains of fifties and captains of tens over the people.

Num. 16:5 And he spake unto Korah and unto all his company, saying, Even to morrow the LORD will shew who *are* his, and *who is* holy; and will cause *him* to come near unto him: even *him* whom **he hath chosen** will he cause to come near unto him.

YLT and he speaketh unto Korah, and unto all his company, saying, 'Morning!- and Jehovah is knowing those who are his, and him who is holy, and hath brought near unto Him; even him whom **He doth fix on** He bringeth near unto Him.

NKJV and he spoke to Korah and all his company, saying, "Tomorrow morning the LORD will show who *is* His and *who is* holy, and will cause *him* to come near to Him. That one whom **He chooses** He will cause to come near to Him.

NASB and he spoke to Korah and all his company, saying, "Tomorrow morning the LORD will show who is His, and who is holy, and will bring *him* near to Himself; even the one whom **He will choose**, He will bring near to Himself.

NIV Then he said to Korah and all his followers: "In the morning the LORD will show who belongs to him and who is holy, and he will make that person come near him. The man **he chooses** he will cause to come near him.

NLT Then he said to Korah and his followers, "Tomorrow morning the LORD will show us who belongs to him and who is holy. The LORD will allow only those whom **he selects** to enter his own presence.

EKLEGÓ – to pick, choose, elect – Except for the missing "Even to morrow" (KJV) or "Morning" (YLT) the rest is a direct translation – whom God has chosen as priests (see whole chapter)

LXX *KAI ELALÉSE PROS KORE KAI PROS PASAN AUTOU TÉN SUNAGÓGÉN LEGÓN EPESKEPTAI KAI*
and spoke to Kore and to all of him the assembly saying has visited and

EGNÓ HO THEOS TOUS ONTAS AUTOU KAI TOUS HAGIOUS KAI PROSÉGAGETO PROS HEAUTON
knows the God the being of him and the holy and led to himself

KAI HOUS ***EXELEXATO*** *HEAUTÓ PROSÉGAGETO PROS HEAUTON*
and whom he chose himself led to himself

engLXX And he spoke to Core and all his assembly, saying, God has visited and known those that are his and who are holy, and has brought them to himself; and whom he has chosen for himself, he has brought to himself.

Num. 16:7 And put fire therein, and put incense in them before the LORD to morrow: and it shall be *that* the man whom the LORD **doth choose**, he *shall be* holy: *ye take* too much upon you, ye sons of Levi.

YLT and put in them fire, and put on them perfume, before Jehovah to-morrow, and it hath been, the man whom Jehovah **chooseth**, he *is* the holy one; - enough of you, sons of Levi.'

NKJV put fire in them and put incense in them before the LORD tomorrow, and it shall be *that* the man whom the LORD **chooses** *shall be* the holy one. *You take* too much upon yourselves, you sons of Levi!"

NASB and put fire in them, and lay incense upon them in the presence of the LORD tomorrow; and the man whom the LORD **chooses** *shall be* the one who is holy. You have gone far enough, you sons of Levi!"

NIV and tomorrow put burning coals and incense in them before the LORD. The man the LORD **chooses** will be the one who is holy. You Levites have gone too far!'

NLT Light fires in them tomorrow, and burn incense before the LORD. Then we will see whom the LORD **chooses** as his holy one. You Levites are the ones who have gone too far!"

EKLEGÓ – to pick, choose, elect - a direct translation – whom the Lord chooses as ministers to Him

LXX *KAI EPITHETE EP AUTA PUR KAI EPITHETE EP AUTA THUMIAMA ENANTI KURIOU*
and put upon them fire and put upon them incense before Lord

AURION KAI ESTAI HO ANÉR HON ***EKLELEKTAI*** *KURIOS HOUTOS HAGIOS*
tomorrow and shall be the man who chooses Lord he holy

HIKANOUSTHÓ HUMIN HUIOI LEUI
empowered you sons of Levi

engLXX and put fire on them, and put incense on them before the Lord to-morrow; and it shall come to pass that the man whom the Lord has chosen, he shall be holy: let it be enough for you, ye sons of Levi.

Num. 17:5 And it shall come to pass, *that* the man's rod, whom **I shall choose**, shall blossom: and I will make to cease from me the murmurings of the children of Israel, whereby they murmur against you.

YLT 'And it hath come to pass, the man's rod on whom **I fix** doth flourish, and I have caused to cease from off me the murmurings of the sons of Israel, which they are murmuring against you.'

NKJV And it shall be *that* the rod of the man whom **I choose** will blossom; thus I will rid Myself of the murmurings of the children of Israel, which they murmur against you."

NASB It will come about that the rod of the man whom **I choose** will sprout. Thus I will lessen from upon Myself the grumblings of the sons of Israel, who are grumbling against you."

NIV The staff belonging to the man **I choose** will sprout, and I will rid myself of this constant grumbling against you by the Israelites.'

NLT Buds will sprout on the staff belonging to the man **I choose**. Then I will finally put an end to the people's murmuring and complaining against you."

EKLEGÓ – to pick, choose, elect - a direct translation – whom God chooses to be high priest

	LXX	*KAI ESTAI HO ANTHRÓPOS HON AN* ***EKLEXÓMAI*** *AUTON HÉ RHABDOS AUTOU* and shall be the man who ever I should choose he the rod of him *EKBLASTÉSEI KAI PERIELÓ AP EMOU TON GOGGUSMON HUIÓN ISRAÉL HA* shall sprout forth and take away from me the grumbling of sons of Israel which *AUTOI GOGGUZOUSIN EPH HUMIN* they grumble against you
	engLXX	And it shall be, the man whom I shall choose, his rod shall blossom; and I will remove from me the murmuring of the children of Israel, which they murmur against you.
Deu. 4:37		And because he loved thy fathers, therefore **he chose** their seed after them, and brought thee out in his sight with his mighty power out of Egypt;
	YLT	'And because that He hath loved thy fathers, **He doth** also **fix** on their seed after them, and doth bring thee out, in His presence, by His great power, from Egypt:
	NKJV	"And because He loved your fathers, therefore **He chose** their descendants after them; and He brought you out of Egypt with His Presence, with His mighty power,
	NASB	Because He loved your fathers, therefore **He chose** their descendants after them. And He personally brought you from Egypt by His great power,
	NIV	Because he loved your ancestors and **chose** their descendants after them, he brought you out of Egypt by his Presence and his great strength,
	NLT	Because he loved your ancestors, **he chose** to bless their descendants, and he personally brought you out of Egypt with a great display of power.

EKLEGÓ – to pick, choose, elect - a direct translation if you read "led you himself" (in the interlinear) as equivalent to "bring thee out, in His presence" – God chose the seed of the fathers of Israel (V.1)

LXX *DIA TO AGAPÉSAI AUTON TOUS PATERAS SOU KAI* ***EXELEXATO*** *TO SPERMA AUTÓN MET*
due to the love him the fathers of you and chose the seed of them after

AUTOUS HUMAS KAI EXÉGAGE SE AUTOS EN TÉ ISCHUI AUTOU TÉ MEGALÉ EX AIGUPTOU
them you and he led you himself in the strength of him the great out of Egypt

engLXX Because he loved thy fathers, he also chose you their seed after them, and he brought thee himself with his great strength out of Egypt,

---

Deu. 7:6 For thou *art* an holy people unto the LORD thy God: the LORD thy God **hath chosen** thee to be a special people unto himself, above all people that *are* upon the face of the earth.

YLT for a holy people *art* thou to Jehovah thy God; on thee hath Jehovah thy God **fixed**, to be to Him for a peculiar people, out of all the peoples who *are* on the face of the ground.

NKJV "For you *are* a holy people to the LORD your God; the LORD your God **has chosen** you to be a people for Himself, a special treasure above all the peoples on the face of the earth.

NASB For you are a holy people to the LORD your God; the LORD your God **has chosen** you to be a people for His own possession out of all the peoples who are on the face of the earth.

NIV For you are a people holy to the LORD your God. The LORD your God **has chosen** you out of all the peoples on the face of the earth to be his people, his treasured possession.

NLT For you are a holy people, who belong to the LORD your God. Of all the people on earth, the LORD your God **has chosen** you to be his own special treasure.

PROAIREÓ – a direct translation – God chose Israel as a nation above all nations

LXX *HOTI LAOS HAGIOS EI KURIÓ TÓ THEÓ SOU KAI SE* ***PROEILETO*** *KURIOS HO THEOS*
since people holy you are to Lord the God of you and you chose Lord the God

SOU EINAI AUTÓ LAON PERIOUSION PARA PANTA TA ETHNÉ HOSA
of you to be to him people especial from all the nations |
as many as

EPI PROSÓPOU TÉS GÉS
upon face of the earth

engLXX For thou art a holy people to the Lord thy God; and the Lord thy God chose thee to be to him a peculiar people beyond all nations that *are* upon the face of the earth.

Deu. 7:7 The LORD did not set his love upon you, nor **choose** you, because ye were more in number than any people; for ye *were* the fewest of all people:

YLT 'Not because of your being more numerous than any of the peoples hath Jehovah delighted in you, and **fixeth** on you, for ye *are* the least of all the peoples,

NKJV "The LORD did not set His love on you nor **choose** you because you were more in number than any other people, for you were the least of all peoples;

NASB "The LORD did not set His love on you nor **choose** you because you were more in number than any of the peoples, for you were the fewest of all peoples,

NIV The LORD did not set his affection on you and **choose** you because you were more numerous than other peoples, for you were the fewest of all peoples.

NLT "The L**ord** did not set his heart on you and **choose** you because you were more numerous than other nations, for you were the smallest of all nations!

EKLEGÓ – to pick, choose, elect - a loose translation with "set his love upon you" rendered as "preferred" (engLXX); the rest is a direct translation – Lord chose Israel from among the nations

LXX *OUCH HOTI POLUPLÉTHEITE PARA PANTA TA ETHNÉ PROEILETO KURIOS HUMAS KAI*
not since numerous than all the nations prefer Lord you and

EXELEXATO *KURIOS HUMAS HUMEIS GAR ESTE OLIGOSTOI PARA PANTA TA ETHNÉ*
chose Lord you you for ye are very few from all the nations

engLXX It was not because ye are more numerous than all *other* nations that the Lord preferred you, and the Lord made choice of you: for ye are fewer in number than all *other* nations.

Deu. 10:15 Only the LORD had a delight in thy fathers to love them, and he **chose** their seed after them, *even* you above all people, as *it is* this day.

EKLEGÓ – to pick, choose, elect - a direct to loose translation with "delight" of the Lord in thy fathers given as "prefer" (LXX-inter) – Lord chose seed of thy fathers (speaking to the people of Israel)

LXX *PLÉN TOUS PATERAS HUMÓN PROEILETO KURIOS AGAPAN AUTOUS KAI* ***EXELEXATO*** *TO*
LXX-inter moreover the fathers of you prefer Lord to love them and chose the

SPERMA AUTÓN MET AUTOUS HUMAS PARA PANTA TA ETHNÉ KATA TÉN HÉMERAN TAUTÉN
seed of them after them you from all the nations | according to the day this

engLXX Only the Lord chose your fathers to love them, and he chose out their seed after them, *even* you, beyond all nations, as at this day.

Deu. 12:5 But unto the place which the LORD your God **shall choose** out of all your tribes to put his name there, *even* unto his habitation shall ye seek, and thither thou shalt come:

YLT but unto the place which Jehovah your God **doth choose** out of all your tribes to put His name there, to His tabernacle ye seek, and thou hast entered thither,

EKLEGÓ – to pick, choose, elect - a divergent translation with "habitation" (KJV) or "tabernacle" (YLT) missing; "out of all your tribes" rendered as "in . . . cities" – God shall choose the place where the temple will be

LXX *ALL É EIS TON TOPON HON AN* ***EKLEXÉTAI*** *KURIOS HO THEOS SOU EN MIA TÓN*
but | only in the place which ever chooses Lord the God of you in midst | of the

POLEÓN HUMÓN EPONOMASAI TO ONOMA AUTOU EKEI KAI EPIKLÉTHÉNAI KAI
cities your to name the name of him there and to be called and

EKZÉTÉSETE KAI ELEUSESTHE EKEI
| and ye shall enter there
ye shall seek after

engLXX But in the place which the Lord thy God shall choose in one of your cities to name his name there, and to be called upon, ye shall even seek *him* out and go thither.

Deu. 12:11 Then there shall be a place which the LORD your God **shall choose** to cause his name to dwell there; thither shall ye bring all that I command you; your burnt offerings, and your sacrifices, your tithes, and the heave offering of your hand, and all your choice[3] vows which ye vow unto the LORD:

EKLEGÓ – to pick, choose, elect - a divergent translation with "choice vows" (KJV) rendered as "choice gift" (engLXX) – the place which God will choose to put His name there for sacrifices.

LXX *KAI ESTAI HO TOPOS HON AN* ***EKLEXÉTAI*** *KURIOS HO THEOS SOU*
and shall be the place which ever chooses Lord the God of you

EPIKLÉTHÉNAI TO ONOMA AUTOU EKEI EKEI OISETE PANTA HOSA EGÓ ENTELLOMAI HUMIN
to be called upon the name of him there there ye shall bring all as many as I give charge to you

SÉMERON TA HOLOKAUTÓMATA HUMÓN KAI TA THUSIASMATA HUMÓN KAI TA EPIDEKATA
today the whole burnt offering of you and the sacrifices of you and the tithes

HUMÓN KAI TAS APARCHAS TÓN CHEIRÓN HUMÓN KAI PAN EKLEKTON[3]
of you and the first-fruits of the hands of you and every choice

TÓN DÓRÓN HUMÓN HOSA AN EUXÉSTHE KURIÓ TÓ THEÓ HUMÓN
of the gifts of you as many as ever should vow to Lord the God of you

3. See MIBCHAR

engLXX And there shall be a place which the Lord thy God shall choose for his name to be called there, thither shall ye bring all things that I order you to-day; your whole-burnt-offerings, and your sacrifices, and your tithes, and the first-fruits of your hands, and every choice gift of yours, whatsoever ye shall vow to the Lord your Gd.

Deu. 12:14 But in the place which the LORD **shall choose** in one of thy tribes, there thou shalt offer thy burnt offerings, and there thou shalt do all that I command thee.

EKLEGÓ – to pick, choose, elect - a divergent translation with "today" (LXX-inter) added – the place which the Lord shall choose out of the tribes

LXX *ALL É EIS TON TOPON HON AN* ***EKLEXÉTAI*** *KURIOS HO THEOS SOU AUTON EN*
LXX-inter but only in the place which ever chooses Lord the God of you it in

MIA TÓN PHULÓN SOU EKEI ANOISETE TA HOLOKAUTÓMATA HUMÓN KAI EKEI
one of the tribes of you there ye shall offer the whole burnt offering of you and there

POIÉSEIS PANTA HOSA EGÓ ENTELLOMAI SOI SÉMERON
you shall do all which I command you today

engLXX save in the place which the Lord thy God shall choose, in one of thy tribes, there shall ye offer your whole-burnt-offerings, and there shalt thou do all things whatsoever I charge thee this day.

Deu. 12:18 But thou must eat them before the LORD thy God in the place which the LORD thy God **shall choose**, thou, and thy son, and thy daughter, and thy manservant, and thy maidservant, and the Levite that *is* within thy gates: and thou shalt rejoice before the LORD thy God in all that thou puttest thine hands unto.

EKLEGÓ – to pick, choose, elect - a divergent translation with "Levite" rendered as "stranger" (engLXX) lit. Gk. Proselyte – the place God will choose for all the people to eat the sacrifices appropriate

LXX *ALL É ENANTION KURIOU TOU THEOU SOU PHAGÉ AUTO EN TÓ TOPÓ HÓ AN*
but only before Lord the God of you eat it in the place which | ever

EKLEXÉTAI *KURIOS HO THEOS SOU AUTÓ SU KAI HO HUIOS SOU KAI HÉ*
chooses Lord the God of you himself you and the sons of you and the

THUGATÉR SOU HO PAIS SOU KAI HÉ PAIDISKÉ SOU KAI HO PROSÉLUTOS HO
daughter of you the | manservant of you and the maidservant | of you and the proselyte who

EN TAIS POLESIN HUMÓN KAI EUPHRANTHÉSÉ ENANTION KURIOU TOU THEOU
in the cities of you and shall rejoice before Lord the God

SOU EPI PANTA HOU EAN EPIBALÉS TÉN CHEIRA SOU
of you upon all which ever should put the hand of you

engLXX But before the Lord thy God thou shalt eat it, in the place which the Lord thy God shall choose for himself, thou, and thy son, and thy daughter, thy man-servant, and thy maid-servant, and the stranger that is within thy gates; and thou shalt rejoice before the Lord thy God, on whatsoever thou shalt lay thine hand.

Deu. 12:21 If the place which the Lord thy God **hath chosen** to put his name there be too far from thee, then thou shalt kill of thy herd and of thy flock, which the Lord hath given thee, as I have commanded thee, and thou shalt eat in thy gates whatsoever thy soul lusteth after.

EKLEGÓ – to pick, choose, elect - a direct translation – the place which the Lord chooses to put His name there

LXX *EAN DE MAKRAN APEXÉ SOU HO TOPOS HON AN* ***EKLEXÉTAI*** *KURIOS HO*
If but far away from you the place which ever chooses Lord the

THEOS SOU EKEI EPIKLÉTHÉNAI TO ONOMA AUTOU EKEI KAI THUSEIS APO TÓN
God of you there to call upon the name of him there and sacrifice from the

BOÓN SOU KAI APO TÓN PROBATÓN SOU HÓN AN DÓ HO THEOS SOI HON
oxen of you and from the sheep of you which | gives the God | which
ever to you

TROPON ENETEILAMÉN SOI KAI PHAGÉ EN TAIS POLESI SOU KATA TÉN
direction commanded to you and eat in the cities of you | the

EPITHUMIAN TÉS PSUCHÉS SOU according to
desire of the soul of you

engLXX And if the place be far from thee, which the Lord thy God shall choose for himself, that his name be called upon it, then thou shalt kill of thy herd and of thy flock which God shall have given thee, even as I commanded thee, and thou shall eat in thy cities according to the desire of thy soul.

Deu. 12:26 Only thy holy things which thou hast, and thy vows, thou shalt take, and go unto the place which the Lord **shall choose**:

YLT Only, thy holy things which thou hast, and thy vows, thou dost take up, and hast gone in unto the place which Jehovah **doth choose**,

EKLEGÓ – to pick, choose, elect - a divergent translation with the addition of "to have his name named upon it" (engLXX) – the place which the Lord shall choose

LXX *PLÉN TA HAGIA SOU EAN GENÉTAI SOI KAI TAS EUCHAS SOU LABÓN HÉXEIS EIS TON TOPON*
Moreover the holy of you if come to you and the prayers of you take coming into the place

HON AN ***EKLEXÉTAI*** *KURIOS HO THEOS SOU EPIKLÉTHÉNAI TO ONOMA AUTOU EKEI*
which ever chooses Lord the God of you to be called upon the name of him there

engLXX But thou shalt take thy holy things, if thou hast any, and thy vowed-offerings, and come to the place which the Lord thy God shall choose to have his name named upon it.

Deu. 14:2 For thou *art* an holy people unto the LORD thy God, and the LORD **hath chosen** thee to be a peculiar people unto himself, above all the nations that *are* upon the earth.

YLT for a holy people *art* thou to Jehovah thy God, and on thee hath Jehovah fixed to be to Him for a people, a peculiar treasure, out of all the peoples who *are* on the face of the ground.

EKLEGÓ – to pick, choose, elect - a direct translation – the Lord chose Israel to be a peculiar people unto Himself

LXX *HOTI LAOS HAGIOS EI KURIÓ TÓ THEÓ SOU KAI SE* ***EXELEXATO*** *KURIOS HO*
since people holy | you are to Lord the God of you and you Choose Lord the

THEOS SOU GENESTHAI SE LAON AUTÓ PERIOUSION APO PANTÓN TÓN
God of you to become you people to him prized from all the

ETHNÓN TÓN EPI PROSÓPOU TÉS GÉS
nations the upon face of the earth

engLXX For thou art a holy people to the Lord thy God, and the Lord thy God has chosen thee to be a peculiar people to himself of all the nations on the face of the earth.

Deu. 14:23 And thou shalt eat before the LORD thy God, in the place which he **shall choose** to place his name there, the tithe of thy corn, of thy wine, and of thine oil, and the firstlings of thy herds and of thy flocks; that thou mayest learn to fear the LORD thy God always.

EKLEGÓ – to pick, choose, elect - a divergent translation with "before the Lord thy God" not rendered – the place which the Lord shall choose to place His name there

LXX *KAI PHAGÉ AUTO EN TÓ TOPÓ HÓ EAN* ***EKLEXÉTAI*** *KURIOS HO THEOS SOU*
and eat it in the place which ever chooses Lord the God of you

EPIKLÉTHÉNAI TO ONOMA AUTOU EKEI OISETE TA EPIDEKATA TOU SITOU SOU
to be called upon the name of him there | the tithes of the grain of you
ye shall bring

KAI TOU OINOU SOU KAI TOU ELAIOU SOU TA PRÓTOTOKA TÓN BOÓN SOU KAI TÓN
and the wine of you and the oil of you the first born of the oxen of you and of the

PROBATÓN SOU HINA MATHÉS PHOBEISTHAI KURION TON THEON SOU PASAS TAS HÉMERAS
sheep of you in order that should learn to fear Lord the God of you all the days

engLXX And thou shalt eat it in the place which the Lord thy God shall choose to have his name called there; ye shall bring the tithe of thy corn and of thy wine, and of thine oil, the first-born of thy herd and of thy flock, that thou mayest learn to fear the Lord thy God always.

Deu. 14:24 And if the way be too long for thee, so that thou art not able to carry it; *or* if the place be too far from thee, which the Lord thy God **shall choose** to set his name there, when the Lord thy God hath blessed thee:

YLT And when the way is too much for thee, that thou art not able to carry it –when the place is too far off from thee which Jehovah thy God **doth choose** to put His name there, when Jehovah thy God doth bless thee; -

EKLEGÓ – to pick, choose, elect - a direct translation – the place which the Lord shall choose to put His name there

LXX *EAN DE MAKRAN GENÉTAI HÉ HODOS APO SOU KAI MÉ DUNÉ ANAPHEREIN AUTA HOTI*
if but far be the way from you and not able to bear them since

MAKRAN APO SOU HO TOPOS HON AN ***EKLEXÉTAI*** *KURIOS HO THEOS SOU EPIKLÉTHÉNAI*
far from you the place which ever chooses Lord the God of you to be called upon

TO ONOMA AUTOU EKEI HOTI EULOGÉSEI SE KURIOS HO THEOS SOU
the name of him there since shall bless you Lord the God of you

engLXX And if the journey be too far for thee, and thou art not able to bring them, because the place *is* far from thee which the Lord thy God shall choose to have his name called there, because the Lord thy God will bless thee;

Deu. 14:25 Then shalt thou turn *it* into money, and bind up the money in thine hand, and shalt go unto the place which the LORD thy God **shall choose**:

EKLEGÓ – to pick, choose, elect - a direct translation – the place which the Lord shall choose

LXX ***KAI APODÓSÉ AUTA ARGURIOU KAI LÉPSÉ TO ARGURION EN TAIS CHERSI SOU***
and shall give up them silver and | the silver in the hands of you
you shall take

KAI POREUSÉ EIS TON TOPON HON AN **EKLEXÉTAI** ***KURIOS HO THEOS SOU AUTON***
and you shall go to the place which ever chooses Lord the God of you him

engLXX then thou shalt sell them for money, and thou shalt take the money in thy hands, and thou shalt go to the place which the Lord thy God shall choose

Deu. 15:20 Thou shalt eat *it* before the LORD thy God year by year in the place which the LORD **shall choose**, thou and thy household.

EKLEGÓ – to pick, choose, elect – a divergent translation with "LORD" following "the LORD thy God" in the Heb. and these two swap places in the Gk. – the place which the Lord shall choose

LXX ***ENANTI KURIOU PHAGÉ AUTO ENIAUTON EX ENIAUTOU EN TÓ TOPÓ HO EAN***
before Lord eat it year out of year in the place which ever

EKLEXÉTAI ***KURIOS HO THEOS SOU SU KAI HO OIKOS SOU***
chooses Lord the God of you you and the house of you

engLXX Thou shalt eat it before the Lord year by year in the place which the Lord thy God shall choose, thou and thy house.

Deu. 16:2 Thou shalt therefore sacrifice the passover unto the LORD thy God, of the flock and the herd, in the place which the LORD **shall choose** to place his name there.

EKLEGÓ – to pick, choose, elect - a divergent translation with "Lord thy God" twice in the LXX and only once in the Heb. – the place which the Lord shall choose to place His name there

LXX *KAI THUSEIS TO PASCHA KURIÓ TÓ THEÓ SOU PROBATA KAI BOAS EN TÓ TOPÓ HÓ EAN*
and sacrifice the Passover to Lord the God of you sheep and oxen in the place which ever

EKLEXÉTAI *KURIOS HO THEOS SOU AUTON EPIKLÉTHÉNAI TO ONOMA AUTOU EKEI*
chooses Lord the God of you him to be called upon the name of him there

engLXX And thou shalt sacrifice the passover to the Lord thy God, sheep and oxen in the place which the Lord thy God shall choose to have his name called upon it.

Deu. 16:6 But at the place which the LORD thy God **shall choose** to place his name in, there thou shalt sacrifice the passover at even, at the going down of the sun, at the season that thou camest forth out of Egypt.

EKLEGÓ – to pick, choose, elect - a direct translation – the place which the Lord shall choose to place His name there

LXX *ALL É EIS TON TOPON HON AN* ***EKLEXÉTAI*** *KURIOS HO THEOS SOU*
but only in the place which ever chooses Lord the God of you

EPIKLÉTHÉNAI TO ONOMA AUTOU EKEI THUSEIS TO PASCHA ESPERAS PROS
to be called upon the name of him there sacrifice the Passover evening towards

DUSMAS HÉLIOU EN TÓ KAIRÓ HÓ EXÉLTHES EX AIGUPTOU
descent of sun in the season which came forth | Egypt
out of

engLXX But in the place which the Lord thy God shall choose, to have his name called there, thou shalt sacrifice the passover at even at the setting of the sun, at the time when thou camest out of Egypt.

Deu. 16:7 And thou shalt roast and eat *it* in the place which the LORD thy God **shall choose**: and thou shalt turn in the morning, and go unto thy tents.

YLT and thou hast cooked and eaten in the place on which Jehovah thy God doth **fix**, and hast turned in the morning, and gone to thy tents;

EKLEGÓ – to pick, choose, elect - a divergent translation with "boil" added – the place which the Lord will choose

LXX *KAI EPSÉSEIS KAI OPTÉSEIS KAI PHAGÉ EN TÓ TOPÓ OU EAN* ***EKLEXÉTAI***
and boil and roast and eat in the place which ever chooses

KURIOS HO THEOS SOU AUTON KAI APOSTRAPHÉSÉ TOPRÓI KAI ELEUSÉ EIS
Lord the God of you him and you shall return | and go to

TOUS OIKOUS SOU in the morning
the houses of you

engLXX And thou shalt boil and roast and eat it in the place, which the Lord thy God shall choose; and thou shalt return in the morning, and go to thy house.

Deu. 16:11 And thou shalt rejoice before the LORD thy God, thou, and thy son, and thy daughter, and thy manservant, and thy maidservant, and the Levite that *is* within thy gates, and the stranger, and the fatherless, and the widow, that *are* among you, in the place which the LORD thy God **hath chosen** to place his name there.

EKLEGÓ – to pick, choose, elect - apart from not rendering "within thy gates", with perhaps the "among you" (engLXX) covering it, as well as the "among you" (KJV) [i.e. two with one], a direct translation – the place where the Lord has chosen to place his name

LXX *KAI EUPHRANTHÉSÉ ENANTION KURIOU TOU THEOU SOU SU KAI HO HUIOS*
and shall rejoice before Lord the God of you you and the son

SOU KAI HÉ THUGATÉR SOU HO PAIS SOU KAI HÉ PAIDISKÉ SOU KAI HO LEUITÉS
of you and the daughter of you the | of you and the | of you and the Levite
manservant maidservant

KAI HO PROSÉLUTOS KAI HO ORPHANOS KAI HÉ CHÉRA HÉ OUSA EN HUMIN EN
and the foreigner and the orphan and the widow the is in you in

TÓ TOPÓ HÓ EAN* EKLEXÉTAI *KURIOS HO THEOS SOU AUTON EPIKLÉTHÉNAI
the place which ever chooses Lord the God of you him to be called upon

TO ONOMA AUTOU EKEI
the name of him there

engLXX And thou shalt rejoice before the Lord thy God, thou and thy son, and thy daughter, thy man-servant and thy maid-servant, and the Levite, and the stranger, and the orphan, and the widow which dwells among you, in whatsoever place the Lord thy God shall choose, that his name should be called there.

Deu. 16:15 Seven days shalt thou keep a solemn feast unto the LORD thy God in the place which the LORD **shall choose**: because the LORD thy God shall bless thee in all thine increase, and in all the works of thine hands, therefore thou shalt surely rejoice.

YLT Seven days thou dost feast before Jehovah thy God, in the place which Jehovah **doth choose**, for Jehovah thy God doth bless thee in all thine increase, and in every work of thy hands, and thou hast been only rejoicing.

EKLEGÓ – to pick, choose, elect - a direct translation – the place which the Lord will choose

LXX ***HEPTA HÉMERAS HEORTASEIS KURIÓ TÓ THEÓ SOU EN TÓ TOPÓ HÓ AN***
seven days you feast to Lord the God of you in the place which |
ever

EKLEXÉTAI *KURIOS HO THEOS SOU AUTÓ EAN DE EULOGÉSÉ SE KURIOS HO THEOS SOU EN*
chooses Lord the God of you it if but shall bless you Lord the God of you in

PASI GENNÉMASI SOU KAI EN PANTI ERGÓ TÓN CHEIRÓN SOU KAI ESÉ EUPHRAINOMENOS
all offspring of you and in all work of the hands of you and shall be cheer

engLXX Seven days shalt thou keep a feast to the Lord thy God in the place which the Lord thy God shall choose for himself; and if the Lord thy God shall bless thee in all thy fruits, and in every work of thy hands, then thou shalt rejoice.

Deu. 16:16 Three times in a year shall all thy males appear before the LORD thy God in the place which he **shall choose**; in the feast of unleavened bread, and in the feast of weeks, and in the feast of tabernacles: and they shall not appear before the LORD empty:

EKLEGÓ – to pick, choose, elect - a direct translation – the place which the Lord shall choose

LXX *TREIS KAIROUS TOU ENIAUTOU OPHTHÉSETAI PAN ARSENIKON SOU ENANTION KURIOU TOU*
three seasons of the year shall appear every male of you before Lord the

THEOU SOU EN TÓ TOPÓ HÓ EAN ***EKLEXÉTAI*** *AUTON KURIOS EN TÉ HEORTÉ TÓN AZUMÓN*
God of you in the place which ever chooses him Lord in the feast of the unleavened

KAI EN TÉ HEORTÉ TÓN HEBDOMADÓN KAI EN TÉ HEORTÉ TÉS SKÉNOPÉGIAS OUK
and in the feast of the sevens and in the feast of the tents not

OPHTHÉSÉ ENÓPION KURIOU TOU THEOU SOU KENOS
shall appear before Lord the God of you empty

engLXX Three times in the year shall all thy males appear before the Lord thy God in the place which the Lord shall choose in the feast of unleavened bread, and in the feast of weeks, and in the feast of tabernacles: thou shalt not appear before the Lord thy God empty.

Deu. 17:8 If there arise a matter too hard for thee in judgment, between blood and blood, between plea and plea, and between stroke and stroke, *being* matters of controversy within thy gates: then shalt thou arise, and get thee up into the place which the LORD thy God **shall choose**;

YLT 'When anything is too hard for thee for judgment, between blood and blood, between plea and plea, and between stroke and stroke - matters of strife within thy gates - then thou hast risen, and gone up unto the place on which Jehovah thy God **doth fix**,

EKLEGÓ – to pick, choose, elect - a loose translation with "within thy gates" given as "in the cities" – the place which the Lord shall choose

LXX *EAN DE ADUNATÉSÉ APO SOU RÉMA EN KRISEI ANAMESON HAIMA HAIMATOS*
if but unable from of you word in judge between blood blood

KAI ANAMESON KRISIS KRISEÓS KAI ANAMESON APHÉ APHÉS KAI ANAMESON
and between judgment judgment and between blow blow and between

ANTILOGIA ANTILOGIAS RÉMATA KRISEÓS EN TAIS POLESIN HUMÓN 9KAI
dispute dispute for matters | of judgment in the cities of you and

ANASTAS ANABÉSÉ EIS TON TOPON HON AN ***EKLEXÉTAI*** *KURIOS HO THEOS SOU EKEI*
rising up attend in the place which ever chooses Lord the God of you there

engLXX And if a matter shall be too hard for thee in judgment, between blood and blood, and between cause and cause, and between stroke and stroke, and between contradiction and contradiction, matters of judgment in your cities; 9then thou shalt arise and go up to the place which the Lord thy God shall choose,

---

Deu. 17:10 And thou shalt do according to the sentence, which they of that place which the LORD **shall choose** shall shew thee; and thou shalt observe to do according to all that they inform thee:

EKLEGÓ – to pick, choose, elect - a direct translation – the place which the Lord chooses

LXX ***KAI POIÉSEIS KATA TO PRAGMA HON AN ANAGGEILÓSI SOI EK TOU TOPOU HOU***
and shall do | according to the deed which ever announce to you | out of the place which

EAN EKLEXÉTAI KURIOS HO THEOS SOU KAI PHULAXÉ POIÉSAI PANTA HOSA
ever chooses Lord the God of you and shall guard to do all as much as

AN NOMOTHETÉTHÉ SOI
ever law established for you

engLXX And thou shalt act according to the thing which they shall report to thee out of the place which the Lord thy God shall choose, and thou shalt observe to do all whatsoever shall have been by law appointed to thee.

Deu. 17:15 Thou shalt in any wise set *him* king over thee, whom the LORD thy God **shall choose**: *one* from among thy brethren shalt thou set king over thee: thou mayest not set a stranger over thee, which *is* not thy brother.

YLT thou dost certainly set over thee a king on whom Jehovah **doth fix**; from the midst of thy brethren thou dost set over thee a king; thou art not able to set over thee a stranger, who is not thy brother.

EKLEGÓ – to pick, choose, elect - a direct translation – the king whom the Lord chooses from your brothers

LXX ***KATHISTÓN KATASTÉSEIS EPI SEAUTON ARCHONTA HON AN EKLEXÉTAI***
placing you shall place over yourself ruler which ever chooses

KURIOS HO THEOS AUTON EK TÓN ADELPHÓN SOU KATASTÉSEIS EPI SEAUTON ARCHONTA
Lord the God him out of the brothers of you you shall place over yourself ruler

OU DUNÉSÉ KATASTÉSAI EPI SEAUTON ANTHRÓPON ALLOTRION HOTI OUK ADELPHOS SOU ESTI
not shall be able to place over yourself man alien since not brother of you is

engLXX	thou shalt surely set over thee the ruler whom the Lord God shall choose: of thy brethren thou shalt set over thee a ruler; thou shalt not have power to set over thee a stranger, because he is not thy brother.
Deu. 18:5	For the LORD thy God **hath chosen** him out of all thy tribes, to stand to minister in the name of the LORD, him and his sons for ever.
YLT	for on him hath Jehovah thy God **fixed**, out of all thy tribes, to stand to serve in the name of Jehovah, He and his sons continually.

EKLEGÓ – to pick, choose, elect - a divergent translation with "to stand to minister in the name of the LORD" (KJV) changed to "to minister and bless in his name" (engLXX); the addition of "among the children of Israel" (engLXX); "for ever" (KJV) not rendered – the tribe of Levi (V.1) whom the Lord has chosen from all the tribes to minister to Him

LXX *HOTI AUTON* ***EXELEXATO*** *KURIOS EK PASÓN TÓN PHULÓN SOU PARESTANAI*
since him chooses Lord out of all the tribes of you to stand

ENANTI KURIOU TOU THEOU LEITOURGEIN KAI EULOGEIN EPI TÓ ONOMATI
before Lord the God to officiate and to bless upon the name

AUTOU AUTOS KAI HOI HUIOI AUTOU EN TOIS HUIOIS ISRAÉL
of him he and the sons of him in the sons of Israel

engLXX	because the Lord has chosen him out of all thy tribes, to stand before the Lord thy God, to minister and bless in his name, himself and his sons among the children of Israel.
Deu. 18:6	And if a Levite come from any of thy gates out of all Israel, where he sojourned, and come with all the desire of his mind unto the place which the LORD **shall choose**;

EKLEGÓ – to pick, choose, elect - a divergent translation with "the Lord" not mentioned as the one choosing – the place which the Lord shall choose

LXX *EAN DE PARAGENÉTAI HO LEUITÉS EK MIAS TÓN POLEÓN EK PANTÓN TÓN*
if but should come the Levite out of one of the cities out of all the
HUIÓN ISRAÉL HOU AUTOS PAROIKEI KATH HOTI EPITHUMEI HÉ PSUCHÉ
sons of Israel which he sojourns that since desires the soul
AUTOU EIS TON TOPON HON AN ***EKLEXÉTAI***
of him in the place which ever chooses

engLXX And if a Levite come from one of the cities of all the children of Israel, where he himself dwells, accordingly as his mind desires, to the place which he shall have chosen,

---

Deu. 21:5 And the priests the sons of Levi shall come near; for them the Lord thy God **hath chosen** to minister unto him, and to bless in the name of the Lord; and by their word shall every controversy and every stroke be *tried*:

YLT 'And the priests, sons of Levi, have come nigh - for on them **hath** Jehovah thy God **fixed** to serve Him, and to bless in the name of Jehovah, and by their mouth is every strife, and every stroke -

NKJV Then the priests, the sons of Levi, shall come near, for the Lord your God **has chosen** them to minister to Him and to bless in the name of the Lord; by their word every controversy and every assault shall be *settled*.

NASB Then the priests, the sons of Levi, shall come near, for the Lord your God **has chosen** them to serve Him and to bless in the name of the Lord; and every dispute and every assault shall be settled by them.

NIV The levitical priests shall step forward, for the Lord your God **has chosen** them to minister and to pronounce blessings in the name of the Lord and to decide all cases of dispute and assault.

NLT Then the Levitical priests must step forward, for the Lord your God **has chosen** them to minister before him and to pronounce blessings in the Lord's name. They are to decide all legal and criminal cases.

EPILEGÓ – pick out, select, remove - a loose translation with "sons" of Levi not rendered, just implied and "to minister unto him" (KJV) given as "to stand by him" (engLXX) – the Levites are whom the Lord chose to minister

LXX ***KAI PROSELEUSONTAI HOI HIEREIS HOI LEUITAI HOTI AUTOUS*** ***EPELEXE***
and shall come forward the priests the Levites since them chose
KURIOS HO THEOS PARESTÉKENAI AUTÓ KAI EULOGEIN EPI TÓ ONOMATI
Lord the God to stand beside him and to bless over the name
AUTOU KAI EPI TÓ STOMATI AUTÓN ESTAI PASA ANTILOGIA KAI PASA APHÉ
of him and upon the mouth of them shall be every dispute and every blow

engLXX And the priests the Levites shall come, because the Lord God has chosen them to stand by him, and to bless in his name, and by their word shall every controversy and every stroke be *decided*.

Deu. 23:16 He shall dwell with thee, *even* among you, in that place which **he shall choose** in one of thy gates, where it liketh him best: thou shalt not oppress him.

YLT with thee he doth dwell, in thy midst, in the place which **he chooseth** within one of thy gates, where it is pleasing to him; thou dost not oppress him.

NKJV He may dwell with you in your midst, in the place which **he chooses** within one of your gates, where it seems best to him; you shall not oppress him.

NASB He shall live with you in your midst, in the place which **he shall choose** in one of your towns where it pleases him; you shall not mistreat him.

NIV Let them live among you wherever they like and in whatever town **they choose**. Do not oppress him.

NLT Let them live among you in any town **they choose**, and do not oppress them.

ARESKÓ – a direct translation – the place where the fleeing slave (V.15) chooses and is pleased to live

LXX *META SOU KATOIKÉSEI EN HUMIN KATOIKÉSEI HOU AN* ***ARESÉ*** *AUTÓ OU*
with you he shall dwell in you he shall dwell which | shall please to him not

THLIPSEIS AUTON ever
afflict him

engLXX He shall dwell with thee, he shall dwell among you where he shall please; thou shalt not afflict him.

Deu. 26:2 That thou shalt take of the first of all the fruit of the earth, which thou shalt bring of thy land that the Lord thy God giveth thee, and shalt put *it* in a basket, and shalt go unto the place which the Lord thy God shall **choose** to place his name there.

EKLEGÓ – to pick, choose, elect - a direct translation – the place which the Lord chooses to place His name there

LXX *KAI LÉPSÉ APO TÉS APARCHÉS TÓN KARPÓN TÉS GÉS SOU HÉS KURIOS HO*
and shall take from the firstfruit of the fruits of the earth of you which Lord the

THEOS SOU DIDÓSI SOI KAI EMBALEIS EIS KARTALLON KAI POREUSÉ EIS TON
God of you shall give to you and shall put into basket and you shall go into the

TOPON HON AN ***EKLEXÉTAI*** *KURIOS HO THEOS SOU EPIKLÉTHÉNAI TO ONOMA AUTOU EKEI*
place which ever chooses Lord the God of you to call upon the name of him there

engLXX that thou shalt take of the first of the fruits of thy land, which the Lord thy God gives thee, and thou shalt put them into a basket, and thou shalt go to the place which the Lord thy God shall choose to have his name called there.

Deu. 30:19 I call heaven and earth to record this day against you, *that* I have set before you life and death, blessing and cursing: therefore **choose** life, that both thou and thy seed may live:

EKLEGÓ – to pick, choose, elect - a direct translation – Moses (29:2) pleads with Israel to choose life over death, blessing over cursing

LXX *DIAMARTUROMAI HUMIN SÉMERON TON TE OURANON KAI TÉN GÉN TÉN ZÓÉN*
I call to testify to you today the both heaven and the earth the life

KAI TON THANATON DEDÓKA PRO PROSÓPOU HUMÓN TÉN EULOGIAN KAI TÉN
and the death I give before face of you the blessing and the

KATARAN ***EKLEXAI*** *TÉN ZÓÉN SU HINA ZÉSÉS SU KAI TO SPERMA SOU*
curse choose the life you | should live you and the seed of you
in order that

engLXX I call both heaven and earth to witness this day against you, I have set before you life and death, the blessing and the curse: choose thou life, that thou and thy seed may live;

Deu. 31:11 When all Israel is come to appear before the Lord thy God in the place which he shall **choose**, thou shalt read this law before all Israel in their hearing.

EKLEGÓ – to pick, choose, elect - a direct translation – the place which the Lord chooses for the law to be read

LXX *EN TÓ SUMPOREUESTHAI PANTA ISRAÉL OPHTHÉNAI ENÓPION KURIOU TOU*
in the going forth all Israel to appear before Lord the

THEOU HUMÓN EN TÓ TOPÓ HÓ AN ***EKLEXÉTAI*** *KURIOS ANAGNÓSESTHE TON*
God of you in the place which ever chooses Lord you shall read the

NOMON TOUTON ENANTION PANTOS ISRAÉL EIS TA ÓTA AUTÓN
law this before all Israel in the ears of them

engLXX when all Israel come together to appear before the Lord your God, in the place which the Lord shall choose, ye shall read this law before all Israel in their ears,

---

Jos. 8:3 So Joshua arose, and all the people of war, to go up against Ai: and Joshua **chose out** thirty thousand mighty men of valour, and sent them away by night.

YLT And Joshua riseth, and all the people of war, to go up to Ai, and Joshua **chooseth** thirty thousand men, mighty ones of valour, and sendeth them away by night,

NKJV So Joshua arose, and all the people of war, to go up against Ai; and Joshua **chose** thirty thousand mighty men of valor and sent them away by night.

NASB So Joshua rose with all the people of war to go up to Ai; and Joshua **chose** 30,000 men, valiant warriors, and sent them out at night.

NIV So Joshua and the whole army moved out to attack Ai. He **chose** thirty thousand of his best fighting men and sent them out at night.

NLT So Joshua and all the fighting men set out to attack Ai. Joshua **chose** 30,000 of his best warriors and sent them out at night.

EPILEGÓ – pick out, select, remove - a direct translation – the 30,000 men Joshua chose to go at night for the next day's ambush

LXX *KAI ANESTÉ IÉSOUS KAI PAS HO LAOS HO POLEMISTÉS ÓSTE ANABÉNAI EIS GAI* ***EPELEXE*** *DE*
who rose up Jesus and all the people the warriors so as to ascend to Gai chose but
IÉSOUS TRIAKONTA CHILIADAS ANDRÓN DUNATOUS EN ISCHUI KAI APESTEILEN AUTOUS NUKTOS
Jesus thirty thousand of men mighty in strength and sent them by night

engLXX And Joshua and all the men of war rose to go up to Gai; and Joshua chose out thirty thousand mighty men, and he sent them away by night.

Jos. 9:27 And Joshua made them that day hewers of wood and drawers of water for the congregation, and for the altar of the LORD, even unto this day, in the place which he should **choose**.

YLT and Joshua maketh them on that day hewers of wood and drawers of water for the company, and for the altar of Jehovah, unto this day, at the place which He doth **choose**.

EKLEGÓ – to pick, choose, elect - a divergent translation with the addition of "therefore the inhabitants of Gabaon became hewers of wood and drawers of water for the altar of God" (engLXX) – the place which the Lord will choose

LXX ***KAI KATESTÉSEN AUTOUS IÉSOUS EN TÉ HÉMERA EKEINÉ XULOKOPOUS KAI HUDROPHOROUS***
and established them Jesus in the day that wood cutters and water carriers

PASÉ TÉ SUNAGÓGÉ KAI TÓ THUSIASTÉRIÓ TOU THEOU DIA TOUTO EGENONTO HOI
to all the congregation and to the altar service of the God therefore became the

KATOIKOUNTES GABAÓN XULOKOPOI KAI HUDROPHOROI TOU THUSIASTÉRIOU TOU THEOU
dwellers of Gabaon wood cutters and water carriers of the altar of the God

HEÓS TÉS SÉMERON HÉMERAS KAI EIS TON TOPON HON AN **EKLEXÉTAI** ***KURIOS***
until this today day and in the place which ever chooses Lord

engLXX And Joshua made them in that day hewers of wood and drawers of water to the whole congregation, and for the altar of God: therefore the inhabitants of Gabaon became hewers of wood and drawers of water for the altar of God until this day, even for the place which the Lord should choose.

Jos. 24:15 And if it seem evil unto you to serve the LORD, **choose** you this day whom ye will serve; whether the gods which your fathers served that *were* on the other side of the flood, or the gods of the Amorites, in whose land ye dwell: but as for me and my house, we will serve the LORD.

YLT and if wrong in your eyes to serve Jehovah - **choose** for you to-day whom ye do serve; - whether the gods whom your fathers served, which *are* beyond the River, or the gods of the Amorite in whose land ye are dwelling; and I and my house -- we serve Jehovah.'

EKLEGÓ – to pick, choose, elect - a divergent translation with the addition of "for he is holy" (engLXX) – Joshua exhorts Israel to choose whom as God they will serve

LXX ***EI DE MÉ ARESKEI HUMIN LATREUEIN KURIÓ*** **EKLEXASTHE** ***HUMIN AUTOIS SÉMERON TINI***
if but not pleasing to you to serve Lord ye choose to you yourselves today whom

LATREUSÉTE EITE TOIS THEOIS TÓN PATERÓN HUMÓN TOIS EN
ye serve whether to the gods of the fathers of you to the in

TÓ PERAN TOU POTAMOU EITE TOIS THEOIS TÓN AMORRAIÓN EN HOIS HUMEIS
the other side of the river whether to the gods of the Amorites in which you

KATOIKEITE EPI TÉS GÉS AUTÓN EGÓ DE KAI HÉ OIKIA MOU LATREUSOMEN
dwell upon the land of them I but and the house of me we shall serve

KURIÓ HOTI HAGIOS ESTI
Lord since holy he is

engLXX But if it seem not good to you to serve the Lord, choose to yourselves this day whom ye will serve, whether the gods of your fathers that were on the other side of the river, or the gods of the Amorites, among whom ye dwell upon their land: but I and my house will serve the Lord, for he is holy.

Jos. 24:22 And Joshua said unto the people, Ye *are* witnesses against yourselves that ye have **chosen** you the LORD, to serve him. And they said, *We are* witnesses.

YLT And Joshua saith unto the people, 'Witnesses ye are against yourselves, that ye have **chosen** for you Jehovah to serve Him (and they say, 'Witnesses!')

EKLEGÓ – to pick, choose, elect - a divergent translation with "And they said, *We are* witnesses" (KJV) not rendered – Israel chooses the Lord to serve Him

LXX *KAI EIPEN IÉSOUS PROS TON LAON MARTURES HUMEIS KATH HUMÓN HOTI*
and he said Jesus to the people witnesses you against you since

HUMEIS ***EXELEXASTHE*** *KURIÓ LATREUEIN AUTÓ*
you chose for Lord to serve him

engLXX And Joshua said to the people, Ye *are* witnesses against yourselves, that ye have chosen the Lord to serve him.

Jud. 5:8 They **chose** new gods; then *was* war in the gates: was there a shield or spear seen among forty thousand in Israel?

YLT He **chooseth** new gods, then war *is* at the gates! A shield is not seen – and a spear among forty thousand in Israel.

EKLEGÓ – to pick, choose, elect - a divergent translation with "war in the gates" (KJV) or "war *is* at the gates" (YLT) rendered as "the cities of rulers fought" (engLXX) – Israel chose new gods [See the contrast with the choice in Jos. 24:22]

LXX ***EXELEXANTO*** *THEOUS KAINOUS TOTE EPOLEMÉSAN POLEIS ARCHONTÓN*
chose gods new then waged war cities of rulers

THUREOS EAN OPHTHÉ KAI LOGCHÉ EN TESSARAKONTA CHILIASIN EN ISRAÉL
shield if see and spear in forty thousand in Israel

engLXX They chose new gods; then the cities of rulers fought; there was not a shield or spear seen among forty thousand in Israel.

Jud. 10:14 Go and cry unto the gods which ye have **chosen**; let them deliver you in the time of your tribulation.

EKLEGÓ – to pick, choose, elect - a direct translation – the gods chosen by the sons of Israel (V.11)

LXX *POREUESTHE KAI BOÉSATE PROS TOUS THEOUS HOUS* ***EXELEXASTHE***
proceed and yell to the gods which ye chose

HEAUTOIS KAI AUTOI SÓSATÓSAN HUMAS EN KAIRÓ THLIPSEÓS HUMÓN
to yourselves and they save you in season of affliction of you

engLXX Go, and cry to the gods whom ye have chosen to yourselves, and let them save you in the time of your affliction.

Jud. 20:15 And the children of Benjamin were numbered at that time out of the cities twenty and six thousand men that drew sword, beside the inhabitants of Gibeah, which were numbered seven hundred **chosen** men.

YLT — And the sons of Benjamin number themselves on that day; out of the cities *are* twenty and six thousand men drawing sword, apart from the inhabitants of Gibeah, *who* numbered themselves, seven hundred **chosen** men;

NKJV — And from their cities at that time the children of Benjamin numbered twenty-six thousand men who drew the sword, besides the inhabitants of Gibeah, who numbered seven hundred **select** men.

NASB — From the cities on that day the sons of Benjamin were numbered, 26,000 men who draw the sword, besides the inhabitants of Gibeah who were numbered, 700 **choice** men.

NIV — At once the Benjaminites mobilised twenty-six thousand swordsmen from their towns, in addition to seven hundred **able young** men from those living in Gibeah.

NLT — In all, 26,000 of their warriors armed with swords arrived in Gibeah to join the 700 **elite** troops who lived there.

EKLEKTOS – a divergent translation with "twenty and six thousand men" (KJV) given as "twenty-three thousand" (engLXX) - the quality of the men of war are prominent in view to the translator with the addition of "able to use both hands alike" (engLXX), their excellence is rendered by the Greek word, as opposed to there being a similar number to choose out in Gibeah

LXX — *KAI EPESKEPÉSAN HOI HUIOI BENIAMIN EN TÉ HÉMERA EKEINÉ APO TÓN POLEÓN EIKOSITREIS*
and numbered the sons of Benjamin in the day that from the cities twenty three

CHILIADES ANÉR HELKÓN RHOMPHAIAN EKTOS TÓN OIKOUNTÓN TÉN GABAA HOI
thousand man wounding sword without of the dwellers of the Gabaa the

EPESKEPÉSAN HEPTAKOSIOI ANDRES ***EKLEKTOI*** *EK PANTOS LAOU AMPHOTERODEXIOI*
numbered seven hundred men choice out of all people ambidextruous

engLXX — And the children of Benjamin from their cities were numbered in that day, twenty-three thousand, *every* man drawing a sword, besides the inhabitants of Gabaa, who were numbered seven hundred chosen men of all the people, able to use both hands alike;

Jud. 20:16		Among all this people *there were* seven hundred **chosen** men lefthanded; every one could sling stones at an hair *breadth*, and not miss.
	YLT	among all this people *are* seven hundred chosen men, bound of their right hand, each of these slinging with a stone at the hair, and he doth not err.

NOT in LXX – it appears the preceding verse [see Jud. 20:15 above - Verse division here differs – see also below (e.g.) 1Sa. 13:2] LXX translated the "lefthanded" (KJV) with "both hands alike" (engLXX) and the number of men "700" was only mentioned in V.15 and not repeated in V.16 in the LXX – so that, the 2nd BACHAR contained in that repeated clause of the two verses 15-16 is left thereby not translated

	LXX	*PANTES HOUTOI SPHENDONÉTAI EN LITHOIS PROS TRICHA KAI OUK EXAMARTANONTES* all these slingers in stones to hair and not miss
	engLXX	All these could sling with stones at a hair, and not miss.
Jud. 20:34		And there came against Gibeah ten thousand **chosen** men out of all Israel, and the battle was sore: but they knew not that evil *was* near them.
	YLT	And they come in over against Gibeah - ten thousand **chosen** men out of all Israel - and the battle *is* grievous, and they have not known that the evil is striking against them.
	NKJV	And ten thousand **select** men from all Israel came against Gibeah, and the battle was fierce. But the Benjamites did not know that disaster *was* upon them.
	NASB	When ten thousand **choice** men from all Israel came against Gibeah, the battle became fierce; but Benjamin did not know that disaster was close to them.
	NIV	Then ten thousand of Israel's **able young** men made a frontal attack on Gibeah. The fighting was so heavy that the Benjaminites did not realise how near disaster was.
	NLT	There were 10,000 **elite** Israelite troops who advanced against Gibeah. The fighting was so heavy that Benjamin didn't realize the impending disaster.

EKLEKTOS – a direct translation – the secondary meaning of BACHAR of "to be chosen: preferred: excellent": *EKLEKTOS* used exactly like *NEANIAS* or *NEANISKOS*: 10,000 elite troops out of Israel

LXX *KAI ÉLTHON EXENANTIAS GABAA DEKA CHILIADES ANDRÓN* ***EKLEKTÓN*** *EK*
and came out of opposite Gabaa ten thousand of men choice out of
PANTOS ISRAÉL KAI PARATAXIS BAREIA KAI AUTOI OUK EGNÓSAN HOTI
of all Israel and side by side heavy and they not know since
PHTHANEI AP AUTOUS HÉ KAKIA
come upon them the evil

engLXX And there came over against Gabaa ten thousand chosen men out of all Israel; and the fight *was* severe; and they knew not that evil was coming upon them.

1Sa. 2:28 And did I **choose** him out of all the tribes of Israel *to be* my priest, to offer upon mine altar, to burn incense, to wear an ephod before me? and did I give unto the house of thy father all the offerings made by fire of the children of Israel?

EKLEGÓ – to pick, choose, elect - a loose translation with "father" added to clarify the "him" chosen (from V.27) – Levi the forefather, hence "father", of Eli God chose as priest to serve and his descendants

LXX *KAI* ***EXELEXAMÉN*** *TON OIKON TOU PATROS SOU EK PANTÓN TÓN SKÉPTRÓN*
1Ki.2:28 and I chose the house of the father of you out of all the tribes
ISRAÉL EMOI HIERATEUEIN TOU ANABAINEIN EPI THUSIASTÉRION MOU KAI
of Israel to me to (be) priest of the to ascend upon altar of me and
THUMIAN THUMIAMA KAI AIREIN EPHOUD KAI EDÓKA TÓ OIKÓ TOU PATROS
burn incense and wear ephod and gave to the house of the father

SOU TA PANTA TOU PUROS HUIÓN ISRAÉL EIS BRÓSIN
of you the all of the of fire of sons of Israel into food

engLXX And I chose the house of thy father out of all the tribes of Israel to minister to me in the priest's office, to go up to my altar, and to burn incense, and to wear an ephod. And I gave to the house of thy father all the offerings by fire of the children of Israel for food.

1Sa. 8:18 And ye shall cry out in that day because of your king which ye shall have **chosen** you; and the Lord will not hear you in that day.

YLT And ye have cried out in that day because of the king whom ye have **chosen** for yourselves, and Jehovah doth not answer you in that day.'

EKLEGÓ – to pick, choose, elect - a divergent translation with the added "because ye have chosen to yourselves a king" – Israel's choosing of a king over the Lord (V.7) [as opposed to whom as king as per 10:24 – see below]

LXX *KAI BOÉSESTHE EN TÉ HÉMERA EKEINÉ EK PROSÓPOU BASILEÓS HUMÓN HOU*
1Ki.8:18 and ye cry in the day that out of face of king of you whom

EXELEXASTHE *HEAUTOIS KAI OUK EPAKOUSETAI KURIOS HUMÓN EN TAIS*
ye chose to yourselves and not hear Lord of you in the

HÉMERAIS EKEINAIS HOTI HUMEIS EXELEXASTHE HEAUTOIS BASILEA
days those since you chose to yourselves a king

engLXX And ye shall cry out in that day because of your king whom ye have chosen to yourselves, and the Lord shall not hear you in those days, because ye have chosen to yourselves a king.

1Sa. 10:24 And Samuel said to all the people, See ye him whom the Lord **hath chosen**, that *there is* none like him among all the people? And all the people shouted, and said, God save the king.

YLT And Samuel saith unto all the people, 'Have ye seen him on whom Jehovah **hath fixed**, for there is none like him among all the people?' And all the people shout, and say, 'Let the king live!'

EKLEGÓ – to pick, choose, elect - a divergent translation with "to himself" (engLXX) added to "the Lord has chosen" (KJV) – the Lord chooses Saul as king (1Sa. 9:27 & V.1 onwards)

LXX **1Ki.10:24**
KAI EIPE SAMOUÉL PROS PANTA TON LAON EI HEÓRAKATE HON ***EKLELEKTAI***
and said Samuel to all the people are ye see whom chose

HEAUTÓ KURIOS HOTI OUK ESTIN HOMOIOS AUTÓ EN PASIN HUMIN KAI
to himself Lord since not is like to him in all to you and

EGNÓSAN PAS HO LAOS KAI EIPAN ZÉTÓ HO BASILEUS
know all the people and they said live the king

engLXX And Samuel said to all the people, Have ye seen whom the Lord has chosen to himself, that there is none like to him among you all? And all the people took notice, and said, Let the king live!

1Sa. 12:13 Now therefore behold the king whom ye **have chosen**, *and* whom ye have desired! and, behold, the LORD hath set a king over you.

EKLEGÓ – to pick, choose, elect - a divergent translation with "*and* whom ye have desired!" (KJV) not rendered – the king whom Israel chose over the Lord

LXX **1Ki.12:13**
KAI NUN IDOU HO BASILEUS HON ***EXELEXASTHE*** *KAI IDOU DEDÓKE KURIOS*
and now see the king whom ye chose and see given Lord

EPH HUMAS BASILEA
over you king

engLXX And now behold the king whom ye have chosen; and behold, the Lord has set a king over you.

1Sa. 13:2 Saul **chose** him three thousand *men* of Israel; *whereof* two thousand were with Saul in Michmash and in mount Beth-el, and a thousand were with Jonathan in Gibeah of Benjamin: and the rest of the people he sent every man to his tent.

YLT — and Saul **chooseth** for himself three thousand *men* out of Israel; and two thousand are with Saul in Michmash, and in the hill-country of Beth-El; and a thousand have been with Jonathan in Gibeah of Benjamin; and the remnant of the people he hath sent each to his tents.

EKLEGÓ – to pick, choose, elect - a direct translation [Note also, like Jud. 20:16 (above) the verse division differences] – Saul chooses 3,000 men out of Israel

LXX **1Ki.13:1-2**

KAI ***EKLEGETAI*** *HEAUTÓ SAOUL TREIS CHILIADAS ANDRÓN EK TÓN ANDRÓN*
and chose for himself Saul three thousand men out of the men

ISRAÉL KAI ÉSAN META SAOUL DISCHILIOI HOI EN MACHMAS KAI EN TÓ OREI
of Israel and they were with Saul two thousand who in Machmas and in the mount

BAITHÉL KAI CHILIOI ÉSAN META IÓNATHAN EN GABAA TOU BENIAMIN KAI TO
Bæthel and thousand they were with Jonathan in Gabaa of the Benjamin and the

KATALOIPON TOU LAOU EXAPESTEILEN HEKASTON EIS TO SKÉNÓMA AUTOU
remainder of the people sent out each into the tent of him

engLXX — And Saul chooses for himself three thousand men of the men of Israel: and there were with Saul two thousand who were in Machmas, and in mount Bæthel, and a thousand were with Jonathan in Gabaa of Benjamin: and he sent the rest of the people every man to his tent.

1Sa. 16:8 — Then Jesse called Abinadab, and made him pass before Samuel. And he said, Neither hath the LORD **chosen** this.

EKLEGÓ – to pick, choose, elect - a direct translation – God did not choose Abinadab son of Jesse

LXX **1Ki.16:8**

KAI EKALESEN IESSAI TON AMINADAB KAI PARÉLTHE KATA PROSÓPON
and called Jesse the Aminadab and went by face

SAMOUÉL KAI EIPEN OUDE TOUTON ***EXELEXATO*** *HO THEOS*
of Samuel and said neither this chose the God

engLXX — And Jessæ called Aminadab, and he passed before Samuel: and he said, Neither has God chosen this one.

1Sa. 16:9 — Then Jesse made Shammah to pass by. And he said, Neither hath the LORD **chosen** this.

EKLEGÓ – to pick, choose, elect - a direct translation – God did not choose Shammah son of Jesse

LXX **1Ki.16:9** — *KAI PARÉGAGEN IESSAI TON SAMA KAI EIPE KAI EN TOUTÓ OUK* ***EXELEXATO*** *KURIOS*
and made pass by Jesse the Sama and said also en this not chose Lord

engLXX — And Jessæ caused Sama to pass by: and he said, Neither has God chosen this one.

1Sa. 16:10 — Again, Jesse made seven of his sons to pass before Samuel. And Samuel said unto Jesse, The LORD hath not **chosen** these.

EKLEGÓ – to pick, choose, elect - a direct translation – God did not choose the seven sons of Jesse presented to Samuel

LXX **1Ki.16:10** — *KAI PARÉGAGEN IESSAI TOUS HEPTA HUIOUS AUTOU ENÓPION SAMOUÉL KAI*
and made pass Jesse the seven sons of him before Samuel and

EIPE SAMOUÉL OUK ***EXELEXATO*** *KURIOS EN TOUTOIS*
said Samuel not chose Lord in these

engLXX — And Jessæ caused his seven sons to pass before Samuel: and Samuel said, the Lord has not chosen these.

1Sa. 17:40 — And he took his staff in his hand, and **chose** him five smooth stones out of the brook, and put them in a shepherd's bag which he had, even in a scrip; and his sling *was* in his hand: and he drew near to the Philistine.

EKLEGÓ – to pick, choose, elect - a divergent translation with "for his store" (engLXX) added – David chose 5 smooth stones out of the brook

LXX *KAI ELABE TÉN BAKTÉRIAN AUTOU EN TÉ CHEIRI AUTOU KAI* ***EXELEXATO***
1Ki. 17:40 and took the staff of him in the hand of him and chose

HEAUTÓ PENTE LITHOUS LEIOUS EK TOU CHEIMARROU KAI ETHETO AUTOUS
for himself five stones smooth out of the stream and put them

EN TÓ KADIÓ TÓ POIMENIKÓ TÓ ONTI AUTÓ EIS SULLOGÉN KAI SPHENDONÉ
in the scrip for the shepherd the being of him into collection and sling

AUTOU EN TÉ CHEIRI AUTOU KAI PROSÉLTHE PROS TON ANDRA TON ALLOPHULON
of him in the hand of him and went to the man the Philistine

engLXX And he took his staff in his hand, and he chose for himself five smooth stones out of the brook, and put them in the shepherd's scrip which he had for his store, and his sling was in his hand; and he approached the Philistine.

1Sa. 20:30 Then Saul's anger was kindled against Jonathan, and he said unto him, Thou son of the perverse rebellious *woman*, do not I know that thou **hast chosen** the son of Jesse to thine own confusion, and unto the confusion of thy mother's nakedness?

YLT And the anger of Saul burneth against Jonathan, and he saith to him, 'Son of a perverse rebellious woman! Have I not known that thou **art fixing** on the son of Jesse to thy shame, and to the shame of the nakedness of thy mother?'

NKJV Then Saul's anger was aroused against Jonathan, and he said to him, "You son of a perverse, rebellious *woman!* Do I not know that you **have chosen** the son of Jesse to your own shame and to the shame of your mother's nakedness?

NASB Then Saul's anger burned against Jonathan and he said to him, "You son of a perverse, rebellious woman! Do I not know that you **are choosing** the son of Jesse to your own shame and to the shame of your mother's nakedness?

NIV Saul's anger flared up at Jonathan and he said to him, 'You son of a perverse and rebellious woman! Don't I know that you **have sided** with the son of Jesse to your own shame and to the shame of the mother who bore you?

NLT Saul boiled with rage at Jonathan. "You stupid son of a whore!" he swore at him. "Do you think I don't know that you **want** him to be king in your place, shaming yourself and your mother?

METOCHOS – accomplice, partaker - a divergent translation with "son of traitorous damsels" (engLXX) given for "son of the perverse rebellious *woman*" (KJV): plural rather than singular and different expletive – words spoken by Saul and thereby in his mind: the result of the choice of David by Jonathan: accomplice

LXX **1Ki.20:30**

KAI ETHUMÓTHÉ ORGÉ SAOUL EPI IÓNATHAN SPHODRA KAI EIPEN AUTÓ HUIE
and incensed angry Saul upon Jonathan greatly and said to him son

KORASIÓN AUTOMOLOUNTÓN OU GAR OIDA HOTI ***METOCHOS*** *EI SU TÓ HUIÓ*
of damsels deserting not for know since partaker are you | son with the

IESSAI EIS AISCHUNÉN SOU KAI EIS AISCHUNÉN APOKALUPSEÓS MÉTROS SOU
of Jesse in shame of you and in shame of uncovering of mother of you

engLXX And Saul was exceedingly angry with Jonathan, and said to him, Thou son of traitorous damsels! For do I not know that thou art an accomplice with the son of Jessæ to thy shame, and to the shame of thy mother's nakedness?

1Sa. 24:2 Then Saul took three thousand **chosen** men out of all Israel, and went to seek David and his men upon the rocks of the wild goats.

YLT And Saul taketh three thousand **chosen** men out of all Israel, and goeth to seek David and his men, on the front of the rocks of the wild goats,

NKJV Then Saul took three thousand **chosen** men from all Israel, and went to seek David and his men on the Rocks of the Wild Goats.

NASB Then Saul took three thousand **chosen** men from all Israel and went to seek David and his men in front of the Rocks of the Wild Goats.

NIV So Saul took three thousand **able young** men from all Israel and set out to look for David and his men near the Crags of the Wild Goats.

NLT So Saul chose 3,000 **elite** troops from all Israel and went to search for David and his men near the rocks of the wild goats.

EKLEKTOS – a divergent translation with "Saul" not rendered – the secondary meaning of BACHAR of "to be chosen: preferred: excellent": *EKLEKTOS* used exactly like *NEANIAS* or *NEANISKOS*

LXX **1Ki.24:3** *KAI ELABE METH HEAUTOU TREIS CHILIADAS ANDRÓN* ***EKLEKTOUS*** *EK PANTOS ISRAÉL KAI*
and took with himself three thousand men choice out of all Israel and

EPOREUTHÉ ZÉTEIN TON DAUID KAI TOUS ANDRAS AUTOU EPI PROSÓPON SADDAIEM
went to seek the David and the men of him upon face of Saddæem

engLXX And he took with him three thousand men, chosen out of all Israel, and went to seek David and his men in front of Saddæem.

1Sa. 26:2 Then Saul arose, and went down to the wilderness of Ziph, having three thousand **chosen** men of Israel with him, to seek David in the wilderness of Ziph.

YLT And Saul riseth, and goeth down unto the wilderness of Ziph, and with him three thousand men, **chosen** ones of Israel, to seek David in the wilderness of Ziph.

NKJV Then Saul arose and went down to the Wilderness of Ziph, having three thousand **chosen** men of Israel with him, to seek David in the Wilderness of Ziph.

NASB So Saul arose and went down to the wilderness of Ziph, having with him three thousand **chosen** men of Israel, to search for David in the wilderness of Ziph.

NIV So Saul went down to the Desert of Ziph, with his three thousand **select** Israelite **troops**, to search there for David.

NLT So Saul took 3,000 of Israel's **elite troops** and went to hunt him down in the wilderness of Ziph.

EKLEKTOS – a direct translation – 3,000 BACHAR; not BACHAR 3,000 i.e. they were already picked: the secondary meaning of BACHAR of "to be chosen: preferred: excellent": *EKLEKTOS* used exactly like *NEANIAS* or *NEANISKOS*

LXX *KAI ANESTÉ SAOUL KAI KATEBÉ EIS TÉN ERÉMON ZIPH KAI MET AUTOU TREIS*
1Ki.26:2 and arose Saul and went into the desert of Ziph and with him three

CHILIADES ANDRÓN ***EKLEKTOI*** *EX ISRAÉL ZÉTEIN TON DAUID EN TÉ ERÉMÓ ZIPH*
thousand of men choice out of Israel to seek the David in the desert of Ziph

engLXX And Saul arose, and went down to the wilderness of Ziph, and with him *went* three thousand men chosen out of Israel, to seek David in the wilderness of Ziph.

2Sa. 6:1 Again, David gathered together all *the* **chosen** *men* of Israel, thirty thousand.

YLT And David gathered again every **chosen one** in Israel, thirty thousand,

NKJV Again David gathered all *the* **choice** *men* of Israel, thirty thousand.

NASB Now David again gathered all the **chosen** men of Israel, thirty thousand.

NIV David again brought together all **the able young men** of Israel – thirty thousand.

NLT Then David again gathered all **the elite troops** in Israel, 30,000 in all.

NEANIAS – young man - a divergent translation with "thirty thousand" rendered as "seventy thousand" - the quality meaning of BACHAR given by "young men": guys in their prime

LXX ***KAI SUNÉGAGEN ETI DAUID PANTA*** **NEANIAN** ***EX ISRAÉL HÓS HEBDOMÉKONTA CHILIADAS***
2Ki.6:1 and gathered yet David all young men | Israel about seventy thousand
out of

engLXX And David again gathered all the young men of Israel, about seventy thousand.

2Sa. 6:21 And David said unto Michal, *It was* before the LORD, which **chose** me before thy father, and before all his house, to appoint me ruler over the people of the LORD, over Israel: therefore will I play before the LORD.

YLT And David saith unto Michal, '- Before Jehovah, who fixed on me above thy father, and above all his house, to appoint me leader over the people of Jehovah, and over Israel, - yea, I played before Jehovah;

EKLEGÓ – to pick, choose, elect - a divergent translation with "dance" added – the Lord chose David as king over Saul (the father of Michal who had rebelled and the Lord had rejected – 1Sa.13:13-14)

LXX ***KAI EIPE DAUID PROS MELCHOL ENÓPION KURIOU ORCHÉSOMAI EULOGÉTOS***
2Ki.6:21 and said David to Melchol before Lord dance bless

KURIOS HOS **EXELEXATO** ***ME HUPER TON PATERA SOU KAI HUPER PANTA TON***
Lord who chose me over the father of you and over all the

OIKON AUTOU TOU KATASTÉSAI ME EIS HÉGOUMENON EPI TON LAON AUTOU
house of him of the to place me into lead over the people of him

EPI TON ISRAÉL KAI PAIXOMAI KAI ORCHÉSOMAI ENÓPION KURIOU
over the Israel and play and dance before Lord

	engLXX	And David said to Melchol, I will dance before the Lord. Blessed *be* the Lord who chose me before thy father, and before all his house, to make me head over his people, even over Israel: therefore I will play, and dance before the Lord.
2Sa. 10:9a		When Joab saw that the front of the battle was against him before and behind, he **chose** of all…
	YLT	and Joab seeth that the front of the battle hath been unto him before and behind, and he **chooseth** of all . . .
	NKJV	When Joab saw that the battle line was against him before and behind, he **chose** some . . .
	NASB	Now when Joab saw that the battle was set against him in front and in the rear, he **selected** . . .
	NIV	Joab saw that there were battle lines in front of him and behind him; so he **selected** some . . .
	NLT	When Joab saw that he would have to fight on both the front and the rear, he **chose** some . . .

EPILEGÓ – pick out, select, remove - a direct translation – Joab chose quality soldiers in the midst of seeing a strong attack on two fronts

LXX	*KAI EIDEN IÓAB HOTI EGENÉTHÉ PROS AUTON ANTIPROSÓPON TOU POLEMOU EK TOU*
2Ki.10:9a	and saw Joab since it be to him facing the war out of the
	KATA PROSÓPON EXENANTIAS KAI EK TOU OPISTHEN KAI ***EPELEXATO*** *EK PANTÓN…*
	against face right opposite and out of the rear and chose out of all
engLXX	And Joab saw that the front of the battle was against him from that which was opposed in front and from behind, and he chose out *some* of all…

2Sa. 10:9b		. . . the **choice** *men* of Israel, and put *them* in array against the Syrians:
	YLT	. . . the **chosen** in Israel, and setteth in array to meet Aram,
	NKJV	. . . the **choice** *men* of Israel and put *them* in battle array against the Syrians.

NASB . . . all the **choice men** of Israel, and arrayed *them* against the Arameans.

NIV . . . of the **best troops** in Israel and deployed them against the Arameans.

NLT . . . of Israel's **elite troops** and placed them under his personal command to fight the Arameans in the fields.

NEANIAS – young man - a direct translation – The second meaning of BACHAR "to be chosen: preferred: excellent": here, soldiers in view, their best being: the fittest in prime of life: the young men:

LXX . . .*TÓN* ***NEANIÓN*** *ISRAÉL KAI PARETAXANTO EX ENANTIAS SURIAS*
2Ki.10:9b the young men of Israel and deployed out of opposite Syria

engLXX . . .the young men of Israel, and they set themselves in array against Syria.

2Sa. 15:15 And the king's servants said unto the king, Behold, thy servants *are ready to do* whatsoever my lord the king **shall appoint**.

YLT And the servants of the king say unto the king, 'According to all that my lord the king **chooseth** - lo, thy servants *do*.'

NKJV And the king's servants said to the king, "We *are* your servants, *ready to do* whatever my lord the king **commands**."

NASB Then the king's servants said to the king, "Behold, your servants *are ready to do* whatever my lord the king **chooses**."

NIV The king's officials answered him, 'Your servants are ready to do whatever our lord the king **chooses**.'

NLT "We are with you," his advisers replied. "Do what you **think is best**."

HAIREÓ – a direct translation – the servants of king David (v.14) willing to do whatever he chose to be done

LXX *KAI EIPON HOI PAIDES TOU BASILEÓS PROS TON BASILEA KATA PANTA HOSA*
2Ki.15:15 and said the servants of the king to the king | according to | all | as much as

HAIREITAI *HO KURIOS HÉMÓN HO BASILEUS IDOU HOI PAIDES SOU*
chooses the Lord of us the king look the servants of you

engLXX And the king's servants said to the king, In all things which our lord the king chooses, behold *we are* thy servants.

2Sa. 16:18 And Hushai said unto Absalom, Nay; but whom the LORD, and this people, and all the men of Israel, **choose**, his will I be, and with him will I abide.

EKLEGÓ – to pick, choose, elect - a divergent translation with "all the men" (KJV) rendered as "every man" (LXX-inter) – who the Lord, the people and all Israel chose as king

LXX **2Ki.16:18** *KAI EIPE CHOUSI PROS ABESSALÓM OUCHI ALLA KATOPISTHEN HOU*
LXX-inter and said Chusi to Abessalom no but after whom

EXELEXATO *KURIOS KAI HO LAOS HOUTOS KAI PAS ANÉR ISRAÉL AUTÓ*
chose Lord and the people this and every man of Israel to him

ESOMAI KAI META AUTOU KATHÉSOMAI
will be and with him sit

engLXX And Chusi said to Abessalom, Nay, but following whom the Lord, and this people, and all Israel have chosen,- his will I be, and with him I will dwell.

2Sa. 17:1 Moreover Ahithophel said unto Absalom, Let me now **choose out** twelve thousand men, and I will arise and pursue after David this night:

YLT And Ahithophel said unto Absalom, 'Let me **choose**, I pray thee, twelve thousand men, and I arise and pursue after David to-night,

NKJV Moreover Ahithophel said to Absalom, "Now let me **choose** twelve thousand men, and I will arise and pursue David tonight.

NASB Furthermore, Ahithophel said to Absalom, "Please let me **choose** 12,000 men that I may arise and pursue David tonight.

NIV Ahithophel said to Absalom, 'I **would choose** twelve thousand men and set out tonight in pursuit of David.

NLT Now Ahithophel urged Absalom, "Let me **choose** 12,000 men to start out after David tonight.

EPILEGÓ – pick out, select, remove - a direct translation – Ahithophel offers to choose 12,000 men with whom to pursue David

LXX *KAI EIPEN ACHITOPHEL PROS ABESSALÓM* ***EPILEXÓ*** *DÉ EMAUTÓ DÓDEKA*
2Ki.17:1 and said Achitopel to Abessalom choose indeed | for myself twelve

CHILIADAS ANDRÓN KAI ANASTÉSOMAI KAI KATADIÓXO OPISÓ DAUID TÉN NUKTA
thousand men and arise and pursue after David the night

engLXX And Achitophel said to Abessalom, Let me now choose out for myself twelve thousand men, and I will arise and follow after David this night:

2Sa. 19:38 And the king answered, Chimham shall go over with me, and I will do to him that which shall seem good unto thee: and whatsoever thou shalt **require** of me, *that* will I do for thee.

YLT And the king saith, 'With me doth Chimham go over, and I do to him that Which *is* good in thine eyes, yea, all that thou dost **fix** on me I do to thee.'

EKLEGÓ – to pick, choose, elect - a divergent translation with "I will do to him that which shall seem good unto thee" (KJV) or "I do to him that which *is* good in thine eyes" (YLT), rendered as "I will do to him what is good in my sight" (engLXX): i.e. the exact opposite – king David promises to do whatever Barzillai (V.33) chooses for him to do for his son (1Ki. 2:7) Chimham

LXX *KAI EIPEN HO BASILEUS MET EMOU DIABÉTÓ CHAMAAN KAGÓ POIÉSÓ AUTÓ*
2Ki.19:38 and said the king with me pass Chamaan and shall do to him

TO AGATHON EN OPHTHALMOIS MOU KAI PANTA HOSA AN ***EKLEXÉ*** *EP EMOI POIÉSÓ SOI*
the good in eyes of me and all whom ever choose by me shall do for you

engLXX And the king said, Let Chamaam go over with me, and I will do to him what is good in my sight; and whatsoever thou shalt choose at my hand, I will do for thee.

2Sa. 24:12 Go and say unto David, Thus saith the LORD, I offer thee three *things*; **choose** thee one of them, that I may do *it* unto thee.

EKLEGÓ – to pick, choose, elect - a direct translation: the missing initial portion "Go and say unto David" is tagged on the end of V.11 in the LXX – King David is given the choice of three things to choose from

LXX 11 *POREUTHÉTI KAI LALÉSON PROS DAUID LEGÓN* 12 *TADE LEGEI KURIOS TRIA*
2Ki.24:12 go and speak to David saying thus says Lord three

EGÓ EIMI AIRÓ EPI SE KAI ***EKLEXAI*** *SEAUTÓ HEN EX AUTÓN KAI POIÉSÓ SOI*
I am bring upon you and choose | for yourself | which | out of | them and will do to you

engLXX Thus saith the Lord, I bring *one of* three things upon thee: now choose thee one of them, and I will do *it* to thee.

1Ki. 3:8 And thy servant *is* in the midst of thy people which thou hast **chosen**, a great people, that cannot be numbered nor counted for multitude.

EKLEGÓ – to pick, choose, elect - a divergent translation with "nor counted for multitude" not rendered – the people of Israel whom the Lord has chosen

LXX *HO DE DOULOS SOU EN MESÓ TOU LAOU SOU HON* ***EXELEXÓ*** *LAON POLUN*
3Ki.3:8 the but servant of you in midst of the people of you whom chose people great

HOS OUK ARITHMÉTHÉSETAI
which not numbered

engLXX But thy servant *is* in the midst of thy people, whom thou hast chosen, a great people, which cannot be numbered.

1Ki. 8:16a Since the day that I brought forth my people Israel out of Egypt, I **chose** no city out of all the tribes of Israel to build an house…

YLT From the day that I brought out My people, even Israel, from Egypt, I have not **fixed** on a city out of all the tribes of Israel, to build a house…

EKLEGÓ – to pick, choose, elect - a direct translation – the Lord is saying he was making a new decision: he had not chosen Jerusalem as the place for a temple, at least up to the time of the exodus from Egypt, and right up until David (V.17)

LXX *APH HÉS HÉMERAS EXÉGAGON TON LAON MOU TON ISRAÉL EX AIGUPTOU OUK*
3Ki.8:16a from which day led the people of me the Israel out of Egypt not

EXELEXAMÉN *EN POLEI EN HENI SKÉPTRÓ ISRAÉL TOU OIKODOMÉSAI OIKON…*
chose in city in one tribe of Israel of the to build house

engLXX From the day that I brought out my people Israel out of Egypt, I have not chosen a city in *any* one tribe of Israel to build a house, (...)

1Ki. 8:16b …that my name might be therein; but I **chose** David to be over my people Israel.

YLT … for My name being there; and I **fix** on David to be over My people Israel.

EKLEGÓ – to pick, choose, elect - a divergent translation with the added clause "but I chose Jerusalem that my name should be there" (engLXX) – the choosing of David by the Lord to be king over the people

LXX **3Ki.8:16** …*TOU EINAI TO ONOMA MOU EKEI KAI EXELEXAMÉN EN HIEROUSALÉM EINAI TO ONOMA*
the to be the name of me there and chose in Jerusalem to be the name

MOU EKEI KAI ***EXELEXAMÉN*** *TON DAUID TOU EINAI EPI TON LAON MOU TON ISRAÉL*
of me there and chose the David the to be upon the people of me the Israel

engLXX …so that my name should be there: but I chose Jerusalem that my name should be there, and I chose David to be over my people Israel.

1Ki. 8:44 If thy people go out to battle against their enemy, whithersoever thou shalt send them, and shall pray unto the LORD toward the city which thou **hast chosen**, and *toward* the house that I have built for thy name:

EKLEGÓ – to pick, choose, elect - a direct translation – a prayer of Solomon (V.26) mentioning the Lord having chosen Jerusalem

LXX **3Ki.8:44** *HOTI EXELEUSETAI HO LAOS SOU EIS POLEMON EPI TOUS ECHTROUS AUTOU EN HODÓ HÉ*
since go the people of you into war upon the enemy of him in way which

EPISTREPSEIS AUTOUS KAI PROSEUXONTAI EN ONOMATI KURIOU HODON TÉS POLEÓS HÉS
turn them and pray in name of Lord way of the city which

EXELEXÓ *EN AUTÉ KAI TOU OIKOU HOU ÓKODOMÉSA TÓ ONOMATI SOU*
chose in she and of the house which built to the name of you

engLXX *If it be* that thy people shall go forth to war against their enemies in the way by which thou shalt turn them, and pray in the name of the Lord toward the city which thou hast chosen, and the house which I have built to thy name,

---

1Ki. 8:48 And *so* return unto thee with all their heart, and with all their soul, in the land of their enemies, which led them away captive, and pray unto thee toward their land, which thou gavest unto their fathers, the city which thou **hast chosen**, and the house which I have built for thy name:

YLT yea, they have turned back unto Thee, with all their heart, and with all their soul, in the land of their enemies who have taken them captive, and have prayed unto Thee the way of their land, which Thou gavest to their fathers, the city which Thou **hast chosen**, and the house which I have builded for Thy name:

EKLEGÓ – to pick, choose, elect - a divergent translation with "enemies, which led them away captive" (KJV) or "their enemies who have taken them captive" (YLT), given as "whither thou hast carried them captives" (engLXX) – Jerusalem, the city which the Lord has chosen

LXX *KAI EPISTREPSÓSI PROS SE EN HOLÉ KARDIA AUTÓN KAI EN HOLÉ PSUCHÉ*
3Ki.8:48 and they shall turn to you in whole heart of them and in whole soul

AUTÓN EN TÉ GÉ ECHTRÓN AUTÓN HOU METÉGAGES AUTOUS KAI PROSEUXONTAI
of them in the land of enemies of them who led them and pray

PROS SE HODON GÉS AUTÓN HÉS EDÓKAS TOIS PATRASIN AUTÓN KAI TÉS POLEÓS HÉS
to you way land of them which gave to the fathers of them and the cities which

EXELEXÓ *KAI TOU OIKOU HOU ÓKODOMÉKA TÓ ONOMATI SOU*
chose and of the house which built to the name of you

engLXX and they shall turn to thee with all their heart, and with all their soul, in the land of their enemies whither thou hast carried them captives, and shall pray to thee toward their land which thou hast given to their fathers, and the city which thou hast chosen, and the house which I have built to thy name:

1Ki. 11:13 Howbeit I will not rend away all the kingdom; *but* will give one tribe to thy son for David my servant's sake, and for Jerusalem's sake which I have **chosen**.

EKLEGÓ – to pick, choose, elect - a direct translation – Jerusalem which the Lord chose

LXX *PLÉN HOLÉN TÉN BASILEIAN OU MÉ LABÓ SKÉPTRON EN DÓSÓ TÓ HUIÓ SOU DIA DAUID TON*
3Ki.11:13 except whole the kingdom in no wise take tribe in shall give to the son | due to David the

DOULON MOU KAI DIA HIEROUSALÉM TÉN POLIN HÉN ***EXELEXAMÉN*** of you
servant of me and due to Jerusalem the city which chose

engLXX Only I will not take away the whole kingdom: I will give one tribe to thy son for David my servant's sake, and for the sake of Jerusalem, the city which I have chosen.

1Ki. 11:32 (But he shall have one tribe for my servant David's sake, and for Jerusalem's sake, the city which I have **chosen** out of all the tribes of Israel:)

YLT and the one tribe he hath for My servant David's sake, and for Jerusalem's sake, the city which I have **fixed on**, out of all the tribes of Israel.

EKLEGÓ – to pick, choose, elect - a divergent translation with "he shall have one tribe" (KJV) given as "he shall have two tribes" (engLXX) – the city which the Lord has chosen out of all the tribes of Israel

LXX *KAI DUO SKÉPTRA ESONTAI AUTÓ DIA TON DOULON MOU DAUID KAI DIA HIEROUSALÉM*
3Ki.11:32 and two tribes shall be to him due to the servant of me David and due to Jerusalem

TÉN POLIN HÉN ***EXELEXAMÉN*** *EN AUTÉ EK PASÓN PHULÓN ISRAÉL*
the city which chose in she out of all tribes of Israel

engLXX Yet he shall have two tribes, for my servant David's sake, and for the sake of Jerusalem, the city which I have chosen out of all the tribes of Israel.

1Ki. 11:34 Howbeit I will not take the whole kingdom out of his hand: but I will make him prince all the days of his life for David my servant's sake, whom I **chose**, because he kept my commandments and my statutes:

YLT And I do not take the whole of the kingdom out of his hand, for prince I make him all days of his life, for the sake of David My servant whom I **chose**, who kept My commands and My statutes;

EKLEGÓ – to pick, choose, elect - a divergent translation with "I will make him prince all the days of his life" (KJV) given as "I will certainly resist him all the days of his life" (engLXX) – David, God's servant whom He chose as king

LXX *KAI OU MÉ LABÓ TÉN BASILEIAN HOLÉN EK CHEIROS AUTOU DIOTI*
3Ki.11:34 and in no wise take the kingdom whole out of hand of him due to

ANTITASSOMENOS ANTITAXOMAI AUTÓ PASAS TAS HÉMERAS TÉS ZÓÉS
resisting shall resist him all the days of the life

AUTOU DIA TON DAUID TON DOULON MOU HON ***EXELEXAMÉN*** *AUTON*
of him due to the David the servant of me whom chose him

engLXX Howbeit I will not take the whole kingdom out of his hand, (for I will certainly resist him all the days of his life,) for David my servant's sake, whom I have chosen.

1Ki. 11:36 And unto his son will I give one tribe, that David my servant may have a light alway before me in Jerusalem, the city which I have **chosen** me to put my name there.

YLT and to his son I give one tribe, for there being a lamp to David My servant all the days before Me in Jerusalem, the city that I have **chosen** to Myself to put My name there.

EKLEGÓ – to pick, choose, elect - a divergent translation with "I give one tribe" (KJV) given as "I will give the two *remaining* tribes" (engLXX) – Jerusalem, the city the Lord chose for Himself to put His name there

LXX *TÓ DE HUIÓ AUTOU DÓSÓ TA DUO SKÉPTRA HOPÓS É THESIS TÓ DOULÓ MOU*
3Ki.11:36 to the but son of him shall give the two tribes so that be setting to the | servant of me

DAUID PASAS TAS HÉMERAS ENÓPION EMOU EN HIEROUSALÉM TÉ POLEI HÉN
David all the days before me in Jerusalem the city which

EXELEXAMÉN *EMAUTÓ TOU THESTHAI TO ONOMA MOU EKEI*
chose for myself the to put the name of me there

engLXX But to his son I will give the two *remaining* tribes, that my servant David may have an establishment continually before me in Jerusalem, the city which I have chosen for myself to put my name there.

1Ki. 12:21 And when Rehoboam was come to Jerusalem, he assembled all the house of Judah, with the tribe of Benjamin, an hundred and fourscore thousand **chosen men**, which were warriors, to fight against the house of Israel, to bring the kingdom again to Rehoboam the son of Solomon.

YLT And Rehoboam cometh to Jerusalem, and assembleth all the house of Judah and the tribe of Benjamin, a hundred and eighty thousand **chosen** warriors, to fight with the house of Israel, to bring back the kingdom to Rehoboam son of Solomon.

NKJV And when Rehoboam came to Jerusalem, he assembled all the house of Judah with the tribe of Benjamin, one hundred and eighty thousand **chosen men** who were warriors, to fight against the house of Israel, that he might restore the kingdom to Rehoboam the son of Solomon.

NASB Now when Rehoboam had come to Jerusalem, he assembled all the house of Judah and the tribe of Benjamin, 180,000 **chosen men** who were warriors, to fight against the house of Israel to restore the kingdom to Rehoboam the son of Solomon.

NIV When Rehoboam arrived in Jerusalem, he mustered all Judah and the tribe of Benjamin – a hundred and eighty thousand **able young men** – to go to war against Israel and to regain the kingdom for Rehoboam son of Solomon.

NLT When Rehoboam arrived at Jerusalem, he mobilized the men of Judah and the tribe of Benjamin—180,000 **select troops**—to fight against the men of Israel and to restore the kingdom to himself.

NEANIAS – young man - a divergent translation with "a hundred and eighty thousand" (YLT) given as "a hundred and twenty thousand" (engLXX) – with warriors in the context, the quality meaning of BACHAR is seen: guys in their prime: young men

LXX *KAI ROBOAM EISÉLTHEN EIS HIEROUSALÉM KAI EXEKKLÉSIASE TÉN*
3Ki.12:21 and Roboam went into Jerusalem and gathered the

SUNAGÓGÉN IOUDA KAI SKÉPTRON BENIAMIN HEKATON KAI EIKOSI CHILIADAS
assembly of Juda and tribe of Benjamin hundred and twenty thousand

NEANIÓN *POIOUNTÓN POLEMON TOU POLEMEIN PROS OIKON ISRAÉL*
young men able for war of the to war to house of Israel

EPISTREPSAI TÉN BASILEIAN ROBOAM HUIÓ SALÓMÓN
to return the kingdom Roboam to son of Solomon

engLXX And Roboam went into Jerusalem, and he assembled the congregation of Juda, and the tribe of Benjamin, a hundred and twenty thousand young men, warriors, to fight against the house of Israel, to recover the kingdom to Roboam the son of Solomon.

1Ki. 14:21 And Rehoboam the son of Solomon reigned in Judah. Rehoboam *was* forty and one years old when he began to reign, and he reigned seventeen years in Jerusalem, the city which the LORD did **choose** out of all the tribes of Israel, to put his name there. And his mother's name *was* Naamah an Ammonitess.

EKLEGÓ – to pick, choose, elect - a direct translation - Jerusalem, the city which the Lord chose to put His name there

LXX *KAI ROBOAM HUIOS SALÓMÓN EBASILEUSEN EPI IOUDAN HUIOS TESSARAKONTA KAI HENOS*
3Ki.14:21 and Roboam son of Solomon reigned over Juda son forty and one

ENIAUTÓN ROBOAM EN TÓ BASILEUEIN AUTON KAI HEPTAKAIDEKA ETÉ EBASILEUSEN EN
before Roboam in the to reign him and seventeen years reigned in

HIEROUSALÉM TÉ POLEI HÉN ***EXELEXATO*** *KURIOS THESTHAI TO ONOMA AUTOU EKEI EK*
Jerusalem the city which chose Lord setting the name of him there out of

PASÓN PHULÓN TOU ISRAÉL KAI TO ONOMA TÉS MÉTROS AUTOU NAAMA HÉ AMMÓNITIS
all of tribes of the Israel and the name of the mother of him Naama the Ammonitess

engLXX And Roboam son of Solomon ruled over Juda. Roboam was forty and one years old when he began to reign, and he reigned seventeen years in the city Jerusalem, which the Lord chose to put his name there out of all the tribes of Israel: and his mother's name *was* Naama the Ammonitess.

1Ki. 18:23 Let them therefore give us two bullocks; and let them **choose** one bullock for themselves, and cut it in pieces, and lay *it* on wood, and put no fire *under*: and I will dress the other bullock, and lay *it* on wood, and put no fire *under*:

YLT and let them give to us two bullocks, and they **choose** for themselves the one bullock, and cut it in pieces, and place *it* on the wood, and place no fire; and I - I prepare the other bullock, and have put *it* on the wood, and fire I do not place; -

EKLEGÓ – to pick, choose, elect - a divergent translation with the 2nd "and lay *it* on wood" (KJV) not translated – the instruction to the prophets of Baal (V.19) to choose one of the bullocks to sacrifice

LXX *DOTÓSAN HÉMIN DUO BOAS KAI* ***EKLEXASTHÓSAN*** *HEAUTOIS TON HENA KAI*
3Ki.18:23 give to us two oxen and choose for yourselves the one and

MELISATÓSAN KAI EPITHETÓSAN EPI TÓN XULÓN KAI PUR MÉ EPITHETÓSAN
dismember and place upon the wood and fire not place

KAI EGÓ POIÉSÓ TON BOUN TON ALLON KAI PUR OU MÉ EPITHÓ
and I shall do the ox the other and fire in no wise place

engLXX Let them give us two oxen, and let them choose one for themselves, and cut it in pieces, and lay it on the wood, and put no fire *on* the wood: and I will dress the other bullock, and put on no fire.

1Ki. 18:25 And Elijah said unto the prophets of Baal, **Choose** you one bullock for yourselves, and dress *it* first; for ye *are* many; and call on the name of your gods, but put no fire *under*.

YLT And Elijah saith to the prophets of Baal, '**Choose** for you the one bullock, and prepare first, for ye *are* the multitude, and call ye in the name of your god, and place no fire.'

EKLEGÓ – to pick, choose, elect - a divergent translation with "Baal" (KJV) given as "shame" (engLXX - cf. Jer. 11:13 where "Baal" is directly translated) – the prophets of Baal instructed to choose one bullock

LXX *KAI EIPEN ÉLIOU TOIS PROPHÉTAIS TÉS AISCHUNÉS* ***EKLEXASTHE*** *HEAUTOIS*
3Ki.18:25 and said Eliu to the prophets of the shame choose ye to yourselves

TON MOSCHON TON HENA KAI POIÉSATE PRÓTOI HOTI POLLOI HUMEIS KAI
the calf the one and prepare first since many you and

EPIKALESASTHE EN ONOMATI THEOU HUMÓN KAI PUR MÉ EPITHÉTE
call ye in name of god of you and fire not place

engLXX And Eliu said to the prophets of shame, Choose to yourselves one calf, and dress it first, for ye *are* many; and call ye on the name of your god; but apply no fire.

2Ki. 21:7 And he set a graven image of the grove that he had made in the house, of which the LORD said to David, and to Solomon his son, In this house, and in Jerusalem, which I have **chosen** out of all tribes of Israel, will I put my name for ever:

YLT And he setteth the graven image of the shrine that he made in the house of which Jehovah said unto David and unto Solomon his son, 'In this house, and in Jerusalem, that I have **chosen** out of all the tribes of Israel, I put My name - to the age;

EKLEGÓ – to pick, choose, elect - a divergent translation with "that he had made" (KJV) not translated – Jerusalem, the place the Lord chose out of all the tribes of Israel to put His name there for ever

LXX *KAI ETHÉKE TO GLUPTON TOU ALSOUS EN TÓ OIKÓ HÓ EIPE KURIOS PROS DAUID KAI PROS*
4Ki.21:7 and display the carving of the grove in the house | which said Lord to David and to

SALÓMÓN TON HUION AUTOU EN TÓ OIKÓ TOUTÓ KAI EN HIEROUSALÉM HÉ
Solomon the son of him in the house this and in Jerusalem which

EXELEXAMÉN *EK PASÓN PHULÓN TOU ISRAÉL KAI THÉSÓ TO ONOMA MOU EIS TON AIÓNA*
chose out of all of tribes of the Israel and set the name of me into the ages

engLXX And he set up the graven image of the grove in the house of which the Lord said to David, and to Solomon his son, In this house, and in Jerusalem which I have chosen out of all the tribes of Israel, will I even place my name for ever.

2Ki. 23:27 And the LORD said, I will remove Judah also out of my sight, as I have removed Israel, and will cast off this city Jerusalem which I have **chosen**, and the house of which I said, My name shall be there.

EKLEGÓ – to pick, choose, elect - a direct translation – Jerusalem which the Lord chose

LXX *KAI EIPE KURIOS KAI GE TON IOUDA APOSTÉSÓ APO TOU PROSÓPOU MOU*
4Ki.23:27 and said Lord and yet the Juda sent from the face of me

KATHÓS APESTÉSA TON ISRAÉL KAI APEÓSOMAI TÉN POLIN TAUTÉN HÉN
as also removed the Israel and thrust away the city this which

EXELEXAMÉN *TÉN HIEROUSALÉM KAI TON OIKON HOU EIPON ESTAI TO ONOMA MOU EKEI*
chose the Jerusalem and the house which said to be the name of me there

engLXX And the Lord said, I will also remove Juda from my presence, as I removed Israel, and will reject this city which I have chosen *even* Jerusalem, and the house *of* which I said, My name shall be there.

1Ch. 15:2 Then David said, None ought to carry the ark of God but the Levites: for them hath the Lord **chosen** to carry the ark of God, and to minister unto him for ever.

EKLEGÓ – to pick, choose, elect - a direct translation – the Lord chose the Levites as carriers of the ark and as ministers unto Him for ever

LXX *TOTE EIPE DAUID OUK ESTIN ARAI TÉN KIBÓTON TOU THEOU ALL É TOUS*
then said David not is to bear the ark of the God but be the

LEUITAS HOTI AUTOUS ***EXELEXATO*** *KURIOS AIREIN TÉN KIBÓTON KURIOU KAI*
Levites since them chose Lord to bear the ark of Lord and

LEITOURGEIN AUTÓ HEÓS AIÓNOS
to minister to him unto ages

engLXX Then said David, It is not *lawful for any* to bear the ark of God, but the Levites; for the Lord has chosen them to bear the ark of the Lord, and to minister to him for ever.

1Ch. 19:10a Now when Joab saw that the battle was set against him before and behind, he **chose out** of all…

YLT And Joab seeth that the front of the battle hath been unto him, before and behind, and he **chooseth out** of all . . .

NKJV When Joab saw that the battle line was set against him before and behind, he **chose** some of . . .

NASB Now when Joab saw that the battle was set against him in front and in the rear, he **selected** from all . . .

NIV Joab saw that there were battle lines in front of him and behind him; so he **selected** some of . . .

NLT When Joab saw that he would have to fight on both the front and the rear, he **chose** some of . . .

EKLEGÓ – to pick, choose, elect - a direct translation – Joab chose quality soldiers as a response to the threat before and behind him

LXX *KAI EIDEN IÓAB HOTI GEGONASIN ANTIPROSÓPOI TOU POLEMEIN PROS AUTON*
and saw Joab since it be face off the war to him

KATA PROSÓPON KAI EXOPISTHE KAI ***EXELEXATO*** *EK PANTOS...*
according to front and behind and chose out of all

engLXX And Joab saw that they were fronting *him* to fight against him before and behind, and he chose *some* out of all...

1Ch. 19:10b	. . . the **choice** of Israel, and put *them* in array against the Syrians.
YLT	. . . the **choice** in Israel, and setteth in array to meet Aram,
NKJV	. . . the **choice men** of Israel and put *them* in battle array against the Syrians.
NASB	. . . the **choice men** of Israel and they arrayed themselves against the Arameans.
NIV	. . . the **best troops** in Israel and deployed them against the Arameans.
NLT	. . . Israel's **elite troops** and placed them under his personal command to fight the Arameans in the fields.

NEANIAS – young man – a direct translation - the secondary meaning of BACHAR of "to be chosen: preferred: excellent": the best troops, those in their prime: young men

LXX ...***NEANIOU*** *EX ISRAÉL KAI PARETAXANTO ENANTION TOU SUROU*
young men out of Israel and set before the Syrian

engLXX ...the young men of Israel, and they set themselves in array against the Syrian.

1Ch. 21:10	Go and tell David, saying, Thus saith the LORD, I offer thee three *things*: **choose** thee one of them, that I may do *it* unto thee.

YLT Go, and thou hast spoken unto David, saying, Thus said Jehovah, Three – I am stretching out unto thee; **choose** for thee one of these, and I do *it* to thee.'

EKLEGÓ – to pick, choose, elect - a direct translation – David is offered three things to choose from

LXX ***POREUOU KAI LALÉSON PROS DAUID LEGÓN HOUTÓ LEGEI KURIOS TRIA HAIRÓ***
go and speak to David saying thus says Lord three take

EGÓ EPI SE* EKLEXAI *SEAUTÓ HEN EX AUTÓN KAI POIÉSÓ SOI
I upon you choose for yourself which | them and I shall do to you
out of

engLXX Go and speak to David, saying, Thus saith the Lord, I bring three things upon thee: choose one of them for thyself, and I will do it to thee.

1Ch. 28:4a Howbeit the LORD God of Israel **chose** me before all the house of my father to be king over Israel for ever: (. . .)

YLT 'And Jehovah, God of Israel, **doth fix on** me out of all the house of my father to be for king over Israel to the age, (. . .)

NKJV However the LORD God of Israel **chose** me above all the house of my father to be king over Israel forever, (. . .)

NASB Yet, the LORD, the God of Israel, **chose** me from all the house of my father to be king over Israel forever. . .

NIV 'Yet the LORD, the God of Israel, **chose** me from my whole family to be king over Israel for ever. . .

NLT "Yet the LORD, the God of Israel, **has chosen** me from among all my father's family to be king over Israel forever. . .

EKLEGÓ – to pick, choose, elect - a direct translation – the Lord chose David (V.2) from all those in his family to be king for ever

LXX *KAI* ***EXELEXATO*** *KURIOS HO THEOS ISRAÉL EN EMOI APO PANTOS OIKOU*
and chose Lord the God of Israel in me from all house

PATROS MOU EINAI BASILEA EPI ISRAÉL EIS TON AIÓNA…
of father of me to be king over Israel into the ages

engLXX Yet the Lord God of Israel chose me out of the whole house of my father to be king over Israel for ever…

1Ch. 28:4b . . . for **he hath chosen** Judah *to be* the ruler; and of the house of Judah, the house of my father; and among the sons of my father he liked me to make *me* king over all Israel:

YLT . . . for on Judah **He hath fixed** for a leader, and in the house of Judah, the house of my father, and among the sons of my father, on me, *me* He hath been pleased to make king over all Israel;

NKJV . . . for **He has chosen** Judah *to be* the ruler; and of the house of Judah, the house of my father, and among the sons of my father, He was pleased with me to make *me* king over all Israel.

NASB . . . For **He has chosen** Judah to be a leader; and in the house of Judah, my father's house, and among the sons of my father He took pleasure in me to make *me* king over all Israel.

NIV . . . **He chose** Judah as leader, and from the tribe of Judah he chose my family, and from my father's sons he was pleased to make me king over all Israel.

NLT . . . For **he has chosen** the tribe of Judah to rule, and from among the families of Judah he chose my father's family. And from among my father's sons the LORD was pleased to make me king over all Israel.

HAIRETIZÓ – to choose – a direct translation - the Lord chose Judah, the house of Jesse, and David among his brothers as king

LXX *KAI EN IOUDA* ***HÉRETIKE*** *TO BASILEION KAI EX OIKOU IOUDA TON OIKON TOU*
and in Juda chose the king and out of house of Juda the house of the

PATROS MOU KAI EN TOIS HUIOIS TOU PATROS MOU EN EMOI ÉTHELÉSE TOU
father of me and in the sons of the father of me in me set of the

GENESTHAI ME EIS BASILEA EPI PANTI ISRAÉL
to be me in king over all Israel

engLXX …and he chose Juda as the kingly *house*, and out of the house of Juda *he chose* the house of my father; and among the sons of my father he preferred me, that I should be king over all Israel.

1Ch. 28:5 And of all my sons, (for the LORD hath given me many sons,) he **hath chosen** Solomon my son to sit upon the throne of the kingdom of the LORD over Israel.

EKLEGÓ – to pick, choose, elect - a direct translation – the Lord chose Solomon as David's son to be the next king

LXX *KAI APO PANTÓN TÓN HUIÓN MOU HOTI POLLOUS HUIOUS EDÓKE MOI KURIOS*
and from all the sons of me since many sons gave to me Lord

EXELEXATO *EN SALÓMÓN TÓ HUIÓ MOU KATHISAI AUTON EPI THRONOU*
chose in Solomon the son of me to sit him upon throne

BASILEIAS KURIOU EPI TON ISRAÉL
of kingdom of Lord over the Israel

engLXX And of all my sons, (for the Lord has given me many sons,) he has chosen Solomon my son, to set him on the throne of the kingdom of the Lord over Israel.

1Ch. 28:6 And he said unto me, Solomon thy son, he shall build my house and my courts: for **I have chosen** him *to be* my son, and I will be his father.

YLT and saith to me, Solomon thy son, he doth build My house, and My courts, for **I have fixed on** him to Me for a son, and I - I am to him for a father,

NKJV Now He said to me, 'It is your son Solomon *who* shall build My house and My courts; for **I have chosen** him *to be* My son, and I will be his Father.

NASB He said to me, 'Your son Solomon is the one who shall build My house and My courts; for **I have chosen him** to be a son to Me, and I will be a father to him.

NIV He said to me, "Solomon your son is the one who will build my house and my courts, for **I have chosen** him to be my son, and I will be his father.

NLT He said to me, 'Your son Solomon will build my Temple and its courtyards, for **I have chosen** him as my son, and I will be his father.

HAIRETIZÓ – to choose – a direct translation – the Lord told David (V.2) that he chose Solomon to build the temple

LXX *KAI EIPE MOI HO THEOS SALÓMÓN HO HUIOS SOU OIKODOMÉSEI TON OIKON MOU KAI TÉN*
and said to me the God Solomon the son of you shall build the house of me and the

AULÉN MOU HOTI ***HÉRETIKA*** *EN AUTÓ EINAI MOU HUION KAGÓ ESOMAI AUTÓ EIS PATERA*
court of me since chose in him to be of me son and I shall be to him to father

engLXX And God said to me, Solomon thy son shall build my house and my court for I have chosen him to be my son, and I will be to him a father.

1Ch. 28:10 Take heed now; for the Lord **hath chosen** thee to build an house for the sanctuary: be strong, and do *it*.

YLT See, now, for Jehovah **hath fixed on** thee to build a house for a sanctuary; be strong, and do.'

NKJV Consider now, for the Lord **has chosen** you to build a house for the sanctuary; be strong, and do it."

NASB Consider now, for the Lord **has chosen** you to build a house for the sanctuary; be courageous and act."

NIV Consider now, for the Lord **has chosen** you to build a house as the sanctuary. Be strong and do the work.'

NLT So take this seriously. The Lord **has chosen** you to build a temple as his sanctuary. Be strong, and do the work."

HAIRETIZÓ – to choose – a direct translation – David tells Solomon (V.9) how the Lord chose him to build Him a house, so to be strong and do it

LXX *IDE NUN HOTI KURIOS* ***HÉRETIKE*** *SE OIKODOMÉSAI AUTÓ OIKON EIS*
look now since Lord chose you to build to him house to

HAGIASMA ISCHUE KAI POIEI
holiness be strong and do

engLXX See now, for the Lord has chosen thee to build him a house for a sanctuary, be strong and do *it.*

1Ch. 29:1 Furthermore David the king said unto all the congregation, Solomon my son, whom alone God **hath chosen**, *is yet* young and tender, and the work *is* great: for the palace *is* not for man, but for the LORD God.

YLT And David the king saith to all the assembly, 'Solomon my son - the one on whom God **hath fixed** - *is* young and tender, and the work *is* great, for not for man is the palace, but for Jehovah God;

NKJV Furthermore King David said to all the congregation: "My son Solomon, whom alone God **has chosen**, *is* young and inexperienced; and the work *is* great, because the temple *is* not for man but for the LORD God.

NASB Then King David said to the entire assembly, "My son Solomon, whom alone God **has chosen**, is still young and inexperienced and the work is great; for the temple is not for man, but for the LORD God.

NIV Then King David said to the whole assembly: 'My son Solomon, the one whom God **has chosen**, is young and inexperienced. The task is great, because this palatial structure is not for man but for the LORD God.

NLT Then King David turned to the entire assembly and said, "My son Solomon, whom God **has** clearly **chosen** as the next king of Israel, is still young and inexperienced. The work ahead of him is enormous, for the temple he will build is not for mere mortals—it is for the LORD God himself!

HAIRETIZÓ – to choose – a divergent translation with "palace" not translated – Solomon is the one chosen by God to be king after David

LXX *KAI EIPE DAUID HO BASILEUS PASÉ TÉ EKKLÉSIA SALÓMÓN HO HUIOS MOU EIS*
and said David the king all the gathering Solomon the son of me to

HON ***HÉRETIKEN*** *EN AUTÓ KURIOS NEOS KAI HAPALOS KAI TO ERGON MEGA*
whom chose in him Lord young and tender and the work great

HOTI OUK ANTHRÓPÓ ALL É KURIÓ THEÓ
since not to man but is for Lord God

engLXX And David the king said to all the congregation, Solomon my son, whom the Lord has chosen, *is* young and tender, and the work *is* great; for *it is* not for man, but for the Lord God.

2Ch. 6:5a Since the day that I brought forth my people out of the land of Egypt I **chose** no city among all the tribes of Israel to build an house in…

EKLEGÓ – to pick, choose, elect - a direct translation – Solomon recounts what David heard from God (V.4) how at the time of the exodus from Egypt the Lord had not chosen a city, as yet, where to build a temple

LXX *APO TÉS HÉMERAS HÉS ANÉGAGON TON LAON MOU EK GÉS AIGUPTOU OUK*
from the day which led the people of me | land of Egypt not
out of

EXELEXAMÉN *EN POLEI APO PASÓN PHULÓN ISRAÉL TOU OIKODOMÉSAI OIKON…*
chose in city from all tribes of Israel of the to build house

engLXX From the day when I brought up my people out of the land of Egypt, I chose no city of all the tribes of Israel, to build a house…

2Ch. 6:5b …that my name might be there; neither **chose** I any man to be a ruler over my people Israel:

EKLEGÓ - to pick, choose, elect - a direct translation - Solomon recounts what David heard from God (V.4) how at the time of the exodus from Egypt the Lord had not chosen any man to be a king over Israel

LXX *TOU EINAI TO ONOMA MOU EKEI KAI OUK* ***EXELEXAMÉN*** *EN ANDRI TOU EINAI*
the to be the name of me there and not chose in man of the to be

EIS HÉGOUMENON EPI TON LAON MOU ISRAÉL
to leader over the people of me Israel

engLXX …that my name should be there; neither did I choose a man to be a leader over my people Israel.

2Ch. 6:6a But I have **chosen** Jerusalem, that my name might be there; (. . .)

EKLEGÓ - to pick, choose, elect - a direct translation – the Lord has (now since the exodus) chosen Jerusalem to place His name there

LXX *KAI* ***EXELEXAMÉN*** *TÉN HIEROUSALÉM GENESTHAI TO ONOMA MOU EKEI…*
and chose the Jerusalem to be the name of me there

engLXX But I chose Jerusalem that my name should be there; (. . .)

2Ch. 6:6b . . . and have **chosen** David to be over my people Israel.

EKLEGÓ - to pick, choose, elect - a direct translation - the Lord has (now since the exodus) chosen David to be king over Israel

LXX *KAI* ***EXELEXAMÉN*** *EN DAUID TOU EINAI EPI TON LAON MOU ISRAÉL*
and chose in David of the to be over the people of me Israel

engLXX . . . and I chose David to be over my people Israel.

2Ch. 6:34 If thy people go out to war against their enemies by the way that thou shalt send them, and they pray unto thee toward this city which thou **hast chosen**, and the house which I have built for thy name;

YLT When Thy people doth go out to battle against its enemies in the way that Thou dost send them, and they have prayed unto Thee the way of this city that Thou **hast fixed on**, and the house that I have built for Thy name:

EKLEGÓ – to pick, choose, elect - a direct translation – the city which the Lord chose

LXX *EAN DE EXELTHÉ HO LAOS SOU EIS POLEMON EPI TOUS ECHTROUS AUTOU EN HODÓ HÉ*
if but go the people of you to war upon the enemy of him in way which

APOSTELEIS AUTOUS KAI PROSEUXÓNTAI PROS SE KATA TÉN HODON TÉS POLEÓS TAUTÉS
send them and pray to you | according to the way of the citiy this

***HÉN EXELEXÓ** EN AUTÉ KAI OIKOU HOU ÓKODOMÉKA TÓ ONOMATI SOU*
which chose in her and house which built for the name of you

engLXX And if thy people shall go forth to war against their enemies by the way by which thou shalt send them, and shall pray to thee toward this city which thou hast chosen, and *toward* the house which I have built to thy name;

2Ch. 6:38 If they return to thee with all their heart and with all their soul in the land of their captivity, whither they have carried them captives, and pray toward their land, which thou gavest unto their fathers, and *toward* the city which thou hast **chosen**, and toward the house which I have built for thy name

EKLEGÓ – to pick, choose, elect - a direct translation – the city which the Lord has chosen

LXX *KAI EPISTREPSÓSI PROS SE EN HOLÉ KARDIA KAI EN HOLÉ PSUCHÉ AUTÓN EN*
and turn to you in whole heart and in whole soul of them in

GÉ AICHMALÓTEUSANTÓN AUTOUS HOPOU ÉCHMALÓTEUSAN AUTOUS KAI
land being taken captive them where took captive them and

PROSEUXÓNTAI HODON GÉS AUTÓN HÉS EDÓKAS TOIS PATRASIN AUTÓN
pray way land of them which gave to the fathers of them

KAI TÉS POLEÓS HÉS ***EXELEXÓ*** *KAI TOU OIKOU HOU ÓKODOMÉSA TÓ ONOMATI SOU*
and of the city which chose and of the house which buit for the name of you

engLXX and *if* they shall turn to thee with all their heart and all their soul in the land of them that carried them captives, whither they carried them captives, and shall pray toward their land which thou gavest to their fathers, and the city which thou didst choose, and the house which I built to thy name:-

---

2Ch. 7:12 And the Lord appeared to Solomon by night, and said unto him, I have heard thy prayer, and have **chosen** this place to myself for an house of sacrifice.

EKLEGÓ – to pick, choose, elect - a direct translation – the Lord agrees that He has chosen Jerusalem as the place for His temple

LXX *KAI ÓPHTHÉ KURIOS TÓ SALÓMÓN TÉN NUKTA KAI EIPEN AUTÓ ÉKOUSA TÉN*
and appeared Lord to the Solomon the night and said to him heard the

PROSEUCHÉS SOU KAI ***EXELEXAMÉN*** *EN TÓ TOPÓ TOUTÓ EMAUTÓ EIS OIKON THUSIAS*
prayer of you and chose in the place this to myself for house of sacrifice

engLXX And the Lord appeared to Solomon by night, and said to him, I have heard thy prayer, and I have chosen this place to myself for a house of sacrifice.

2Ch. 7:16 For now have I **chosen** and sanctified this house, that my name may be there for ever: and mine eyes and mine heart shall be there perpetually.

YLT and now, I have chosen and sanctified this house for My name being there unto the age; yea, Mine eyes and My heart have been there all the days.

EKLEGÓ – to pick, choose, elect - a direct translation – the temple in Jerusalem which the lord has chosen for His name to be there

LXX *KAI NUN* ***EXELEXAMÉN*** *KAI HÉGIAKA TON OIKON TOUTON TOU EINAI ONOMA*
and now chose and sanctified the house this of the to be name

MOU EKEI HEÓS AIÓNOS KAI ESONTAI HOI OPHTHALMOI MOU KAI HÉ KARDIA
of me there unto ages and shall be the eyes of me and the heart

MOU EKEI PASAS TAS HÉMERAS
of me there all the days

engLXX And now I have chosen and sanctified this house, that my name should be there for ever: and my eyes and my heart shall be there always.

2Ch. 11:1 And when Rehoboam was come to Jerusalem, he gathered of the house of Judah and Benjamin an hundred and fourscore thousand **chosen** *men*, which were warriors, to fight against Israel, that he might bring the kingdom again to Rehoboam.

YLT And Rehoboam cometh in to Jerusalem, and assembleth the house of Judah and Benjamin, a hundred and eighty thousand **chosen** warriors, to fight with Israel, to bring back the kingdom to Rehoboam.

NKJV Now when Rehoboam came to Jerusalem, he assembled from the house of Judah and Benjamin one hundred and eighty thousand **chosen** *men* who were warriors, to fight against Israel, that he might restore the kingdom to Rehoboam.

NASB Now when Rehoboam had come to Jerusalem, he assembled the house of Judah and Benjamin, 180,000 **chosen men** who were warriors, to fight against Israel to restore the kingdom to Rehoboam.

NIV When Rehoboam arrived in Jerusalem, he mustered Judah and Benjamin - a hundred and eighty thousand **able young men** – to go to war against Israel and to regain the kingdom for Rehoboam.

NLT When Rehoboam arrived at Jerusalem, he mobilized the men of Judah and Benjamin—180,000 **select troops**—to fight against Israel and to restore the kingdom to himself.

NEANISKOS - young man, boy – a divergent translation with "to fight against Israel" (KJV) rendered as "he waged war with Israel" (engLXX) as seen in context since in Vss 2-3 we read how no one fought - the quality meaning of BACHAR given by "young men": guys in their prime

LXX *KAI ÉLTHE ROBOAM EIS HIEROUSALÉM KAI EXEKKLÉSIASE TON IOUDAN KAI BENIAMIN*
and came Roboam into Jerusalem and gathered the Judah and Benjamin

HEKATON OGDOÉKONTA CHILIADAS ***NEANISKÓN*** *POIOUNTÓN*
hundred eighty thousand young men able

POLEMON KAI EPOLEMEI PROS ISRAÉL TOU EPISTREPSAI TÉN BASILEIAN TÓ ROBOAM
to war and made war unto Israel of the turn the kingdom to the Roboam

engLXX And Roboam came to Jerusalem; and he assembled Juda and Benjamin, a hundred and eighty thousand young men fit for war, and he waged war with Israel to recover the kingdom to Roboam.

2Ch. 12:13 So king Rehoboam strengthened himself in Jerusalem, and reigned: for Rehoboam *was* one and forty years old when he began to reign, and he reigned seventeen years in Jerusalem, the city which the LORD had **chosen** out of all the tribes of Israel, to put his name there. And his mother's name *was* Naamah an Ammonitess.

EKLEGÓ – to pick, choose, elect - a direct translation – Jerusalem, the city which the Lord chose out of all the tribes of Israel, to put His name there

LXX *KAI KATISCHUSEN HO BASILEUS ROBOAM EN HIEROUSALÉM KAI EBASILEUSE*
and grew strong the king Roboam in Jerusalem and reigned

KAI TESSARAKONTA KAI HENOS ETÓN ROBOAM EN TÓ BASILEUSAI AUTON
and forty and one years Roboam in the reign him

KAI HEPTAKAIDEKA ETÉ EBASILEUSEN EN HIEROUSALÉM EN TÉ POLEI HÉ
and seventeen years reigned in Jerusalem in the city which

EXELEXATO *KURIOS EPONOMASAI TO ONOMA AUTOU EKEI EK PASÓN PHULÓN*
chose Lord to name the name of him there out of all tribes

HUIÓN ISRAÉL KAI TO ONOMA TÉS MÉTROS AUTOU NOOMMA HÉ AMANITIS
of sons of Israel and the name of the mother of him Noomma the Ammanitess

engLXX So king Roboam strengthened *himself* in Jerusalem, and reigned: and Roboam was forty and one years old when he began to reign, and he reigned seventeen years in Jerusalem, in the city which the Lord chose out of all the tribes of the children of Israel to call his name there: and his mother's name was Noomma the Ammanitess.

2Ch. 13:3a And Abijah set the battle in array with an army of valiant men of war, *even* four hundred thousand **chosen** men: (. . .)

YLT And Abijah directeth the war with a force of mighty men of war, four hundred thousand **chosen** men, (. . .)

NKJV Abijah set the battle in order with an army of valiant warriors, four hundred thousand **choice** men . . .

NASB Abijah began the battle with an army of valiant warriors, 400,000 **chosen** men, (. . .)

NIV Abijah went into battle with an army of four hundred thousand **able** fighting men, (. . .)

NLT Judah, led by King Abijah, fielded 400,000 **select** warriors, (. . .)

DUNATOS - strong, mighty, able – a direct translation - the quality meaning of BACHAR given by "valiant" (KJV) men of war portrayed as: strong, mighty

LXX *KAI PARETAXATO ABIA EN DUNAMEI POLEMISTAIS DUNAMEÓS TETRAKOSIAIS*
and deployed Abia in force of warriors of power four hundred

	CHILIASIN ANDRÓN ***DUNATÓN***... thousand men mighty
engLXX	And Abia set the battle in array with an army, with mighty men of war, *even* four hundred thousand mighty men: (. . .)
2Ch. 13:3b	. . . Jeroboam also set the battle in array against him with eight hundred thousand **chosen** men, *being* mighty men of valour.
YLT	. . . and Jeroboam hath set in array with him battle, with eight hundred thousand **chosen** men, mighty of valour.
NKJV	. . . Jeroboam also drew up in battle formation against him with eight hundred thousand **choice** men, mighty men of valor.
NASB	. . . while Jeroboam drew up in battle formation against him with 800,000 **chosen** men who were valiant warriors.
NIV	. . . and Jeroboam drew up a battle line against him with eight hundred thousand **able** troops.
NLT	. . . while Jeroboam mustered 800,000 **select** troops from Israel.

DUNATOS - strong, mighty, able – a direct translation - the quality meaning of BACHAR given by the soldiers arrayed, the "men of valour" (KJV) portrayed as: strong, mighty

LXX	...*KAI IEROBOAM PARETAXATO PROS AUTON POLEMON EN OKTAKOSIAIS* and Jeroboam deployed to him war in eight hundred *CHILIASI* ***DUNATOI*** *POLEMISTAI DUNAMEÓS* thousand mighty warriors of power
engLXX	...and Jeroboam set the battle in array against him with eight hundred thousand, *they were* mighty warriors of the host.

2Ch. 13:17 — And Abijah and his people slew them with a great slaughter: so there fell down slain of Israel five hundred thousand **chosen** men.

YLT — and Abijah and his people smite among them a great smiting, and there fall wounded of Israel five hundred thousand **chosen** men.

NKJV — Then Abijah and his people struck them with a great slaughter; so five hundred thousand **choice** men of Israel fell slain.

NASB — Abijah and his people defeated them with a great slaughter, so that 500,000 **chosen** men of Israel fell slain.

NIV — Abijah and his troops inflicted heavy losses on them, so that there were five hundred thousand casualties among Israel's **able** men.

NLT — Abijah and his army inflicted heavy losses on them; 500,000 of Israel's **select** troops were killed that day.

DUNATOS - strong, mighty, able – a direct translation - the quality meaning of BACHAR given by the 500,000 fallen Israel soldiers mentioned honourably as: strong, mighty

LXX — *KAI EPATAXEN EN AUTOIS ABIA KAI HO LAOS AUTOU PLÉGÉN MEGALÉN KAI*
and beat in them Abia and the people of him struck great and

EPESON TRAUMATIAI APO ISRAÉL PENTAKOSIAI CHILIADES ANDRES ***DUNATOI***
fell slain from Israel five hundred thousand men able

engLXX — And Abia and his people smote them with a great slaughter: and there fell slain of Israel five hundred thousand mighty men.

2Ch. 25:5 — Moreover Amaziah gathered Judah together, and made them captains over thousands, and captains over hundreds, according to the houses of *their* fathers, throughout all Judah and Benjamin: and he numbered them from twenty years old and above, and found them three hundred thousand **choice** *men*, *able* to go forth to war, that could handle spear and shield.

YLT And Amaziah gathereth Judah, and appointeth them, according to the house of the fathers, for heads of the thousands, and for heads of the hundreds, for all Judah and Benjamin; and he inspecteth them from a son of twenty years and upward, and findeth them three hundred thousand **chosen ones**, going forth to the host, holding spear and target.

NKJV Moreover Amaziah gathered Judah together and set over them captains of thousands and captains of hundreds, according to *their* fathers' houses, throughout all Judah and Benjamin; and he numbered them from twenty years old and above, and found them to be three hundred thousand **choice** *men*, *able* to go to war, who could handle spear and shield.

NASB Moreover, Amaziah assembled Judah and appointed them according to *their* fathers' households under commanders of thousands and commanders of hundreds throughout Judah and Benjamin; and he took a census of those from twenty years old and upward and found them to be 300,000 **choice** men, *able* to go to war *and* handle spear and shield.

NIV Amaziah called the people of Judah together and assigned them according to their families to commanders of thousands and commanders of hundreds for all Judah and Benjamin. He then mustered those twenty years old or more and found that there were three hundred thousand **men fit for** military service, able to handle the spear and shield.

NLT Then Amaziah organized the army, assigning generals and captains for all Judah and Benjamin. He took a census and found that he had an army of 300,000 **select** troops, twenty years old and older, all trained in the use of spear and shield.

DUNATOS - strong, mighty, able – a divergent translation with "Judah and Benjamin" (KJV) rendered as "Juda and Jerusalem" (engLXX) – the secondary quality meaning of BACHAR given by the 300,000 soldiers mentioned as: strong, mighty

LXX *KAI SUNÉGAGEN AMASIAS TON OIKON IOUDA KAI ANESTÉSEN AUTOUS KAT*
and gathered Amasias the house of Juda and established them according to

OIKOUS PATRIÓN AUTÓN EIS CHILIARCHOUS KAI HEKATONTARCHOUS EN PANTI IOUDA KAI
houses of fathers of them into thousand-rulers and hundred-rulers in all Juda and

HIEROUSALÉM KAI ÉRITHMÉSEN AUTOUS APO EIKOSAETOUS KAI EPANÓ KAI HEUREN AUTOUS
Jerusalem and numbered them from twenty years and up and found them

TRIAKOSIAS CHILIADAS EXELTHEIN EIS POLEMON ***DUNATOUS*** *KRATOUNTAS DORU KAI THUREON*
three hundred thousand to go to war able strong in spear and shield

engLXX And Amasias assembled the house of Juda, and appointed them according to the houses of their families for captains of thousands and captains of hundreds in all Juda and Jerusalem: and he numbered them from twenty years old and upwards, and found them three hundred thousand able to go out to war, holding spear and shield.

2Ch. 29:11 My sons, be not now negligent: for the Lord **hath chosen** you to stand before him, to serve him, and that ye should minister unto him, and burn incense.

YLT My sons, be not now at rest, for on you **hath** Jehovah **fixed** to stand before Him, to serve Him, and to be to Him ministering and making perfume.

NKJV My sons, do not be negligent now, for the Lord **has chosen** you to stand before Him, to serve Him, and that you should minister to Him and burn incense."

NASB My sons, do not be negligent now, for the Lord **has chosen** you to stand before Him, to minister to Him, and to be His ministers and burn incense."

NIV My sons, do not be negligent now, for the Lord **has chosen** you to stand before him and serve him, to minister before him and to burn incense.'

NLT My sons, do not neglect your duties any longer! The Lord **has chosen** you to stand in his presence, to minister to him, and to lead the people in worship and present offerings to him."

HAIRETIZÓ – to choose – a divergent translation with "My sons" not translated – king Hezekiah (V.1) speaks to the Levites (V.4) and reminds them the Lord chose them for the job of ministering to Him in the temple

LXX *KAI NUN MÉ DIALIPÉTE HOTI EN HUMIN* ***HÉRETIKE*** *KURIOS STÉNAI ENANTION*
and now not cease since in you chose Lord to stand before
AUTOU LEITOURGEIN KAI EINAI AUTÓ LEITOURGOUNTAS KAI THUMIÓNTAS
him to officiate and to be to him ministers and incense burners

engLXX And now be not wanting *to your duty*, for the Lord has chosen you to stand before him to minister, and to be ministers and burners of incense to him.

2Ch. 33:7 And he set a carved image, the idol which he had made, in the house of God, of which God had said to David and to Solomon his son, in this house, and in Jerusalem, which I have **chosen** before all the tribes of Israel, will I put my name for ever:

EKLEGÓ – to pick, choose, elect - a divergent translation with the added clause "the molten *statue*" (engLXX) – God said that he chose Jerusalem out of all the tribes of Israel to put His name there

LXX *KAI ETHÉKE TO GLUPTON TO CHÓNEUTON EIKONA HÉN EPOIÉSEN EN OIKÓ THEOU HOU EIPE*
and put the carved the molten image which made in house of God which said
THEOS PROS DAUID KAI PROS SALÓMÓN HUION AUTOU EN TÓ OIKÓ TOUTÓ KAI HIEROUSALÉM
God to David and to Solomon son of him in the house this and Jerusalem
HÉN ***EXELEXAMÉN*** *EK PASÓN PHULÓN ISRAÉL THÉSÓ TO ONOMA MOU EIS TON AIÓNA*
which chose out of all tribes of Israel put the name of me into the ages

engLXX And he set the graven *image*, the molten *statue*, the idol which he made, in the house of God, of which God had said to David and to Solomon his son, In this house, and Jerusalem, which I have chosen out of all the tribes of Israel, I will put my name for ever;

Neh. 1:9 But *if* ye turn unto me, and keep my commandments, and do them; though there were of you cast out unto the uttermost part of the heaven, *yet* will I gather them from thence, and will bring them unto the place that I have **chosen** to set my name there.

EKLEGÓ – to pick, choose, elect - a direct translation – Jerusalem (V.2), the place which the Lord chose to set His name there

LXX *KAI EAN EPISTREPSÉTE PROS ME KAI PHULAXÉTE TAS ENTOLAS MOU KAI*
and if turn to me and guard the commands of me and
POIÉSÉTE AUTAS EAN É HÉ DIASPORA HUMÓN AP AKROU TOU OURANOU
do them if be the scattered you from highest of the heaven
EKEITHEN SUNAXÓ AUTOUS KAI EISAXÓ AUTOUS EIS TON TOPON HON
from there gather them and bring them into the place which
EXELEXAMÉN *KATASKÉNÓSAI TO ONOMA MOU EKEI*
chose to establish the name of me there

engLXX But if ye turn again to me, and keep my commandments, and do them; if ye should be scattered under the utmost *bound* of heaven, thence will I gather them, and I will bring them into the place which I have chosen to cause my name to dwell there.

Neh. 9:7 Thou *art* the Lord the God, who didst **choose** Abram, and broughtest him forth out of Ur of the Chaldees, and gavest him the name of Abraham;

YLT Thou *art* He, O Jehovah God, who didst **fix** on Abraham, and didst bring him out from Ur of the Chaldeans, and didst make his name Abraham,

EKLEGÓ – to pick, choose, elect - a divergent translation with "Ur" not translated – the Lord chose Abram to lead him out of the land of the Chaldees

	LXX	*SU EI KURIOS HO THEOS SU* ***EXELEXÓ*** *EN ABRAM KAI EXÉGAGES AUTON EK* you are Lord the God you chose in Abram and led him out of *TÉS CHÓRAS TÓN CHALDAIÓN KAI EPETHÉKAS AUTÓ ONOMA ABRAAM* the region of the Chaldeans and placed to him name Abraham
	engLXX	Thou art the Lord God, thou didst choose Abram, and broughtest him out of the land of the Chaldeans, and gavest him the name of Abraam:
Job 7:15		So that my soul **chooseth** strangling, *and* death rather than my life.
	YLT	And my soul **chooseth** strangling, death rather than my bones.
	NKJV	So that my soul **chooses** strangling *and* death rather than my body.
	NASB	So that my soul **would choose** suffocation, death rather than my pains.
	NIV	so that I **prefer** strangling and death, rather than this body of mine.
	NLT	I **would rather** be strangled - rather die than suffer like this.

APALLASSÓ – to set free, to separate – a divergent translation with "death rather than my life" (KJV) or "Death rather than my bones" (YLT) given as "yet *keep* my bones from death" (engLXX) - the word for soul in Greek *PSUCHÉ* is used for either "soul" or "life" so that: separate spirit from soul can be perceived as, soul separated from the living and, in that sense render the Hebrew, so "my soul chooseth strangling" (KJV) i.e. my soul chooses death, rendered as "Thou wilt separate life from my spirit" (engLXX): the verb "chooseth" given as "separate"

	LXX	***APALLAXEIS*** *APO PNEUMATOS MOU TÉN PSUCHÉN MOU APO DE THANATOU TA OSTA MOU* set free from spirit of me the soul of me from but death the bones of me
	engLXX	Thou wilt separate life from my spirit; and yet *keep* my bones from death.
Job 9:14		How much less shall I answer him, *and* **choose out** my words *to reason* with him?
	YLT	How much less do I - I answer Him? **Choose out** my words with Him?
	NKJV	How then can I answer Him, *and* **choose** my words *to reason* with Him?

NASB How then can I answer Him, *and* **choose** my words before Him?
NIV How then can I dispute with him? **How can I find** words **to argue** with him?
NLT So who am I, that **I should try to** answer God or even **reason** with him?

DIAKRINÓ – to judge, decide – a divergent translation with the action of Job to "choose out" his words with God, rendered as God doing the action of "judge my cause" (engLXX)

LXX *EAN DE MOU HUPAKOUSETAI É* ***DIAKRINEI*** *TA RÉMATA MOU*
if but of me hear or judge the sayings of me

engLXX Oh then that he would hearken to me, or judge my cause.

Job 15:5 For thy mouth uttereth thine iniquity, and thou **choosest** the tongue of the crafty.
YLT For thy mouth teacheth thine iniquity, and thou **chooseth** the tongue of the subtile.
NKJV For your iniquity teaches your mouth, and you **choose** the tongue of the crafty.
NASB "For your guilt teaches your mouth, and you **choose** the language of the crafty.
NIV Your sin prompts your mouth; you **adopt** the tongue of the crafty.
NLT Your sins are telling your mouth what to say. Your words **are based on** clever deception.

DIAKRINÓ – to judge, decide – a divergent translation with "thou choosest the tongue of the crafty" (KJV) or "of the subtile" (YLT): an emphasis on Job (See 12:1 up to 14:22 then replied to by Eliphaz in 15:1 onwards) accused here in Verse 5 as one who speaketh evil: as if Job was subtile/crafty of tongue, rendered in the LXX as not judging or discerning the words of God

LXX *ENOCHOS EI RÉMASI STOMATOS SOU OUDE* ***DIEKRINAS*** *RÉMATA DUNASTÓN*
liable to if saying of mouth of you nor judge sayings of mighty

engLXX Thou art guilty by the words of thy mouth, neither hast thou discerned the words of the mighty.

Job 29:25 I **chose** out their way, and sat chief, and dwelt as a king in the army, as one *that* comforteth the mourners.

EKLEGÓ – to pick, choose, elect - a direct translation – Job (V.1) mentions how he (used to) choose for others what to do

LXX ***EXELEXAMÉN*** *HODON AUTÓN KAI EKATHISA ARCHÓN KAI KATESKÉNOUN HÓSEI*
chose way of them and sat ruler and encamp as

BASILEUS EN MONOZÓNOIS HON TROPON PATHEINOUS PARAKALÓN
king in single armed whose manner mourners comforting

engLXX I chose out their way, and sat chief, and dwelt as a king in the midst of warriors, as one comforting mourners.

Job 34:4		**Let us choose** to us judgment: let us know among ourselves what *is* good.
	YLT	Judgment **let us choose** for ourselves, let us know among ourselves what *is* good.
	NKJV	**Let us choose** justice for ourselves; let us know among ourselves what *is* good.
	NASB	**Let us choose** for ourselves what is right; let us know among ourselves what is good.
	NIV	**Let us discern** for ourselves what is right; let us learn together what is good.
	NLT	So **let us discern** for ourselves what is right; let us learn together what is good.

HAIREÓ - to choose, prefer – a direct translation – Elihu (V.1) calls on Job and friends to choose or check out wise (V.2) judgment.

LXX *KRISIN* ***ELÓMETHA*** *HEAUTOIS GNÓMEN ANAMESON HEAUTÓN HO TI KALON*
judgment choose for ourselves know in the midst of ourselves the what good

engLXX Let us choose judgment to ourselves: let us know among ourselves what is right.

Job 34:33		*Should it be* according to thy mind? He will recompense it, whether thou refuse, or whether thou **choose**; and not I: therefore speak what thou knowest.
	YLT	By thee doth He recompense, that thou hast refused - That thou **dost choose**, and not I? And what thou hast known, speak.

NLT "Must God tailor his justice to your demands?
But you have rejected him!
The **choice is** yours, not mine.
Go ahead, share your wisdom with us.

EKLEGÓ – to pick, choose, elect - for the sake of comprehension I have added the paraphrasing of the NLT [this is where paraphrases have their best use cf. below Job 36:21] a direct translation – Elihu (V.1) suggests Job chooses whether what he (Elihu) has stated is valid or not

LXX ***MÉ APO SOU APOTISEI AUTÉN HOTI SU APÓSÉ HOTI SU*** ***EKLEXÉ*** ***KAI OUK EGÓ***
not from of you repay her since you | since you chose and not I
thrust away

KAI TI EGNÓS LALÉSON
and what know speak

engLXX Will he take vengeance for it on thee, whereas thou wilt put *it* far *from thee*? For thou shalt choose, and not I; and what thou knowest, speak thou.

Job 36:21 Take heed, regard not iniquity: for this **hast thou chosen** rather than affliction.
YLT Take heed - do not turn unto iniquity, for on this **thou hast fixed** rather than *on* affliction.
NKJV Take heed, do not turn to iniquity, for **you have chosen** this rather than affliction.
NASB "Be careful, do not turn to evil, for **you have preferred** this to affliction.
NIV Beware of turning to evil, which **you seem to prefer** to affliction.
NLT Be on guard! Turn back from evil, for God sent this suffering to keep you from a life of evil.

EXAIREÓ - to choose, select out, take out – a direct translation - Elihu (V.1) accuses Job of choosing iniquity instead of poverty

	LXX	*ALLA PHULAXAI MÉ PRAXÉS ATOPA EPI TOUTÓN GAR* ***EXEILÓ*** *APO PTÓCHEIAS* but guard not act out of place | over this for chose from poverty
	engLXX	But take heed lest thou do that which is wrong: for of this thou has made choice because of poverty.
Psa. 25:12		What man *is* he that feareth the LORD? him shall he teach in the way *that* he **shall choose**.
	YLT	Who *is* this - the man fearing Jehovah? He directeth him in the way He **doth choose**.
	NKJV	Who *is* the man that fears the LORD? Him shall He[4] teach in the way He[4] **chooses**.
	NASB	Who is the man who fears the LORD? He will instruct him in the way he **should choose**.
	NIV	Who, then, are those who fear the Lord? He will instruct them in the ways they **should choose**[5].
	NLT	Who are those who fear the LORD? He will show them the path they **should choose**.

HAIRETIZÓ – to choose – a direct translation – this can be read either as, the Lord choosing the way or, the man choosing the way, wherein the Lord gives instruction

	LXX **24:12**	*TIS ESTIN ANTHRÓPOS HO PHOBOUMENOS TON KURION NOMOTHETÉSEI AUTÓ* who is man the fear the Lord law instruct to him *EN HODÓ HÉ* ***HÉRETISATO*** in way which chose
	engLXX	Who is the man that fears the Lord? He shall instruct him in the way which he has chosen.
Psa. 33:12		Blessed *is* the nation whose God *is* the LORD; *and* the people *whom* he hath **chosen** for his own inheritance.

4. [[4]or, "he"]
5. [[5]or, "*ways he* ***chooses***"]

EKLEGÓ – to pick, choose, elect - a direct translation – Israel the people whom the Lord has chosen

LXX **32:12** ***MAKARION TO ETHNOS HOU ESTI KURIOS HO THEOS AUTOU LAOS HON***
blessed the nation where is Lord the God of him people whom

EXELEXATO ***EIS KLÉRONOMIAN HEAUTÓ***
chose into inheritance to himself

engLXX Blessed is the nation whose God is the Lord; the people whom he has chosen for his own inheritance.

Psa. 47:4 He shall **choose** our inheritance for us, the excellency of Jacob whom he loved. Selah.

YLT He doth **choose** for us our inheritance, the excellency of Jacob that He loves. Selah.

EKLEGÓ – to pick, choose, elect - a direct translation – as part of the context (V.3), the Lord has chosen the kind of outcome, the inheritance, for Israel

LXX **46:4** ***EXELEXATO*** ***HÉMIN TÉN KLÉRONOMIAN AUTOU TÉN KALLONÉN IAKÓB HÉN***
chose to us the inheritance of him the beauty of Jacob which

ÉGAPÉSE DIAPSALMA
loved Pause

engLXX He has chosen out his inheritance for us, the beauty of Jacob which he loved. Pause.

Psa. 65:4 Blessed *is the man whom* thou **choosest**, and causest to approach *unto thee, that* he may dwell in thy courts: we shall be satisfied with the goodness of thy house, *even* of thy holy temple.

YLT O the happiness of *him whom* Thou **choosest**, and drawest near, he inhabiteth Thy courts, we are satisfied with the goodness of Thy house, Thy holy temple.

EKLEGÓ – to pick, choose, elect - a direct translation – whom the Lord chooses to approach Him

LXX **64:4** *MAKARIOS HON* ***EXELEXÓ*** *KAI PROSELABOU KATASKÉNÓSEI EN TAIS AULAIS*
blessed whom chose and took to yourself encamp in the courts

SOU PLÉSTHÉSOMETHA EN TOIS AGATHOIS TOU OIKOU SOU HAGIOS HO NAOS SOU
of you filled in the good of the house of you holy the temple of you

engLXX Blessed *is he* whom thou hast chosen and adopted; he shall dwell in thy courts; we shall be filled with the good things of thy house; thy temple is holy.

Psa. 78:67 Moreover he refused the tabernacle of Joseph, and **chose** not the tribe of Ephraim:

EKLEGÓ – to pick, choose, elect - a direct translation – the Lord did not choose the tribe of Ephraim

LXX **77:67** *KAI APÓSATO TO SKÉNÓMA IÓSÉPH KAI TÉN PHULÉN EPHRAIM OUK* ***EXELEXATO***
and thrust away the tent of Joseph and the tribe of Ephraim not chose

engLXX And he rejected the tabernacle of Joseph, and chose not the tribe of Ephraim;

Psa. 78:68 But **chose** the tribe of Judah, the mount Zion which he loved.

EKLEGÓ – to pick, choose, elect - a direct translation – the Lord chose the tribe of Judah

LXX **77:68** *KAI* ***EXELEXATO*** *TÉN PHULÉN IOUDA TO OROS TO SIÓN HO ÉGAPÉSE*
and chose the tribe of Juda the mountain the Zion which loved

engLXX but chose the tribe of Juda, the mount Sion which he loved.

Psa. 78:70 He **chose** David also his servant, and took him from the sheepfolds:

EKLEGÓ – to pick, choose, elect - a direct translation – the Lord chose David

LXX **77:70** *KAI* ***EXELEXATO*** *DAUID TON DOULON AUTOU KAI ANELABEN AUTON EK TÓN*
and chose David the servant of him and took him out of the

POIMNIÓN TÓN PROBATÓN
flocks of the sheep

engLXX He chose David also his servant, and took him up from the flocks of sheep.

Psa. 84:10 For a day in thy courts *is* better than a thousand. I **had rather** be a doorkeeper in the house of my God, than to dwell in the tents of wickedness.

YLT For good *is* a day in Thy courts, O Teacher! I **have chosen rather** to be at the threshold, in the house of my God, than to dwell in tents of wickedness.

EKLEGÓ – to pick, choose, elect - a loose translation with "be a doorkeeper" (KJV) or "be at the threshold" (YLT), given as "be an abject" (engLXX) – any job in house of God is preferred over being in dwellings of the wicked

LXX **83:10** *HOTI KREISSÓN HÉMERA MIA EN TAIS AULAIS SOU HUPER CHILIADAS*
since better day one in the courts of you rather than thousands

EXELEXAMÉN *PARARRIPTEISTHAI EN TÓ OIKÓ TOU THEOU MALLON É*
chose cast aside in the house of the God more than

OIKEIN ME EN SKÉNÓMASIN AMARTÓLÓN
to live me in tents of sinners

engLXX For one day in thy courts is better than thousands. I would rather be an abject in the house of God, than dwell in the tents of sinners.

Psa. 89:19 Then thou spakest in vision to thy holy one, and saidst, I have laid help upon *one that is* mighty; I have exalted *one* **chosen** out of the people.

YLT Then Thou hast spoken in vision, to Thy saint, yea, Thou sayest, I have placed help upon a mighty one, exalted a **chosen one** out of the people,

NKJV Then You spoke in a vision to Your holy one, and said: "I have given help to *one who is* mighty; I have exalted **one chosen** from the people.

NASB Once You spoke in vision to Your godly ones, and said, "I have given help to one who is mighty; I have exalted **one chosen** from the people.

NIV Once you spoke in a vision, to your faithful people you said: "I have bestowed strength on a warrior; I have raised up **a young man** from among the people.

NLT Long ago you spoke in a vision to your faithful people. You said, "I have raised up a warrior. I have **selected** him from the common people to be king.

EKLEKTOS – a divergent translation with "to thy holy one" (KJV) or "to thy saint" (YLT), given as "to thy children" (engLXX): note also NASB, NIV & NLT: the person in view is likely Samuel (the holy one or saint to whom vision was given) since Samuel was the one to mention God had chosen another to take king Saul's place as per 1 Samuel 13:13-14: the ongoing context helps us see this likeliness as David is shown as the one chosen (V.20) – the secondary quality meaning of BACHAR: a particular chosen one is in view, a "mighty one", David (V.20), so a quality guy: choice

LXX **88:19** *TOTE ELALÉSAS EN HORASEI TOIS HUIOIS SOU KAI EIPAS ETHEMÉN*
then spoke in vision to the sons of you and said placed

BOÉTHEIAN EPI DUNATON HUPSÓSA ***EKLEKTON*** *EK TOU LAOU MOU*
aid upon mighty raising choice out of the people of me

engLXX Then thou spokest in vision to thy children, and saidst, I have laid help on a mighty one; I have exalted one chosen out of my people.

Psa. 105:26 He sent Moses his servant; *and* Aaron whom he had **chosen**.

EKLEGÓ – to pick, choose, elect - a direct translation – the Lord chose Moses and Aaron to show His signs among Egypt (the land of Ham Vss.23 & 27)

LXX *EXAPESTEILE MÓUSÉN TON DOULON AUTOU AARÓN HON* ***EXELEXATO*** *AUTON*
104:26 sent out Moses the servant of him Aaron whom chose him

engLXX He sent forth Moses his servant, *and* Aaron whom he had chosen.

Psa. 119:30 I **have chosen** the way of truth: thy judgments have I laid *before me.*
YLT The way of faithfulness I **have chosen**, thy judgments I have compared,
NKJV I **have chosen** the way of truth; Your judgments I have laid *before me.*
NASB I **have chosen** the faithful way; I have placed Your ordinances *before me.*
NIV I **have chosen** the way of faithfulness; I have set my heart on your laws.
NLT I **have chosen** to be faithful; I have determined to live by your regulations.

HAIRETIZÓ – to choose – a loose translation with "have I laid" (KJV) or "I have compared" (YLT), given as "have not forgotten" (engLXX) – the way of truth is chosen

LXX *HODON ALÉTHEIAS* ***HÉRETISAMÉN*** *KAI TA KRIMATA SOU OUK EPELATHOMÉN*
118:30 way of truth chose and the judgments of you not forget

engLXX I have chosen the way of truth; and have not forgotten thy judgments.

Psa. 119:173 Let thine hand help me; for I have **chosen** thy precepts.

HAIRETIZÓ - to choose – a direct translation – the written words of the Lord are chosen

LXX *GENESTHÓ HÉ CHEIR SOU TOU SÓSAI ME HOTI TAS ENTOLAS SOU* ***HÉRETISAMÉN***
118:173 be the hand of you of the to save me since the | commandments of you chose

engLXX Let thine hand be *prompt* to save me; for I have chosen thy commandments.

Psa. 132:13 For the Lord hath **chosen** Zion; he hath desired *it* for his habitation.

EKLEGÓ – to pick, choose, elect - a direct translation – the Lord has chosen Zion

	LXX	***HOTI* EXELEXATO *KURIOS TÉN SIÓN HÉRETISATO AUTÉN EIS KATOIKIAN HEAUTÓ***
	131:13	since chose Lord the Zion chose her into dwelling for himself
	engLXX	For the Lord has elected Sion, he has chosen her for a habitation for himself, *saying,*
Psa. 135:4		For the LORD hath **chosen** Jacob unto himself, *and* Israel for his peculiar treasure.

EKLEGÓ – to pick, choose, elect - a direct translation – the Lord has chosen Jacob

	LXX	***HOTI TON IAKÓB* EXELEXATO *HEAUTÓ HO KURIOS ISRAÉL EIS PERIOUSIASMON HEAUTÓ***
	134:4	since the Jacob chose for himself the Lord Israel into prized treasure for hiimself
	engLXX	For the Lord has chosen Jacob for himself, *and* Israel for his peculiar treasure.
Pro. 1:29		For that they hated knowledge, and did not **choose** the fear of the LORD:
	YLT	Because that they have hated knowledge, and the fear of Jehovah **have** not **chosen**.
	NKJV	Because they hated knowledge, and **did** not **choose** the fear of the LORD,
	NASB	Because they hated knowledge and **did** not **choose** the fear of the LORD.
	NIV	since they hated knowledge and **did** not **choose** to fear the LORD.
	NLT	For they hated knowledge and **chose** not to fear the LORD.

PROAIREÓ - to choose, prefer – a divergent translation with "knowledge" (KJV) given as "wisdom" (engLXX); "fear of the Lord" (KJV) as "word of the Lord" (engLXX) – (V.22) the simple, the scorners, the fools, have not chosen the word of the Lord

	LXX	***EMISÉSAN GAR SOPHIAN TON DE LOGON TOU KURIOU OU* PROEILANTO**
		hated for wisdom the but word of the Lord not chose
	engLXX	For they hated wisdom, and did not choose the word of the Lord:

Pro. 3:31		Envy thou not the oppressor, and **choose** none of his ways.
	YTL	Be not envious of a man of violence, nor **fix** thou on any of his ways.
	NKJV	Do not envy the oppressor, and **choose** none of his ways;
	NASB	Do not envy a man of violence and **do** not **choose** any of his ways.
	NIV	Do not envy the violent or **choose** any of their ways.
	NLT	Don't envy violent people or **copy** their ways.

ZÉLOÓ - to esteem, emulate, strive after – a divergent translation with "envy thou not the oppressor" (KJV) or "Be not envious of a man of violence" (YLT), given as "Procure not the reproaches of bad men" (engLXX) – to go after the ways of a violent man

	LXX	*MÉ KTÉSÉ KAKÓN ANDRÓN ONEIDÉ MÉDE* ***ZÉLÓSÉS*** *TAS HODOUS AUTÓN* not acquire of bad men scorn neither emulate the ways of them
	engLXX	Procure not the reproaches of bad men, neither do thou covet their ways.
Pro. 8:10		Receive my instruction, and not silver; and knowledge rather than **choice** gold.
	YLT	Receive my instruction, and not silver, and knowledge rather than **choice** gold.
	NKJV	Receive my instruction, and not silver, and knowledge rather than **choice** gold;
	NASB	"Take my instruction and not silver, and knowledge rather than **choicest** gold.
	NIV	Choose my instruction instead of silver, knowledge rather than **choice** gold,
	NLT	Choose my instruction rather than silver, and knowledge rather than **pure** gold.

DOKIMAZÓ - to approve, assay, test – a direct translation – the quality meaning of BACHAR: to be chosen, preferred, excellent: top gold, so given as choice gold which can only be obtained by purifying: tested gold

	LXX	*LABETE PAIDEIAN KAI MÉ ARGURION KAI GNÓSIN HUPER CHRUSION* ***DEDOKIMASMENON*** receive child rearing and not silver and knowledge over gold tried
	engLXX	Receive instruction, and not silver; and knowledge rather than tried gold.

Pro. 8:19 My fruit *is* better than gold, yea, than fine gold; and my revenue than **choice** silver.

YLT Better *is* my fruit than gold, even fine gold, and mine increase than **choice** silver.

NKJV My fruit *is* better than gold, yes, than fine gold, and my revenue than **choice** silver.

NASB "My fruit is better than gold, even pure gold, and my yield better than **choicest** silver.

NIV My fruit is better than fine gold; what I yield surpasses **choice** silver.

NLT My gifts are better than gold, even the purest gold, my wages better than **sterling** silver!

EKLEKTOS – a divergent translation with "fine gold" (KJV) given as "precious stones" (engLXX) – the secondary meaning of BACHAR of "to be chosen: preferred: excellent": *EKLEKTOS* used exactly like *NEANIAS* or *NEANISKOS*: the chosen, quality of the silver, is expressed by choice [see also CHARUTS for the gold]

LXX *BELTION EME KARPIZESTHAI*[6] *HUPER CHRUSION*[7] *KAI LITHON TIMION TA DE*
best my enjoy fruit over gold and stones precious the but

EMA GENNÉMATA KREISSÓ ARGURIOU ***EKLEKTOU***
my produce better of silver of choice

engLXX *It is* better to have my fruit than *to have* gold and precious stones; and my produce is better than choice silver.

Pro. 10:20 The tongue of the just *is as* **choice** silver: the heart of the wicked *is* little worth.

YLT The tongue of the righteous *is* **chosen** silver, the heart of the wicked – as a little thing.

NKJV The tongue of the righteous *is* **choice** silver; the heart of the wicked *is worth* little.

NASB The tongue of the righteous is *as* **choice** silver, the heart of the wicked is *worth* little.

---

6. See PERI
7. See CHARUTS

NIV The tongue of the righteous is **choice** silver, but the heart of the wicked is of little value.

NLT The words of the godly are like **sterling** silver; the heart of a fool is worthless.

PUROÓ - burn up with fire, purify, purge – a divergent translation with "little worth" (KJV) or "little thing" (YLT), given as "shall fail" (engLXX) – the secondary meaning of BACHAR of "to be chosen: preferred: excellent": chosen silver as the object chosen is seen as quality and this is given by being tested: tried by fire

LXX *ARGUROS* ***PEPURÓMENOS*** *GLÓSSA DIKAIOU KARDIA DE ASEBOUS EKLEIPSEI*
silver fire purified tongue of righteous heart but impious fails

engLXX The tongue of the just is tried silver; but the heart of the ungodly shall fail.

Pro. 16:16 How much better *is it* to get wisdom than gold! And to get understanding rather to **be chosen** than silver!

YLT To get wisdom - how much better than gold, and to get understanding to **be chosen** than silver!

NKJV How much better *it is* to get wisdom than gold! And to get understanding is to **be chosen** rather than silver.

NASB How much better it is to get wisdom than gold! And to get understanding is to **be chosen** above silver.

NIV How much better to get wisdom than gold, **to get** understanding rather than silver! [i.e. NOT translated]

NLT How much better to get wisdom than gold, and good judgment than silver! [i.e. NOT translated]

HAIRETOS aNT - to be chosen, elected – a divergent translation with the added "brood" (engLXX)/ "nests" (LXX-inter) of wisdom – intelligence/prudence is to be chosen over silver

LXX *NOSSIAI SOPHIAS HAIRETÓTERAI CHRUSIOU NOSSIAI DE PHRONESEÓS*

LXX-inter nests of wisdom to choose of gold nests but of intelligence

HAIRETÓTERAI *HUPER ARGURION*
to choose over silver

engLXX The brood of wisdom is more to be chosen than gold, and the brood of prudence more to be chosen than silver.

Pro. 21:3 To do justice and judgment *is* **more acceptable** to the LORD than sacrifice.
YLT To do righteousness and judgment, **is chosen** of Jehovah rather than sacrifice.
NKJV To do righteousness and justice *is* **more acceptable** to the LORD than sacrifice.
NASB To do righteousness and justice **is desired** by the LORD more than sacrifice.
NIV To do what is right and just **is more acceptable** to the LORD than sacrifice.
NLT The LORD **is more pleased** when we do what is right and just than when we offer him sacrifices.

ARESTOS - acceptable, pleasing – a divergent translation with "judgment" (KJV) rendered as "to speak truth" (engLXX) - the only place where BACHAR is given as "acceptable": to do right: justice and appropriate judgment chosen, is preferred over doing shedding blood in sacrifices: more acceptable

LXX *POIEIN DIKAIA KAI ALÉTHEUEIN* ***ARESTA*** *PARA THEÓ MALLON É THUSIÓN AIMA*
to do right and to truth pleasing more to God rather than sacrifice blood

engLXX To do justly and to speak truth, are more pleasing to God than the blood of sacrifices.

Pro. 22:1 A good name *is* rather **to be chosen** than great riches, *and* loving favour rather than silver and gold.
YLT A name **is chosen** rather than much wealth, than silver and than gold – good grace.
NKJV A *good* name **is to be chosen** rather than great riches, loving favor rather than silver and gold.
NASB A *good* name **is to be** more **desired** than great wealth, favor is better than silver and gold.
NIV A good name **is** more **desirable** than great riches; to be esteemed is better than silver or gold.
NLT **Choose** a good reputation over great riches; being held in high esteem is better than silver or gold.

HAIRETOS aNT - to be chosen, elected – a direct translation – a good name is more to be chosen over wealth

LXX ***HAIRETÓTERON*** *ONOMA KALON É PLOUTOS POLUS HUPER DE ARGURION KAI*
chose name good than wealth much more but silver and

CHRUSION CHARIS AGATHÉ
Gold favour good

engLXX A fair name is better than much wealth, and good favour is above silver and gold.

Ecc. 9:4 For to him that is **joined**[8] to all the living there is hope: for a living dog is better than a dead lion.

NOT in LXX - See Note 8 below

LXX *HOTI TIS HOS* ***KOINÓNEI***[8] *PROS PANTAS TOUS ZÓNTAS ESTIN ELPIS HOTI HO*
since one who communes to all the living is hope since the

KUÓN HO ZÓN AUTOS AGATHOS HUPER TON LEONTA TON NEKRON
dog the living he good over the lion the dead

engLXX For who is he that has fellowship with all the living? There is hope *of him*: for a living dog is better than a dead lion.

Sng. 5:15 His legs *are as* pillars of marble, set upon sockets of fine gold: his countenance *is* as Lebanon, **excellent** as the cedars.

YLT His limbs pillars of marble, founded on sockets of fine gold, his appearance as Lebanon, **choice** as the cedars.

NKJV His legs *are* pillars of marble set on bases of fine gold. His countenance *is* like Lebanon, **excellent** as the cedars.

NASB “His legs are pillars of alabaster set on pedestals of pure gold; his appearance is like Lebanon **choice** as the cedars.

8. BACHAR not translated, but the word CHABAR next to it

NIV His legs are pillars of marble set on bases of pure gold. His appearance is like Lebanon, **choice** as its cedars.

NLT His legs are like marble pillars set in sockets of finest gold. His posture is stately, like the **noble** cedars of Lebanon.

EKLEKTOS – a direct translation – the secondary meaning of BACHAR of "to be chosen: preferred: excellent": *EKLEKTOS* used exactly like *NEANIAS* or *NEANISKOS*: the quality in view, the emphasis on choice given by *EKLEKTOS*: the paramount thing that came to mind with "Lebanon" in the bible is its cedars where they appear together as words 21 times for their beauty, strength and abundance: the maiden speaks of her beloved man as choice as the cedars in looks

LXX *KNÉMAI AUTOU STULOI MARMARINOI TETHEMELIÓMENOI EPI BASEIS CHRUSAS*
legs of him columns marble founded upon bases of gold

EIDOS AUTOU HÓS LIBANOS ***EKLEKTOS*** *HÓS KEDROI*
form of him as Lebanon choice as cedars

engLXX His legs are marble pillars set on golden sockets: his form is as Libanus, choice as the cedars.

Isa. 1:29 For they shall be ashamed of the oaks which ye have desired, and ye shall be confounded for the gardens that ye **have chosen**.

YLT For *men* are ashamed because of the oaks that ye have desired, and ye are confounded because of the gardens that ye **have chosen**.

NKJV For they shall be ashamed of the terebinth trees which you have desired; and you shall be embarrassed because of the gardens which you **have chosen**.

NASB Surely you will be ashamed of the oaks which you have desired, and you will be embarrassed at the gardens which you **have chosen**.

NIV 'You will be ashamed because of the sacred oaks in which you have delighted; you will be disgraced because of the gardens that you **have chosen**.

NLT You will be ashamed of your idol worship in groves of sacred oaks. You will blush because you worshiped in gardens dedicated to idols.
[i.e. NOT translated]

EPITHUMEÓ - desired, coveted – a loose translation with "oaks" (KJV) given as "idols" (engLXX) – the only place where BACHAR is translated by *EPITHUMEÓ*: the gardens where idols and false gods were worshipped are desired (chosen) resulting in the people being made ashamed

LXX *DIOTI AISCHUNTHÉSONTAI APO TÓN EIDÓLÓN AUTÓN HA AUTOI ÉBOULONTO*
for ashamed from the idols of them which they wished

KAI ÉSCHUNTHÉSAN EPI TOIS KÉPOIS HA ***EPETHUMÉSAN***
and ashamed upon the gardens which desired

engLXX For they shall be ashamed of their idols, which they delighted in, and they are made ashamed of the gardens which they coveted.

Isa. 7:15 Butter and honey shall he eat, that he may know to refuse the evil, and **choose** the good.

YLT Butter and honey he doth eat, when he knoweth to refuse evil, and to **fix** on good.

EKLEGÓ – to pick, choose, elect - a direct translation with "before" (engLXX) seen in the "when" (YLT): direct does not equal "literal" – the Son of the virgin (V.14) shall choose good

LXX *BOUTURON KAI MELI PHAGETAI PRINÉ GNÓNAI AUTON É PROELESTHAI*
butter and honey eat before to know him or to prefer

PONÉRA ***EKLEXASTHAI*** *TO AGATHON*
evil choose the good

engLXX Butter and honey shall he eat, before he knows either to prefer evil, *or* choose the good.

Isa. 7:16 For before the child shall know to refuse the evil, and **choose** the good, the land that thou abhorrest shall be forsaken of both her kings.

YLT For before the youth doth know to refuse evil, and to **fix** on good, forsaken is the land thou art vexed with, because of her two kings.

EKLEGÓ – to pick, choose, elect - a direct translation – there is a time for a child to know to refuse evil and choose good instead: here, in reference to the Son of the virgin (V.14) also

LXX *DIOTI PRINÉ GNÓNAI TO PAIDION AGATHON É KAKON APEITHEI PONÉRIA* ***EKLEXASTHAI*** *TO*
for before to know the child good or bad resisting evil choose the

AGATHON KAI KATALEIPHTHÉSETAI HÉ GÉ HÉN SU PHOBÉ APO PROSÓPOU TÓN DUO BASILEÓN
good and abandoned the land which you fear from face of the two kings

engLXX For before the child shall know good or evil, he refuses evil, to choose the good; and the land shall be forsaken which thou art afraid of because of the two kings.

Isa. 14:1 For the Lord will have mercy on Jacob, and will yet **choose** Israel, and set them in their own land: and the strangers shall be joined with them, and they shall cleave to the house of Jacob.

YLT Because Jehovah loveth Jacob, and hath **fixed** again on Israel, and given them rest on their own land, and joined hath been the sojourner to them, and they have been admitted to the house of Jacob.

EKLEGÓ – to pick, choose, elect - a direct translation – the Lord will again choose Israel

LXX *KAI ELEÉSEI KURIOS TON IAKÓB KAI* ***EKLEXETAI*** *ETI TON ISRAÉL KAI*
and mercy Lord the Jacob and choose yet the Israel and

ANAPAUSONTAI EPI TÉS GÉS AUTÓN KAI HO GEIÓRAS PROSTETHÉSETAI PROS
rest upon the land of them and the foreigner added to

AUTOUS KAI PROSTETHÉSETAI PROS TON OIKON IAKÓB
them and added to the house of Jacob

engLXX And the Lord will have mercy on Jacob, and will yet choose Israel, and they shall rest on their land: and the stranger shall be added to them, yea, shall be added to the house of Jacob.

Isa. 40:20 He that *is* so impoverished that he hath no oblation **chooseth** a tree *that* will not rot; he seeketh unto him a cunning workman to prepare a graven image, *that* shall not be moved.

YLT He who is poor *by* heave-offerings, a tree not rotten doth **choose**, a skilful artizan he seeketh for it, to establish a graven image - not moved.

EKLEGÓ – to pick, choose, elect - a divergent translation with "impoverished" (KJV) or "poor" (YLT), not translated – the choosing of a wood that will last

LXX *XULON GAR ASÉPTON* ***EKLEGETAI*** *TEKTÓN KAI SOPHÓS ZÉTÉSEI PÓS STÉSEI*
tree for hardwood chooses sculptor and wise seeks how to station

EIKONA AUTOU KAI HINA MÉ SALEUÉTAI
image of him and | not shake
in order that

engLXX For the artificer chooses out a wood that will not rot, and will wisely enquire how he shall set up his image, and *that so* that it should not be moved.

Isa. 41:8 But thou, Israel, *art* my servant, Jacob whom I have **chosen**, the seed of Abraham my friend.

YLT - And thou, O Israel, My servant, Jacob, whom I have **chosen**, seed of Abraham, My lover,

EKLEGÓ – to pick, choose, elect - a divergent translation with "my friend" (KJV) or "My lover" (YLT), given as "whom I have loved" (engLXX) – the Lord chose Jacob

LXX *SU DE ISRAÉL PAIS MOU IAKÓB KAI HON* ***EXELEXAMÉN*** *SPERMA ABRAAM HON ÉGAPÉSA*
you but Israel | of me Jacob and whom chose seed of Abraam whom loved
young servant

engLXX But thou, Israel, art my servant Jacob, and he whom I have chosen, the seed of Abraam, whom I have loved:

Isa. 41:9 *Thou* whom I have taken from the ends of the earth, and called thee from the chief men thereof, and said unto thee, Thou *art* my servant; I have **chosen** thee, and not cast thee away.

YLT Whom I have taken hold of, from the ends of the earth, and from its near places I have called thee, and I say to thee, My servant Thou *art*, I have **chosen** thee, and not rejected thee.

EKLEGÓ – to pick, choose, elect - a loose translation with "chief men" (KJV) or "near places" (YLT), given as "high places" – Jacob (V.8) whom the Lord has chosen

LXX ***OU ANTELABOMÉN AP AKRÓN TÉS GÉS KAI EK TÓN SKOPIÓN AUTÉS EKALESA***
not took from farthest of the earth and | out of the heights of her called

SE KAI EIPA SOI PAIS MOU EI ***EXELEXAMÉN*** ***SE KAI OUK EGKATELIPON SE***
you and said to you | young servant of me are chosen you and not abandon you

engLXX whom I have taken hold of from the ends of the earth, and from the high places of it I have called thee, and said to thee, Thou art my servant; I have chosen thee, and I have not forsaken thee.

Isa. 41:24 Behold, ye *are* of nothing, and your work of nought: an abomination *is he that* **chooseth** you.

YLT Lo, ye *are* of nothing, and your work of nought, an abomination – it **fixeth** on you.

EKLEGÓ – to pick, choose, elect - a divergent translation with "ye of nothing" (KJV) given as "whence ye are" (engLXX) – The nations who war with Israel (V.12), Isles (V.1) [other than Israel; against God] Heb. "abomination chooses you" (KJV) [connects or is a result of their waywardness]: Gk. "An abomination out of the earth" (engLXX) chosen

LXX ***HOTI POTHEN ESTE HUMEIS KAI POTHEN HÉ ERGASIA HUMÓN EK GÉS***
since whence ye are you and whence the works of you out of earth

BDELUGMA ***EXELEXANTO*** *HUMAS*
abomination chosen you

engLXX whence ye are, and whence is your work: they have chosen you an abomination out of the earth.

Isa. 43:10 Ye *are* my witnesses, saith the LORD, and my servant whom I have **chosen**: that ye may know and believe me, and understand that I *am* he: before me there was no God formed, neither shall there be after me.

YLT Ye *are* My witnesses, an affirmation of Jehovah, and My servant whom I have **chosen**, so that ye know and give credence to Me, and understand that I *am* He, before Me there was no God formed, and after Me there is none.

EKLEGÓ – to pick, choose, elect - a loose translation with "saith the LORD" (KJV) or "an affirmation of Jehovah" (YLT), given as "I *too am* a witness, saith the Lord God" (engLXX) – Israel (v.1) is the servant whom the Lord has chosen

LXX *GINESTHE MOI MARTURES KAI EGÓ MARTUS LEGEI KURIOS HO THEOS KAI HO*
be ye to me witnesses and I witness says Lord the God and the

PAIS MOU HON ***EXELEXAMÉN*** *HINA GNÓTE KAI PISTEUSÉTE KAI SUNÉTE HOTI*
| of me whom chosen in order that | and believe and perceive since
young servant ye should know

EGÓ EIMI EMPROSTHEN MOU OUK EGENETO ALLOS THEOS KAI MET EME OUK ESTAI
I am before me not be another god and after me not shall be

engLXX Be ye my witnesses, and I *too am* a witness, saith the Lord God, and my servant whom I have chosen: that ye may know, and believe, and understand that I am *he*: before me there was no other God, and after me there shall be none.

Isa. 44:1 Yet now hear, O Jacob my servant; and Israel, whom I have **chosen**:

EKLEGÓ – to pick, choose, elect - a direct translation – Israel whom the Lord has chosen

	LXX	***NUN DE AKOUSON IAKÓB HO PAIS MOU KAI ISRAÉL HON* EXELEXAMÉN** now but hear Jacob the | of me and Israel whom chosen young servant
	engLXX	But now hear, Jacob my servant; and Israel, whom I have chosen.
Isa. 44:2		Thus saith the LORD that made thee, and formed thee from the womb, *which* will help thee; Fear not, O Jacob, my servant; and thou, Jesurun, whom I have **chosen**.
	YLT	Thus said Jehovah, thy Maker, and thy Former, From the womb He doth help thee; fear not, my servant Jacob, and Jeshurun, whom I have **fixed** on.

EKLEGÓ – to pick, choose, elect - a divergent translation with "Jesurun" (KJV) or "Jeshurun" (YLT), given as "beloved Israel" (engLXX) – Israel whom the Lord has chosen

	LXX	*HOUTÓ LEGEI KURIOS HO THEOS HO POÉSAS SE KAI HO PLASAS SE EK KOILIAS ETI* this says Lord the God who made you and who shaped you out of body yet ***BOÉTHÉTHÉSÉ MÉ PHOBOU PAIS MOU IAKÓB KAI ÉGAPÉMENOS ISRAÉL HON* EXELEXAMÉN** helped not fear | of me Jacob and loved Israel whom chosen young servant
	engLXX	Thus saith the Lord God that made thee, and he that formed thee from the womb; Thou shalt yet be helped: fear not, my servant Jacob; and beloved Israel, whom I have chosen.
Isa. 48:10		Behold, I have refined thee, but not with silver; I **have chosen** thee in the furnace of affliction.
	YLT	Lo, I have refined thee, and not with silver, I **have chosen** thee in a furnace of affliction.
	NKJV	Behold, I have refined you, but not as silver; I **have tested** you in the furnace of affliction.
	NASB	"Behold, I have refined you, but not as silver; I **have tested** you in the furnace of affliction.
	NIV	See, I have refined you, though not as silver; I **have tested** you in the furnace of affliction.
	NLT	I have refined you, but not as silver is refined. Rather, I **have refined** you in the furnace of suffering.

EXAIREÓ - to choose, select out, take out – a divergent translation with, "I have refined" (KJV) given as "I have sold" (engLXX) – chosen whilst in affliction

LXX *IDOU PEPRAKA SE OUCH HENEKEN ARGURIOU* ***EXEILAMÉN*** *DE SE EK KAMINOU*
look bartered you not on account of silver chose but you out of furnace

PTÓCHEIAS
poverty
i.e. took you out

engLXX Behold, I have sold thee, *but* not for silver; but I have rescued thee from the furnace of affliction.

Isa. 49:7 Thus saith the LORD, the Redeemer of Israel, *and* his Holy One, to him whom man despiseth, to him whom the nation abhorreth, to a servant of rulers, Kings shall see and arise, princes also shall worship, because of the LORD that is faithful, *and* the Holy One of Israel, and he shall **choose** thee.

YLT Thus said Jehovah, Redeemer of Israel, His Holy One, to the despised in soul, to the abominated of a nation, to the servant of rulers: 'Kings see, and have risen, princes, and worship, for the sake of Jehovah, who is faithful, the Holy of Israel, and He **chooseth** thee.'

EKLEGÓ – to pick, choose, elect - a divergent translation with "servant" (KJV) rendered as "servants" (engLXX) – The Lord chooses Israel (V.3) but a prophetic look at the Messiah (V.6 "light to the Gentiles")

LXX *HOUTÓS LEGEI KURIOS HO RUSAMENOS SE HO THEOS ISRAÉL HAGIASETE TON*
this says Lord the rescuing you the God of Israel holy ye the

PHAULIZONTA TÉN PSUCHÉN AUTOU TON BDELUSSOMENON HUPO TÓN
despises the life of him the abhorred by the

ETHNÓN TÓN DOULÓN TÓN ARCHONTÓN BASILEIS OPSONTAI AUTON KAI
nations the servants of the rulers kings see him and

ANASTÉSONTAI ARCHONTES KAI PROSKUNÉSOUSIN AUTÓ HENEKEN KURIOU
arise rulers and obey him on account of Lord

HOTI PISTOS ESTIN HO HAGIOS ISRAÉL KAI ***EXELEXAMÉN*** *SE*
since faithful is the holy of Israel and chosen you

engLXX Thus saith the Lord that delivered thee, the God of Israel, Sanctify him that despises his life, him that is abhorred by the nations that are the servants of princes: kings shall behold him, and princes shall arise, and shall worship him, for the Lord's sake: for the Holy One of Israel is faithful, and I have chosen thee.

Isa. 56:4 For thus saith the LORD unto the eunuchs that keep my sabbaths, and **choose** *the things* that please me, and take hold of my covenant;

EKLEGÓ – to pick, choose, elect - a direct translation – eunuchs (that) choose the things that please the Lord

LXX *TADE LEGEI KURIOS TOIS EUNOUCHOIS HOSOI AN PHULAXÓNTAI TA SABBATA*
thus says Lord to the eunuchs | any guard the sabbaths
as many as

MOU KAI ***EKLEXÓNTAI*** *HA EGÓ THELÓ KAI ANTECHÓNTAI TÉS DIATHÉKÉS MOU*
of me and choose what I wish and hold of the covenant of me

engLXX Thus saith the Lord to the eunuchs, as many as shall keep my sabbaths, and choose the things which I take pleasure in, and take hold of my covenant;

Isa. 58:5 Is it such a fast that I have **chosen**? a day for a man to afflict his soul? *Is it* to bow down his head as a bulrush, and to spread sackcloth and ashes *under him*? Wilt thou call this a fast, and an acceptable day to the LORD?

YLT Like this is the fast that I **choose**? The day of a man's afflicting his soul? To bow as a reed his head, and sackcloth and ashes spread out? This dost thou call a fast, and a desirable day - to Jehovah?

EKLEGÓ – to pick, choose, elect - a divergent translation with "to the LORD" (KJV) not translated – the fast which the Lord has not chosen

LXX *OU TAUTÉN TÉN NÉSTEIAN* ***EXELEXAMÉN*** *KAI HÉMERAN TAPEINOUN ANTHRÓPON TÉN*
not this the fast chose and day to humble man the

PSUCHÉN AUTOU OUD AN KAMPSÉS HÓS KRIKON TON TRACHÉLON SOU KAI SAKKON KAI
soul of him nor even bend as hook the neck of you and sackcloth and

SPODON HUPOSTRÓSÉ OUD HOUTÓ KALESETE NÉSTEIAN DEKTÉN
ashes spread nor this call fast acceptable

engLXX I have not chosen this fast, nor *such* a day for a man to afflict his soul; neither though thou shouldest bend down thy neck as a ring, and spread under thee sackcloth and ashes, neither thus shall ye call a fast acceptable.

Isa. 58:6 *Is* not this the fast that I have **chosen**? To loose the bands of wickedness, to undo the heavy burdens, and to let the oppressed go free, and that ye break every yoke?

YLT Is not this the fast that I **chose** - To loose the bands of wickedness, to shake off the burdens of the yoke, and to send out the oppressed free, and every yoke ye draw off?

EKLEGÓ – to pick, choose, elect - a loose translation with "break every yoke" (KJV) given as "cancel every unjust account" (engLXX) – the fast the Lord has chosen

LXX *OUCHI TOIAUTÉN NÉSTEIAN* ***EXELEXAMÉN*** *LEGEI KURIOS ALLA LUE PANTA SUNDESMON*
not such fast chose says Lord but loose every bond

ADIKIAS DIALUE STRAGGALIAS BIAIÓN SUNALLAGMATÓN APOSTELLE TETHRAUSMENOUS
of injustice untie perverseness violent exchanges send devastated

EN APHESEI KAI PASAN SUGGRAPHÉN ADIKON DIASPA
in release and all writ unjust tear apart

engLXX I have not chosen such a fast, saith the Lord; but do thou loose every burden of iniquity, do thou untie the knots of hard bargains, set the bruised free, and cancel every unjust account.

Isa. 65:12		Therefore will I number you to the sword, and ye shall all bow down to the slaughter: because when I called, ye did not answer; when I spake, ye did not hear; but did evil before mine eyes, and did **choose** *that* wherein I delighted not.

EKLEGÓ – to pick, choose, elect - a direct translation – the people provoking God to anger (V.3), the apostate people (V.2 YLT), choose what the Lord does not delight in

LXX ***EGÓ PARADÓSÓ HUMAS EIS MACHAIRAN PANTES EN SPHAGÉ PESEISTHE HOTI***
I shall deliver you into sword all in slaughter fall since

ELALÉSA HUMAS KAI OUCH HUPÉKOUSATE ELALÉSA KAI PARÉKOUSATE KAI
spoke you and not listened spoke and disregarded and

EPOIÉSATE TO PONÉRON ENANTION EMOU KAI HA OUK EBOULOMÉN ***EXELEXASTHE***
did the evil before me and what not desired chose

engLXX I will deliver you up to the sword, ye shall all fall by slaughter: for I called you, and ye hearkened not; I spoke, and ye refused to hear; and ye did evil in my sight, and chose the things wherein I delighted not.

Isa. 66:3		He that killeth an ox *is as if* he slew a man; he that sacrificeth a lamb, *as if* he cut off a dog's neck; he that offereth an oblation, *as if he offered* swine's blood; he that burneth incense, *as if* he blessed an idol. Yea, they have **chosen** their own ways, and their soul delighteth in their abominations.
	YLT	Whoso slaughtereth the ox smiteth a man, whoso sacrificeth the lamb beheadeth a dog, whoso is bringing up a present - The blood of a sow, whoso is making mention of frankincense, is blessing iniquity. Yea, they have **fixed** on their own ways, and in their abominations their soul hath delighted.

EKLEGÓ – to pick, choose, elect - a divergent translation with "Whoso slaughtereth the ox smiteth a man, whoso sacrificeth the lamb beheadeth a dog" (YLT) rendered as "But the transgressor that sacrifices a calf to me, is as he that kills a dog" (engLXX) – the wicked [the proud in contrast to the humble (V.2)] have chosen their own ways

LXX *HO DE ANOMOS HO THUÓN MOI MOSCHON HÓS HO APOKTENNÓN KUNA HO DE*
the but unlawful who sacrifices to me calf as the slayer dog the but

ANAPHERÓN SEMIDALIN HÓS AIMA HUEION HO DIDOUS LIBANON EIS
offering fine flour as blood of pig the giving frankincense into

MNÉMOSUNON HÓS BLASPHÉMOS KAI AUTOI ***EXELEXANTO*** *TAS HODOUS*
memorial as blasphemer and they chose the ways

AUTÓN KAI TA BDELUGMATA AUTÓN HÉ PSUCHÉ AUTÓN ÉTHELÉSE
of them and the abominations of them the soul of them desired

engLXX But the transgressor that sacrifices a calf to me, is as he that kills a dog; and he that offers fine flour, as *one that offers* swine's blood; he that gives frankincense for a memorial, is as a blasphemer. Yet they have chosen their own ways, and their soul has delighted in their abominations.

Isa. 66:4a I also will **choose** their delusions, and will bring their fears upon them; because when I called, none did answer; (…)

YLT I also - I **fix** on their vexations, and their fears I bring in to them, because I have called, and there is none answering, (…)

EKLEGÓ – to pick, choose, elect - a divergent translation with "fears" (KJV) rendered as "sins" (engLXX) – the Lord chooses the delusions (KJV), the vexations (YLT), the mockeries (LXX), of the wicked

LXX *KAI EGÓ* ***EKLEXOMAI*** *TA EMPAIGMATA AUTÓN KAI TAS HAMARTIAS*
and I chose the mockeries of them and the sins

ANTAPODÓSÓ AUTOIS HOTI EKALESA AUTOUS KAI OUCH HUPÉKOUSAN MOU…
recompense to them since called them and not give ear of me

engLXX I also will choose their mockeries, and will recompense their sins upon them; because I called them, and they did not hearken to me; (…)

Isa. 66:4b		. . . when I spake, they did not hear: but they did evil before mine eyes, and **chose** *that* in which I delighted not.
	YLT	. . . I spake, and they have not hearkened, and they do the evil things in Mine eyes, and on that which I desired not - **fixed**.

EKLEGÓ – to pick, choose, elect - a direct translation – the proud choose that which the Lord does not delight in

LXX	…*ELALÉSA KAI OUK ÉKOUSAN KAI EPOIÉSAN TO PONÉRON ENANTION EMOU* spoke and not hear and did the evil before me *KAI HA OUK ÉBOULOMÉN* ***EXELEXANTO*** and what not desire chose
engLXX	…I spoke, and they heard not: and they did evil before me, and chose the things wherein I delighted not.

Jer. 8:3		And death **shall be chosen** rather than life by all the residue of them that remain of this evil family, which remain in all the places whither I have driven them, saith the LORD of hosts.
	YLT	And **chosen is** death rather than life by all the remnant who are left of this evil family, in all the remaining places, whither I have driven them, an affirmation of Jehovah of Hosts.
	NKJV	Then death **shall be chosen** rather than life by all the residue of those who remain of this evil family, who remain in all the places where I have driven them," says the LORD of hosts.
	NASB	And death **will be chosen** rather than life by all the remnant that remains of this evil family, that remains in all the places to which I have driven them," declares the LORD of hosts.
	NIV	Wherever I banish them, all the survivors of this evil nation **will prefer** death to life, declares the LORD Almighty."
	NLT	And the people of this evil nation who survive **will wish** to die rather than live where I will send them. I, the LORD of Heaven's Armies, have spoken!

HAIREÓ – a divergent translation with “evil” not rendered – the evil nation, by their very acts of evil, choose death rather than life

LXX *HOTI* ***EILONTO*** *TON THANATON É TÉN ZÓÉN KAI PASI TOIS KATALOIPOIS TOIS*
since chose the death | rather than the life and all to the remaining to the

KATALEIPHTHEISIN APO TÉS GENEAS EKEINÉS EN PANTI TOPÓ HOU EAN
left behind from the kindred that in every place which ever

EXÓSÓ AUTOUS EKEI 4*HOTI TADE LEGEI KURIOS*…
push out them there since thus says Lord

engLXX because they chose death rather than life, even to all the remnant that are left of that family, in every place whither I shall drive them out. 4For thus saith the Lord, (…)

Jer. 33:24 Considerest thou not what this people have spoken, saying, The two families which the LORD hath **chosen**, he hath even cast them off? Thus they have despised my people, that they should be no more a nation before them.

NOT in LXX - Jeremiah 33:14-26 is not translated in the LXX: many portions of Jeremiah are found out of place in the LXX: this section is not found at all

Jer. 49:19 Behold, he shall come up like a lion from the swelling of Jordan against the habitation of the strong: but I will suddenly make him run away from her: and who *is* a **chosen** *man*, *that* I may appoint over her? For who *is* like me? And who will appoint me the time? And who *is* that shepherd that will stand before me?

YLT Lo, as a lion he cometh up, because of the rising of the Jordan, unto the enduring habitation, but I cause to rest, I cause him to run from off her, and who is **chosen**? Concerning her I lay a charge, for who is like Me? And who conveneth Me? And who *is* this shepherd who standeth before Me?

NKJV "Behold, he shall come up like a lion from the flooding of the Jordan against the habitation of the strong; but I will suddenly make him run away from her. And who *is* a **chosen** *man that* I may appoint over her? For who *is* like Me? Who will arraign Me? And who *is* that shepherd who will withstand Me?"

NASB Behold, one will come up like a lion from the thickets of the Jordan against a perennially watered pasture; for in an instant I will make him run away from it, and whoever is **chosen** I shall appoint over it. For who is like Me, and who will summon Me *into court*? And who then is the shepherd who can stand against Me?"

NIV "Like a lion coming up from Jordan's thickets to a rich pasture-land, I will chase Edom from its land in an instant. Who is the **chosen one** I will appoint for this? Who is like me and who can challenge me? And what shepherd can stand against me?"

NLT I will come like a lion from the thickets of the Jordan, leaping on the sheep in the pasture. I will chase Edom from its land, and I will appoint the leader of my **choice**. For who is like me, and who can challenge me? What ruler can oppose my will?"

EPHISTÉMI - set up, establish – a divergent translation with "young men" (engLXX) added – the secondary meaning of BACHAR of "to be chosen: preferred: excellent": the Heb. is about someone suitable the Lord appoints; the Gk. is divergent and about young men [cf. 50:44 below]

LXX **29:19** *IDOU HÓSPER LEÓN ANABÉSETAI EK MESOU TOU IORDANOU EIS TOPON*
look as lion arise out of midst of the Jordan into place

AITHAM HOTI TACHU EKDIÓXÓ AUTOUS AP AUTÉS KAI TOUS NEANISKOUS EP
Aitham since quickly drive out them from her and the young men upon

AUTÉN ***EPISTÉSATE*** *HOTI TIS HÓSPER EGÓ KAI TIS ANTISTÉSETAI MOI KAI TIS*
her set since who as I and who oppose me and who

HOUTOS POIMÉN HOS STÉSETAI KATA PROSÓPON MOU
this shepherd whom stand in face of me

	engLXX	Behold, he shall come up as a lion out of the midst of Jordan to the place of Ætham: for I will speedily drive them from it, and do ye set the young men against her: for who is like me? And who will withstand me? And who *is* this shepherd, who shall confront me?
Jer. 50:44		Behold, he shall come up like a lion from the swelling of Jordan unto the habitation of the strong: but I will make them suddenly run away from her: and who *is* a **chosen** *man*, *that* I may appoint over her? for who *is* like me? and who will appoint me the time? And who *is* that shepherd that will stand before me?
	YLT	Lo, as a lion he cometh up, because of the rising of the Jordan, unto the enduring habitation, but I cause to rest, I cause them to run from off her. And who is chosen? On her I lay a charge, for who *is* like Me? And who doth convene Me? And who *is* this shepherd who standeth before Me?
	NKJV	"Behold, he shall come up like a lion from the flooding of the Jordan against the habitation of the strong; but I will make them suddenly run away from her. And who *is* a **chosen** *man that* I may appoint over her? For who *is* like Me? Who will arraign Me? And who *is* that shepherd who will withstand Me?"
	NASB	"Behold, one will come up like a lion from the thicket of the Jordan to a perennially watered pasture; for in an instant I will make them run away from it, and whoever is **chosen** I will appoint over it. For who is like Me, and who will summon Me *into court*? And who then is the shepherd who can stand before Me?"
	NIV	Like a lion coming up from Jordan's thickets to a rich pasture-land, I will chase Babylon from its land in an instant. Who is the **chosen one** I will appoint for this? Who is like me and who can challenge me? And what shepherd can stand against me?'
	NLT	"I will come like a lion from the thickets of the Jordan, leaping on the sheep in the pasture. I will chase Babylon from its land, and I will appoint the leader of my **choice**. For who is like me, and who can challenge me? What ruler can oppose my will?"

EPHISTÉMI - set up, establish – a divergent translation with "youths" (engLXX) added – the secondary meaning of BACHAR of "to be chosen: preferred: excellent": the Heb. is about someone suitable the Lord appoints; the Gk. is divergent and about young men [cf. 49:19 above]

LXX **27:44** *IDOU HÓSPER LEÓN ANABÉSETAI APO TOU IORDANOU EIS GAITHAN HOTI*
look as lion rises from the Jordan into Aithan since

TACHEÓS EKDIÓXÓ AUTOUS AP AUTÉS KAI PANTA NEANISKON EP AUTÉN
quickly drive out them from her and every young man upon her

EPISTÉSÓ *HOTI TIS HÓSPER EGÓ KAI TIS ANTISTÉSETAI MOI KAI TIS HOUTOS*
set since who as I and who oppose me and who this

POIMÉN HOS STÉSETAI KATA PROSÓPON MOU
shepherd whom stand in face of me

engLXX Behold, he shall come up as a lion from Jordan to Gaethan; for I will speedily drive them from her, and I will set all the youths against her: for who is like me? And who will resist me? And who is this shepherd who will stand before me?

Eze. 20:5 And say unto them, Thus saith the Lord GOD; In the day when I **chose** Israel, and lifted up mine hand unto the seed of the house of Jacob, and made myself known unto them in the land of Egypt, when I lifted up mine hand unto them, saying, I *am* the LORD your God;

YLT and thou hast said unto them: thus said the Lord Jehovah: in the day of My **fixing** on Israel, I lift up My hand, to the seed of the house of Jacob, and am known to them in the land of Egypt, and I lift up My hand to them, saying, I *am* Jehovah your God.

HAIRETIZÓ - to choose – a divergent translation with "GOD" (KJV) or "Jehovah" (YLT) not rendered – the day when the Lord chose Israel

LXX *KAI EREIS PROS AUTOUS TADE LEGEI KURIOS APH HÉS HÉMERAS* ***HÉRETIKA*** *TON OIKON*
and say to them thus says Lord from which day chose the house of

ISRAÉL KAI EGNÓRISTHÉN TÓ SPERMATI OIKOU IAKÓB KAI EGNÓSTHÉN AUTOIS EN GÉ
Israel and made known to the seed of house of Jacob and known to them in land

AIGUPTOU KAI ENTELABOMÉN TÉ CHEIRI MOU AUTÓN LEGÓN EGÓ KURIOS HO THEOS HUMÓN
of Egypt and took with the hand of me of them saying I Lord the God of you

engLXX and thou shalt say to them, Thus saith the Lord; From the day that I chose the house of Israel, and became known to the seed of the house of Jacob, and was known to them in the land of Egypt, and helped them with my hand, saying, I am the Lord your God;

Hag. 2:23 In that day, saith the LORD of hosts, will I take thee, O Zerubbabel, my servant, the son of Shealtiel, saith the LORD, and will make thee as a signet: for I have **chosen** thee, saith the LORD of hosts.

YLT In that day - an affirmation of Jehovah of Hosts, I take thee, Zerubbabel, son of Shealtiel, My servant - an affirmation of Jehovah, and have set thee as a signet, for on thee I have **fixed**, an affirmation of Jehovah of Hosts!

HAIRETIZÓ - to choose – a direct translation, even with "hosts" given as "Almighty" – the Lord has chosen Zerubbabel

LXX **2:24** *EN TÉ HÉMERA EKEINÉ LEGEI KURIOS PANTOKRATÓR LÉPSOMAI SE ZOROBABEL TON TOU*
in the day that says Lord Almighty take you Zerubabel the of the

SALATHIEL TON DOULON MOU LEGEI KURIOS KAI THÉSOMAI SE HÓS SPHRAGIDA DIOTI
Salathiel the servant of me says Lord and set you as seal since

SE ***HÉRETISA*** *LEGEI KURIOS PANTOKRATÓR*
you chose says Lord Almighty

engLXX In that day, saith the Lord Almighty, I will take thee, O Zorobabel, the son of Salathiel, my servant, saith the Lord, and will make thee as a seal: for I have chosen thee, saith the Lord Almighty.

Zec. 1:17 Cry yet, saying, Thus saith the LORD of hosts; My cities through prosperity shall yet be spread abroad; and the LORD shall yet comfort Zion, and shall yet **choose** Jerusalem.

YLT Again call, saying: Thus said Jehovah of Hosts, again do my cities overflow from good, and Jehovah hath again comforted Zion, and He hath **fixed** again on Jerusalem.'

HAIRETIZÓ - to choose – a divergent translation with "angel" added (cf. V.14) – the Lord shall choose Jerusalem (again)

LXX *KAI EIPE PROS ME HO AGGELOS HO LALÓN EN EMOI ETI ANAKRAGE LEGÓN*
and says to me the angel the speaking in me yet shout saying

TADE LEGEI KURIOS PANTOKRATÓR ETI DIACHUTHÉSONTAI POLEIS EN
thus says Lord Almighty yet dispersed cities in

AGATHOIS KAI ELEÉSEI KURIOS ETI TÉN SIÓN KAI ***HAIRETIEI*** *TÉN HIEROUSALÉM*
good and mercy Lord yet with the Zion and choose the Jerusalem

engLXX And the angel that spoke with me said to me, Cry yet, and say, Thus saith the Lord Almighty; Yet shall cities be spread abroad through prosperity; and the Lord shall yet have mercy upon Sion, and shall choose Jerusalem.

Zec. 2:12 And the LORD shall inherit Judah his portion in the holy land, and shall **choose** Jerusalem again.

HAIRETIZÓ - to choose – a direct translation (with the word "land" assumed) – the Lord will yet choose Jerusalem

LXX **2:16** *KAI KATAKLÉRONOMÉSEI KURIOS TON IOUDAN TÉN MERIDA AUTOU EPI TÉN*
and inherit Lord the Juda the portion of him upon the

HAGIAN KAI ***HAIRETIEI*** *ETI TÉN HIEROUSALÉM*
holy and choose yet the Jerusalem

engLXX And the Lord shall inherit Juda his portion in the holy *land*, and he will yet choose Jerusalem.

Zec. 3:2 — And the LORD said unto Satan, The LORD rebuke thee, O Satan; even the LORD that hath **chosen** Jerusalem rebuke thee: *is* not this a brand plucked out of the fire?

YLT — And Jehovah saith unto the Adversary: 'Jehovah doth push against thee, O Adversary, Yea, push against thee doth Jehovah, who is **fixing** on Jerusalem, is not this a brand delivered from fire?'

EKLEGÓ – to pick, choose, elect - a divergent translation with "behold" (engLXX) added – the Lord chooses Jerusalem

LXX

KAI EIPE KURIOS PROS TON DIABOLON EPITIMÉSAI KURIOS EN SOI DIABOLE KAI
and said Lord to the Devil admonish Lord in you Devil and

EPITIMÉSAI KURIOS EN SOI HO ***EKLEXAMENOS*** *TÉN HIEROUSALÉM OUK IDOU*
admonish Lord in you who chose the Jerusalem not look

TOUTO HÓS DALOS EXESPASMENOS EK PUROS
this whom firebrand pulled out out of fire

engLXX — And the Lord said to the Devil, The Lord rebuke thee, O Devil, even the Lord that has chosen Jerusalem rebuke thee: behold! Is not this as a brand plucked from the fire?

2 - BACHIR

Translated into Greek in the LXX

EKLEKTOS	**13**	**2Sa. 21:6; 1Ch. 16:13; Psa. 89:3; Psa. 105:6 Psa. 105:43; Psa. 106:5; Psa. 106:23 Isa. 42:1; Isa. 43:20; Isa. 45:4; Isa. 65:9 Isa. 65:15; Isa. 65:22**
TOTAL	13	

Translated into English - Both KJV related

Ys Conc.	Count	Ss Conc. No. H 972	Count
chosen	7	chosen	8
chosen one	1	elect	4
elect	4	chose	1
choose	1		
TOTAL	13	TOTAL	13

Refs		Text quotes KJV unless otherwise stated
2Sa. 21:6		Let seven men of his sons be delivered unto us, and we will hang them up unto the LORD in Gibeah of Saul, *whom* the LORD **did choose**. And the king said, I will give *them*. KJV margin: Or, ***chosen*** *of the LORD*
	YLT	let there be given to us seven men of his sons, and we have hanged them before Jehovah, in the height of Saul, **the chosen** of Jehovah.' And the king saith, 'I do give;'
	NKJV	let seven men of his descendants be delivered to us, and we will hang them before the LORD in Gibeah of Saul, *whom* the LORD **chose**." And the king said, "I will give *them*."
	NASB	let seven men from his sons be given to us, and we will hang them before the LORD in Gibeah of Saul, **the chosen** of the LORD." And the king said, "I will give *them*."
	NIV	let seven of his male descendants be given to us to be killed and their bodies exposed before the LORD at Gibeah of Saul – the LORD's **chosen one**.' So the king said, 'I will give them to you.'
	NLT	So let seven of Saul's sons be handed over to us, and we will execute them before the LORD at Gibeon, on **the mountain** of the LORD." "All right," the king said, "I will do it."

EKLEKTOS – a divergent translation with the addition of "in the sun" in the (engLXX): it appears Sir Lancelot's translation used a different Gk. text of the LXX since the Gk. word *HÉLIOS* for "sun" is not there in the LXX we are using: the Gk. text here is a direct translation – we know from the time of Samuel being sent by the Lord to find Saul, to be made the 1st king of Israel, that Saul was "higher than any of the people from his shoulder and upward" (1Sa. 10:23YLT) a truly choice man of Jehovah; the NLT and the others too could also be seen to refer to the place Gibeah (KJV) Gibeon (NLT) as being the choice place

[See [1] below]

LXX **2Ki.21:6**

DOTÓ HÉMIN HEPTA ANDRAS EK TÓN HUIÓN AUTOU KAI EXÉLIASÓMEN AUTOUS
give us seven men out of the sons of him and we shall hang them

TÓ KURIÓ EN TÓ GABAÓN SAOUL ***EKLEKTOUS*** *KURIOU KAI EIPEN HO BASILEUS EGÓ DÓSÓ*
to the Lord in the Gabaon of Saul choice of Lord and said the king I shall give

	engLXX	Let one give us seven men of his sons, and let us hang them up in the sun to the Lord in Gabaon of Saul, as chosen out for the Lord. And the king said, I will give *them*.
1Ch. 16:13		O ye seed of Israel his servant, ye children of Jacob, **his chosen ones**.
	YLT	O seed of Israel, His servant, O sons of Jacob, **His chosen ones**!
	NKJV	O seed of Israel His servant, you children of Jacob, **His chosen ones**!
	NASB	O seed of Israel His servant, sons of Jacob, **His chosen ones**!
	NIV	you his servants, the descendants of Israel, **his chosen ones**, the children of Jacob.
	NLT	you children of his servant Israel, you descendants of Jacob, **his chosen ones**.

EKLEKTOS – a direct translation – to God the seed of Israel is choice, previously named Jacob, but it is of note that the prophets kept mentioning how if any wicked were found in the midst, they were removed, thus retaining excellence in the remaining seed

[See [1] below]

	LXX	*SPERMA ISRAÉL PAIDES AUTOU HUIOI IAKÓB* ***EKLEKTOI*** *AUTOU* seed of Israel | of him sons of Jacob choice of him young servants
	engLXX	*ye* seed of Israel his servants, *ye* seed of Jacob his chosen ones.
Psa. 89:3		I have made a covenant **with my chosen**, I have sworn unto David my servant,
	YLT	I have made a covenant **for My chosen**, I have sworn to David My servant:
	NKJV	"I have made a covenant **with My chosen**, I have sworn to My servant David:
	NASB	"I have made a covenant **with My chosen**; I have sworn to David My servant,
	NIV	You said, 'I have made a covenant **with my chosen one**, I have sworn to David my servant,
	NLT	The Lord said, "I have made a covenant with David, **my chosen** servant. I have sworn this oath to him:

EKLEKTOS – a divergent translation making the singular into the plural: "chosen ones" (engLXX) instead of "chosen" (KJV) when only David is in view Vss 3-4 - as per V.4 (NKJV) God deemed David highly "Your seed I will establish forever, and build up your throne to all generations", a man after His own heart (1Sa. 13:14): excellent David

[See [1] below]

	LXX **88:3**	*DIETHEMÉN DIATHÉKÉN TOIS* ***EKLEKTOIS*** *MOU ÓMOSA DAUID TÓ DOULÓ MOU* ordained covenant with the choice of me sworn David the servant of me
	engLXX	I made a covenant with my chosen ones, I sware unto David my servant.
Psa. 105:6		O ye seed of Abraham his servant, ye children of Jacob **his chosen**.
	YLT	O seed of Abraham, His servant, O sons of Jacob, **His chosen ones**.
	NKJV	O seed of Abraham His servant, you children of Jacob, **His chosen ones**!
	NASB	O seed of Abraham His servant, you children of Jacob, **His chosen ones**!
	NIV	you his servants, the descendants of Abraham, **his chosen ones**, the children of Jacob.
	NLT	you children of his servant Abraham, you descendants of Jacob, **his chosen ones**.

EKLEKTOS – a divergent translation making the singular into the plural: "servants" (engLXX) instead of "servant" (KJV) when only Abraham is in view as the "servant" - to God the seed of Jacob is choice, but it is of note that the prophets kept mentioning how if any wicked were found in the midst, they were removed, thus retaining excellence in the remaining seed

[See [1] below]

	LXX **104:6**	*SPERMA ABRAAM DOULOI AUTOU HUIOI IAKÓB* ***EKLEKTOI*** *AUTOU* seed of abraham servants of him sons of Jacob choice of him
	engLXX	*ye* seed of Abraam, his servants, *ye* children of Jacob, his chosen ones.
Psa. 105:43		And he brought forth his people with joy, ***and*** **his chosen** with gladness:
	YLT	And He bringeth forth His people with joy, with singing **His chosen ones**.

NKJV	He brought out His people with joy, **His chosen ones** with gladness.
NASB	And He brought forth His people with joy, **His chosen ones** with a joyful shout.
NIV	He brought out his people with rejoicing, **his chosen ones** with shouts of joy;
NLT	So he brought his people out of Egypt with joy, **his chosen ones** with rejoicing.

EKLEKTOS – a direct translation – in Exodus 15:20-21 (NKJV) we read "Miriam the prophetess, the sister of Aaron, took the timbrel in her hand; and all the women went out after her with timbrels and with dances. And Miriam answered them: 'Sing to the LORD, for He has triumphed gloriously! The horse and its rider He has thrown into the sea!' ": a time of much rejoicing. Miriam is one of those identified alongside Moses and Aaron as choice: e.g. as per Micah 6:4 (NKJV) "For I brought you up from the land of Egypt, I redeemed you from the house of bondage; and I sent before you Moses, Aaron, and Miriam." - to God the seed of Jacob is choice, but it is of note that the prophets kept mentioning how if any wicked were found in the midst, they were removed, thus retaining excellence in the remaining seed

[See [1] below]

LXX **104:43**	*KAI EXÉGAGE TON LAON AUTOU EN AGALLIASEI KAI TOUS* ***EKLEKTOUS*** *AUTOU* and led out the people of him in exultation and the choice of him *EN EUPHROSUNÉ* in gladness
engLXX	And he brought out his people with exultation, and his chosen with joy;

Psa. 106:5 That I may see the good of **thy chosen**, that I may rejoice in the gladness of thy nation, that I may glory with thine inheritance.

YLT	To look on the good of **Thy chosen ones**, to rejoice in the joy of Thy nation, to boast myself with Thine inheritance.
NKJV	That I may see the benefit of **Your chosen ones**, that I may rejoice in the gladness of Your nation, that I may glory with Your inheritance.

NASB That I may see the prosperity of **Your chosen ones**, that I may rejoice in the gladness of Your nation, that I may glory with Your inheritance.

NIV that I may enjoy the prosperity of **your chosen ones**, that I may share in the joy of your nation and join your inheritance in giving praise.

NLT Let me share in the prosperity of **your chosen ones**. Let me rejoice in the joy of your people; let me praise you with those who are your heritage.

EKLEKTOS – a divergent translation with "that I may glory" (KJV) or "to boast myself" (YLT), rendered as "that we may glory" (engLXX): from a singular to a plural – the nation of Israel is choice before the Lord and is limited in blessing in the good and the rejoicing to the righteous as per the Lord's direct covenant with the nation (see Deu. 30) and the specific context "O the happiness of those keeping judgment, doing righteousness at all times." (106:3 YLT)

[See [1] below]

LXX **105:5**
*TOU IDEIN EN TÉ CHRÉSTOTÉTI TÓN **EKLEKTÓN** SOU TOU EUPHRANTHÉNAI EN*
the to see in the gracious of the choice of you of the to be glad in

TÉ EUPHROSUNÉ TOU ETHNOUS SOU TOU EPAINEISTHAI META TÉS KLÉRONOMIAS SOU
the gladness of the nation of you of the praise with the Inheritance of you

engLXX that we may behold the good of thine elect, that we may rejoice in the gladness of thy nation, that we may glory with thine inheritance.

Psa. 106:23 Therefore he said that he would destroy them, had not Moses **his chosen** stood before him in the breach, to turn away his wrath, lest he should destroy *them*.

YLT And He saith to destroy them, unless Moses, **His chosen one**, had stood in the breach before Him, to turn back His wrath from destroying.

NKJV Therefore He said that He would destroy them, had not Moses **His chosen one** stood before Him in the breach, to turn away His wrath, lest He destroy *them*.

NASB Therefore He said that He would destroy them, had not Moses **His chosen one** stood in the breach before Him, to turn away His wrath from destroying *them*.

NIV So he said he would destroy them – had not Moses, **his chosen one**, stood in the breach before him to keep his wrath from destroying them.

NLT So he declared he would destroy them. But Moses, **his chosen one**, stepped between the Lord and the people. He begged him to turn from his anger and not destroy them.

EKLEKTOS – a direct translation – Moses was mentioned as "the man Moses *is* very humble, more than any of the men who *are* on the face of the ground" (Num. 12:3 YLT) and Jesus said "whoever humbles himself as this little child is the greatest in the kingdom of heaven" (Matthew 18:4 NKJV) so, we know Moses as excellent in God's eyes: choice

[See [1] below]

LXX **105:23**
KAI EIPE TOU EXOLOTHREUSAI AUTOUS EI MÉ MÓUSÉS HO ***EKLEKTOS*** *AUTOU*
and said of the to utterly destroy them if not Moses the choice of him

ESTÉ EN TÉ THRAUSEI ENÓPION AUTOU TOU APOSTREPSAI APO THUMOU
stood in the breach before him of the to turn from raging

ORGÉS AUTOU TOU MÉ EXOLOTHREUSAI
anger of him of the not to utterly destroy

engLXX So he said that he would have destroyed them, had not Moses his chosen stood before him in the breach, to turn *him* away from the fierceness of his anger, so that he should not destroy them.

Isa. 42:1 Behold my servant, whom I uphold; **mine elect**, *in whom* my soul delighteth; I have put my spirit upon him: he shall bring forth judgment to the Gentiles.

YLT Lo, My servant, I take hold on him, **My chosen one** - My soul hath accepted, I have put My Spirit upon him, judgment to nations he bringeth forth.

NKJV "Behold! My Servant whom I uphold, **My Elect One** *in whom* My soul delights! I have put My Spirit upon Him; He will bring forth justice to the Gentiles.

NASB "Behold, My Servant, whom I uphold; **My chosen one** *in whom* My soul delights. I have put My Spirit upon Him; He will bring forth justice to the nations.

NIV 'Here is my servant, whom I uphold, **my chosen one** in whom I delight; I will put my Spirit on him, and he will bring justice to the nations.

NLT "Look at my servant, whom I strengthen. He is **my chosen one**, who pleases me. I have put my Spirit upon him. He will bring justice to the nations.

EKLEKTOS – a divergent translation with the addition of "Jacob" and "Israel": the passage from Vss 1-7 is a prophetic word about the coming Messiah: Jesus e.g. "a light to the Gentiles" (V.6 NKJV) fulfilled in "A light to bring *revelation* to the Gentiles" (Luke 2:32 NKJV) – As this is about the Eternal Son of God: God manifest in the flesh (1 Timothy 3:16 KJV/NKJV/YLT – Quoted by Ignatius of Antioch 1st century AD *Magnesians 8:2* et al), He is not chosen or picked out, but is Excellent, choice

[See [1] below]

LXX ***IAKÓB HO PAIS MOU ANTILÉPSOMAI AUTOU ISRAÉL HO EKLEKTOS MOU PROSEDEXATO***
Jacob the | of me shall take hold of him Israel the choice of me accepted
young servant

AUTON HÉ PSUCHÉ MOU EDÓKA TO PNEUMA MOU EP AUTON KRISIN
him the soul of me gave the spirit of me upon him judgment

TOIS ETHNESIN EXOISEI
to the nations shall bring forth

engLXX Jacob is my servant, I will help him: Israel is my chosen, my soul has accepted him; I have put my Spirit upon him; he shall bring forth judgement to the Gentiles.

Isa. 43:20 The beast of the field shall honour me, the dragons and the owls: because I give waters in the wilderness, *and* rivers in the desert, to give drink to my people, **my chosen**.

YLT Honour me doth the beast of the field, dragons and daughters of an ostrich, for I have given in a wilderness waters, floods in a desolate place, to give drink to My people - **My chosen**.

NKJV The beast of the field will honor Me, the jackals and the ostriches, because I give waters in the wilderness *and* rivers in the desert, to give drink to My people, **My chosen**.

NASB "The beasts of the field will glorify Me, the jackals and the ostriches, because I have given waters in the wilderness and rivers in the desert, to give drink to **My chosen** people.

NIV The wild animals honour me, the jackals and the owls, because I provide water in the wilderness and streams in the wasteland, to give drink to my people, **my chosen**,

NLT The wild animals in the fields will thank me, the jackals and owls, too, for giving them water in the desert. Yes, I will make rivers in the dry wasteland so **my chosen** people can be refreshed.

EKLEKTOS – a direct to loose translation as it is arguable on the accuracy of "owls", "ostriches" when "dragons" are in the original, though the NKJV renders that as "jackals", as does the NASB, NIV, NLT - to God His people, the seed of Israel is choice "This people I have formed for Myself, My praise they recount." (V.21 YLT), but it is of note that the prophet mentions how the wicked are judged Vss 22-28, they are removed, thus retaining excellence in the remaining seed: a choice people: excellent

[See [1] below]

LXX *EULOGÉSOUSI ME TA THÉRIA TOU AGROU SEIRÉNES KAI THUGATERES*
shall bless me the wild beasts of the field sirens and daughters

STROUTHÓN HOTI EDÓKA EN TÉ ERÉMÓ HUDÓR KAI POTAMOUS EN TÉ
of ostriches since gave in the desert water and rivers in the

ANUDRÓ POTISAI TO GENOS MOU TO ***EKLEKTON***
waterless to water the race of me the choice

engLXX the beasts of the field shall bless me, the owls and young ostriches; for I have given water in the wilderness, and rivers in the dry land, to give drink to my chosen race,

---

Isa. 45:4 For Jacob my servant's sake, and Israel **mine elect**, I have even called thee by thy name: I have surnamed thee, though thou hast not known me.

YLT For the sake of my servant Jacob, and of Israel **My chosen**, I call also thee by thy name, I surname thee, and thou hast not known Me.

NKJV For Jacob My servant's sake, and Israel **My elect**, I have even called you by your name; I have named you, though you have not known Me.

NASB "For the sake of Jacob My servant, and Israel **My chosen *one***, I have also called you by your name; I have given you a title of honor though you have not known Me.

NIV For the sake of Jacob my servant, of Israel **my chosen**, I summon you by name and bestow on you a title of honour, though you do not acknowledge me.

NLT "And why have I called you for this work? Why did I call you by name when you did not know me? It is for the sake of Jacob my servant, Israel **my chosen one**.

EKLEKTOS – a divergent translation with "I have surnamed thee" (KJV) or "I surname thee" (YLT), rendered as "and accept thee" (engLXX) – Jacob was renamed Israel after his wrestling match: The Lord said "Thy name is no more called Jacob, but Israel; for thou hast been a prince with God and with men, and dost prevail" (Gen. 32:28 YLT) so, it was due to his excellence in prevailing that he was choice

[See [1] below]

LXX *HENEKEN TOU PAIDOS MOU IAKÓB KAI ISRAÉL TOU* ***EKLEKTOU*** *MOU EGÓ*
for the sake of the | of me Jacob and Israel of the choice of me I
young servant

KALESÓ SE TÓ ONOMATI SOU KAI PROSDEXOMAI SE SU DE OUK EGNÓS ME
call you with the name of you and accept you you but not known me

engLXX For the sake of my servant Jacob, and Israel mine elect, I will call thee by thy name, and accept thee: but thou hast not known me.

Isa. 65:9 And I will bring forth a seed out of Jacob, and out of Judah an inheritor of my mountains: **and mine elect** shall inherit it, and my servants shall dwell there.

YLT And I have brought out from Jacob a seed, and from Judah a possessor of My mount, and possess it do **My chosen ones**, and My servants do dwell there.

NKJV I will bring forth descendants from Jacob, and from Judah an heir of My mountains; **My elect** shall inherit it, and My servants shall dwell there.

NASB "I will bring forth offspring from Jacob, and an heir of My mountains from Judah; even **My chosen ones** shall inherit it, and My servants will dwell there.

NIV I will bring forth descendants from Jacob, and from Judah those who will possess my mountains; **my chosen people** will inherit them, and there will my servants live.

NLT I will preserve a remnant of the people of Israel and of Judah to possess my land. **Those I choose** will inherit it, and my servants will live there.

EKLEKTOS – a direct translation – following the express retaining of the few from the many V.8 following much testing and purifying, the remainder will be the choice

[See [1] below]

LXX *KAI EXAXÓ TO EX IAKÓB SPERMA KAI EX IOUDA KAI KLÉRONOMÉSEI TO*
and lead out the out of Jacob seed and out of Juda and shall inherit the

OROS TO HAGION MOU KAI KLÉRONOMÉSOUSIN HOI ***EKLEKTOI*** *MOU KAI HOI*
mountain the holy of me and shall inherit the choice of me and the

		DOULOI MOU KAI KATOIKÉSOUSIN EKEI servants of me and shall dwell there
	engLXX	And I will lead forth the seed *that came* of Jacob and of Juda, and they shall inherit my holy mountain: and mine elect and my servants shall inherit it, and shall dwell there.
Isa. 65:15		And ye shall leave your name for a curse **unto my chosen**: for the Lord GOD shall slay thee, and call his servants by another name:
	YLT	And ye have left your name for an oath for **My chosen ones**, and the Lord Jehovah hath put thee to death, and to His servants He giveth another name.
	NKJV	You shall leave your name as a curse to **My chosen**; for the Lord GOD will slay you, and call His servants by another name;
	NASB	"You will leave your name for a curse to **My chosen ones**, and the Lord GOD will slay you. But My servants will be called by another name.
	NIV	You will leave your name for **my chosen ones** to use in their curses; the Sovereign LORD will put you to death, but to his servants he will give another name.
	NLT	Your name will be a curse word among **my people**, for the Sovereign LORD will destroy you and will call his true servants by another name.

EKLEKTOS – a divergent translation with "His servants" (KJV) rendered as "my servants" (engLXX): from a third party to a first party event – the wicked and unbelieving in the midst of Israel Vss11-12 shames all of Israel so that, at the end, what the faithful are named by will be different: these faithful are the choice in view in contrast to the unfaithful

[See [1] below]

LXX	*KATALEIPSETE GAR TO ONOMA HUMÓN EIS PLÉSMONÉN TOIS* ***EKLEKTOIS*** *MOU HUMAS* shall leave behind for the name of you into satiety to the choice of me you

		DE ANELEI KURIOS TOIS DE DOULEUOUSI MOI KLÉTHÉSETAI ONOMA KAINON
		but take up Lord to the but serve to me shall be called name new
	engLXX	For ye shall leave your name for a loathing to my chosen, and the Lord shall destroy you: but my servants shall be called by a new name,
Isa. 65:22		They shall not build, and another inhabit; they shall not plant, and another eat: for as the days of a tree *are* the days of my people, **and mine elect** shall long enjoy the work of their hands. [23] They shall not labour in vain…
	YLT	They do not build, and another inhabit, they do not plant, and another eat, for as the days of a tree *are* the days of My people, and the work of their hands wear out do **My chosen ones**. [23]They labour not for a vain thing…
	NKJV	They shall not build and another inhabit; they shall not plant and another eat; for as the days of a tree, *so shall* be the days of My people, and **My elect** shall long enjoy the work of their hands. [23]They shall not labor in vain...
	NASB	"They will not build and another inhabit, they will not plant and another eat; for as the lifetime of a tree, *so will be* the days of My people, and **My chosen ones** will wear out the work of their hands. [23]They will not labor in vain…
	NIV	No longer will they build houses and others live in them, or plant and others eat. For as the days of a tree, so will be the days of my people; **my chosen ones** will long enjoy the work of their hands. [23]They will not labour in vain…
	NLT	Unlike the past, invaders will not take their houses and confiscate their vineyards. For my people will live as long as trees, and **my chosen ones** will have time to enjoy their hard-won gains. [23]They will not work in vain...

EKLEKTOS – a divergent translation with the words "of life" (engLXX) added – the remaining people, faithful and true, are choice [see V.9 and V.15 above][See [1] below]

LXX 65:22-23a

OU MÉ OIKODOMÉSOUSI KAI ALLOI ENOIKÉSOUSI KAI OU MÉ PHUTEUSOUSI
in no wise build and others dwell in and in no wise shall plant

KAI ALLOI PHAGONTAI KATA GAR TAS HÉMERAS TOU XULOU TÉS ZÓÉS
and others eat according to for the days of the tree of the life

ESONTAI HAI HÉMERAI TOU LAOU MOU TA GAR ERGA TÓN PONÓN AUTÓN
shall be the days of the people of me the for works of the effort of them

PALAIÓSOUSIN [23] *HOI* ***EKLEKTOI*** *MOU OU KOPIASOUSIN EIS KENON . . .*
shall grow old the choice of me not they shall labour into void

engLXX They shall by no means build, and others inhabit; and they shall by no means plant, and others eat: for as the days of the tree of life shall be the days of my people, they shall long enjoy the fruits of their labours.[23] My chosen shall not toil in vain . . .

---

1. It is of note that every instance of BACHIR is rendered as *EKLEKTOS* by the LXX translators. We have other Hebrew words only translated by *EKLEKTOS* too, but each of these BEROMIM, CHOPHESH, BOCHAN, and MANNAMIM occur only once. It is the abundant wealth of use of *EKLEKTOS* for other words, seen in the realm of "quality" or "excellence" in contrast to, and *clear* undisputed absence of, anything else, that indicate the later translation of both *EKLEKTOS* and here BACHIR, as "chosen" to be a divergence from the original.
This reality expanded upon and clarified step by step in the analysis of this complete work - with every place the Hebrew words associated with ***EKLEKTOS*** presented and, with all the LXX renderings of every one of those places displayed in the reference section - all backing this truth.
So that, all the renderings throughout of the Heb. word BACHIR and the Gk. word *EKLEKTOS* as "chosen" or, "elect" in Eng. are the product of later lexicons and later translations: They are here, as such, only as faithful to the text of these publications – that is to say, the KJV, the YLT, the NKJV, the NASV, the NIV, the NLT, the engLXX - but as seen by the analysis of the root use-age identified by the independent comparison of the translated undisputed Heb. words, *EKLEKTOS* and BACHIR have only reasonable ground to mean "to be chosen: preferred: excellent, choice, high quality".

3 - BACHUR

Translated into Greek in the LXX

EKLEKTOS		**5**	***EKLEKTOS*:**
NEANISKOS	(young man, boy)	34	**2 Kings 8:12; Psalm 78:31**
NEANIAS	(young man, youth)	2	**Lamentations 1:15**
ANÉR	(man, husband)	1	**Lamentations 5:13**
NOT in LXX		3	**Lamentations 5:14**
	TOTAL	45	

Translated into English - Both KJV related

Ys Conc.	Count	Ss Conc. No. H 970	Count
choice young man	1	young man	42
chosen	1	the chosen	1
young	1	young	1
young man	42	not translated	1
TOTAL	45	TOTAL	45

Refs | **Text quotes KJV unless otherwise stated**

Deu. 32:25 — The sword without, and terror within, shall destroy both the **young man** and the virgin, the suckling *also* with the man of gray hairs.

YLT — Without bereave doth the sword, and at the inner-chambers - fear, both **youth** and virgin, suckling with man of grey hair.

NEANISKOS - young man, boy – a direct translation – the young man mentioned generically that as well as the virgin (maiden), will be affected

LXX — *EXÓTHEN ATEKNÓSEI AUTOUS MACHAIRA KAI EK TÓN TAMIEIÓN PHOBOS*
without make childless them sword and out of the closet fear

***NEANISKOS** SUN PARTHENÓ THÉLAZÓN META KATHESTÉKOTOS PRESBUTOU*
young man with virgin suckling with being placed elder

engLXX — Without, the sword shall bereave them of children, and terror *shall issue* out of the secret chambers; the young man shall perish with the virgin, the suckling with him who has grown old.

Jud. 14:10 — So his father went down unto the woman: and Samson made there a feast; for so used the **young men** to do.

NEANISKOS - young man, boy – a divergent translation with the addition of "for seven days" (engLXX) – young men apparently had a custom to hold a feast: young men

LXX — *KAI KATEBÉ HO PATÉR AUTOU PROS TÉN GUNAIKA KAI EPOIÉSEN EKEI*
and went down the father of him to the woman and made there

*SAMPSÓN POTON HÉMERAS HEPTA HOTI HOUTÓS POIOUSIN HOI **NEANISKOI***
Samson banquet days seven since thus they did the young men

engLXX — And his father went down to the woman, and Sampson made there a banquet for seven days, for so the young men are used to do.

Rut. 3:10 And he said, Blessed *be* thou of the LORD, my daughter: *for* thou hast shewed more kindness in the latter end than at the beginning, inasmuch as thou followedst not **young men**, whether poor or rich.

NEANIAS - young man, youth – a divergent translation with the addition of "Booz" (engLXX) – Ruth is complimented for not going after: young men

LXX ***KAI EIPE BOOZ EULOGÉMENÉ SU TÓ KURIÓ THEÓ THUGATER HOTI ÉGATHUNAS***
and said Booz blessed you the Lord God daughter since did good

TO ELEOS SOU TO ESCHATON HUPER TO PRÓTON MÉ POREUTHÉNAI SE OPISÓ
the mercy of you the last over the first not go you after

NEANIÓN ***EITOI PTÓCHOS EITOI PLOUSIOS***
young men whether poor whether rich

engLXX And Booz said, Blessed *be* thou of the Lord God, *my* daughter, for thou hast made thy latter kindness greater than the former, in that thou followest not after young men, whether *any be* poor or rich.

1Sa. 8:16 And he will take your menservants, and your maidservants, and your goodliest **young men**, and your asses, and put *them* to his work.

YLT And your men-servants, and your maid-servants, and your **young men** – the best, and your asses, he doth take, and hath prepared for his own work;

NOT in LXX – a divergent translation with the whole clause "and your goodliest young men" (KJV) or "and your young men – the best" (YLT), not translated – this missing clause contains BACHUR

LXX ***KAI TOUS DOULOUS HUMÓN KAI TAS DOULAS HUMÓN KAI TA BOUKOLIA HUMÓN***
1Ki.8:16 and the slaves of you and the maids of you and the herds of you

TA AGATHA KAI TOUS ONOUS HUMÓN LÉPSETAI KAI APODEKATÓSEI EIS TA ERGA AUTOU
the good and the donkeys of you shall take and take a tenth into the works of him

engLXX And he will take your servants, and your handmaids, and your good herds and your asses, and will take the tenth of them for his works.

1Sa. 9:2 And he had a son, whose name *was* Saul, a choice **young man**, and a goodly: and *there was* not among the children of Israel a goodlier person than he: from his shoulders and upward *he was* higher than any of the people.

YLT and he hath a son, and his name *is* Saul, a choice **youth** and goodly, and there is not a man among the sons of Israel goodlier than he – from his shoulder and upward, higher than any of the people.

ANÉR – a [particular] man; husband cf. *LDM* – a divergent translation with "choice" (KJV) rendered as "of great stature" (engLXX) – instead of young man, just man is given: the other word for "man" in Greek *ANTHRÓPOS* refers to "any man" and in plural: to a crowd, which can include others; but *ANÉR* refers to "a [particular] man" when it is not used for "husband", so that in plural it always refers to a particular group of men - a [particular] man, here Saul

LXX *KAI TOUTÓ HUIOS KAI ONOMA AUTÓ SAOUL EUMEGETHÉS* ***ANÉR*** *AGATHOS KAI*
1Ki.9:2 and this son and name for him Saul large man good and

OUK ÉN EN HUIOIS ISRAÉL AGATHOS HUPER AUTON HUPERÓMIAN KAI EPANÓ
not was in sons of Israel good over him head and shoulders and above

HUPSÉLOS HUPER PASAN TÉN GÉN
high over all the land

engLXX And this man *had* a son, and his name was Saul, of great stature, a goodly man; and there was not among the sons of Israel a goodlier than he, high above all the people from his shoulders and upward.

2Ki. 8:12 And Hazael said, Why weepeth my lord? And he answered, Because I know the evil that thou wilt do unto the children of Israel: their strong holds wilt thou set on fire, and their **young men** wilt thou slay with the sword, and wilt dash their children, and rip up their women with child.

YLT And Hazael saith, `Wherefore is my lord weeping?' and he saith, `Because I have known the evil that thou dost to the sons of Israel – their fenced places thou dost send into fire, and their **young men** with sword thou dost slay, and their sucklings thou dost dash to pieces, and their pregnant women thou dost rip up.'

NKJV And Hazael said, "Why is my lord weeping?" And he answered, "Because I know the evil that you will do to the children of Israel: Their strongholds you will set on fire, and their **young men** you will kill with the sword; and you will dash their children, and rip open their women with child."

NASB Hazael said, "Why does my lord weep?" Then he answered, "Because I know the evil that you will do to the sons of Israel: their strongholds you will set on fire, and their **young men** you will kill with the sword, and their little ones you will dash in pieces, and their women with child you will rip up."

NIV "Why is my lord weeping?" asked Hazael. "Because I know the harm you will do to the Israelites," he answered. "You will set fire to their fortified places, kill their **young men** with the sword, dash their little children to the ground, and rip open their pregnant women."

NLT "What's the matter, my lord?" Hazael asked him. Elisha replied, "I know the terrible things you will do to the people of Israel. You will burn their fortified cities, kill their **young men** with the sword, dash their little children to the ground, and rip open their pregnant women!"

EKLEKTOS – a direct translation – since young men are seen as men in their prime: e.g. the best soldier material, these are given as *EKLEKTOS* "choice men" (engLXX)

LXX *KAI EIPEN AZAÉL TI HOTI HO KURIOS MOU KLAIEI KAI EIPEN HOTI OIDA HOSA*
4Ki.8:12 and said Azael why since the Lord of me weeps and said since saw as many as

POIÉSEIS TOIS HUIOIS ISRAÉL KAKA TA OCHURÓMATA AUTÓN EXAPOSTELEIS
shall do to the sons of Israel bad the fortresses of them send out

EN PURI KAI TOUS ***EKLEKTOUS*** *AUTÓN EN RHOMPHAIA APOKTENEIS KAI TA*
in fire and the choice of them in broadsword kill and the

NÉPIA AUTÓN ENSEISEIS KAI TAS EN GASTRI ECHOUSAS AUTÓN ANARRÉXEIS
infants of them shall dash and the in womb having of them shall gut

engLXX And Azael said, Why does my lord weep? And he said, Because I know all the evil that thou wilt do to the children of Israel: thou wilt utterly destroy their strong holds with fire, and thou wilt slay their choice men with the sword, and thou wilt dash their infants *against the ground*, and their women with child thou wilt rip up.

2Ch. 36:17a Therefore he brought upon them the king of the Chaldees, who slew their **young men** with the sword in the house of their sanctuary, (. . .)

YLT And He causeth to go up against them the king of the Chaldeans, and he slayeth their **chosen ones** by the sword in the house of their sanctuary, (. . .)

NEANISKOS - young man, boy – a divergent translation with "their sanctuary" (KJV) rendered as "his sanctuary" (engLXX) - the young men killed by the sword in Jerusalem (V.11)

LXX *KAI ÉGAGEN EP AUTOUS BASILEA CHALDAIÓN KAI APEKTEINE TOUS*
and led upon them king of Chaldeans and killed the

NEANISKOUS *AUTÓN EN RHOMPHAIA EN OIKÓ HAGIASMATOS AUTOU* . . .
young men of them in broadsword in house of sanctuary of him

engLXX And he brought against them the king of the Chaldeans, and slew their young men with the sword in the house of his sanctuary, (. . .)

2Ch. 36:17b . . . and had no compassion upon **young man** or maiden, old man, or him that stooped for age: he gave *them* all into his hand.

YLT . . . and hath had no pity on **young man** and virgin, old man and very aged - the whole He hath given into his hand.

NOT in LXX – a divergent translation with "young man" (KJV) rendered as "Sedekias" (engLXX) – word not translated and instead another put in its place

LXX . . . ***KAI OUK EPHEISATO TOU SEDEKIOU KAI TAS PARTHENOUS AUTÓN OUK***
and not spare the Sedekias and the virgins of them not

ÉLEÉSE KAI TOUS PRESBUTEROUS AUTÓN APÉGAGON TA PANTA PAREDÓKEN
mercied and the elders of them took away the all deliver

EN CHERSIN AUTÓN
in hands of them

engLXX . . . and did not spare Sedekias, and had no mercy upon their virgins, and they led away their old men: he delivered all things into their hands.

Psa. 78:31 The wrath of God came upon them, and slew the fattest of them, and smote down **the chosen** *men* of Israel.

YLT And the anger of God hath gone up against them, and He slayeth among their fat ones, and **youths** of Israel He caused to bend.

NKJV The wrath of God came against them, and slew the stoutest of them, and struck down the **choice** *men* of Israel.

NASB The anger of God rose against them and killed some of their stoutest ones, and subdued the **choice men** of Israel.

NIV God's anger rose against them; he put to death the sturdiest among them, cutting down the **young men** of Israel.

NLT the anger of God rose against them, and he killed their strongest men. He struck down the **finest** of Israel's **young men**.

EKLEKTOS – a direct translation - since young men are seen as men in their prime: e.g. the best physical shape, these are given as *EKLEKTOS*: "choice men" (engLXX)

LXX **77:31**	*KAI ORGÉ TOU THEOU ANEBÉ EP AUTOUS KAI APEKTEINEN EN TOIS* and anger of the God arose upon them and killed in the
	PIOSIN AUTÓN KAI TOUS ***EKLEKTOUS*** *TOU ISRAÉL SUNEPODISEN* plenty of them and the choice of the Israel bound feet
engLXX	then the indignation of God rose up against them, and slew the fattest of them, and overthrew the choice men of Israel.

Psa. 78:63	The fire consumed their **young men**; and their maidens were not given to marriage.
YLT	His **young men** hath fire consumed, and His virgins have not been praised.

NEANISKOS - young man, boy – a divergent translation with "not given to marriage" (KJV) or "have not been praised" (YLT), rendered as "mourned not" (engLXX) – the young men of Israel consumed by fire as a result of their persistent rebellion (Vss 56-59)

LXX **77:63**	*TOUS* ***NEASNISKOUS*** *AUTÓN KATEPHAGE PUR KAI HAI PARTHENOI AUTÓN OUK EPENTHÉSAN* the young men of them devoured fire and the virgins of them not mourned
engLXX	Fire devoured their young men; and their virgins mourned not.

Psa. 148:12	Both **young men**, and maidens; old men, and children:

NEANISKOS - young man, boy – a direct translation – part of a list from V.7 of categories of people or created beings or things called upon to praise God: young men

LXX	***NEANISKOI*** *KAI PARTHENOI PRESBUTAI META NEÓTERÓN* young men and virgins elders with young
engLXX	young men and virgins, old men with youths:

Pro. 20:29 — The glory of **young men** *is* their strength: and the beauty of old men *is* the gray head.

YLT — The beauty of **young men** is their strength, and the honour of old men is grey hairs.

NEANIAS - young man, youth – a divergent translation with the youths "strength" not mentioned, but instead "wisdom" being added and placed in view – a contrast between old men versus young men and what each are best known for: young men

LXX — ***KOSMOS*** ***NEANIAIS*** ***SOPHIA DOXA DE PRESBUTERÓN POLIAI***
ornament to young men wisdom glory but elders greys

engLXX — Wisdom is an ornament to young men; and grey *hairs* are the glory of old men.

Ecc. 11:9 — Rejoice, O **young man**, in thy youth[1]; and let thy heart cheer thee in the days of thy youth[2], and walk in the ways of thine heart, and in the sight of thine eyes: but know thou, that for all these *things* God will bring thee into judgment.

YLT — Rejoice, O **young man**, in thy childhood[1], and let thy heart gladden thee in days of thy youth[2], and walk in the ways of thy heart, and in the sight of thine eyes, and know thou that for all these, doth God bring thee into judgment.

NEANISKOS - young man, boy – a divergent translation with "in the sight of thine eyes" (KJV) rendered as "not in the sight of thine eyes" (engLXX):the opposite – advice being given to a generic young man

LXX — ***EUPHRAINOU NEANISKE*** *EN NEOTÉTI*[1] ***SOU KAI AGATHUNATÓ SE HÉ KARDIA***
rejoice young man in youth of you and let cheer you the heart

SOU EN HÉMERAIS NEOTÉTOS[2] ***SOU KAI PERIPATEI EN HODOIS KARDIAS SOU***
of you in days of youth of you and walk in ways of heart of you

1. Heb. YALEDUTH
2. See BECHURIM/BECHUROTH

AMÓMOS KAI MÉ EN HORASEI OPHTHALMÓN SOU KAI GNÓTHI HOTI EPI PASI
blameless and not in seeing of eyes of you and know since upon all

TOUTOIS AXEI SE HO THEOS EN KRISEI
these carry you the God in judgment

engLXX Rejoice, O young man, in thy youth; and let thy heart cheer thee in the days of thy youth, and walk in the ways of thy heart blameless, but not in the sight of thine eyes: yet know that for all these things God will bring thee into judgement.

Isa. 9:17 Therefore the Lord shall have no joy in their **young men**, neither shall have mercy on their fatherless and widows: for every one *is* an hypocrite and an evildoer, and every mouth speaketh folly. For all this his anger is not turned away, but his hand *is* stretched out still.

YLT Therefore, over its **young men** the Lord rejoiceth not, and its orphans, and its widows He pitieth not, for every one *is* profane, and an evil doer, and every mouth is speaking folly. With all this not turned back hath His anger, and still His hand is stretched out.

NEANISKOS - young man, boy – a direct translation – the Lord's judgment here will include every category of people in the land: young men will not be rejoiced over

LXX *DIATOUTO EPI TOUS* ***NEANISKOUS*** *AUTÓN OUK EUPHRANTHÉSETAI HO KURIOS*
therefore upon the young men of them not shall be gladdened the Lord

KAI TOUS ORPHANOUS AUTÓN KAI TAS CHÉRAS AUTÓN OUK ELEÉSEI HOTI
and the orphans of them and the widows of them not mercied since

PANTES ANOMOI KAI PONÉROI KAI PAN STOMA LALEI ADIKA EPI PASI TOUTOIS
all lawless and evil and every mouth speaks | upon all for these
unrighteousness

OUK APESTRAPHÉ HO THUMOS ALL ETI HÉ CHEIR HUPSÉLÉ
not turn back the rage but yet the hand uplifted

	engLXX	Therefore the Lord shall not take pleasure in their young men, neither shall he have pity on their orphans or on their widows: for they are all transgressors and wicked, and every mouth speaks unjustly. For all this *his* anger is not turned away, but *his* hand is yet exalted.
Isa. 23:4		Be thou ashamed, O Zidon: for the sea hath spoken, *even* the strength of the sea, saying, I travail not, nor bring forth children, neither do I nourish up **young men**, *nor* bring up virgins.
	YLT	Be ashamed, O Zidon; for the sea spake, the strength of the sea, saying: 'I have not been pained, nor have I brought forth, nor have I nourished **young men**, *nor* brought up virgins.'

NEANISKOS - young man, boy – a direct translation – a portion of the prophecy against Tyre as, Tyre and Sidon, side by side, traded abundantly by sea: the "sea" here is a type for Tyre itself, as the main port and harbour which will be utterly destroyed, so that: young men as well as virgins are no longer brought up in Tyre

LXX *AISCHUNTHÉTI SIDÓN EIPEN HÉ THALASSA HÉ DE ISCHUS TÉS THALASSÉS EIPEN OUK*
be dishonoured Sidon said the sea the but strength of the sea said not

ÓDINON OUDE ETEKON OUDE EXETHREPSA ***NEANISKOUS*** *OUDE HUPSÓSA PARTHENOUS*
travail nor engender nor reared young men nor raised up virgins

	engLXX	Be ashamed, O Sidon: the sea has said, yea, the strength of the sea has said, I have not travailed, nor brought forth, nor have I brought up young men, nor reared virgins.
Isa. 31:8		Then shall the Assyrian fall with the sword, not of a mighty man; and the sword, not of a mean man, shall devour him: but he shall flee from the sword, and his **young men** shall be discomfited.
	YLT	And fallen hath Asshur by sword, not of the high, yea, a sword - not of the low, doth consume him, and he hath fled for himself from the face of a sword, and his **young men** become tributary.

NEANISKOS - young man, boy – a divergent translation with "he shall flee from the sword" (KJV) or "he hath fled for himself from the face of a sword" (YLT), rendered as "neither shall he flee from the face of the sword" (engLXX): the opposite – young men of Assyria will be subjugated

LXX *KAI PESEITAI ASSOUR OU MACHAIRA ANDROS OUDE MACHAIRA ANTHRÓPOU*
and shall fall Assyria not sword of [particular] man | neither sword of man

KATAPHAGETAI AUTON KAI PHEUXETAI OUK APO PROSÓPOU MACHAIRAS HOI
devour him and escape not from face of sword the

DE ***NEANISKOI*** *ESONTAI EIS HÉTTÉMA*
but young men shall be into overcome

engLXX And the Assyrian shall fall: not the sword of a great man, nor the sword of a mean man shall devour him; neither shall he flee from the face of the sword: but the young men shall be overthrown:

Isa. 40:30 Even the youths shall faint and be weary, and the **young men** shall utterly fall:

NEANISKOS - young man, boy – a divergent translation with the addition of "and the choice *men*" (engLXX) – young men fail in contrast to those who wait on the Lord (V.31): their youth is no help to them in contrast

LXX *PEINASOUSI GAR NEÓTEROI KAI KOPIASOUSI* ***NEANISKOI*** *KAI EKLEKTOI*[3]
hungered for youth and wearied young men and choice

ANISCHUES ESONTAI
without strength shall be

engLXX For the young *men* shall hunger, and the youths shall be weary, and the choice *men* shall be powerless:

Isa. 42:22 But this *is* a people robbed and spoiled; *they are* all of them snared in holes[4], and they are hid in prison houses: they are for a prey, and none delivereth; for a spoil, and none saith, Restore.

3. *EKLEKTOS* is not from a Heb. word & is a LXX addition. See a*EKLEKTOS* chapter
4. NOT in LXX – it appears neither in the English of the KJV and YLT, nor in the Gk. of the LXX. The word BACHUR is not – strictly speaking (in the Heb.) – clearly in view, but more like BECHURIM, but with Ss listing above as "not translated", I have added it here. The Heb. word appears similar to that of Numbers 11:28 [see BECHURIM/BECHUROTH]

YLT And this *is* a people seized and spoiled, snared in holes[4] - all of them, and in houses of restraint they were hidden, they have been for a prey, and there is no deliverer, a spoil, and none is saying, 'Restore.'

LXX *KAI EIDON KAI EGENETO HO LAOS PEPRONOMEUMENOS KAI DIÉRPASMENOS*
and I saw and came to be the people were despoiled and plundered

HÉ GAR PAGIS EN TOIS TAMEIOIS PANTACHOU KAI EN OIKOIS HAMA HOPOU
the for snare in the closet everywhere and in house together where

EKRUPSAN AUTOUS EGENONTO EIS PRONOMÉN KAI OUK ÉN EXAIROUMENOS
hid them became into spoil and not was escape

HARPAGMA KAI OUK ÉN HO LEGÓN APODOS
prey and not was the spoken give back

engLXX And I beheld, and the people were spoiled and plundered: for *there is* a snare in the secret chambers everywhere, and in the houses also, where they have hidden them: they became a spoil, and there was no one that delivered the prey, and there was none who said, Restore.

Isa. 62:5 For *as* a **young man** marrieth a virgin, *so* shall thy sons marry thee: and *as* the bridegroom rejoiceth over the bride, *so* shall thy God rejoice over thee.

YLT For a **young man** doth marry a virgin, thy Builders do marry thee, with the joy of a bridegroom over a bride, rejoice over thee doth thy God.

NEANISKOS - young man, boy – a loose translation with "marrieth" (KJV) rendered as "lives with" (engLXX) – young men and their wives pictured, the husband with joy over his bride, so likewise the Lord with his people will rejoice

LXX *KAI HÓS SUNOIKÓN* ***NEANISKOS*** *PARTHENÓ HOUTÓ KATOIKÉSOUSIN HOI HUIOI*
and as dwell with young man with virgin thus shall dwell the sons

SOU KAI ESTAI HON TROPON EUPHRANTHÉSETAI NUMPHIOS EPI NUMPHÉ
of you and shall be the manner shall be glad groom over bride

HOUTÓS EUPHRANTHÉSETAI KURIOS EPI SOI
so will be glad Lord over you

engLXX And as a young man lives with a virgin, so shall thy sons dwell in *thee*: and it shall come to pass *that* as a bridegroom will rejoice over a bride, so will the Lord rejoice over thee.

Jer. 6:11 Therefore I am full of the fury of the LORD; I am weary with holding in: I will pour it out upon the children abroad, and upon the assembly of **young men** together: for even the husband with the wife shall be taken, the aged with *him that is* full of days.

YLT And with the fury of Jehovah I have been filled, (I have been weary of containing,) to pour *it* on the suckling in the street, and on the assembly of **youths** together, for even husband with wife are captured, an elder with one full of days,

NEANISKOS - young man, boy – a divergent translation with "LORD" (KJV) not translated – young men gathered together will receive the Lord's fury

LXX *KAI TON THUMON MOU EPLÉSA KAI EPESCHON KAI OU SUNETELESA AUTOUS*
and the rage of me filled and I kept back and not finish entirely them

EKCHEÓ EPI NÉPIA EXÓTHEN KAI EPI SUNAGÓGÉN ***NEANISKÓN*** *HAMA HOTI*
shall pour out upon children outside and upon gathered young men together since

ANÉR KAI GUNÉ SULLÉPHTHÉSONTAI PRESBUTEROS META PLÉROUS HÉMERÓN
man and woman shall be seized elder with full of days

engLXX And I allowed my wrath to come to full, yet I kept *it* in, and did not utterly destroy them: I will pour it out on the children without, and on the assembly of young men together: for man and woman shall be taken together, the old man with him that is full of days.

Jer. 9:21 For death is come up into our windows, *and* is entered into our palaces, to cut off the children from without, *and* the **young men** from the streets.

YLT For death hath come up into our windows, it hath come into our palaces, to cut off the suckling from without, **young men** from the broad places.

NEANISKOS - young man, boy – a divergent translation with "palaces" (KJV) given as "land" (engLXX) – young men in the streets will receive their death

LXX *HOTI ANEBÉ THANATOS DIA TÓN THURIDÓN HUMÓN EISÉLTHEN EIS TÉN GÉN*
since arisen death through the windows of you entered into the land

HUMÓN TOU EKTRIPSAI NÉPIA EXÓTHEN KAI ***NEANISKOUS*** *APO TÓN PLATEIÓN*
of you of the wipe out children outside and young men from the streets

engLXX For death has come up through your windows, it has entered into our land, to destroy the infants without, and the young men from the streets.

Jer. 11:22 Therefore thus saith the LORD of hosts, Behold, I will punish them: the **young men** shall die by the sword; their sons and their daughters shall die by famine:

YLT Therefore, thus said Jehovah of Hosts: 'Lo, I am seeing after them, the **chosen ones** die by sword, their sons and their daughters die by famine,

NEANISKOS - young man, boy – a divergent translation with "Therefore thus saith the LORD of hosts" (KJV) or "Therefore, thus said Jehovah of Hosts" (YLT), not rendered: perhaps since the LXX translator did translate it at the beginning of V.21 he thought there was no need to do so again here, as a continuation of what the Lord was saying(?) – young men shall die by the sword

LXX *IDOU EGÓ EPISKEPSOMAI EP AUTOUS HOI* ***NEANISKOI*** *AUTÓN EN MACHAIRA APOTHANOUNTAI*
look I shall visit upon them the young men of them in sword shall die

KAI HOI HUIOI AUTÓN KAI HAI THUGATERES AUTÓN TELEUTÉSOUSIN EN LIMÓ
and the sons of them and the daughters of them they shall end in famine

	engLXX	behold, I will visit them: their young men shall die by the sword; and their sons and their daughters shall die of famine:
Jer. 15:8		Their widows are increased to me above the sand of the seas: I have brought upon them against the mother of the **young men** a spoiler at noonday: I have caused *him* to fall upon it suddenly, and terrors upon the city.
	YLT	Its widows have been more to Me than the sand of the seas, I brought in to them - against the mother - a **young man** - a spoiler - at noon. I caused to fall upon her suddenly, wrath and trouble.

NEANISKOS - young man, boy – a direct translation – young men e.g. enemy soldiers coming in at noon to cause destruction (LXX), or a single one (YLT) or, the children [young men] of mothers (KJV, NKJV) who are the victims as per ongoing context (V.9)

LXX

EPLÉTHUNTHÉSAN HAI CHÉRAI AUTÓN HUPER TÉN AMMON TÉS THALASSÉS
multiplied the widows of them more than the sand of the sea

EPÉGAGON EPI MÉTERA ***NEANISKOUS*** *TALAIPÓRIAN EN MESÉMBRIA*
brought upon mother young men misery in midday

EPERRIPSA EP AUTÉN EXAIPHNÉS TROMON KAI SPOUDÉN
cast upon her sudden trembling and anxiety

	engLXX	Their widows have been multiplied more than the sand of the sea: I have brought young men against the mother, *even* distress at noon-day: I have suddenly cast upon her trembling and anxiety.
Jer. 18:21		Therefore deliver up their children to the famine, and pour out their *blood* by the force of the sword; and let their wives be bereaved of their children, and *be* widows; and let their men be put to death; *let* their **young men** *be* slain by the sword in battle.

NEANISKOS - young man, boy – a direct translation – young men killed by the sword in fighting

LXX *DIATOUTO DOS TOUS HUIOUS AUTÓN EIS LIMON KAI ATHROISON AUTOUS EIS*
therefore give the sons of them into famine and gather them into

CHEIRAS MACHAIRAS GENESTHÓSAN HAI GUNAIKES AUTÓN ATEKNOI KAI
hands of swords let become the wives of them childless and

CHÉRAI KAI HOI ANDRES AUTÓN GENESTHÓSAN ANÉRÉMENOI THANATÓ KAI
widows and the men of them let become taken up with death and

HOI ***NEANISKOI*** *AUTÓN PEPTÓKOTES MACHAIRA EN POLEMÓ*
the young men of them fall by sword in war

engLXX Therefore do thou deliver their sons to famine, and gather them to the power of the sword: let their women be childless and widows; and let their men be cut off by death, and their young men fall by the sword in war.

Jer. 31:13 Then shall the virgin rejoice in the dance, both **young men** and old together: for I will turn their mourning into joy, and will comfort them, and make them rejoice from their sorrow.

YLT Then rejoice doth a virgin in a chorus, both **young men** and old men – together, and I have turned their mourning to joy, and have comforted them, and gladdened them above their sorrow,

NEANISKOS - young man, boy – a divergent translation with "their sorrow" (KJV) not translated – young men and old will rejoice when the Lord restores Israel (V.11)

LXX *TOTE CHARÉSONTAI PARTHENOI EN SUNAGÓGÉ* ***NEANISKÓN*** *KAI PRESBUTAI CHARÉSONTAI*
38:13 then shall rejoice virgins in assembly of young men and elders shall rejoice

KAI STREPSÓ TO PENTHOS AUTÓN EIS CHARMONÉN KAI POIÉSÓ AUTOUS EUPHRAINOMENOUS
and shall turn the mourning of them into joyfulness and shall make them glad

engLXX Then shall the virgins rejoice in the assembly of youth, and the old men shall rejoice; and I will turn their mourning into joy, and will make them merry.

Jer. 48:15		Moab is spoiled, and gone up *out of* her cities, and his chosen[5] **young men** are gone down to the slaughter, saith the King, whose name *is* the LORD of hosts.
	YLT	Spoiled is Moab, and her cities hath one gone up, and the choice of its **young men** have gone down to slaughter, an affirmation of the King, Jehovah of Hosts *is* His name.

NEANISKOS - young man, boy - a divergent translation with "saith the King, whose name *is* the LORD of hosts" (KJV) not translated – the best young men will perish from Moab

LXX **31:15**	*ÓLETO MÓAB POLIS AUTOU KAI EKLEKTOI*[5] ***NEANISKOI*** *AUTOU KATEBÉSAN EIS SPHAGÉN* destroyed Moab city of him and choice young men of him gone down into slaughter
engLXX	Moab is ruined, *even* his city, and his choice young men have gone down to slaughter.

Jer. 49:26		Therefore her **young men** shall fall in her streets, and all the men of war shall be cut off in that day, saith the LORD of hosts.
	YLT	Therefore fall do her **young men** in her broad places, and all the men of war are cut off in that day, an affirmation of Jehovah of Hosts.

NEANISKOS - young man, boy – a divergent translation with "in that day" (KJV) not translated – young men of Damascus (Vs. 24 & 27) shall fall [cf. 50:30 below]

LXX **30:26**	*DIATOUTO PESOUNTAI* ***NEANISKOI*** *EN PLATEIAIS SOU KAI PANTES HOI ANDRES* therefore shall fall young men en streets of you and all the men *HOI POLEMISTAI SOU PESOUNTAI PHÉSI KURIOS* the warriors of you shall fall says Lord
engLXX	Therefore shall the young men fall in thy streets, and all thy warriors shall fall, saith the Lord.

5. See MIBCHAR

Jer. 50:30 Therefore shall her **young men** fall in the streets, and all her men of war shall be cut off in that day, saith the LORD.

YLT Therefore fall do her **young men** in her broad places, and all her men of war are cut off in that day, an affirmation of Jehovah.

NEANISKOS - young man, boy - a divergent translation with "in that day" (KJV) not translated – young men of Babylon (V.29) shall fall [cf. 49:26 above]

LXX **27:30** *DIATOUTO PESOUNTAI HOI* ***NEANISKOI*** *AUTÉS EN TAIS PLATEIAIS AUTÉS KAI*
therefore shall fall the young men of her in the streets of her and

PANTES HOI ANDRES HOI POLEMISTAI AUTÉS RIPHÉSONTAI EIPE KURIOS
all the men the warriors of her shall be cast down says Lord

engLXX Therefore shall her young men fall in the streets, and all her warriors shall be cast down, saith the Lord.

Jer. 51:3 Against *him that* bendeth let the archer bend his bow, and against *him that* lifteth himself up in his brigandine: and spare ye not her **young men**; destroy ye utterly all her host.

YLT Let not the treader tread his bow, nor lift himself up in his coat of mail, nor have ye pity on her **young men**, devote ye to destruction all her host.

NEANISKOS - young man, boy – a divergent translation with "and against *him that* lifteth himself up in his brigandine" (KJV) or "nor lift himself up in his coat of mail" (YLT), rendered as "and him that has armour put it on" (engLXX): instead of being against the person putting on armour, the LXX translator renders an instruction to put it on: opposite – there is to be no pity on the young men of Babylon (V. 2)

LXX **28:3** *TEINETÓ HO TEINÓN TO TOXON AUTOU KAI PERITHESTHÓ HÓ ESTIN HOPLA AUTOU KAI*
stretch the archer the bow of him and put on what is weapons of him and

MÉ PHEISÉSTHE EPI TOUS ***NEANISKOUS*** *AUTÉS KAI APHANISATE PASAN TÉN DUNAMIN AUTÉS*
not spare upon the young men of her and obliterate all the force of her

engLXX Let the archer bend his bow, and him that has armour put it on: and spare ye not her young men, but destroy ye all her host.

Jer. 51:22 With thee also will I break in pieces man and woman; and with thee will I break in pieces old and young; and with thee will I break in pieces the **young man** and the maid;

YLT And I have broken in pieces by thee man and woman, and I have broken in pieces by thee old and young, and I have broken in pieces by thee **young man** and virgin,

NEANISKOS - young man, boy – a divergent translation with the clause "and with thee will I break in pieces old and young" (KJV) omitted from translation – both young men and virgin of Babylon (Vs. 1 & 2) will be: broken in pieces (Heb.) scattered (Gk.)

LXX **28:22** *KAI DIASKORPIÓ EN SOI* ***NEANISKON*** *KAI PARTHENON KAI DIASKORPIÓ EN SOI*
and I shall scatter in you young man and virgin and shall scatter in you

ANDRA KAI GUNAIKA
man and woman

engLXX And by thee I will scatter youth and maid; and by thee I will scatter man and woman.

Lam. 1:15 The Lord hath trodden under foot all my mighty *men* in the midst of me: he hath called an assembly against me to crush my **young men**: the Lord hath trodden the virgin, the daughter of Judah, *as* in a winepress. 16For these *things* I weep; (. . .)

YLT Trodden down all my mighty ones hath the Lord in my midst, He proclaimed against me an appointed time, to destroy my **young men**, a wine-press hath the Lord trodden, to the virgin daughter of Judah. 16For these I am weeping, (. . .)

NKJV “The Lord has trampled underfoot all my mighty *men* in my midst; He has called an assembly against me to crush my **young men**; the Lord trampled *as* in a winepress the virgin daughter of Judah. [16]For these *things* I weep; (. . .)

NASB “The Lord has rejected all my strong men in my midst; He has called an appointed time against me to crush my **young men**; the Lord has trodden *as in* a wine press the virgin daughter of Judah. [16]For these things I weep; (. . .)

NIV ‘The Lord has rejected all the warriors in my midst; he has summoned an army against me to crush my **young men**. In his winepress the Lord has trampled Virgin Daughter Judah. [16]This is why I weep . . .

NLT “The Lord has treated my mighty men with contempt. At his command a great army has come to crush my **young warriors**. The Lord has trampled his beloved city like grapes are trampled in a winepress. [16]For all these things I weep; (. . .)

EKLEKTOS – a loose translation with “trodden under” (KJV) or “trodden down” (YLT), rendered as “cut off” (engLXX) – the young men, being the best (to fight as soldiers), and “mighty *men*” (KJV), “strong men” (engLXX) already mentioned, in the preceding clause, here the LXX translator continues the quality emphasis with *EKLEKTOS*: “choice men” (engLXX)

LXX *SAMECH EXÉRE PANTAS TOUS ISCHUROUS MOU HO KURIOS EK MESOU MOU*
SAMECH lift out all the strong of me the Lord out of midst of me

EKALESEN EP EME KAIRON TOU SUNTRIPSAI ***EKLEKTOUS*** *MOU LÉNON*
called upon me season of the to break choice of me vat

EPATÉSE KURIOS PARTHENÓ THUGATRI IOUDA EPI TOUTOIS EGÓ KLAIÓ
trod Lord for virgin daughter of Juda upon for these I weep

engLXX SAMECH. The Lord has cut off all my strong men from the midst of me: he has summoned against me a time for crushing my choice men: the Lord has trodden a wine-press for the virgin daughter of Juda: for these things I weep.

Lam. 1:18 The LORD is righteous; for I have rebelled against his commandment: hear, I pray you, all people, and behold my sorrow: my virgins and my **young men** are gone into captivity.

YLT Righteous is Jehovah, for His mouth I have provoked. Hear, I pray you, all ye peoples, and see my pain, my virgins and my **young men** have gone into captivity.

NEANISKOS - young man, boy – a direct translation – young men and the virgins of Jerusalem (V. 17) are gone into captivity

LXX ***TSADÉ DIKAIOS ESTI KURIOS HOTI STOMA AUTOU PAREPIKRANA AKOUSATE DÉ***
TSADE righteous is Lord since mouth of him greatly embittered hear indeed

PANTES HOI LAOI KAI IDETE TO ALGOS MOU PARTHENOI MOU KAI **NEANISKOI**
all the people and look the pain of me virgins of me and young men

MOU EPOREUTHÉSAN EN AICHMALÓSIA
of me were gone in captivity

engLXX TSADE. The Lord is righteous; for I have provoked his mouth: hear, I pray you, all people, and behold my grief: my virgins and my young men are gone into captivity.

Lam. 2:21 The young and the old lie on the ground in the streets: my virgins and my **young men** are fallen by the sword; thou hast slain *them* in the day of thine anger; thou hast killed, *and* not pitied.

YLT Lain on the earth *in* out-places have young and old, my virgins and my **young men** have fallen by the sword, Thou hast slain in a day of Thine anger, Thou hast slaughtered - Thou hast not pitied.

NEANISKOS - young man, boy – a divergent translation with "fallen by the sword" (KJV) rendered as "gone into captivity" (engLXX) – virgins and young men share in the same fate

LXX ***CHSEN EKOIMÉTHÉSAN EIS TÉN EXODON PAIDARION KAI PRESBUTÉS PARTHENOI MOU KAI***
CHSEN laid out into the way out boy and old virgins of me and

***NEANISKOI** MOU EPOREUTHÉSAN EN AICHMALÓSIA EN RHOMPHAIA KAI EN LIMÓ*
young men of me went in captivity in broadswordand in famine

APEKTEINAS EN HÉMERA ORGÉS SOU EMAGEIREUSAS OUK EPHEISÓ
killed in day of anger of you cut up not spared

engLXX CHSEN. The child and old man have lain down in the street: my virgins and my young men are gone into captivity: thou hast slain *them* with the sword and with famine; in the day of thy wrath thou hast mangled *them*, thou has not spared.

Lam. 5:13 They took the **young men** to grind, and the children fell under the wood.
YLT **Young men** to grind they have taken, and youths with wood have stumbled.
NKJV **Young men** ground at the millstones; boys staggered under *loads of* wood.
NASB **Young men** worked at the grinding mill, and youths stumbled under *loads* of wood.
NIV **Young men** toil at the millstones; boys stagger under loads of wood.
NLT **Young men** are led away to work at millstones, and boys stagger under heavy loads of wood.

EKLEKTOS – a divergent translation with "took . . . to grind" (KJV) rendered as "lifted up *the voice in* weeping" (engLXX) – young men (Heb.) *EKLEKTOS* (Gk.): The engLXX translates "chosen men" according to lexicon records and post 1st century use of *EKLEKTOS* in spite of following the Gk. and doing right by it, as per his earlier "choice men" (engLXX 2 Ki. 8:12; Psa. 78:31; Lam. 1:15) - [cf. Lam. 5:14 below]

LXX ***EKLEKTOI** KLAUTHMON ANELABON KAI NEANISKOI EN XULÓ ÉSTHENÉSAN*
choice weeping raised and young men in tree weakened

engLXX The chosen men lifted up *the voice in* weeping, and the youths fainted under the wood.

Lam. 5:14 The elders have ceased from the gate, the **young men** from their musick.
YLT The aged from the gate have ceased, **young men** from their song.

NKJV	The elders have ceased *gathering at* the gate, and the **young men** from their music.
NASB	Elders are gone from the gate, **young men** from their music.
NIV	The elders are gone from the city gate; the **young men** have stopped their music.
NLT	The elders no longer sit in the city gates; the **young men** no longer dance and sing.

EKLEKTOS - a direct translation – in contrast to the elders, the young men are mentioned: young men (Heb.) *EKLEKTOS* (Gk.): The engLXX translates "chosen men" according to lexicon records and post 1st century use of *EKLEKTOS* in spite of following the Gk. and doing right by it, as per his earlier "choice men" (engLXX 2 Ki. 8:12; Psa. 78:31; Lam. 1:15) - [cf. Lam. 5:13 above]

LXX *KAI PRESBUTAI APO PULÉS KATEPAUSAN* ***EKLEKTOI*** *EK PSALMÓN AUTÓN KATEPAUSAN*
and elders from gate ceased choice out of psalms of them ceased

engLXX And the elders ceased from the gate, the chosen men ceased from their music.

Eze. 9:6

Slay utterly old *and* **young**, both maids, and little children, and women: but come not near any man upon whom *is* the mark; and begin at my sanctuary. Then they began at the ancient men which *were* before the house.

YLT aged, **young man**, and virgin, and infant, and women, ye do slay – to destruction; and against any man on whom *is* the mark ye do not go nigh, and from My sanctuary ye begin.' 7And they begin among the aged men who *are* before the house . . .

NEANISKOS - young man, boy – a direct translation – all are to be slain who have not the mark: young man [generic] as part of a list of categories of people on the list

LXX *PRESBUTERON KAI* ***NEANISKON*** *KAI PARTHENON KAI NÉPIA KAI GUNAIKAS*
elder and young man and virgin and infants and women

APOKTEINATE EIS EXALEIPSIN EPI DE PANTAS EPH HOUS ESTI TO SÉMEION MÉ
kill into wiped out upon but all upon whom is the sign not

EGGISÉTE APO TÓN HAGIÓN MOU ARXASTHE KAI ÉRXANTO APO TÓN
should go near from the holy of me begin and they began from the

ANDRÓN TÓN PRESBUTERÓN HOI ÉSAN ESÓ EN TÓ OIKÓ
men of the elders the they were inside in the house

engLXX Slay utterly old man and youth, and virgin, and infants, and women: but go ye not nigh any on whom is the mark: begin at my sanctuary. So they began with the elder men who were within in the house.

Eze. 23:6 *Which were* clothed with blue, captains and rulers, all of them desirable **young men**, horsemen riding upon horses.

YLT Clothed with blue - governors and prefects, desirable **young men** all of them, horsemen, riding on horses,

NEANISKOS - young man, boy – a direct translation – Assyrian (V.5) soldiers looking resplendent: desirable young men [cf. 23:12 below]

LXX *ENDEDUKOTAS HUAKINTHINA HÉGOUMENOUS KAI STRATÉGOUS* ***NEANISKOI***
clothed blue leaders and commanders young men

KAI EPILEKTOI[6] *PANTES HIPPEIS HIPPAZOMENOI EPH HIPPÓN*
and choice all horsemen riding upon horses

engLXX clothed with purple, princes and captains; *they were* young men and choice, all horsemen riding on horses.

Eze. 23:12 She doted upon the Assyrians *her* neighbours, captains and rulers clothed most gorgeously, horsemen riding upon horses, all of them desirable **young men**.

YLT On sons of Asshur she hath doted, governors and prefects, neighbouring ones - clothed in perfection, horsemen, riding on horses, desirable **young men** all of them.

6. See separate chapter for *EPILEKTOS*

NEANISKOS - young man, boy – a direct translation – Assyrian (V.5) soldiers looking resplendent: desirable young men [cf. 23:6 above]

LXX *EPI TOUS HUIOUS TÓN ASSURIÓN EPETHETO HÉGOUMENOUS KAI*
upon the sons of the Assyrians doted leaders and
STRATÉGOUS TOUS EGGUS AUTÉS ENDEDUKOTAS EUPARUPHA HIPPEIS
commanders the near of her clothed elegantly horsemen
HIPPAZOMENOUS EPH HIPPÓN ***NEANISKOI*** *EPILEKTOI*[7] *PANTES*
riding upon horses young men choice all

engLXX She doted upon the sons of the Assyrians, princes and captains, her neighbours, clothed with fine linen, horsemen riding on horses; *they were* all choice young men.

Eze. 23:23 The Babylonians, and all the Chaldeans, Pekod, and Shoa, and Koa, *and* all the Assyrians with them: all of them desirable **young men**, captains and rulers, great lords and renowned, all of them riding upon horses.

YLT Sons of Babylon, and of all Chaldea, Pekod, and Shoa, and Koa, all the sons of Asshur with them, desirable **young men**, governors and prefects, all of them - rulers and proclaimed ones, riding on horses, all of them.

NEANISKOS - young man, boy – a direct translation – desirable young men

LXX *HUIOUS BABULÓNOS KAI PANTAS TOUS CHALDAIOUS PHAKOUK KAI SOUE KAI*
sons of Babylon and all the Chaldeans Phakoud and Soue and

7. See separate chapter for *EPILEKTOS* [same family as *EKLEKTOS* with not much discernible difference in meaning, except perhaps "over" or "higher" emphasis added from ***EPI*** in contrast to "outer" from of Excellence (from *EK*)] – [see Eze. 23:23 below]

HUCHOUE KAI PANTAS HUIOUS ASSURIÓN MET AUTÓN ***NEANISKOUS***
Huchoue and all sons of Assyria with them young men

EPILEKTOUS[8] *HÉGEMONAS KAI STRATÉGOUS PANTAS TRISSOUS KAI*
choice leaders and commanders all tribunes and

ONOMASTOUS HIPPEUONTAS EPH HIPPÓN
renowned riding upon horses

engLXX the children of Babylon, and all the Chaldeans, Phacuc, and Sue, and Hychue, and all the sons of the Assyrians with them; choice young men, governors and captains, all princes and renowned, riding on horses.

Eze. 30:17 The **young men** of Aven and of Pibeseth shall fall by the sword: and these *cities* shall go into captivity.

YLT The **youths** of Aven and Pi-Beseth by sword do fall, and these into captivity do go.

NEANISKOS - young man, boy – a divergent translation with "women" added – young men of specified cities shall die by the sword

LXX ***NEANISKOI*** *HÉLIOUPOLEÓS KAI BOUBASTOU EN MACHAIRA PESOUNTAI KAI*
young men of Heliopolis and Bubastum in sword shall fall and

HAI GUNAIKES EN AICHMALÓSIA POREUSONTAI
the women in captivity shall go

engLXX The youths of Heliopolis and Bubastum shall fall by the sword, and the women shall go into captivity.

8. See separate chapter for *EPILEKTOS* [same family as *EKLEKTOS* with not much discernible difference in meaning, except perhaps "over" or "higher" emphasis added from *EPI* in contrast to "outer" form of Excellence (from *EK*)] – [see Eze. 23:12 above]

Joe. 2:28 And it shall come to pass afterward, *that* I will pour out my spirit upon all flesh; and your sons and your daughters shall prophesy, your old men shall dream dreams, your **young men** shall see visions:

YLT And it hath come to pass afterwards, I do pour out My Spirit on all flesh, and prophesied have your sons and your daughters, your old men do dream dreams, your **young men** do see visions.

NEANISKOS - young man, boy – a direct translation – this is the passage Peter quotes loosely in Acts 2:17 swapping round the order at the end: the young men seeing visions first, and then the old men dreaming dreams - young men prophesied as seeing visions

LXX *KAI ESTAI META TAUTA KAI EKCHEÓ APO TOU PNEUMATOS MOU EPI PASAN*
and shall be after these and shall pour out from the spirit of me upon all

SARKA KAI PROPHÉTEUSOUSIN HOI HUIOI HUMÓN KAI HAI THUGATERES
flesh and shall prophesy the sons of you and the daughters

HUMÓN KAI HOI PRESBUTEROI HUMÓN ENUPNIA ENUPNIASTHÉSONTAI KAI HOI
of you and the elders of you dreams shall dream and the

***NEANISKOI** HUMÓN HORASEIS OPSONTAI*
young men of you visions shall see

engLXX And it shall come to pass afterward, that I will pour out of my Spirit upon all flesh; and your sons and your daughters shall prophesy, and your old men shall dream dreams, and your young men shall see visions.

Amo. 2:11 And I raised up of your sons for prophets, and of your **young men** for Nazarites. *Is it* not even thus, O ye children of Israel? Saith the LORD.

YLT And I raise of your sons for prophets, and of your **choice ones** for Nazarites, is not this true, O sons of Israel? An affirmation of Jehovah.

NEANISKOS - young man, boy – a direct translation – the Lord reminds Israel how he made young men into dedicated – consecrated – servants, but they went on to make them drunk (V.12)

LXX *KAI ELABON EK TÓN HUIÓN HUMÓN EIS PROPHÉTAS KAI EK TÓN* ***NEANISKÓN***
and raised out of the sons of you into prophets and out of the young men
HUMÓN EIS HAGIASMON MÉ OUK ESTI TAUTA HUIOI ISRAÉL LEGEI KURIOS
of you into sanctification not not is these sons of Israel says Lord

engLXX And I took of your sons for prophets, and of your young men for consecration. Are not these things so, ye sons of Israel? Saith the Lord.

Amo. 4:10 I have sent among you the pestilence after the manner of Egypt: your **young men** have I slain with the sword, and have taken away your horses; and I have made the stink of your camps to come up unto your nostrils: yet have ye not returned unto me, saith the LORD.

YLT I have sent among you pestilence by the way of Egypt, I have slain by sword your **choice ones**, with your captive horses, and I cause the stink of your camps to come up - even into your nostrils, and ye have not turned back unto Me, an affirmation of Jehovah.

NEANISKOS - young man, boy – a divergent translation with "I have made the stink of your camps to come up unto your nostrils" (KJV) or "I cause the stink of your camps to come up - even into your nostrils" (YLT), rendered as "in my wrath against you I set fire to your camps" (engLXX) – young men killed by the sword

LXX *EXAPESTEILA EIS HUMAS THANATON EN HODÓ AIGUPTOU KAI APEKTEINA EN*
I sent out into you death in way of Egypt and I killed in
RHOMPHAIA TOUS ***NEANISKOUS*** *HUMÓN META AICHMALÓSIAS HIPPÓN SOU KAI*
broadsword the young men of you with captivity horses of you and

ANÉGAGON EN PURI TAS PAREMBOLAS EN TÉ ORGÉ HUMÓN KAI OUD HÓS
I led in fire the camps in the anger of you and neither as

EPESTREPSATE PROS ME LEGEI KURIOS
ye returned to me says Lord

engLXX I sent pestilence among you by the way of Egypt, and slew your young men with the sword, together with thy horses that were taken captive; and in my wrath against you I set fire to your camps: yet not even thus did ye return to me, saith the Lord.

Amo. 8:13 In that day shall the fair virgins and **young men** faint for thirst.

NEANISKOS - young man, boy – a direct translation – young men and virgins will faint with thirst

LXX *EN TÉ HÉMERA EKEINÉ EKLEIPSOUSIN HAI PARTHENOI HAI KALAI KAI HOI*
in the day that shall dissipate the virgins the good and the

NEANISKOI *EN DIPSEI*
young men in thirst

engLXX In that day shall the fair virgins and the young men faint for thirst;

Zec. 9:17 For how great *is* his goodness, and how great *is* his beauty! Corn shall make the **young men** cheerful, and new wine the maids.

YLT For what His goodness! And what His beauty! Corn the **young men**, and new wine the virgins - make fruitful!

NEANISKOS - young man, boy – a divergent translation with "For how great *is* his goodness, and how great *is* his beauty!" (KJV) or "For what His goodness! And what His beauty!" (YLT), rendered as "For if he has anything good, and if he has anything fair" (engLXX) – young men given corn: perhaps with new wine mentioned for the virgins, "corn" may be a reference to a type of beer

LXX *HOTI EI TI AGATHON AUTOU KAI EI TI KALON PAR AUTOU SITOS* ***NEANISKOIS***
since if any good of him and if any good from him corn for young men

KAI OINOS EUÓDIAZÓN EIS PARTHENOUS
and wine being fragrant into virgins

engLXX For if he has anything good, and if he has anything fair, the young *men shall have* corn, and *there shall be* fragrant wine to the virgins.

4 - BAR

From BARAR - to clean. to purify

Translated into Greek in the LXX

EKLEKTOS		**2**		**Song of Songs 6:9; Song of Songs 6:10**
KATHAROS	(clean, pure)	2		
AMEMPTOS	(blameless)	1		
EUTHUS	(straight, direct)	1		
TÉLAUGÉS	(far shining)	1	aNT	
	TOTAL	7		

Translated into English - Both KJV related

Ys Conc.	Count	Ss Conc. No. H 1305	Count
choice	1	clean	3
clean	3	pure	2
clear	1	choice	1
pure	2	clear	1
TOTAL	7	TOTAL	7

Refs	**Text quotes KJV unless otherwise stated**
Job 11:4	For thou hast said, My doctrine *is* pure, and I am **clean** in thine eyes.
YLT	And thou sayest, 'Pure *is* my discourse, And **clean** I have been in Thine eyes.'

AMEMPTOS – blameless, without reproach - A divergent translation with "doctrine" (KJV) or "discourse" (YLT), rendered as "works" (engLXX) - "clean" in the sense of free from wrongdoing, means "blameless"

LXX	*MÉ GAR LEGE HOTI KATHAROS EIMI TOIS ERGOIS KAI* ***AMEMPTOS*** *ENANTION AUTOU* not for say since clean I am with the works and blameless before him
engLXX	For say not, I am pure in my works, and blameless before him.
Psa. 19:8	The statutes of the LORD *are* right, rejoicing the heart: the commandment of the LORD *is* **pure**, enlightening the eyes.

TÉLAUGÉS aNT – far shining, bright - A loose translation in that "pure" (KJV) is given as "bright shining" (LXX-inter) - Perhaps in the mention of the commandment "enlightens the eyes", the idea of purity is expressed by how much it was enlightening by "bright shining": in that sense it is not loose, but expressive of the connection with pure in ability to shine

LXX **18:8**	*TA DIKAIÓMATA KURIOU EUTHEA EUPHRAINONTA KARDIAN HÉ ENTOLÉ KURIOU*
LXX-inter	the ordinances of Lord straight making glad heart the commands of Lord
	TÉLAUGÉS *PHÓTIZOUSA OPHTHALMOUS* far shining lighting eyes
engLXX	The ordinances of the Lord are right, rejoicing the heart: the commandment of the Lord is bright, enlightening the eyes.
Psa. 24:4	He that hath clean hands, and a **pure** heart; who hath not lifted up his soul unto vanity, nor sworn deceitfully.

KATHAROS – clean, pure - A direct translation - The whole verse points to the cleanness of heart: pure

LXX 23:4 *ATHÓOS CHERSI KAI* ***KATHAROS*** *TÉ KARDIA HOS OUK ELABEN EPI MATAIÓ TÉN*
scot free hands and pure the heart who not taken upon vain the

PSUCHÉN AUTOU KAI OUK ÓMOSEN EPI DOLÓ TÓ PLÉSION AUTOU
soul of him and not swear upon cunning to the near of him

engLXX He that is innocent in his hands and pure in his heart; who has not lifted up his soul to vanity, nor sworn deceitfully to his neighbour.

Psa. 73:1 [A Psalm of Asaph] Truly God *is* good to Israel, *even* to such as are of a **clean** heart.

EUTHUS – straight, direct - A direct translation - A clean heart is a straight heart: frank, true

LXX 72:1 *PSALMOS TÓ ASAPH HÓS AGATHOS HO THEOS TÓ ISRAÉL TOIS* ***EUTHESI*** *KARDIA*
Psalm to the Asaph how good the God to the Israel to the straight with heart

engLXX A Psalm for Asaph. How good is God to Israel, to the upright in heart!

Pro. 14:4 Where no oxen *are*, the crib *is* **clean**: but much increase *is* by the strength of the ox.

KATHAROS – clean, pure - A direct translation - where there is no activity, the place of dwelling is without dirt – it is clean and empty of "produce"

LXX *HOU MÉ EISI BOES PHATNAI* ***KATHARAI*** *HOU DE POLLA GENNÉMATA PHANERA*
where no are oxen crib clean where but much produce manifest

BOOS ISCHUS
ox strong

engLXX Where no oxen are, the cribs are clean; but where there is abundant produce, the strength of the ox is apparent.

Sng. 6:9 My dove, my undefiled is *but* one; she *is* the *only* one of her mother, she *is* the **choice** *one* of her that bare her. The daughters saw her, and blessed her; *yea*, the queens and the concubines, and they praised her.

YLT One is my dove, my perfect one, one she *is* of her mother, the **choice one** she *is* of her that bare her, daughters saw, and pronounce her happy, queens and concubines, and they praise her.

NKJV My dove, my perfect one, is the only one, the only one of her mother, the **favorite** of the one who bore her. The daughters saw her and called her blessed, the queens and the concubines, and they praised her.

NASB *But* my dove, my perfect one, is unique: she is her mother's only *daughter*; she is the **pure** *child* of the one who bore her. The maidens saw her and called her blessed, the queens and the concubines *also*, and they praised her, *saying*,

NIV but my dove, my perfect one, is unique, the only daughter of her mother, the **favourite** of the one who bore her. The young women saw her and called her blessed; the queens and concubines praised her.

NLT I would still choose my dove, my perfect one— the **favorite** of her mother, dearly loved by the one who bore her. The young women see her and praise her; even queens and royal concubines sing her praises:

EKLEKTOS – A direct translation - "undefiled" or "perfect", she is thus to her mother "choice": excellent and highest quality

LXX **6:8** *MIA ESTI PERISTERA MOU TELEIA MOU MIA ESTI TÉ MÉTRI AUTÉS* ***EKLEKTÉ***
my is dove of me perfect of me my is to the mother of her choice

ESTI TÉ TEKOUSÉ AUTÉN EIDOSAN AUTÉN THUGATERES KAI MAKARIOUSIN
is the engender her saw her daughters and bless

AUTÉN BASILISSAI KAI GE PALLAKAI AINESOUSIN AUTÉN
her queens and indeed concubines shall praise her

engLXX My dove, my perfect one is one; she is the *only* one of her mother; she is the choice of her that bore her. The daughters saw her, and the queens will pronounce her blessed, yea, and the concubines, and they will praise her.

Sng. 6:10 Who *is* she *that* looketh forth as the morning, fair as the moon, **clear** as the sun, *and* terrible as *an army* with banners?

YLT 'Who *is* this that is looking forth as morning, fair as the moon - **clear** as the sun, awe-inspiring as bannered hosts?'

NKJV Who is she *who* looks forth as the morning, fair as the moon, **clear** as the sun, awesome as *an army* with banners?

NASB 'Who is this that grows like the dawn, as beautiful as the full moon, as **pure** as the sun, as awesome as an army with banners?'

NIV Who is this that appears like the dawn, fair as the moon, **bright** as the sun, majestic as the stars in procession?

NLT "Who is this, arising like the dawn, as fair as the moon, as **bright** as the sun, as majestic as an army with billowing banners?"

EKLEKTOS – A direct translation - The sun is the pure light, as it follows the moon in contrast: "clear" or "choice": the best there is

LXX **6:9** *TIS AUTÉ HÉ EKKUPTOUSA HÓSEI ORTHROS KALÉ HÓS SELÉNÉ* ***EKLEKTÉ*** *HÓS*
who she the looking out as dawn fair as moon choice as

HO HÉLIOS THAMBOS HÓS TETAGMENAI
the sun amazing as set in array [soldiers]

engLXX Who is this that looks forth as the morning, fair as the moon, choice as the sun, terrible as *armies* set in array?

5 - BARAR

Translated into Greek in the LXX

EKLEKTOS		**8**	***EKLEKTOS*:**
EKLEGÓ	(to pick, choose)	2	**2 Samuel 22:27a; 2 Samuel 22:27b**
KATHAROS	(clean, pure)	2	**1 Chronicles 7:40; 1 Chronicles 9:22**
PUROÓ	(burn up, purify)	2	**Nehemiah 5:18; Psalm 18:26a**
APHORIZÓ	(to define, determine)	1	**Psalm 18:26b; Isaiah 49:2**
DIAKRINÓ	(to decide, judge)	1	
PARASKEUAZÓ	(make ready)	1	
NOT in LXX		1	
TOTAL		18	

Translated into English - Both KJV related

Ys Conc. = to purify (P.165)	Count	Ss Conc. No. H 1305	Count
manifest	1	pure	5
purge out	1	choice	2

	choice	2	chosen	2
	chosen	2	clean	2
	polished	1	clearly	1
	pure	1	manifest	1
	clearly	1	bright	1
	be clean	1	purge out	1
Partic.	pure	2	polished	1
	purge	1	purge	1
	cleanse	1	purified	1
	make bright	1		
	be purified	1		
	shew self pure	2		
	TOTAL	18	TOTAL	18

Refs	**Text quotes KJV unless otherwise stated**
2Sa. 22:27a	With the **pure** thou wilt shew thyself pure; and with the froward thou wilt shew thyself unsavoury.
YLT	With the **pure** Thou shewest Thyself pure, and with the perverse Thou shewest Thyself a wrestler.
NKJV	With the **pure** You will show Yourself pure; and with the devious You will show Yourself shrewd.
NASB	With the **pure** You show Yourself pure, and with the perverted You show Yourself astute.
NIV	to the **pure** you show yourself pure, but to the devious you show yourself shrewd.
NLT	To the **pure** you show yourself pure, but to the crooked you show yourself shrewd.

EKLEKTOS – a direct translation – the pure, the excellent

LXX	*KAI*	*META*	***EKLEKTOU***	*EKLEKTOS*	*ESÉ*	*KAI*	*META*	*STREBLOU*	*STREBLÓTHÉSÉ*
2Ki.22:27a	and	with	choice	choice	I shall be	and	with	crooked	crooked

engLXX and with the excellent thou wilt be excellent, and with the froward thou will be froward.

2Sa. 22:27b With the pure thou wilt shew thyself **pure**; and with the froward thou wilt shew thyself unsavoury.

YLT With the pure Thou shewest Thyself **pure**, and with the perverse Thou shewest Thyself a wrestler.

NKJV With the pure You will show Yourself **pure**; and with the devious You will show Yourself shrewd.

NASB With the pure You show Yourself **pure**, and with the perverted You show Yourself astute.

NIV to the pure you show yourself **pure**, but to the devious you show yourself shrewd.

NLT To the pure you show yourself **pure**, but to the crooked you show yourself shrewd.

EKLEKTOS - a direct translation – the pure, the excellent

LXX	*KAI*	*META*	*EKLEKTOU*	***EKLEKTOS***	*ESÉ*	*KAI*	*META*	*STREBLOU*	*STREBLÓTHÉSÉ*
2Ki.22:27b	and	with	choice	choice	I shall be	and	with	crooked	crooked

engLXX and with the excellent thou wilt be excellent, and with the froward thou will be froward.

1Ch. 7:40 All these *were* the children of Asher, heads of *their* father's house, **choice** *and* mighty men of valour, chief of the princes. And the number throughout the genealogy of them that were apt to the war *and* to battle *was* twenty and six thousand men.

YLT All these *are* sons of Asher, heads of the house of the fathers, **chosen ones**, mighty in valour, heads of the princes, with their genealogy, for the host, for battle, their number *is* twenty and six thousand men.

NKJV All these *were* the children of Asher, heads of *their* fathers' houses, **choice men**, mighty men of valor, chief leaders. And they were recorded by genealogies among the army fit for battle; their number *was* twenty-six thousand.

NASB All these *were* the sons of Asher, heads of the fathers' houses, **choice** and mighty men of valor, heads of the princes. And the number of them enrolled by genealogy for service in war was 26,000 men.

NIV All these were descendants of Asher – heads of families, **choice men**, brave warriors and outstanding leaders. The number of men ready for battle, as listed in their genealogy, was 26,000.

NLT Each of these descendants of Asher was the head of an ancestral clan. They were all **select men**—mighty warriors and outstanding leaders. The total number of men available for military service was 26,000, as listed in their genealogical records.

EKLEKTOS – a divergent translation with "throughout the genealogy" (KJV) or "with their genealogy" (YLT), not rendered – choice, mighty men of valour

LXX *PANTES HOUTOI HUIOI ASÉR PANTES ARCHONTES PATRIÓN* ***EKLEKTOI***
all these sons of Aser and chiefs of families choice

ISCHUROI DUNAMEI ARCHONTES HÉGOUMENOI HO ARITHMOS AUTÓN EIS
strong powerful chiefs leading the number of them into

PARATAXIN TOU POLEMEIN ARITHMOS AUTÓN ANDRES EIKOSIEX CHILIADES
array of the war number of them men twenty-six thousand

engLXX All these *were* the sons of Aser, all heads of families, choice, mighty men, chief leaders: their number for battle array- their number *was* twenty-six thousand men.

1Ch. 9:22 All these *which were* **chosen** to be porters in the gates *were* two hundred and twelve. These were reckoned by their genealogy in their villages, whom David and Samuel the seer did ordain in their set office.

YLT All of those who are **chosen** for gatekeepers at the thresholds *are* two hundred and twelve; they *are* in their villages, by their genealogy; they whom David and Samuel the seer appointed in their office.

NKJV All those **chosen** as gatekeepers *were* two hundred and twelve. They were recorded by their genealogy, in their villages. David and Samuel the seer had appointed them to their trusted office.

NASB All these who were **chosen** to be gatekeepers at the thresholds were 212. These were enrolled by genealogy in their villages, whom David and Samuel the seer appointed in their office of trust.

NIV Altogether, those **chosen** to be gatekeepers at the thresholds numbered 212. They were registered by genealogy in their villages. The gatekeepers had been assigned to their positions of trust by David and Samuel the seer.

NLT In all, there were 212 gatekeepers in those days, and they were **listed** according to the genealogies in their villages. David and Samuel the seer had appointed their ancestors because they were reliable men.

EKLEKTOS – a divergent translation with "in their villages" (KJV) rendered as "in their courts" (engLXX) – Ys in his Conc. places the "chosen" and that of 1Ch. 16:41 (see below) under the header "*to purify*" BARAR P. 165: The use of BARAR here as opposed to BACHAR means purification was involved: the translator two chapters earlier is clearly following the pattern of the LXX of quality for the word *EKLEKTOS* [see 7:40 above] and uses a well used word for "chosen" seven chapters later [see 16:41 below]: with a preparation involved due to the root "to purify" from barar the "choosing" here is not independent of quality: they are clean

LXX *PANTES HOI **EKLEKTOI** EPI TÉS PULÉS EN TAIS PULAIS DIAKOSIOI KAI*
all the choice upon the gate in the gates two-hundred and

DEKADUO HOUTOI EN TAIS AULAIS AUTÓN HO KATALOCHISMOS AUTÓN
twelve these in the courts of them the distribution of them

TOUTOUS ESTÉSE DAUID KAI SAMOUÉL HO BLEPÓN TÉ PISTEI AUTÓN
these established David and Samuel the seer the trust of them

engLXX All the chosen porters in the gates *were* two hundred and twelve, these *were* in their courts, *this was* their distribution: these David and Samuel the seer established in their charge.

1Ch. 16:41 And with them Heman and Jeduthun, and the rest that were **chosen**, who were expressed by name, to give thanks to the LORD, because his mercy *endureth* for ever;

YLT And with them *are* Heman and Jeduthun, and the rest of those **chosen**, who were defined by name, to give thanks to Jehovah, for to the age *is* His kindness,

NKJV and with them Heman and Jeduthun and the rest who were **chosen**, who were designated by name, to give thanks to the LORD, because His mercy *endures* forever;

NASB With them *were* Heman and Jeduthun, and the rest who were **chosen**, who were designated by name, to give thanks to the LORD, because His lovingkindness is everlasting.

NIV With them were Heman and Jeduthun and the rest of those **chosen** and designated by name to give thanks to the LORD, 'for his love endures for ever.'

NLT David also **appointed** Heman, Jeduthun, and the others chosen by name to give thanks to the LORD, for "his faithful love endures forever."

EKLEGÓ - to pick, choose, elect – a direct translation – Ys in his Conc. places the "chosen" and that of 1Ch. 9:22 (see above) under the header "*to purify*" BARAR P. 165: the purified, then picked by name to the job of praising God

LXX *KAI MET AUTOU AIMAN KAI IDITHOUN KAI HOI LOIPOI* ***EKLEGENTES*** *EP*
and with of him Aiman and idithon and the rest chosen out upon

ONOMATOS TOU AINEIN TON KURION HOTI EIS TON AIÓNA TO ELEOS AUTOU
name of the to praise the Lord since into the ages the mercy of him

engLXX And with him *were* Aeman and Idithun, and the rest chosen out by name to praise the Lord, for his mercy *endures* for ever.

Neh. 5:18 Now *that* which was prepared *for me* daily *was* one ox *and* six **choice** sheep; also fowls were prepared for me, and once in ten days store of all sorts of wine: yet for all this required not I the bread of the governor, because the bondage was heavy upon this people.

YLT and that which hath been prepared for one day *is* one ox, six **fat** sheep, also fowls have been prepared for me, and once in ten days of all wines abundantly, and with this, the bread of the governor I have not sought, for heavy is the service on this people.

NKJV Now *that* which was prepared *for me* daily *was* one ox *and* six **choice** Sheep; also fowl were prepared for me, and once every ten days an abundance of all kinds of wine; yet in spite of this I did not demand the governor's provisions, because the bondage was heavy on this people.

NASB Now that which was prepared for each day was one ox *and* six **choice** sheep, also birds were prepared for me; and once in ten days all sorts of wine *were furnished* in abundance. Yet for all this I did not demand the governor's food *allowance*, because the servitude was heavy on this people.

NIV Each day one ox, six **choice** sheep and some poultry were prepared for me, and every ten days an abundant supply of wine of all kinds. In spite of all this, I never demanded the food allotted to the governor, because the demands were heavy on these people.

NLT The provisions I paid for each day included one ox, six **choice** sheep or goats, and a large number of poultry. And every ten days we needed a large supply of all kinds of wine. Yet I refused to claim the governor's food allowance because the people already carried a heavy burden.

EKLEKTOS – a divergent translation with "also fowls were prepared for me" (KJV) rendered as "and a goat" (engLXX) or, just added – six fat sheep meaning they are quality: choice: how Ys saw "fat" from "pure, clean/to purify" i.e. from the root meaning of BARAR is unclear, but equally "choice", which can be seen from something purified, made clean, so it can from an animal raised to be good to eat by fattening it up

LXX *KAI ÉN GINOMENON EIS HÉMERAN MIAN MOSCHOS EIS KAI PROBATA EX*
and in coming into day one calf into and sheep out of

EKLEKTA *KAI CHIMAROS EGINONTO MOI KAI ANAMESON DEKA HÉMERÓN EN*
choice and male goat came to me and in midst ten days in

PASIN OINOS TÓ PLÉTHEI KAI SUN TOUTOIS ARTOUS TÉS BIAS OUK EZÉTÉSA
all wine for the multitude and with these bread of the force not seek

HOTI BAREIA HÉ DOULEIA EPI TON LAON TOUTON
since heavy the slavery upon the people this

engLXX And there came *to me* for one day one calf, and I had six choice sheep and a goat; and every ten days wine in abundance of all sorts: yet with these I required not the bread of extortion, because the bondage was heavy upon this people.

Job 33:3 My words *shall be of* the uprightness of my heart: and my lips shall utter knowledge **clearly**.
YLT Of the uprightness of my heart *are* my sayings, and knowledge have my lips **clearly** spoken.

KATHAROS - clean, pure, clear – a direct [remember, this does not mean literal] translation: it means the original can be read in a sense that is possible to see in the rendered – clear knowledge, truth is uttered in clean and untarnished words

LXX *KATHARA MOU HÉ KARDIA RÉMASI SUNESIS DE CHEILEÓN MOU* ***KATHARA*** *NOÉSEI*
clean of me the heart sayings understanding but lips of me clean shall consider

engLXX My heart *shall be found* pure by *my* words; and the understanding of my lips shall meditate purity.

Psa. 18:26a With the **pure** thou wilt shew thyself pure; and with the froward thou wilt shew thyself froward.
YLT With the **pure** Thou showest Thyself pure, and with the perverse showest Thyself a wrestler,
NKJV With the **pure** You will show Yourself pure; and with the devious You will show Yourself shrewd.
NASB With the **pure** You show Yourself pure, and with the crooked You show Yourself astute.
NIV to the **pure** you show yourself pure, but to the devious you show yourself shrewd.
NLT To the **pure** you show yourself pure, but to the crooked you show yourself shrewd.

EKLEKTOS – a direct translation – the pure are the excellent: the choice of the world

	LXX	*KAI META* ***EKLEKTOU*** *EKLEKTOS ESÉ KAI META STREBLOU DIASTREPSEIS*
	17:26a	and with choice choice shall be and with crooked shall turn aside from
	engLXX	And with the excellent *man* thou wilt be excellent; and with the perverse thou wilt shew frowardness.
Psa. 18:26b		With the pure thou wilt shew thyself **pure**; and with the froward thou wilt shew thyself froward.
	YLT	With the pure Thou showest Thyself **pure**, and with the perverse showest Thyself a wrestler,
	NKJV	With the pure You will show Yourself **pure**; and with the devious You will show Yourself shrewd.
	NASB	With the pure You show Yourself **pure**, and with the crooked You show Yourself astute.
	NIV	to the pure you show yourself **pure**, but to the devious you show yourself shrewd.
	NLT	To the pure you show yourself **pure**, but to the crooked you show yourself shrewd.

EKLEKTOS - a direct translation – God shows Himself pure to those who are

	LXX	*KAI META EKLEKTOU* ***EKLEKTOS*** *ESÉ KAI META STREBLOU DIASTREPSEIS*
	17:26b	and with choice choice shall be and with crooked shall turn aside from
	engLXX	And with the excellent *man* thou wilt be excellent; and with the perverse thou wilt shew frowardness.
Ecc. 3:18		I said in mine heart concerning the estate of the sons of men, that God might **manifest** them, and that they might see that they themselves are beasts.
	YLT	I said in my heart concerning the matter of the sons of man that God might **cleanse** them, so as to see that they themselves *are* beasts.
	NKJV	I said in my heart, "Concerning the estate of the sons of men, God **tests** them, that they may see that they themselves are *like* beasts."
	NASB	I said to myself concerning the sons of men, "God has surely **tested** them in order for them to see that they are but beasts."
	NIV	I also said to myself, 'As for humans, God **tests** them so that they may see that they are like the animals.
	NLT	I also thought about the human condition—how God **proves** to people that they are like animals.

DIAKRINÓ - to decide, judge, distinguish – a divergent translation with "the estate of the sons of men" (KJV or "the matter of the sons of men" (YLT), rendered as "the speech of the sons of men" (engLXX) – God's examination of the life of someone reveals things, as they are brought to His light, and thereby cleansed in recognising they are "beasts": the Gk. has it as judge, but the manifestation itself is a form of judgment by enabling the sight for men to see themselves

LXX *EIPA EGÓ EN KARDIA MOU PERI LALIAS HUIÓN TOU ANTHRÓPOU HOTI*
said I in heart of me about talk of sons of the man since

DIAKRINEI *AUTOUS HO THEOS KAI TOU DEIXAI HOTI AUTOI KTÉNÉ EISI*
judge them the God and the to show since they beasts are

engLXX I said in my heart, concerning the speech of the sons of man, God will judge them, and that to shew that they are beasts.

Isa. 49:2 And he hath made my mouth like a sharp sword; in the shadow of his hand hath he hid me, and made me a **polished** shaft; in his quiver hath he hid me;

YLT And he maketh my mouth as a sharp sword, in the shadow of His hand He hath hid me, and He maketh me for a **clear** arrow, in His quiver He hath hid me.

NKJV And He has made My mouth like a sharp sword; in the shadow of His hand He has hidden Me, and made Me a **polished** shaft; in His quiver He has hidden Me."

NASB He has made My mouth like a sharp sword, in the shadow of His hand He has concealed Me; and He has also made Me a **select** arrow, He has hidden Me in His quiver.

NIV He made my mouth like a sharpened sword, in the shadow of his hand he hid me; he made me into a **polished** arrow and concealed me in his quiver.

NLT He made my words of judgment as sharp as a sword. He has hidden me in the shadow of his hand. I am like a **sharp** arrow in his quiver.

EKLEKTOS – a direct translation – A highly cleaned shaft of an arrow is made to run smooth and thus becomes one of the best arrows: choice

LXX *KAI ETHÉKE TO STOMA MOU HÓS MACHAIRAN OXEIAN KAI HUPO TÉN SKEPÉN*
and made the mouth of me as sword sharp and under the protection

TÉS CHEIROS AUTOU EKRUPSE ME ETHÉKE ME HÓS BELOS ***EKLEKTON*** *KAI EN*
of the hand of him hid me made me as arrow choice and in

TÉ PHARETRA AUTOU EKRUPSE ME
the quiver of him hid me

engLXX and he has made my mouth as a sharp sword, and he has hid me under the shadow of his hand; he has made me as a choice shaft, and he has hid me in his quiver;

Isa. 52:11 Depart ye, depart ye, go ye out from thence, touch no unclean *thing*; go ye out of the midst of her; be ye **clean**, that bear the vessels of the LORD.

YLT Turn aside, turn aside, go out thence, the unclean touch not, go out from her midst, be ye **pure**, who are bearing the weapons of Jehovah.

APHORIZÓ - to define, determine, set apart – a direct translation – to be kept clean and pure by separating in having determined what is and is not holy

LXX *APOSTÉTE APOSTÉTE EXELTHATE EKEITHEN KAI AKATHARTOU MÉ HAPSÉSTHE*
leave leave go forth from thence and unclean not touch

EXELTHETE EK MESOU AUTÉS ***APHORISTHÉTE*** *HOI PHERONTES TA SKEUÉ KURIOU*
go forth out of midst of her separate ye the bearers the vessels of Lord

engLXX Depart ye, depart, go out from thence, and touch not the unclean thing; go ye out from the midst of her; separate yourselves, ye that bear the vessels of the Lord.

Jer. 4:11 — At that time shall it be said to this people and to Jerusalem, A dry wind of the high places in the wilderness toward the daughter of my people, not to fan, nor to **cleanse**,

YLT — At that time it is said of this people, and of Jerusalem: 'A dry wind of high places in the wilderness,' The way of the daughter of My people, (not for winnowing, nor for **cleansing**,)

KATHAROS - clean, pure, clear – a divergent translation with "A dry wind of the high places" (KJV) or "A dry wind of high places" (YLT), rendered as "a spirit of error" (engLXX) – the wind being sent from the Lord is not a light hot breeze useful for drying cut crops, cleaning up by blowing away the chaff, but instead a destructive forceful wind. Well portrayed in the NLT: "not a gentle breeze useful for winnowing grain. [12]It is a roaring blast sent by me! Now I will pronounce your destruction!"

LXX — *EN TÓ KAIRÓ EKEINÓ EROUSI TÓ LAÓ TOUTÓ KAI TÉ HIEROUSALÉM PNEUMA PLANÉSEÓS EN*
In the season that shall say to the people this and the Jerusalem spirit of delusion in

TÉ ERÉMÓ HODOS TÉS THUGATROS TOU LAOU MOU OUK EIS ***KATHARON*** *OUD EIS HAGION*
the desert way of the daughter of the people of me not into purity nor into holiness

engLXX — At that time they shall say to this people and to Jerusalem, *There is* a spirit of error in the wilderness: the way of the daughter of my people is not to purity, nor to holiness.

Jer. 51:11 — Make **bright** the arrows; gather the shields: the LORD hath raised up the spirit of the kings of the Medes: for his device *is* against Babylon, to destroy it; because it *is* the vengeance of the LORD, the vengeance of his temple.

YLT — **Cleanse** ye the arrows, fill the shields, stirred up hath Jehovah the spirit of the kings of Madia, for against Babylon His device *is* to destroy it, for the vengeance of Jehovah it *is*, the vengeance of His temple.

PARASKEUAZÓ – to make ready, prepare – a divergent translation with "temple" (KJV) rendered as "people" (engLXX) – cleaning or polishing the arrows, prepares them for use: this causes them to shine and reflect light and thus appear bright

LXX 28:11

PARASKEUAZETE *TA TOXEUMATA PLÉROUTE TAS PHARETRAS ÉGEIRE KURIOS TO*
prepare ye the arrows fill ye the quivers arouse Lord the

PNEUMA BASILEÓS MÉDÓN HOTI EIS BABULÓNA HÉ ORGÉ AUTOU TOU EXOLOTHREUSAI
spirit of king of Medes since into Babylon the anger of him of the to utterly destroy

AUTÉN HOTI EKDIKÉSIS KURIOU ESTIN EKDIKÉSIS LAOU AUTOU ESTIN
her since vengeance of Lord it is vengeance of people of him it is

engLXX Prepare the arrows; fill the quivers: the Lord has stirred up the spirit of the king of the Medes: for his wrath is against Babylon, to destroy it utterly; for it is the Lord's vengeance, it is the vengeance of his people.

Eze. 20:38 And I **will purge out** from among you the rebels, and them that transgress against me: I will bring them forth out of the country where they sojourn, and they shall not enter into the land of Israel: and ye shall know that I *am* the LORD.

YLT And **cleared out** from you the rebels, and them transgressing against Me, from the land of their sojournings I bring them out, and unto the land of Israel they come not, and ye have known that I *am* Jehovah.

NKJV I **will purge** the rebels from among you, and those who transgress against Me; I will bring them out of the country where they sojourn, but they shall not enter the land of Israel. Then you will know that I *am* the LORD.

NASB and I **will purge** from you the rebels and those who transgress against Me; I will bring them out of the land where they sojourn, but they will not enter the land of Israel. Thus you will know that I am the LORD.

NIV I **will purge** you of those who revolt and rebel against me. Although I will bring them out of the land where they are living, yet they will not enter the land of Israel. Then you will know that I am the LORD.

NLT I **will purge** you of all those who rebel and revolt against me. I will bring them out of the countries where they are in exile, but they will never enter the land of Israel. Then you will know that I am the LORD.

EKLEGÓ - to pick, choose, elect – a divergent translation with an added "Lord" (engLXX) – to clean, purge out, pick out the wicked from the land of Israel

LXX *KAI* ***EKLEXÓ*** *EX HUMÓN TOUS ASEBEIS KAI TOUS APHESTÉKOTAS DIOTI EK*
and I shall choose out of you the impious and the revolters because | out of

TÉS PAROIKESIAS AUTÓN EXAXÓ AUTOUS KAI EIS TÉN GÉN TOU ISRAÉL OUK
the sojourning of them I will lead them and into the land of the Israel not

EISELEUSONTAI KAI EPIGNÓSESTHE DIOTI EGÓ KURIOS KURIOS
shall enter and shall know because I Lord Lord

engLXX And I will separate from among you the ungodly and the revolters; for I will lead them forth out of their place of sojourning, and they shall not enter into the land of Israel: and ye shall know that I am the Lord, *even* the Lord.

Dan. 11:35 And *some* of them of understanding shall fall, to try them, and to **purge**, and to make *them* white, *even* to the time of the end: because *it is* yet for a time appointed.

YLT And some of the teachers do stumble for refining by them, and for **purifying**, and for making white - till the end of the time, for *it is* yet for a time appointed.

PUROÓ - burn up, purify, purge – a divergent translation with "to make *them* white" (KJV) not rendered [see 12:10 below where it is] – those understanding will be purified by fire of tribulation before the end [see comment at 12:10 below]

LXX *KAI APO TÓN SUNIENTÓN ASTHENÉSOUSI TOU* ***PURÓSAI*** *AUTOUS KAI TOU*
and from of the perceiving shall weaken of the to purify them and of the

EKLEXASTHAI KAI TOU APOKALUPHTHÉNAI HEÓS KAIROU PERAS HOTI ETI EIS KAIRON
to choose and of the to be uncovered until season complete since yet into season

engLXX And *some* of them that understand shall fall, to try them as with fire, and to test *them*, and that they may be manifested at the time of the end, for the matter *is* yet for a *set* time.

Dan. 12:10 Many shall be **purified**, and made white, and tried; but the wicked shall do wickedly: and none of the wicked shall understand; but the wise shall understand.

YLT **Purify** themselves, yea, make themselves white, yea, refined are many: and the wicked have done wickedly, and none of the wicked understand, and those acting wisely do understand;

PUROÓ - burn up, purify, purge – a loose translation as "with fire" (engLXX) is added – to be made clean, purified by the fire of tribulation [the prophetic end time season of tribulation understood immediately before the 2nd coming e.g. "after the tribulation of those days . . . the Son of Man will appear" Matthew 24:29-30 NKJV - see also 11:35 above]

LXX *EKLEGÓSI KAI EKLEUKANTHÓSI KAI* ***PURÓTHÓSI*** *KAI HAGIASTHÓSI POLLOI KAI*
shall be chosen and whitened and purified and sanctified many and

ANOMÉSÓSIN ANOMOI KAI OU SUNÉSOUSI PANTES ANOMOI KAI HOI NOÉMONES SUNÉSOUSI
shall act lawlessly lawless and not understand all lawless and the Intelligent shall understand

engLXX Many must be tested, and thoroughly whitened, and tried with fire, and sanctified; but the transgressors shall transgress: and none of the transgressors shall understand; but the wise shall understand.

Zep. 3:9 For then will I turn to the people a **pure** language, that they may all call upon the name of the LORD, to serve him with one consent.

YLT For then do I turn unto peoples a **pure** lip, to call all of them by the name of Jehovah, to serve Him *with* one shoulder.

NOT in LXX – a divergent translation as the word in view is not translated

LXX *HOTI TOTE METASTREPSÓ EPI LAOUS GLÓSSAN EIS GENEAN AUTÉS TOU EPIKALEISTHAI*
since then I turn upon people tongue into generation of her of the to call upon

PANTAS TO ONOMA KURIOU TOU DOULEUEIN AUTÓ HUPO ZUGON HENA
all the name of Lord of the to serve him under yoke one

engLXX For then will I turn to the peoples a tongue for her generation, that all may call on the name of the Lord, to serve him under one yoke.

6 - BARI

Translated into Greek in the LXX

EKLEKTOS		**9**		***EKLEKTOS*:**
ASTEIOS	(handsome)	1		**Genesis 41:2; Genesis 41:4; Genesis 41:5**
ISCHUROS	(strong, mighty)	1		**Genesis 41:7; Genesis 41:18; Genesis 41:20**
PACHUS	(stout)	1	aNT	**1 Kings 4:23; Habakkuk 1:16**
STEREÓMA	(firm)	1		**Zechariah 11:16**
TOTAL		13		

Translated into English - Both KJV related

Ys Conc.	Count	Ss Conc. No. H 1277	Count
fat	1+4[1]	fat	5
fatter	1	rank (Old Eng. = complete)	2
firm	1	fatfleshed	2
plenteous	1	firm	1

1 See Ys Conc. P.331

rank	2	fatter	1
fatfleshed	2	fed	1
fed	1[2]	plenteous	1
TOTAL	13	TOTAL	13

Refs		**Text quotes KJV unless otherwise stated**
Gen. 41:2		And, behold, there came up out of the river seven well favoured kine and **fatfleshed**; and they fed in a meadow.
	YLT	and lo, from the River coming up are seven kine, of fair appearance, and **fat** *in* flesh, and they feed among the reeds;
	NKJV	Suddenly there came up out of the river seven cows, fine looking and **fat**; and they fed in the meadow.
	NASB	And lo, from the Nile there came up seven cows, sleek and **fat**; and they grazed in the marsh grass.
	NIV	when out of the river there came up seven cows, sleek and **fat**, and they grazed among the reeds.
	NLT	In his dream he saw seven **fat**, healthy cows come up out of the river and begin grazing in the marsh grass.

EKLEKTOS – a direct translation – the seven fat cows that came out of the Nile in Pharaoh's dream (V.1)

LXX *KAI IDOU HÓSPER EK TOU POTAMOU ANEBAINON HEPTA BOES KALAI TÓ EIDEI*
and look even as out of the river came up seven oxen fair to the sight

*KAI **EKLEKTAI** TAIS SARXI KAI EBOSKONTO EN TÓ AXEI*
and choice with the flesh and grazing in the sedge

2. See Ys Conc. P.339

	engLXX	And lo, there came up as it were out of the river seven cows, fair in appearance, and choice of flesh, and they fed on the sedge.
Gen. 41:4		And the ill favoured and leanfleshed kine did eat up the seven well favoured and **fat** kine. So Pharaoh awoke.
	YLT	and the kine of bad appearance and lean *in* flesh eat up the seven kine of fair appearance, and **fat** - and Pharaoh awaketh.
	NKJV	And the ugly and gaunt cows ate up the seven fine looking and **fat** cows. So Pharaoh awoke.
	NASB	The ugly and gaunt cows ate up the seven sleek and **fat** cows. Then Pharaoh awoke.
	NIV	And the cows that were ugly and gaunt ate up the seven sleek, **fat** cows. Then Pharaoh woke up.
	NLT	Then the scrawny, thin cows ate the seven healthy, **fat** cows! At this point in the dream, Pharaoh woke up.

EKLEKTOS – a divergent translation with the added "seven" for the ill favoured cows – the seven fat cows that came out of the Nile in Pharaoh's dream (V.1) eaten up by the seven famished ones

	LXX	*KAI KATEPHAGON HAI HEPTA BOES HAI AISCHRAI KAI LEPTAI TAIS SARXI TAS* and ate the seven oxen the reproachful and thin with the flesh the *HEPTA BOAS TAS KALAS TÓ EIDEI KAI TAS* ***EKLEKTAS*** *TAIS SARXI ÉGERTHÉ DE PHARAÓ* seven oxen the fair to the sight and the choice with the flesh roused but Pharaoh
	engLXX	And the seven ill-favoured and lean cows devoured the seven well-favoured and choice-fleshed cows; and Pharao awoke.
Gen. 41:5		And he slept and dreamed the second time: and, behold, seven ears of corn came up upon one stalk, **rank** and good.
	YLT	And he sleepeth, and dreameth a second time, and lo, seven ears are coming up on one stalk, **fat** and good,

NKJV He slept and dreamed a second time; and suddenly seven heads of grain came up on one stalk, **plump** and good.

NASB He fell asleep and dreamed a second time; and behold, seven ears of grain came up on a single stalk, **plump** and good.

NIV He fell asleep again and had a second dream: seven ears of corn, **healthy** and good, were growing on a single stalk.

NLT But he fell asleep again and had a second dream. This time he saw seven heads of grain, **plump** and beautiful, growing on a single stalk.

EKLEKTOS – a divergent translation omitting to translate "he slept" (KJV) – "rank" in the old English sense of excessive: fat ears of corn in the second dream of Pharaoh

LXX *KAI ENUPNIASTHÉ TO DEUTERON KAI IDOU HEPTA STACHUES ANEBAINON EN*
and dreamed the second and look seven ears came up in

TÓ PUTHMENI HENI ***EKLEKTOI*** *KAI KALOI*
the stem one choice and good

engLXX And he dreamed again. And, behold, seven ears came up on one stalk, choice and good.

Gen. 41:7

And the seven thin ears devoured the seven **rank** and full ears. And Pharaoh awoke, and, behold, *it was* a dream.

YLT and the thin ears swallow the seven **fat** and full ears - and Pharaoh awaketh, and lo, a dream.

NKJV And the seven thin heads devoured the seven **plump** and full heads. So Pharaoh awoke, and indeed, *it was* a dream.

NASB The thin ears swallowed up the seven **plump** and full ears. Then Pharaoh awoke, and behold, *it was* a dream.

NIV The thin ears of corn swallowed up the seven healthy, **full** ears. Then Pharaoh woke up; it had been a dream.

NLT And these thin heads swallowed up the seven **plump**, well-formed heads! Then Pharaoh woke up again and realized it was a dream.

EKLEKTOS – a divergent translation with "wind devoured" (engLXX) an addition - "rank" (KJV) in the old English sense of excessive: fat ears of corn in Pharaoh's second dream eaten up by the seven emaciated ones

LXX *KAI KATEPION HOI HEPTA STACHUES HOI LEPTOI KAI ANEMOPHTHOROI TOUS HEPTA*
and consumed the seven ears the thin and wind destroyed the seven

STACHUAS TOUS ***EKLEKTOUS*** *KAI TOUS PLÉREIS ÉGERTHÉ DE PHARAÓ KAI ÉN ENUPNION*
ears the choice and the full arose but Pharaoh and was dream

engLXX And the seven thin ears and blasted with the wind devoured the seven choice and full ears; and Pharao awoke, and it was a dream.

Gen. 41:18 And, behold, there came up out of the river seven kine, **fatfleshed** and well favoured; and they fed in a meadow:

YLT and lo, out of the River coming up are seven kine, **fat** *in* flesh, and of fair form, and they feed among the reeds;

NKJV Suddenly seven cows came up out of the river, fine looking and **fat**; and they fed in the meadow.

NASB and behold, seven cows, **fat** and sleek came up out of the Nile, and they grazed in the marsh grass.

NIV when out of the river there came up seven cows, **fat** and sleek, and they grazed among the reeds.

NLT and I saw seven **fat**, healthy cows come up out of the river and begin grazing in the marsh grass.

EKLEKTOS – a divergent translation with "behold" (KJV) not rendered – the seven fat cows in Pharaoh's dream as he retells it to Joseph (V.15)

LXX *KAI HÓSPER EK TOU POTAMOU ANEBAINON HEPTA BOES KALAI TÓ EIDEI KAI*
and even as out of the river came up seven oxen fair to the sight and

***EKLEKTAI** TAIS SARXI KAI ENEMONTO EN TÓ AXEI*
choice with the flesh and graze in the sedge

engLXX and there came up as it were out of the river, seven cows well-favoured and choice-fleshed, and they fed on the sedge.

Gen. 41:20 And the lean and the ill favoured kine did eat up the first seven **fat** kine:

YLT 'And the lean and the bad kine eat up the first seven **fat** kine,

NKJV And the gaunt and ugly cows ate up the first seven, the **fat** cows.

NASB and the lean and ugly cows ate up the first seven **fat** cows.

NIV The lean, ugly cows ate up the seven **fat** cows that came up first.

NLT These thin, scrawny cows ate the seven **fat** cows.

EKLEKTOS - a divergent translation with the added "seven" (KJV) for the ill favoured cows – the seven fat cows eaten up by the seven emaciated ones

LXX *KAI KATEPHAGON HAI HEPTA BOES HAI AISCHRAI KAI LEPTAI TAS HEPTA BOAS*
and ate up the seven oxen the reproachful and thin the seven oxen

*TAS PRÓTAS TAS KALAS KAI TAS **EKLEKTAS***
the first the fair and the choice

engLXX And the seven ill-favoured and thin cows ate up the seven first good and choice cows.

Jdg. 3:17 And he brought the present unto Eglon king of Moab: and Eglon *was* a very **fat** man.

YLT and he bringeth near the present to Eglon king of Moab, and Eglon *is* a very **fat** man.

ASTEIOS – handsome, pretty – a divergent translation with "present" (KJV) rendered as "presents" (engLXX) – a very fat man (Heb.); a very handsome man (Gk.): the story is hindered by the divergent "handsome" since the assassination involved Eglon's extreme largesse (V.22)

LXX *KAI EPOREUTHÉ KAI PROSÉNEGKE TA DÓRA TÓ EGLÓM BASILEI MÓAB KAI*
and conveyed and brought the gifts to the Eglom king of Moab and

EGLÓM ANÉR ***ASTEIOS*** *SPHODRA*
Eglom man handsome exceedingly

engLXX And he went, and brought the presents to Eglom king of Moab, and Eglom *was* a very handsome man.

1Ki. 4:23 Ten **fat** oxen, and twenty oxen out of the pastures, and an hundred sheep, beside harts, and roebucks, and fallowdeer, and fatted fowl.

YLT ten **fat** oxen, and twenty feeding oxen, and a hundred sheep, apart from hart, and roe, and fallow-deer, and fatted beasts of the stalls,

NKJV ten **fatted** oxen, twenty oxen from the pastures, and one hundred sheep, besides deer, gazelles, roebucks, and fatted fowl.

NASB ten **fat** oxen, twenty pasture-fed oxen, a hundred sheep besides deer, gazelles, roebucks, and fattened fowl.

NIV ten head of **stall-fed** cattle, twenty of pasture-fed cattle and a hundred sheep and goats, as well as deer, gazelles, roebucks and choice fowl.

NLT also 10 oxen from the **fattening** pens, 20 pasture-fed cattle, 100 sheep or goats, as well as deer, gazelles, roe deer, and choice poultry.

EKLEKTOS - a divergent translation with "harts, and roebucks, and fallowdeer, and fatted fowl" (KJV) or "hart, and roe, and fallow-deer, and fatted beasts of the stalls" (YLT), rendered much shorter by "stags, and choice fatted does" (engLXX) – just like the other examples of quality cattle with this Hebrew word: ten fat cows

LXX *KAI DEKA MOSCHOI* ***EKLEKTOI*** *KAI EIKOSI BOES NOMADES KAI HEKATON*
3Ki.4:23 and ten calves choice and twenty oxen grazing and hundred

PROBATA EKTOS ELAPHÓN KAI DORKADÓN[3] *EKLEKTÓN*[4] *SITEUTA*
sheep outside of stags and does choice fatted

engLXX and ten choice calves, and twenty pastured oxen, and a hundred sheep, besides stags, and choice fatted does.

Psa. 73:4 For *there are* no bands in their death: but their strength *is* **firm**.

YLT V.3 . . . there are no bands at their death, V.4 And their might *is* **firm**.

STEREÓMA – firm, strength, solid – a divergent translation with "strength" (KJV) or "might" (YLT), rendered as "affliction" (engLXX) – Heb. firm in strength (KJV) or in might (YLT); Gk. firm in plague, affliction

LXX **72:4** *HOTI OUK ESTIN ANANEUSIS EN TÓ THANATÓ AUTÓN KAI* ***STEREÓMA*** *EN TÉ MASTIGI AUTÓN*
since not is return up in the death of them and firm in the scourge of them

engLXX For there is no sign of reluctance in their death: and *they have* firmness under their affliction.

Eze. 34:3 Ye eat the fat, and ye clothe you with the wool, ye kill them that are **fed**: *but* ye feed not the flock.

YLT The fat ye do eat, and the wool ye put on, the **fed** one ye slaughter, the flock ye feed not.

PACHUS aNT – stout, thick, fat – a loose translation with "the fat" (KJV) given as "the milk" (engLXX) – fatted sheep slaughtered

LXX *IDOU TO GALA KATESTHETE KAI TA ERIA PERIBALLESTHE KAI TO* ***PACHU***
look the milk ye devour and the wool put around and the stout

SPHAZETE KAI TA PROBATA MOU OU BOSKETE
ye slay and the sheep of me not ye graze

---

3. See TSEBI
4. See the a*EKLEKTOS* chapter

engLXX Behold, ye feed on the milk, and clothe yourselves with the wool, and slay the fat: but ye feed not my sheep.

Dan. 1:15 And at the end of ten days their countenances appeared fairer and **fatter** in flesh than all the children which did eat the portion of the king's meat.

YLT and at the end of ten days their appearance hath appeared better and **fatter** in flesh then any of the lads who are eating the king's portion of food.

ISCHUROS - strong, mighty – a direct translation – Daniel and his companions (V.11) appeared strong and fit after eating all that was within the Heb. law

LXX *KAI META TO TELOS TÓN DEKA HÉMERÓN HÓRATHÉSAN HAI IDEAI AUTÓN*
and after the end of the ten days looked the form of them

AGATHAI KAI ***ISCHURAI*** *TAIS SARXIN HUPER TA PAIDARIA TA ESTHONTA TÉN*
fairer and stronger with the flesh more than the children the eating the

TRAPEZAN TOU BASILEÓS
table of the king

engLXX And at the end of the ten days their countenances appeared fairer and stouter in flesh, than the children that fed at the king's table.

Hab. 1:16 Therefore they sacrifice unto their net, and burn incense unto their drag; because by them their portion *is* fat, and their meat **plenteous**.

YLT Therefore he doth sacrifice to his net, and doth make perfume to his drag, for by them *is* his portion fertile, and his food **fat**.

NKJV Therefore they sacrifice to their net, and burn incense to their dragnet; because by them their share *is* sumptuous and their food **plentious**.

NASB Therefore they offer a sacrifice to their net and burn incense to their fishing net; because through these things their catch is large, and their food is **plentiful**.

NIV Therefore he sacrifices to his net and burns incense to his drag-net, for by his net he lives in luxury and enjoys the **choicest** food.

NLT Then they will worship their nets and burn incense in front of them. "These nets are the gods who have made us **rich**!" They will claim.

EKLEKTOS – a direct translation – choice meat from a good catch

LXX *HENEKEN TOUTOU THUSEI TÉ SAGÉNÉ AUTOU KAI THUMIASEI TÓ AMPHIBLÉSTRÓ AUTOU*
therefore of this sacrifice the dragnet of him and burn incense to the casting net of him

HOTI EN AUTOIS ELIPANE MERIDA AUTOU KAI TA BRÓMATA AUTOU ***EKLEKTA***
since in them fat portion of him and the food of him choice

engLXX Therefore will he sacrifice to his drag, and burn incense to his casting-net, because by them he has made his portion fat, and his meats choice.

Zec. 11:16 For, lo, I will raise up a shepherd in the land, *which* shall not visit those that be cut off, neither shall seek the young one, nor heal that that is broken, nor feed that that standeth still: but he shall eat the flesh of the **fat**, and tear their claws in pieces.

YLT For lo, I am raising up a shepherd in the land, the cut off he doth not inspect, the shaken off he doth not seek, and the broken he doth not heal, the standing he doth not sustain, and the flesh of the **fat** he doth eat, and their hoofs he doth break off.

NKJV For indeed I will raise up a shepherd in the land *who* will not care for those who are cut off, nor seek the young, nor heal those that are broken, nor feed those that still stand. But he will eat the flesh of the **fat** and tear their hooves in pieces.

NASB For behold, I am going to raise up a shepherd in the land who will not care for the perishing, seek the scattered, heal the broken, or sustain the one standing, but will devour the flesh of the **fat** *sheep* and tear off their hoofs.

NIV For I am going to raise up a shepherd over the land who will not care for the lost, or seek the young, or heal the injured, or feed the healthy, but will eat the meat of the **choice** sheep, tearing off their hooves.

NLT This illustrates how I will give this nation a shepherd who will not care for those who are dying, nor look after the young, nor heal the injured, nor feed the healthy. Instead, this shepherd will eat the meat of the **fattest** sheep and tear off their hooves.

EKLEKTOS – a divergent translation with "tear their claws in pieces" (KJV) or "their hoofs he doth break off" (YLT), rendered as "dislocate the joints *of their necks*" (engLXX) - the fatted sheep devoured by the bad shepherd

LXX *DIOTI IDOU EGÓ EXEGEIRÓ POIMENA EPI TÉN GÉN TO EKLIMPANON OU MÉ*
for look I raise shepherd over the land the omit in no wise

EPISKEPSÉTAI KAI TO ESKORPISMENON OU MÉ ZÉTÉSÉ KAI TO
look after and the dispersed in no wise seek and the

SUNTETRIMMENON OU MÉ IASÉTAI KAI TO HOLOKLÉRON OU MÉ KATEUTHUNÉ
broken in no wise heal and the whole in no wise conduct

*KAI TA KREA TÓN **EKLEKTÓN** KATAPHAGETAI KAI TOUS ASTRAGALOUS AUTÓN EKSTREPSEI*
and the meat of the choice devour and the vertebrae of them twist

engLXX For, behold, I *will* raise up a shepherd against the land: he shall not visit that which is perishing, and he shall not seek that which is scattered, and he shall not heal that which is bruised, nor guide that which is whole: but he shall devour the flesh of the choice *ones*, and shall dislocate the joints *of their necks*.

7 - BECHURIM/BECHUROTH

Translated into Greek in the LXX

EKLEKTOS		**1**	**Numbers 11:28**
NEOTÉS	(youth)	2	
TOTAL		3	

Translated into English - Both KJV related

Ys Conc.	Count	Ss Conc. No. H 979	Count
BECHUROTH		**BECHUROTH**	
youth	2	youth	2
BECHURIM			
young men	1	young men	1
TOTAL	3	TOTAL	3

Refs	Text quotes KJV unless otherwise stated
Num. 11:28	And Joshua the son of Nun, the servant of Moses, *one* of his **young men**, answered and said, My lord Moses, forbid them.
YLT	And Joshua son of Nun, minister of Moses, *one* of his **young men**, answereth and saith, 'My lord Moses, restrain them.'
NKJV	So Joshua the son of Nun, Moses' assistant, *one* of his **choice men**, answered and said, "Moses my lord, forbid them!"
NASB	Then Joshua the son of Nun, the attendant of Moses from his **youth**, said, "Moses, my lord, restrain them."
NIV	Joshua son of Nun, who had been Moses' assistant since **youth**, spoke up and said, 'Moses, my lord, stop them!'
NLT	Joshua son of Nun, who had been Moses' assistant since his **youth**, protested, "Moses, my master, make them stop!"

EKLEKTOS – a divergent translation with "of his" omitted – a young man is a guy in his prime of life and this, let alone being Joshua, the servant of Moses, the excellent, quality rendering of *EKLEKTOS* is used by the translator: a youth

LXX *KAI APOKRITHEIS IÉSOUS HO TOU NAUÉ HO PARESTÉKÓS MÓUSÉ HO*
and answered Jesus the of the Naue who stood beside Moses the

EKLEKTOS *EIPE KURIE MÓUSÉ KÓLUSON AUTOUS*
choice said Lord Moses prevent them

engLXX And Joshua the son of Naue, who attended on Moses, the chosen one, said, *My* lord Moses, forbid them

Ecc. 11:9 Rejoice, O young man[1], in thy youth[2]; and let thy heart cheer thee in the days of thy **youth**, and walk in the ways of thine heart, and in the sight of thine eyes: but know thou, that for all these *things* God will bring thee into judgment.

NEOTÉS - youth – a divergent translation with "in the sight of thine eyes" (KJV) rendered as "not in the sight of thine eyes" (engLXX): the opposite – in the days of youth

LXX *EUPHRAINOU NEANISKE*[1] *EN NEOTÉTI SOU KAI AGATHUNATÓ SE HÉ KARDIA*
rejoice young man in youth of you and let cheer you the heart

SOU EN HÉMERAIS ***NEOTÉTOS*** *SOU KAI PERIPATEI EN HODOIS KARDIAS SOU*
of you in days of youth of you and walk in ways of heart of you

AMÓMOS KAI MÉ EN HORASEI OPHTHALMÓN SOU KAI GNÓTHI HOTI EPI PASI
blameless and not in seeing of eyes of you and know since upon all

TOUTOIS AXEI SE HO THEOS EN KRISEI
these carry you the God in judgment

engLXX Rejoice, O young man, in thy youth; and let thy heart cheer thee in the days of thy youth, and walk in the ways of thy heart blameless, but not in the sight of thine eyes: yet know that for all these things God will bring thee into judgement.

Ecc. 12:1 Remember now thy Creator in the days of thy **youth**, while the evil days come not, nor the years draw nigh, when thou shalt say, I have no pleasure in them;

NEOTÉS - youth – a direct translation – the days of thy youth

LXX *KAI MNÉSTHÉTI TOU KTISANTOS SE EN HÉMERAIS* ***NEOTÉTOS*** *SOU HEÓS*
and remember of the creator you in days of youth of you until

---

1. See BACHUR
2. Heb. YALEDUTH

HOTOU MÉ ELTHÓSIN HAI HÉMERAI TÉS KAKIAS KAI PHTHASÓUSIN ETÉ EN
until not come the days of the evil and anticipated years in

HOIS EREIS OUK ESTI MOI EN AUTOIS THELÉMA
which shall say not is to me in them pleasure

engLXX And remember thy Creator in the days of thy youth, before the days of evil come, and the years overtake *thee* in which thou shalt say, I have no pleasure in them.

8 - BEROMIM

Translated into Greek in the LXX

EKLEKTOS	**1**	**Ezekiel 27:24**
TOTAL	1	

Translated into English - Both KJV related

Ys Conc.	Count	Ss Conc. No. H 1264	Count
rich apparel	1	rich apparel	1
TOTAL	1	TOTAL	1

Refs.	Text quotes KJV unless otherwise stated
Eze. 27:24	These *were* thy merchants in all sorts of *things*, in blue clothes, and broidered work, and in chests of **rich apparel**, bound with cords, and made of cedar, among thy merchandise.
YLT	They *are* thy merchants for perfect things, for wrappings of blue, and embroidery, and for treasuries of **rich apparel**, with cords bound and girded, for thy merchandise,
NKJV	These *were* your merchants in choice items—in purple clothes, in embroidered garments, in chests of **multicolored apparel**, in strong twined cords, which were in your marketplace.

NASB They traded with you in choice garments, in clothes of blue and embroidered work, and in carpets of **many colors** and tightly wound cords, which were among your merchandise.

NIV In your market-place they traded with you beautiful garments, blue fabric, embroidered work and **multicoloured rugs** with cords twisted and tightly knotted.

NLT They brought choice fabrics to trade—blue cloth, embroidery, and **multicolored carpets** rolled up and bound with cords.

EKLEKTOS – A loose translation missing words like "clothes" and "embroidery", but the connection with stores/chests/treasury gives us the word as translating "rich apparel".

LXX *PHERONTES EMPORIAN HUAKINTHON KAI THÉSAUROUS* ***EKLEKTOUS***
bring commerce of blue and treasures choice

DEDEMENOUS SCHOINIOIS KAI KUPARISSINA
bound with chords and cypress

engLXX bringing *for* merchandise blue, and choice stores bound with cords, and cypress wood.

9 - BOCHAN

Translated into Greek in the LXX

EKLEKTOS	**1**	**Isaiah 28:16**
TOTAL	1	

Translated into English - Both KJV related

Ys Conc.	Count	Ss Conc. No. H 976	Count
tried	1	tried	1
TOTAL	1	TOTAL	1

Refs	Text quotes KJV unless otherwise stated
Isa. 28:16	Therefore thus saith the Lord God, Behold, I lay in Zion for a foundation a stone, a **tried** stone, a precious corner *stone*, a sure foundation: he that believeth shall not make haste.
YLT	Therefore, thus said the Lord Jehovah: 'Lo, I am laying a foundation in Zion, a stone - a **tried** stone, a corner stone precious, a settled foundation, he who is believing doth not make haste.

NKJV Therefore thus says the Lord God:

"Behold, I lay in Zion a stone for a foundation, a **tried** stone, a precious cornerstone, a sure foundation; whoever believes will not act hastily.

NASB Therefore thus says the Lord God,

"Behold, I am laying in Zion a stone, a **tested** stone, a costly cornerstone *for* the foundation, firmly placed. He who believes *in it* will not be disturbed.

NIV So this is what the Sovereign LORD says:

'See, I lay a stone in Zion, a **tested** stone, a precious cornerstone for a sure foundation; the one who relies on it will never be stricken with panic.

NLT Therefore, this is what the Sovereign LORD says:

"Look! I am placing a foundation stone in Jerusalem, a **firm and tested** stone. It is a precious cornerstone that is safe to build on. Whoever believes need never be shaken.

EKLEKTOS – A loose translation with "shall not make haste" (KJV) rendered as "shall by no means be ashamed" (engLXX) - The tested stone being tried is the highest quality stone fit for a cornerstone position

LXX *DIATOUTO HOUTÓ LEGEI KURIOS KURIOS IDOU EGÓ EMBALLÓ EIS TA THEMELIA*
therefore thus says Lord Lord look I put into the foundations

SIÓN LITHON POLUTELÉ ***EKLEKTON*** *AKROGÓNIAION ENTIMON EIS TA*
Zion stone costly choice cornering valuable into the

THEMELIA AUTÉS KAI HO PISTEUÓN OU MÉ KATAISCHUNTHÉ
foundations of her and the believing in no wise dishonour

engLXX Therefore thus saith the Lord, *even* the Lord, Behold, I lay for the foundations of Sion a costly stone, a choice, a corner-stone, a precious *stone*, for its foundations; and he that believes *on him* shall by no means be ashamed.

10 - CHARUTS

Translated into Greek in the LXX

EKLEKTOS		**1**		**Proverbs 12:24**
CHRUSION	(gold)	6		
ANDREIOS	(manly, vigorous)	2	aNT	
DIKÉ	(judgment, vengeance)	2		
CHRUSOS	(gold)	1		
KATHAROS	(pure, honest)	1		
PRIÓN	(saw)	1	aNT	
SKLÉROTÉS	(hard, rigid)	1		
TEICHOS	(wall)	1		
TROCHOS	(wheel)	1		
NOT in LXX		1		
TOTAL		18		

Translated into English - Both KJV related

	Ys Conc.	Count	Ss Conc. No. H 2742	Count
	CHARUTS[a]			
	diligent	5	gold	6
	sharp	1	diligent	5
	decision	2	decision	2
	sharp pointed thing	1	threshing instrument	2
	threshing instrument	2	sharp	1
	wall	1	sharp things	1
	CHARUTS[b]		wall	1
[-2 as per Ys Conc. page 426]	gold	4		
[As per page Ys Conc. 426]	fine gold	2		
	TOTAL	18	TOTAL	18

Refs	**Text quotes KJV unless otherwise stated**
Job 41:30	Sharp stones *are* under him: he spreadeth **sharp pointed things** upon the mire.
YLT	Under him *are* sharp points of clay, He spreadeth **gold** on the mire.

CHRUSOS – gold – a divergent translation with "of the sea" (engLXX) added - two meanings of CHARUTS as Ys. Conc shows above: here KJV reads the one of sharp/diligent [Similar in NKJV, NIV, NASB, NLT]; YLT reads the other of gold as does the LXX, hence one of the Greek words rendering gold is employed. Normally context provides enough to "tell" which of two meanings is correct: here either appears possible.

LXX **41:21** *HÉ STRÓMNÉ AUTOU OBELISKOI OXEIS PAS DE* ***CHRUSOS*** *THALASSÉS HUP*
the bedding of him stakes sharp all but gold of sea under

AUTON HÓSPER PÉLOS AMUTHTHÉTOS
him as clay aplenty

engLXX His lair is *formed of* sharp points; and all the gold of the sea under him is an immense *quantity of* clay.

Psa. 68:13 Though ye have lien among the pots, *yet shall ye be* as the wings of a dove covered with silver, and her feathers with yellow **gold**.

YLT Though ye do lie between two boundaries, wings of a dove covered with silver, and her pinions with yellow **gold**.

CHRUSION – gold - a direct translation - the gold meaning is given as the colour of the dove portions

LXX **67:13** *ÉAN KOIMÉTHÉTE ANAMESON TÓN KLÉRÓN PTERUGES PERISTERAS*
If should sleep among the lots wings of dove

PERIÉRGURÓMENAI KAI TA METAPHRENA AUTÉS EN CHLÓROTÉTI ***CHRUSIOU***
silver covered and the upper back of her in yellowness of gold

engLXX Even if ye should lie among the lots, *ye shall have* the wings of a dove covered with silver, and her breast with yellow gold.

Pro. 3:14 For the merchandise of it *is* better than the merchandise of silver, and the gain thereof than fine **gold**.

YLT For better *is* her merchandise than the merchandise of silver, and than **gold** - her increase.

CHRUSION – gold – a divergent translation with the second "merchandise" (KJV) not rendered - the gold meaning is given alongside silver: precious, but not as much as wisdom (V.13)

LXX *KREISSON GAR AUTÉN EMPOREUESTHAI É* ***CHRUSIOU*** *KAI ARGURIOU THÉSAUROUS*
better for her to merchandise than of gold and of silver stores

engLXX For it is better to traffic for her, than for treasures of gold and silver.

Pro. 8:10 Receive my instruction, and not silver; and knowledge rather than choice **gold**.

CHRUSION – gold - A direct translation - the gold meaning given: of higher value is education.

LXX *LABETE PAIDEIAN KAI MÉ ARGURION KAI GNÓSIN HUPER* ***CHRUSION*** *DEDOKIMASMENON*
receive ye instruction and not silver and knowledge above gold tested

engLXX Receive instruction, and not silver; and knowledge rather than tried gold.

Pro. 8:19 My fruit *is* better than **gold**, yea, than fine gold; and my revenue than choice silver.

CHRUSION – gold - a divergent translation with “fine gold” (KJV) given as “precious stones” (engLXX) – the gold meaning is given alongside another precious metal silver: both showing as another high quality material that is also less worthy than wisdom’s (V.12) produce.

LXX *BELTION EME KARPIZESTHAI*[1] *HUPER* ***CHRUSION*** *KAI LITHON TIMION TA DE*
best my enjoy fruit above gold and stone precious the but

EMA GENNÉMATA KREISSÓ ARGURIOU EKLEKTOU[2]
my produce better of silver of choice

engLXX *It is* better to have my fruit than *to have* gold and precious stones; and my produce is better than choice silver.

1. See PERI
2 See BACHAR

Pro. 10:4 He becometh poor that dealeth *with* a slack hand: but the hand of the **diligent** maketh rich.

YLT Poor *is* he who is working - a slothful hand, and the hand of the **diligent** maketh rich.

ANDREIOS aNT – manly, vigorous – a divergent translation with added section "a son who is instructed shall be wise, and shall use the fool for a servant." (engLXX) - the Gk. word used for "diligent" means "manly" [*ANÉR* (Genitive *ANDROS*) = a man/a husband] – or "vigorous".

LXX *PENIA ANDRA TAPEINOI CHEIRES DE* ***ANDREIÓN*** *PLOUTIZOUSIN HUIOS*
poverty man humbles hands but vigorous enrich son

PEPAIDEUMENOS SOPHOS ESTAI TÓ DE APHRONI DIAKONÓ CHRÉSETAI
corrected wise shall be to the but foolish for servant shall treat

engLXX Poverty brings a man low: but the hands of the vigorous make rich. A son who is instructed shall be wise, and shall use the fool for a servant.

Pro. 12:24 The hand of the **diligent** shall bear rule: but the slothful shall be under tribute.

YLT The hand of the **diligent** ruleth, and slothfulness becometh tributary.

NKJV The hand of the **diligent** will rule, but the slothful will be put to forced labor.

NASB The hand of the **diligent** will rule, but the slack *hand* will be put to forced labor.

NIV **Diligent** hands will rule, but laziness ends in forced labour.

NLT **Work hard** and become a leader; be lazy and become a slave.

EKLEKTOS – first clause is a direct translation with "the diligent" identified by *EKLEKTOS*; the second clause is loose in translation with "slothful" or "slothfulness" given as "deceitful".

LXX *CHEIR* ***EKLEKTÓN*** *KRATÉSEI EUCHERÓS DOLIOI DE ESONTAI EN PRONOMÉ*
hand of choice shall prevail easily deceitful but shall be in captivity

engLXX The hand of chosen men shall easily obtain rule; but the deceitful shall be for a prey.

Pro. 12:27 The slothful *man* roasteth not that which he took in hunting: but the substance of a **diligent** man *is* precious.

YLT The slothful roasteth not his hunting, and the wealth of a **diligent** man is precious.

KATHAROS – pure, honest - a divergent translation with the possession of the diligent man as precious rendered as the "blameless man" (engLXX) as the precious entity instead - the "diligent" is given as "pure"

LXX *OUK EPITEUXETAI DOLIOS THÉRAS KTÉMA DE TIMION ANÉR* ***KATHAROS***
not successful deceitful hunt property but precious man pure

engLXX A deceitful man shall catch no game; but a blameless man is a precious possession.

Pro. 13:4 The soul of the sluggard desireth, and *hath* nothing: but the soul of the **diligent** shall be made fat.

ANDREIOS aNT – manly, vigorous - A divergent translation with "soul" not translated - the word in the genitive plural, used for "of the diligent" (KJV), means "manly" [*ANÉR* (Genitive *ANDROS*) = a man/a husband] – or "vigorous".

LXX *EN EPITHUMIAIS ESTI PAS AERGOS CHEIRES DE* ***ANDREIÓN*** *EN EPIMELEIA*
in desire is every idle hands but vigorous in takes care

engLXX Every slothful man desires, but the hands of the active are diligent.

Pro. 16:16 How much better *is it* to get wisdom than **gold**! And to get understanding rather to be chosen than silver!

CHRUSION – gold - a loose translation with "get wisdom" (KJV) given as "to choose nests/broods of wisdom" (engLXX) - Gold is given as of less value than wisdom.

LXX *NOSSIAI SOPHIAS HAIRETÓTERAI* ***CHRUSIOU*** *NOSSIAI DE PHRONÉSEÓS*
nests of wisdom to choose of gold nests but of prudence

HAIRETÓTERAI HUPER ARGURION
to choose above silver

engLXX The brood of wisdom is more to be chosen than gold, and the brood of prudence more to be chosen than silver.

Pro. 21:5 The thoughts of the **diligent** *tend* only to plenteousness; but of every one *that is* hasty only to want.

YLT The purposes of the **diligent** *are* only to advantage, and of every hasty one, only to want.

NOT in LXX - LXX skips from Verse 4 to Verse 6 missing out Verse 5 altogether.

So follows: Verses 4-6 in KJV followed by 4-6 as per the LXX of Samuel Bagster: i.e. no verse 5 at all.

Pro. 21:4-6 An high look, and a proud heart, *and* the plowing of the wicked, *is* sin. The thoughts of the diligent *tend* only to plenteousness; but of every one *that is* hasty only to want. The getting of treasures by a lying tongue *is* a vanity tossed to and fro of them that seek death.

LXX [4]*MEGALOPHRÓN EN HUBDEI THRASUKARDIOS LAMPTÉR DE ASEBÓN*
high-minded in insolence bold-hearted torch but of impious

[6]*HAMARTIA HO ENERGÓN THÉSAURISMATA GLÓSSÉ PSEUDEI MATAIA DIÓKEI*
sin the producing treasures tongue lying vanity pursues

EPI PAGIDAS THANATOU
upon snare of death

engLXX A high-minded man is stout-hearted in *his* pride; and the lamp of the wicked is sin. He that gathers treasures with a lying tongue pursue vanity *on* to the snares of death.

Isa. 28:27 For the fitches are not threshed with a **threshing instrument**, neither is a cart wheel turned about upon the cummin; but the fitches are beaten out with a staff, and the cummin with a rod.

YLT For not with a **sharp-pointed thing** threshed are fitches, and the wheel of a cart on cummin turned round, for with a staff beaten out are fitches, and cummin with a rod.

SKLÉROTÉS – hard, rigid - A divergent translation with "and the cummin with a rod" (KJV) given as "and the cumin shall be eaten with bread" (engLXX) - un-translated "threshing instrument" (KJV) or "sharp-pointed thing" (YLT) given as "hardness"

LXX *OU GAR META* ***SKLÉROTÉTOS*** *KATHAIRETAI TO MELANTHION OUDE TROCHOS*
not for with hardness cleansed the pepperwort neither wheel

HAMAXÉS PERIAXEI EPI TO KUMINON ALLA RHABDÓ TINASSETAI TO
of wagon lead about upon the cumin but with rod threshed the

MELANTHION TO DE KUMINON META ARTOU BRÓTHÉSETAI
pepperwort the but cumin with bread shall be eaten

engLXX For the black poppy is not cleansed with harsh treatment, nor will a wagon-wheel pass over the cumin; but the black poppy is threshed with a rod, and the cumin shall be eaten with bread;

Isa. 41:15 Behold, I will make thee a new **sharp** threshing instrument having teeth: thou shalt thresh the mountains, and beat *them* small, and shalt make the hills as chaff.

YLT Lo, I have set thee for a new **sharp** threshing instrument, possessing teeth, thou threshest mountains, and beatest small, and hills as chaff thou makest.

TROCHOS – wheel - a loose translation with "sharp threshing instrument" (KJV) given as "wheels" (engLXX) of agricultural type machinery which, "having teeth" (KJV), are given as "saw-shaped" (engLXX) – the men of Israel (V.14) are encouraged to see themselves as the Lord will make them as effective tools to clear out their enemies

LXX *IDOU EPOIÉSA SE HÓS* ***TROCHOUS*** *HAMAXÉS ALOÓNTAS KAINOUS PRISTÉROEIDEIS KAI*
look made you as wheels of wagon threshing new toothed and

ALOÉSEIS ORÉ KAI LEPTUNEIS BOUNOUS KAI HÓS CHNOUN THÉSEIS
thresh mountain and thin out hills and as dust make

engLXX Behold, I have made thee as new saw-shaped threshing wheels of a waggon; and thou shalt thresh the mountains, and beat the hills to powder, and make *them* as chaff:

Dan. 9:25 Know therefore and understand, *that* from the going forth of the commandment to restore and to build Jerusalem unto the Messiah the Prince *shall be* seven weeks, and threescore and two weeks: the street shall be built again, and the **wall**, even in troublous times.

YLT And thou dost know, and dost consider wisely, from the going forth of the word to restore and to build Jerusalem till Messiah the Leader *is* seven weeks, and sixty and two weeks: the broad place hath been built again, and the **rampart**, even in the distress of the times.

TEICHOS – wall, fortification - a direct translation - a wall of the city given for CHARUTS: perhaps with thinking that as this was built in troubled times, the diligent or furtive building, was envisaged by the "wall" – Nehemiah gives a great account of that rebuilding

LXX *KAI GNÓSÉ KAI SUNÉSEIS APO EXODOU LOGOU TOU APOKRITHÉNAI KAI TOU OIKODOMÉSAI*
and know and appreciate from exit of word of the answer and of the to build

HIEROUSALÉM HEÓS CHRISTOU HÉGOUMENOU HEBDOMADES HEPTA KAI HEBDOMADES
Jerusalem until anointed leading sevens seven and sevens

EXÉKONTADUO KAI EPISTREPSEI KAI OIKODOMÉTHÉSETAI PLATEIA KAI ***TEICHOS*** *KAI*
sixty two and return and built broad and wall and

EKKENÓTHÉSONTAI HOI KAIROI
empty out the seasons

engLXX And thou shalt know and understand, that from the going forth of the command for the answer and for the building of Jerusalem until Christ the prince *there shall be* seven weeks, and sixty-two weeks; and then *the time* shall return, and the street shall be built, and the wall, and the times shall be exhausted.

Joe. 3:14a Multitudes, multitudes in the valley of **decision**: . . .

YLT Multitudes, multitudes *are* in the valley of **decision**, (. . .)

DIKÉ – judgment, vengeance - a divergent translation with "multitudes, multitudes" (KJV) given as "noises have resounded" (engLXX) - "judgment" (engLXX) is given for "decision" (KJV): perhaps the idea of sharp instruments diligently used on the day as per a "sickle" (V.13) [or e.g. as per Isa. 41:15 above also] was a "decision/judgment" time: the valley of Jehoshaphat (V.12) as a large flat area is seen as the place of the final battle

LXX *ÉCHOI EXÉCHÉSAN EN TÉ KOILADI TÉS* ***DIKÉS*** . . .
4:14a sounds resounded in the valley of the judgment

engLXX Noises have resounded in the valley of judgment: (. . .)

Joe. 3:14b . . . for the day of the LORD *is* near in the valley of **decision**.

YLT . . . For near *is* the day of Jehovah in the valley of **decision**.

DIKÉ – judgment, vengeance - a direct translation - "judgment" (engLXX) is given for "decision" (KJV): perhaps the idea of sharp instruments diligently used on the day as per a "sickle" (V.13) [or e.g. as per Isa. 41:15 above also] was a "decision/judgment" time: the valley of Jehoshaphat (V.12) as a large flat area is seen as the place of the final battle

LXX . . . *HOTI EGGUS HÉMERA KURIOU EN TÉ KOILADI TÉS* ***DIKÉS***
4:14b since near day of Lord in the valley of the judgment

engLXX . . . for the day of the Lord is near in the valley of judgment.

Amo. 1:3 Thus saith the LORD; For three transgressions of Damascus, and for four, I will not turn away *the punishment* thereof; because they have threshed Gilead with **threshing instruments** of iron:

YLT Thus said Jehovah: For three transgressions of Damascus, and for four, I do not reverse it, because of their threshing Gilead with **sharp- pointed** irons,

PRIÓN aNT – saw - a divergent translation with the addition of "the women with child" - "threshing instruments" or "sharp pointed" given as "saws"

LXX *KAI EIPE KURIOS EPI TAIS TRISIN ASEBEIAIS DAMASKOU KAI EPI TAIS*
and said Lord upon the three impious of Damascus and upon the

TESSARSIN OUK APOSTRAPHÉSOMAI AUTON ANTH HÓN EPRIZON ***PRIOSI***
four not turn from him because they sawed |

DIDÉROIS TAS EN GASTRI ECHOUSAS TÓN EN GALAAD with saw
iron the in womb having of the in Gilead

engLXX And the Lord said, For three sins of Damascus, and for four, I will not turn away from it; because they sawed with iron saws the women with child of the Galaadites.

Zec. 9:3 And Tyrus did build herself a strong hold, and heaped up silver as the dust, and fine **gold** as the mire of the streets.

CHRUSION – gold - a direct translation - "gold" was so abundant in Tyre that it is described as the mire in the thoroughfares

LXX *KAI ÓKODOMÉSE TUROS OCHURÓMATA AUTÉ KAI ETHÉSAURISEN*
and built Tyrus fortress she and stored

ARGURION HÓS CHOUN KAI SUNÉGAGE ***CHRUSION*** *HÓS PÉLON HODÓN*
silver as dust and gathered gold as clay of way

engLXX And Tyrus built strong-holds for herself, and heaped up silver as dust, and gathered gold as the mire of the ways.

11 - CHEMDAH/CHAMUDOTH

Translated into Greek in the LXX

EKLEKTOS		4		***EKLEKTOS*:**
EPITHUMÉTOS	(desirable)	11	aNT	**Jeremiah 3:19; Jeremiah 25:34**
EPITHUMIA	(desire, yearning)	5		**Haggai 2:7; Zechariah 7:14**
EPAINOS	(praise)	1		
EPITHUMÉMA	(object of desire)	1	aNT	
HÓRAIOS	(beautiful)	1		
KALOS	(good)	1		
KALLOS	(beauty)	1	aNT	
TOTAL		25		

Translated into English - Both KJV related

Ys Conc.	Count	Ss Conc. No. H 2532	Count
CHEMDAH		**CHEMDAH**	
desire	4	pleasant	12
goodly	1	desire	4
pleasant	11	beloved	3
precious	1	goodly	2
CHAMUDOTH		precious	4
pleasant things	1		
precious things	1		
greatly beloved	3		
goodly	1		
precious	2		
TOTAL	25	TOTAL	25

Refs	**Text quotes KJV unless otherwise stated**
Gen. 27:15	And Rebekah took **goodly** raiment of her eldest son Esau, which *were* with her in the house, and put them upon Jacob her younger son:

KALOS – good - a direct translation – the good clothes of Esau

LXX *KAI LABOUSA REBEKKA TÉN STOLÉN HÉSAU TOU HUIOU AUTÉS TOU*
and took Rebekah the robe of Esau of the son of her the

PRESBUTEROU TÉN ***KALÉN*** *HÉ ÉN PAR AUTÉ EN TÓ OIKÓ ENEDUSEN AUTÉN*
elder the good which in by her in the house put her

IAKÓB TON HUION AUTÉS TON NEÓTERON
Jacob the son of her the newer

engLXX And Rebecca having taken the fine raiment of her elder son Esau which was with her in the house, put it on Jacob her younger son.

1Sa. 9:20 And as for thine asses that were lost three days ago, set not thy mind on them; for they are found. And on whom *is* all the **desire** of Israel? *Is it* not on thee, and on all thy father's house?

YLT As to the asses which are lost to thee this day three days, set not thy heart to them, for they have been found; and to whom *is* all the **desire** of Israel?' Is it not to thee and to all thy father's house?'

HÓRAIOS – beautiful, well-formed, graceful – a direct translation – Saul is seen as the beauty of Israel, the one desired

LXX *KAI PERI TÓN ONÓN SOU TÓN APOLÓLUIÓN SÉMERON TRITAIÓN MÉ THÉS*
1Ki.9:20 and about the asses of you of the lost today three not put

TÉN KARDIAN SOU AUTAIS HOTI HEURÉNTAI KAI TINI TA ***HÓRAIA*** *TOU ISRAÉL*
the heart of you to them since found and what the beautiful of the Israel

OU SOI KAI TÓ OIKÓ TOU PATROS SOU
not to you and | house of the father of you
to the

engLXX And concerning thine asses that have been lost now these three days, care not for them, for they are found. And to whom does the excellency of Israel belong? Does it not to thee and to thy father's house?

2Ch. 20:25 And when Jehoshaphat and his people came to take away the spoil of them, they found among them in abundance both riches with the dead bodies, and **precious** jewels, which they stripped off for themselves, more than they could carry away: and they were three days in gathering of the spoil, it was so much.

YLT and Jehoshaphat cometh in, and his people, to seize their spoil, and they find among them, in abundance, both goods and carcases, and **desirable** vessels, and they take spoil to themselves without prohibition, and they are three days seizing the spoil, for it *is* abundant.

EPITHUMÉTOS aNT – (to be) desired, desirable – a divergent translation with "dead bodies" (KJV) or "carcases" (YLT), not translated - desirable vessels

LXX *KAI EXÉLTHEN IÓSAPHAT KAI HO LAOS AUTOU SKULEUSAI TA SKULA AUTÓN*
and came Josaphat and the people of him to despoil the spoil of them

KAI HEURON KTÉNÉ POLLA KAI APOSKEUN KAI SKULA KAI SKEUÉ ***EPITHUMÉTA***
and found cattle much and stuff and spoil and items desirable

KAI ESKULEUSAN EN AUTOIS KAI EGENONTO HÉMERAI TREIS SKULEUONTÓN
and despoiled in them and it be days three gathering

AUTÓN TA SKULA HOTI POLLA ÉN
of them the spoil since much was

engLXX And Josaphat and his people went out to spoil them, and they found much cattle, and furniture, and spoils, and precious things: and they spoiled them, and they were three days gathering the spoil, for it was abundant.

2Ch. 21:20 Thirty and two years old was he when he began to reign, and he reigned in Jerusalem eight years, and departed without being **desired**. Howbeit they buried him in the city of David, but not in the sepulchres of the kings.

YLT A son of thirty and two *years* was he in his reigning, and eight years he hath reigned in Jerusalem, and he goeth without **desire**, and they bury him in the city of David, and not in the graves of the kings.

EPAINOS – praise, approval, commendation – a direct translation – Jehoram (V.5) finished reigning without honour, without being desired: not praised

LXX ***ÉN TRIAKONTA KAI DUO ETÓN HOTE EBASILEUSE KAI OKTÓ ETÉ EBASILEUSEN***
was thirty and two years when reigned and eight years reigned

EN HIEROUSALÉM KAI EPOREUTHÉ OUK EN* EPAINÓ *KAI ETAPHÉ EN POLEI
in Jerusalem and went not in praise and buried in city

DAUID KAI OUK EN TAPHOIS TÓN BASILEÓN
of David and not in tombs of the kings

engLXX He was thirty and two years old when he began to reign, and he reigned eight years in Jerusalem. And he departed without honour, and was buried in the city of David, but not in the tombs of the kings.

2Ch. 32:27 And Hezekiah had exceeding much riches and honour: and he made himself treasuries for silver, and for gold, and for precious stones, and for spices, and for shields, and for all manner of **pleasant** jewels;

YLT And Hezekiah hath riches and honour very much, and treasures he hath made to himself of silver, and of gold, and of precious stone, and of spices, and of shields, and of all *kinds* of **desirable** vessels,

EPITHUMÉTOS aNT - (to be) desired, desirable – a divergent translation with "shields" (KJV) not rendered – desirable vessels

LXX ***KAI EGENETO TÓ EZEKIA PLOUTOS KAI DOXA POLLÉ SPHODRA KAI***
and came to be the Hezekiah rich and glory much exceedingly and

THÉSAUROUS EPOIÉSEN AUTÓ ARGURIOU KAI CHRUSIOU KAI TOU LITHOU TOU
Stores made for him silver and gold and of the stones the

TIMIOU KAI EIS TA ARÓMATA KAI HOPLOTHÉKAS KAI EIS SKEUÉ ***EPITHUMÉTA***
precious and into the aromatics and storehouses and into vessels desirable

engLXX And Ezekias had wealth and very great glory: and he made for himself treasuries of gold, and silver, and precious stones, also for spices, and stores for arms, and for precious vessels;

2Ch. 36:10 And when the year was expired, king Nebuchadnezzar sent, and brought him to Babylon, with the **goodly** vessels of the house of the LORD, and made Zedekiah his brother king over Judah and Jerusalem.

EPITHUMÉTOS aNT - (to be) desired, desirable – a divergent translation with "made Zedekiah his brother king" (KJV) rendered as "made Sedekias his father's brother king" (engLXX): brother turned into uncle – the precious vessels from the temple brought alongside with king Jehoiachin (V.9) to Babylon

LXX *KAI EPISTREPHONTOS TOU ENIAUTOU APESTEILEN HO BASILEUS*
and turn of the year sent the king

NABOUCHODONOSOR KAI EISÉNEGKEN AUTON EIS BABULÓNA META TÓN
Nabuchadnezzar and brought him into Babylon with the

SKEUÓN TÓN ***EPITHUMÉTÓN*** *OIKOU KURIOU KAI EBASILEUSE SEDEKIAN*
vessels the desirable of house of Lord and reigned Zedekiah

ADELPHON TOU PATROS AUTOU EPI IOUDAN KAI HIEROUSALÉM
brother of the father of him over Juda and Jerusalem

engLXX And at the turn of the year, king Nabuchodonosor sent, and brought him to Babylon, with the precious vessels of the house of the Lord, and made Sedekias his father's brother king over Juda and Jerusalem.

Ezr. 8:27 Also twenty basons of gold, of a thousand drams; and two vessels of fine copper, **precious** as gold.

YLT and basins of gold twenty, of a thousand drams, and two vessels of good shining brass, **desirable** as gold.

EPITHUMÉTOS aNT - (to be) desired, desirable – a divergent translation with "two" (KJV) rendered as "superior" (engLXX) – desirable gold

LXX *KAI CHAPHOURÉ CHRUSOI EIKOSI EIS TÉN HODON CHILIOI KAI SKEUÉ*
and bowls gold twenty into the way thousands and vessels

CHALKOU STILBONTOS AGATHOU DIAPHORA ***EPITHUMÉTA*** *EN CHRUSIÓ*
of brass shining good diverse desirable in gold

engLXX and twenty golden bowls, *weighing* about a thousand drachms, and superior vessels of fine shining brass, *precious* as gold.

Psa. 106:24 Yea, they despised the **pleasant** land, they believed not his word:

YLT And they kick against the **desirable** land, they have not given credence to His word.

EPITHUMÉTOS aNT - (to be) desired, desirable – a direct translation – the desirable land

LXX **105:24** *KAI EXOUDENÓSAN GÉN* ***EPITHUMÉTÉN*** *KAI OUK EPISTEUSAN TÓ LOGÓ AUTOU*
and despise land desired and not believed the word of him

engLXX Moreover they set at nought the desirable land, and believed not his word.

Isa. 2:16 And upon all the ships of Tarshish, and upon all **pleasant** pictures.

YLT And for all ships of Tarshish, and for all **desirable** pictures.

NKJV Upon all the ships of Tarshish, and upon all the **beautiful** sloops.

NASB Against all the ships of Tarshish and against all the **beautiful** craft.

NIV for every trading ship and every **stately** vessel.

NLT He will destroy all the great trading ships and every **magnificent** vessel.

KALLOS aNT – beauty – a divergent translation with "Tarshish" (KJV) rendered as "sea" (engLXX) – beautiful appearance, form, craft: the Heb. word SEKIYYAH "pictures" (KJV) occurs only once in OT and it is unclear as to distinct meaning

	LXX	*KAI EPI PAN PLOION THALASSÉS KAI EPI PASAN THEAN PLOIÓN* ***KALLOUS*** and upon every boat of sea and upon every view of ships beauty
	engLXX	and upon every ship of the sea, and upon every display of fine ships.
Jer. 3:19		But I said, How shall I put thee among the children, and give thee a **pleasant** land, a goodly[1] heritage of the hosts of nations? and I said, Thou shalt call me, My father; and shalt not turn away from me.
	YLT	And I have said, How do I put thee among the sons, and give to thee a **desirable** land, a beauteous[1] inheritance of the hosts of nations, and I say, My father - ye do call to Me, and from after Me ye do not turn back.
	NKJV	"But I said: 'How can I put you among the children and give you a **pleasant** land, a beautiful heritage of the hosts of nations?' And I said: 'You shall call Me, "My Father," and not turn away from Me.'
	NASB	"Then I said, 'How I would set you among My sons and give you a **pleasant** land, the most beautiful inheritance of the nations!' and I said, 'You shall call Me, My Father, and not turn away from following Me.'
	NIV	'I myself said, '"How gladly would I treat you like my children and give you a **pleasant** land, the most beautiful inheritance of any nation." I thought you would call me "Father" and not turn away from following me.
	NLT	"I thought to myself, 'I would love to treat you as my own children!' I wanted nothing more than to give you this **beautiful** land— the finest possession in the world. I looked forward to your calling me 'Father,' and I wanted you never to turn from me.

1 See TSEBI

EKLEKTOS – a loose translation with "hosts of nations" (KJV) given as "Almighty God of the Gentiles" (engLXX) – a choice land

LXX *KAI EGÓ EIPA GENOITO KURIE HOTI TAXÓ SE EIS TEKNA KAI DÓSÓ SOI GÉN*
and I said it be Lord since | you into children and | to you land
shall arrange shall give

EKLEKTÉN *KLÉRONOMIAN THEOU PANTOKRATOROS ETHNÓN KAI EIPA*
choice inheritance of God Almighty of nations and said

PATERA KALESETE ME KAI AP EMOU OUK APOSTRAPHÉSESTHE
Father ye call me and from me not ye turn

engLXX And I said, So be it, Lord, for *thou saidst* I will set thee among children, and will give thee a choice land, the inheritance of the Almighty God of the Gentiles: and I said, Ye shall call me Father; and ye shall not turn away from me.

Jer. 12:10 Many pastors have destroyed my vineyard, they have trodden my portion under foot, they have made my **pleasant** portion a desolate wilderness.

YLT Many shepherds did destroy My vineyard, they have trodden down My portion, they have made My **desirable** portion become a wilderness – a desolation.

EPITHUMÉTOS aNT - (to be) desired, desirable – a loose translation with "trodden" (KJV) rendered as "defiled" (engLXX) – the Lord's desirable portion of land

LXX *POIMENES POLLOI DIEPHTHEIRAN TON AMPELÓNA MOU EMOLUNAN TÉN*
shepherds many ruined the vineyard of me defiled the

MERIDA MOU EDÓKAN TÉN MERIDA TÉN ***EPITHUMÉTÉN*** *MOU EIS ERÉMON ABATON*
portion of me gave the portion the desirable of me into desert untrodden

	engLXX	Many shepherds have destroyed my vineyard, they have defiled my portion, they have made my desirable portion a trackless wilderness;
Jer. 25:34		Howl, ye shepherds, and cry; and wallow yourselves *in the ashes*, ye principal of the flock: for the days of your slaughter and of your dispersions are accomplished; and ye shall fall like a **pleasant** vessel.
	YLT	Howl, ye shepherds, and cry, and roll yourselves, ye honourable of the flock, for full have been your days, for slaughtering, and *for* your scatterings, and ye have fallen as a **desirable** vessel.
	NKJV	"Wail, shepherds, and cry! Roll about *in the ashes*, you leaders of the flock! For the days of your slaughter and your dispersions are fulfilled; you shall fall like a **precious** vessel.
	NASB	"Wail, you shepherds, and cry; and wallow *in ashes*, you masters of the flock; for the days of your slaughter and your dispersions have come, and you will fall like a **choice** vessel.
	NIV	Weep and wail, you shepherds; roll in the dust, you leaders of the flock. For your time to be slaughtered has come; you will fall like **the best** of the rams.
	NLT	Weep and moan, you evil shepherds! Roll in the dust, you leaders of the flock! The time of your slaughter has arrived; you will fall and shatter like a **fragile** vase.

EKLEKTOS – a divergent translation with "vessel" (KJV) given as "rams" (engLXX) – desirable vessel (Heb.) - choice rams (Gk.)

LXX **32:34**

ALALAXATE POIMENES KAI KEKRAXATE KAI KOPTESTHE HOI KRIOI TÓN
shout shepherds and cry out and smite the chest the rams of the

PROBATÓN HOTI EPLÉRÓTHÉSAN HAI HÉMERAI HUMÓN EIS SPHAGÉN KAI
sheep since filled the days of you into slaughter and

PESEISTHE HÓSPER HOI KRIOI HOI ***EKLEKTOI***
ye fall even as the rams the choice

	engLXX	Howl, ye shepherds, and cry; and lament, ye rams of the flock: for your days have been completed for slaughter, and ye shall fall as the choice rams.
Eze. 26:12		And they shall make a spoil of thy riches, and make a prey of thy merchandise: and they shall break down thy walls, and destroy thy **pleasant** houses: and they shall lay thy stones and thy timber and thy dust in the midst of the water.
	YLT	And they have spoiled thy wealth, and they have plundered thy merchandise, and they have thrown down thy walls, and thy **desirable** houses they break down, and thy stones, and thy wood, and thy dust, In the midst of the waters they place.

EPITHUMÉTOS aNT - (to be) desired, desirable – a divergent translation with "riches" (KJV) or "wealth" (YLT), given as "power" (engLXX) – pleasant houses

LXX

KAI PRONOMEUSEI TÉN DUNAMIN SOU KAI SKULEUSEI TA HUPARCHONTA SOU
and plundered the power of you and despoiled the resources of you

KAI KATABALEI TA TEICHÉ SOU KAI TOUS OIKOUS SOU TOUS ***EPITHUMÉTOUS***
and throw down the walls of you and the houses of you the desirable

KATHELEI KAI TOUS LITHOUS SOU KAI TA XULA SOU KAI TON CHOUN SOU EIS
demolish and the stones of you and the trees of you and the dust of you into

MESON TÉS THALASSÉS SOU EMBALEI
midst of the sea of you cast

	engLXX	And he shall prey upon thy power, and plunder thy substance, and shall cast down thy walls, and break down thy pleasant houses: and he shall cast thy stones and thy timber and thy dust into the midst of thy sea.
Dan. 9:23		At the beginning of thy supplications the commandment came forth, and I am come to shew *thee*; for thou *art* greatly **beloved**: therefore understand the matter, and consider the vision.

EPITHUMIA – desire, yearning - a direct translation – Daniel (V.2) is much beloved

LXX *EN ARCHÉ TÉS DEÉSEÓS SOU EXÉLTHE LOGOS KAI EGÓ ÉLTHON TOU*
in beginning of the entreaty of you went word and I came the

ANAGGEILAI SOI HOTI ANÉR ***EPITHUMIÓN*** *EI SU KAI ENNOÉTHÉTI EN TÓ*
to announce to you since man desirable are you and consider in the

RHÉMATI KAI SUNES EN TÉ OPTASIA
saying and perceive in the vision

engLXX At the beginning of thy supplication the word came forth, and I am come to tell thee; for thou art a man much beloved: therefore consider the matter, understand the vision.

Dan. 10:3 I ate no **pleasant** bread, neither came flesh nor wine in my mouth, neither did I anoint myself at all, till three whole weeks were fulfilled.

EPITHUMIA - desire, yearning – a direct translation [though divergent in the engLXX "with oil" (engLXX) is added: "oil" is not in the LXX itself] – pleasant bread

LXX *ARTON* ***EPITHUMIÓN*** *OUK EPHAGON KAI KREAS KAI OINOS OUK EISÉLTHEN EIS*
bread desirable not eat and meat and wine not entered into

TO STOMA MOU KAI ALEIMMA OUK ÉLEIPSAMÉN HEÓS PLÉRÓSEÓS TRIÓN
the mouth of me and anointing not anointed until completion of three

HEBDOMADÓN HÉMERÓN
sevens of days

engLXX I ate no pleasant bread, and no flesh or wine entered into my mouth, neither did I anoint myself with oil, until three whole weeks were accomplished.

Dan. 10:11 And he said unto me, O Daniel, a man greatly **beloved**, understand the words that I speak unto thee, and stand upright: for unto thee am I now sent. And when he had spoken this word unto me, I stood trembling.

EPITHUMIA - desire, yearning – a direct translation – Daniel, a greatly beloved man

LXX *KAI EIPE PROS ME DANIÉL ANÉR* ***EPITHUMIÓN*** *SUNES EN TOIS LOGOIS HOIS EGÓ LALÓ*
and said to me Daniel man desirable perceive in the words which I speak

PROS SE KAI STÉTHI EPI TÉ STASEI SOU HOTI NUN APESTALÉN PROS SE KAI EN TÓ
to you and stand upon the placing of you since now sent to you and in the

LALÉSAI AUTON PROS ME TON LOGON TOUTON ANESTÉN ENTROMOS
speaking it to me the word this arose trembling

engLXX And he said to me, O Daniel, man greatly beloved, understand the words which I speak to thee, and stand upright: for I am now sent to thee. And when he had spoken to me this word, I stood trembling.

Dan. 10:19 And said, O man greatly **beloved**, fear not: peace *be* unto thee, be strong, yea, be strong. And when he had spoken unto me, I was strengthened, and said, Let my lord speak; for thou hast strengthened me.

EPITHUMIA - desire, yearning – a loose translation with "be strong, yea, be strong" (KJV) rendered as "quit thyself like a man, and be strong" (engLXX) – Daniel (V.11), a man greatly beloved

LXX *KAI EIPE MOI MÉ PHOBOU ANÉR* ***EPITHUMIÓN*** *EIRÉNÉ SOI ANDRIZOU KAI*
and said to me not fear man desirable peace to you manly and

ISCHUE KAI EN TÓ LALÉSAI AUTON MET EMOU ISCHUSA KAI EIPA LALEITÓ HO
strong and in the speaking it with me strengthened and said speak the

KURIOS MOU HOTI ENISCHUSAS ME
Lord of me since strengthened me

engLXX and said to me, Fear not, man greatly beloved: peace be to thee, quit thyself like a man, and be strong. And when he had spoken with me, I received strength, and said, Let my lord speak; for thou hast strengthened me.

Dan. 11:8 And shall also carry captives into Egypt their gods, with their princes, *and* with their **precious** vessels of silver and of gold; and he shall continue *more* years than the king of the north.

YLT and also their gods, with their princes, with their **desirable** vessels of silver and gold, into captivity he bringeth *into* Egypt; and he doth stand more years than the king of the north.

EPITHUMÉTOS aNT - (to be) desired, desirable – a divergent translation with "molten" (engLXX) added – desirable vessels of silver and gold

LXX *KAI GE TOUS THEOUS AUTÓN META TÓN CHÓNEUTÓN AUTÓN PAN SKEUOS*
and indeed the gods of you with the molten of them all vessels

EPITHUMÉTON *AUTÓN ARGURIOU KAI CHRUSIOU META AICHMALÓSIAS OISEI*
desirable of them silver and gold with captivity carry

EIS AIGUPTON KAI AUTOS STÉSETAI HUPER BASILEA TOU BORRA
into Egypt and he shall stand over king of the north

engLXX Yea, he shall carry with a body of captives into Egypt their gods with their molten *images, and* all their precious vessels of silver and gold; and he shall last longer than the king of the north.

Dan. 11:37 Neither shall he regard the God of his fathers, nor the **desire** of women, nor regard any god: for he shall magnify himself above all.

YLT And unto the God of his fathers he doth not attend, nor to the **desire** of women, yea, to any god he doth not attend, for against all he magnifieth himself.

EPITHUMIA - desire, yearning – a divergent translation with the first "God" (KJV) rendered as "gods" (engLXX) – desire of women

LXX *KAI EPI PANTAS THEOUS TÓN PATERÓN AUTOU OU SUNÉSEI KAI* ***EPITHUMIA***
and upon all gods of the fathers of him not recognise and desirable

GUNAIKÓN KAI EPI PAN THEON OU SUNÉSEI HOTI EPI PANTAS MEGALUNTHÉSETAI
women and upon every god not recognise since over all will magnify

engLXX And he shall not regard any gods of his fathers, nor the desire of women, neither shall he regard any deity: for he shall magnify himself above all.

Dan. 11:38 But in his estate shall he honour the God of forces: and a god whom his fathers knew not shall he honour with gold, and silver, and with precious stones, and **pleasant things**.

YLT And to the god of strongholds, on his station, he giveth honour; yea, to a god whom his fathers knew not he giveth honour, with gold, and with silver, and with precious stone, and with **desirable** things.

EPITHUMÉMA aNT - desire, yearning – a direct translation – desirable things

LXX *KAI THEON MAÓZEIM EPI TOPOU AUTOU DOXASEI KAI THEON HON OUK*
and god of strength over place of him glorify and god which not

EGNÓSAN HOI PATERES AUTOU DOXASEI EN CHRUSÓ KAI ARGURÓ KAI LITHÓ
know the fathers of him glorify in gold and silver and stones

TIMIÓ KAI EN ***EPITHUMÉMASI***
precious and in desirable

engLXX And he shall honour the god of forces on his place: and a god whom his fathers knew not he shall honour with gold, and silver, and precious stones, and desirable things.

Dan. 11:43 But he shall have power over the treasures of gold and of silver, and over all the **precious** things of Egypt: and the Libyans and the Ethiopians *shall be* at his steps.

YLT and he hath ruled over treasures of gold and of silver, and over all the **desirable** things of Egypt, and Lubim and Cushim *are* at his steps.

EPITHUMÉTOS aNT - (to be) desired, desirable – a divergent translation with "treasures" (KJV) rendered as "secret" (engLXX) – the desirable things of Egypt

LXX *KAI KURIEUSEI EN TOIS APOKRUPHOIS TOU CHRUSOU KAI TOU ARGUROU KAI EN PASIN*
and shall lord in the concealed of the gold and the silver and in all

EPITHUMÉTOIS *AIGUPTOU KAI LIBUÓN KAI AITHIOPÓN EN TOIS OCHURÓMASIN AUTÓN*
desirables of Egypt and Libyans and Ethiopians in the strongholds of them

engLXX And he shall have the mastery over the secret *treasures* of gold and silver, and over all the desirable *possessions* of Egypt, and of the Libyans and Ethiopians in their strongholds.

Hos. 13:15 Though he be fruitful among *his* brethren, an east wind shall come, the wind of the LORD shall come up from the wilderness, and his spring shall become dry, and his fountain shall be dried up: he shall spoil the treasure of all **pleasant** vessels.

YLT Though he among brethren produceth fruit, come in doth an east wind, a wind of Jehovah, from a wilderness it is coming up, and it drieth up his fountain, and become dry doth his spring, it - it spoileth a treasure – every **desirable** vessel.

EPITHUMÉTOS aNT - (to be) desired, desirable – a divergent translation with "be fruitful among *his* brethren" (KJV) or "among brethren produceth fruit" (YLT), rendered as "will cause a division among *his* brethren" (engLXX) – desirable vessels

LXX *DIOTI HOUTOS ANAMESON ADELPHÓN DIASTELEI EPAXEI KAUSÓNA ANEMON*
forasmuch this in between brothers separate bring burning wind

KURIOS EK TÉS ERÉMOU EP AUTON KAI ANAXÉRANEI TAS PHLEBAS AUTOU
Lord out of the desert upon him and dry up the arteries of him

EXERÉMÓSEI TAS PÉGAS AUTOU AUTOS KATAXÉRANEI TÉN GÉN AUTOU KAI
desolate the springs of him he dry up the land of him and

PANTA TA SKEUÉ TA ***EPITHUMÉTA*** *AUTOU*
all the vessels the desirable of him

engLXX Forasmuch as he will cause a division among *his* brethren, the Lord shall bring upon him an east wind from the desert, and shall dry up his veins *and* quite drain his fountains: he shall dry up his land, and *spoil* all his precious vessels.

Nah. 2:9 Take ye the spoil of silver, take the spoil of gold: for *there is* none end of the store *and* glory out of all the **pleasant** furniture.

YLT Seize ye silver, seize ye gold, and there is no end to the prepared things, *to* the abundance of all **desirable** vessels.

EPITHUMÉTOS aNT - (to be) desired, desirable – a divergent translation with "none end of the store" (KJV) or "no end to the prepared things" (YLT), rendered as "was no end of their adorning" (engLXX) [NB – not the common meaning of *KOSMOS*: "world", but "adornment"] – desirable vessels

LXX **2:9** *DIÉRPAZON TO ARGURION DIÉRPAZON TO CHRUSION KAI OUK ÉN PERAS TOU*
plunder the silver plunder the gold and not was limit of the

KOSMOU AUTÉS BEBARUNTAI EPI PANTA TA SKEUÉ TA ***EPITHUMÉTA*** *AUTÉS*
decoration of her weighed down upon all the vessels the desirable of her

engLXX They plundered the silver, they plundered the gold, and there was no end of their adorning; they were loaded *with it* upon all their pleasant vessels.

Hag. 2:7 And I will shake all nations, and the **desire** of all nations shall come: and I will fill this house with glory, saith the Lord of hosts.

YLT And I have shaken all the nations, and they have come *to* the **desire** of all the nations, and I have filled this house *with* honour, said Jehovah of Hosts.

NKJV and I will shake all nations, and they shall come to the **Desire** of All Nations, and I will fill this temple with glory,' says the LORD of hosts.

NASB I will shake all the nations; and [2]they will come with the **wealth** of all nations, and I will fill this house with glory,' says the Lord of hosts.

NIV I will shake all nations, and what is **desired** by all nations will come, and I will fill this house with glory," says the LORD Almighty.

NLT I will shake all the nations, and the **treasures** of all the nations will be brought to this Temple. I will fill this place with glory, says the LORD of Heaven's Armies.

EKLEKTOS – a direct translation (bearing in mind the NASB) – I favour the NKJV: Jesus, the Desire of all nation, at His return (cf. Zechariah 12-14): The Excellent

LXX **2:8** *KAI SUSSEISÓ PANTA TA ETHNÉ KAI HÉXEI TA* ***EKLEKTA*** *PANTÓN TÓN ETHNÓN*
and I shall shake all the nations and | shall come the choice of all of the nations

KAI PLÉSÓ TON OIKON TOUTON DOXÉS LEGEI KURIOS PANTOKRATÓR
and | I shall fill the house this with glory says Lord Almighty

engLXX and I will shake all nations, and the choice *portions* of all the nations shall come: and I will fill this house with glory, saith the Lord Almighty.

Zec. 7:14 But I scattered them with a whirlwind among all the nations whom they knew not. Thus the land was desolate after them, that no man passed through nor returned: for they laid the **pleasant** land desolate.

YLT And I toss them on all the nations, that they have not known, the land hath been desolate behind them, of any passing by and turning back, and they set a **desirable** land for a desolation!

2. Or *the desire of all nations will come*

NKJV “But I scattered them with a whirlwind among all the nations which they had not known. Thus the land became desolate after them, so that no one passed through or returned; for they made the **pleasant** land desolate.”

NASB “but I scattered them with a storm wind among all the nations whom they have not known. Thus the land is desolated behind them so that no one went back and forth, for they made the **pleasant** land desolate.”

NIV “I scattered them with a whirlwind among all the nations, where they were strangers. The land they left behind them was so desolate that no one travelled through it. This is how they made the **pleasant** land desolate.”

NLT As with a whirlwind, I scattered them among the distant nations, where they lived as strangers. Their land became so desolate that no one even traveled through it. They turned their **pleasant** land into a desert.”

EKLEKTOS – a direct translation – the pleasant land Israel recounted by the Lord

LXX *KAI EKBALÓ AUTOUS EIS PANTA TA ETHNÉ HA OUK EGNÓSAN KAI HÉ GÉ*
and cast out them into all the nations which not knew and the land

APHANISTHÉSETAI KATOPISTHEN AUTÓN EK DIODEUONTOS KAI EX
destroy behind of them out of travel through and out of

ANASTREPHONTOS KAI ETAXAN GÉN ***EKLEKTÉN*** *EIS APHANISMON*
returning and set land choice into destruction

engLXX And I will cast them out among all the nations, whom they know not; and the land behind them shall be made utterly destitute of any going through or returning: yea they have made the choice land a desolation.

12 - CHEPHETS

Translated into Greek in the LXX

EKLEKTOS		**1**		**Isaiah 54:12**
THELÉMA	(desire, will)	19		
PRAGMA	(deed, act)	4		
CHREIA	(need)	3		
AXIOS	(worthy)	2		
THELÉTOS	(wished for, desired)	2	aNT	
ACHRÉSTOS	(unprofitable, useless)	1		
BOULOMAI	(to will, wish)	1		
BOULEU-Ó/OMAI	(take counsel)	1		
ERGON	(work)	1		
EUCHRÉSTOS	(useful, serviceable)	1		
MELÓ	(to care)	1		
THELÓ	(to be willing)	1		
NOT in LXX		1		
TOTAL		39		

Translated into English - Both KJV related

Ys Conc.	Count	Ss Conc. No. H 2656	Count
delight	3	pleasure	16
desire	8+1[1]	desire	12
matter	1	delight	3
pleasure	15+1[2]	purpose	3
purpose	3	acceptable	1
thing to be desired	1	delightsome	1
thing to desire	1	matter	1
acceptable	1	pleasant	1
delightsome	1	willingly	1
desire		(vb.)	1
pleasant	1		
willingly	1		
TOTAL	39	TOTAL	39

1. See Ys Conc. pages 247-248
2. See Ys Conc. page 759

Refs — **Text quotes KJV unless otherwise stated**

1Sa. 15:22 — And Samuel said, Hath the LORD *as great* **delight** in burnt offerings and sacrifices, as in obeying the voice of the LORD? Behold, to obey *is* better than sacrifice, *and* to hearken than the fat of rams.

THELÉTOS aNT - wished for, desired – a divergent translation with "good" (engLXX) added to "sacrifice" [the last mention] – the Lord wishes far more, for being obedient than for sacrifices

LXX **1Ki.15:22**
KAI EIPE SAMOUÉL EI ***THELÉTON*** *TÓ KURIÓ HOLOKAUTÓMATA KAI THUSIAS*
and said Samuel are desiring to the Lord burnt offerings and sacrifices

HÓS TO AKOUSAI PHÓNÉS KURIOU IDOU AKOÉ HUPER THUSIAN AGATHÉN KAI
as the to hear voice of Lord Look listening above sacrifice good and

HÉ EPAKROASIS HUPER STEAR KRIÓN
the taking heed above fat of rams

engLXX — And Samuel said, Does the Lord take pleasure in whole-burnt-offerings and sacrifices, as in hearing the words of the Lord? Behold, obedience *is* better than a good sacrifice, and hearkening than the fat of rams.

1Sa. 18:25 — And Saul said, Thus shall ye say to David, The king **desireth** not any dowry, but an hundred foreskins of the Philistines, to be avenged of the king's enemies. But Saul thought to make David fall by the hand of the Philistines.

BOULOMAI - to will, wish, prefer – a direct translation – Saul willed not to have funds, but David's life (so he thought) so, he asked for David to go and fight his enemies with "spoils" from them

LXX **1Ki.18:25**
KAI EIPE SAOUL TADE EREITE TÓ DAUID OU ***BOULETAI*** *HO BASILEUS EN DOMATI ALL É EN*
and said Saul thus shall say to the David not wills the king in gift but only in

HEKATON AKROBUSTIAIS ALLOPHULÓN EKDIKÉSAI ECHTHROUS TOU BASILEÓS KAI SAOUL
hundred foreskins of Philistines to avenge enemies of the king and Saul

		ELOGISATO EMBALEIN AUTON EIS CHEIRAS TÓN ALLOPHULÓN
		reasoned to throw him into hands of the Philistines
	engLXX	And Saul said, Thus shall ye speak to David, The king wants no gift but a hundred foreskins of the Philistines, to avenge himself on the king's enemies. Now Saul thought to cast him into the hands of the Philistines.
2Sa. 23:5		Although my house *be* not so with God; yet he hath made with me an everlasting covenant, ordered in all *things*, and sure: for *this is* all my salvation, and all *my* **desire**, although he make *it* not to grow. [6]But *the sons* of Belial…
	YLT	For - not so *is* my house with God; For - a covenant age-during He made with me, arranged in all things, and kept; for - all my salvation, and all **desire**, for - He hath not caused *it* to spring up. [6]As to the worthless…

THELÉMA - desire, will, wish, decree – a divergent translation with the "to grow" (KJV) or "to spring up" (YLT), well rendered by "flourish" (engLXX), is nevertheless connected to the next clause in the following verse by the word "wicked" (engLXX) instead of David's own house – Vss 1-7 are the "the last words of David" (V.1). Vss 5-7 is a prophetic section including a recall here in V.5 of God's promise to David that from his loins will come Jesus [one who will rule for ever]. Yet, he begins by saying that his "house" is "not so with God" (KJV): his family line would not be as faithful, yet God made a promise. So that, he ends with that, it has not yet happened this promise, as expressed by "he make *it* not" (KJV) "not caused *it*" (YLT) i.e. not yet. He goes on about the wicked (V.6) and his last words in V.7 gives us "And the man who cometh against them is filled with iron and the staff of a spear, and with fire they are utterly burnt in the cessation." (2Sa. 23:7 YLT).

The very last king from David's house: Jesus, will rule with iron (Psalm 2:9; Revelation 2:27) and deal finally i.e. cause a "cessation" with the wicked – David's desire is to see, his "salvation", the fulfilment

LXX	***OU GAR HOUTÓS HO OIKOS MOU META ISCHUROU DIATHÉKÉN GAR AIÓNION***
2Ki.23:5	not for thus the house of me with strength covenant for ever

ETHETO MOI HETOIMÉN EN PANTI KAIRÓ PEPHULAGMENÉN HOTI PASA
put with me at hand in every season being guarded since all

SÓTÉRIA MOU KAI PAN ***THELÉMA*** *HOTI OU MÉ BLASTÉSÉ HO PARANOMOS*
salvation of me and all desire since in no wise shall sprout the lawbreaker

engLXX For my house *is* not so with the Mighty One: for he has made an everlasting covenant with me, ready, guarded at every time; for all my salvation and all my desire *is*, that the wicked should not flourish.

1Ki. 5:8 And Hiram sent to Solomon, saying, I have considered the things which thou sentest to me for: *and* I will do all thy **desire** concerning timber of cedar, and concerning timber of fir.

YLT And Hiram sendeth unto Solomon, saying, 'I have heard that which thou hast sent unto me, I do all thy **desire** concerning cedar-wood, and fir- wood,

THELÉMA - desire, will, wish, decree – a divergent translation omitting to translate "Hiram" (KJV): the LXX translator had already done so in the preceding verse and, though again mentioned in the Heb. did not repeat – Solomon (V.7) desired wood from the land of king Hiram

LXX
3Ki.5:8

KAI APESTEILE PROS SALÓMÓN LEGÓN AKÉKOA PERI PANTÓN HÓN
and sent to Solomon saying I listened about all the

APESTALKAS PROS ME EGÓ POIÉSÓ PAN ***THELÉMA*** *SOU XULA KEDRINA KAI PEUKINA*
sent to me I will do all desire of you trees cedar and of pines

engLXX And he sent to Solomon, saying, I have listened concerning all that thou hast sent to me for: I will do all thy will: *as for* timber of cedar and fir,

---

1Ki. 5:9 My servants shall bring *them* down from Lebanon unto the sea: and I will convey them by sea in floats unto the place that thou shalt appoint me, and will cause them to be discharged there, and thou shalt receive *them*: and thou shalt accomplish my **desire**, in giving food for my household.

THELÉMA - desire, will, wish, decree – a divergent translation with the second "sea" not translated – the desire of king Hiram (V.7-8) that his household be provided with victuals (his land was rich in forests, but not so rich in pasture…)

LXX *HOI DOULOI MOU KATAXOUSIN AUTA EK TOU LIBANOU EIS TÉN THALASSAN*
3Ki.5:9 the servants of me | them out of the Lebanon into the sea
they shall lead down

EGÓ THÉSOMAI AUTA SCHEDIAS HEÓS TOU TOPOU HOU EAN APOSTEILÉS
I will put them on rafts unto the place which ever send

PROS ME KAI EKTINAXÓ AUTA EKEI KAI SU AREIS KAI POIÉSEIS TO ***THELÉMA***
to me and shake off them there and you shall lift and shall do the desire

MOU TOU DOUNAI ARTOUS TÓ OIKÓ MOU
of me the to give bread to the house of me

engLXX my servants shall bring them down from Libanus to the sea: I will form them *into* rafts, *and bring them* to the place which thou shalt send to me *about*; and I will land them there, and thou shalt take *them* up: and thou shalt do my will, in giving bread to my household.

1Ki. 5:10 So Hiram gave Solomon cedar trees and fir trees *according to* all his **desire**.

THELÉMA - desire, will, wish, decree – a direct translation – Solomon desired good wood

LXX *KAI ÉN CHIRAM DIDOUS TÓ SALÓMÓN KEDROUS KAI PEUKAS KAI PAN* ***THELÉMA*** *AUTOU*
3Ki.5:10 and was Chiram giving to the Solomon cedars and of pines and all desire of him

engLXX So Chiram gave to Solomon cedars, and fir trees, and all his desire.

1Ki. 9:11 (*Now* Hiram the king of Tyre had furnished Solomon with cedar trees and fir trees, and with gold, according to all his **desire**,) that then king Solomon gave Hiram twenty cities in the land of Galilee.

THELÉMA - desire, will, wish, decree – a divergent translation with the second "Solomon" (KJV) not translated – Solomon got all he desired from Hiram

LXX ***CHIRAM BASILEUS TUROU ANTELABETO TOU SALÓMÓN EN XULOIS KEDRINOIS KAI EN XULOIS***
3Ki.9:11 Chiram king of Tyre assisted of the Solomon in trees cedar and in trees

PEUKINOIS KAI EN CHRUSIÓ KAI EN PANTI **THELÉMATI** ***AUTOU TOTE EDÓKEN HO***
of pine and in gold and in all desire of him then gave the

BASILEUS TÓ CHIRAM EIKOSI POLEIS EN TÉ GÉ TÉ GALILAIA
king to the Chiram twenty cities in the land the Galilee

engLXX Chiram king of Tyre helped Solomon with cedar wood, and fir wood, and with gold, and all that he wished for: then the king gave Chiram twenty cities in the land of Galilee.

1Ki. 10:13 And king Solomon gave unto the queen of Sheba all her **desire**, whatsoever she asked, beside *that* which Solomon gave her of his royal bounty. So she turned and went to her own country, she and her servants.

YLT And king Solomon gave to the queen of Sheba all her **desire** that she asked, apart from that which he gave to her as a memorial of king Solomon, and she turneth and goeth to her land, she and her servants.

THELÓ - to be willing, to please, to delight in - a divergent translation with "of his royal bounty" (KJV) or "as a memorial" (YLT), given as "by the hand" (engLXX) – the queen of Sheba was given by Solomon all that she delighted in

LXX ***KAI HO BASILEUS SALÓMÓN EDÓKE TÉ BASILISSÉ SABA PANTA HOSA***
3Ki.10:13 and the king Solomon gave the queen Saba all as

ÉTHELÉSEN ***HOSA ÉTÉSATO EKTOS PANTÓN HÓN EDEDÓKEI AUTÉ DIA***
desired as she asked outside of all which gave she through

CHEIROS TOU BASILEÓS SALÓMÓN KAI APESTRAPHÉ KAI ÉLTHEN EIS TÉN GÉN
hand of the king Solomon and she turned back and came into the land

		AUTÉS AUTÉ KAI PANTES HOI PAIDES AUTÉS of her she and all the young servants of her
	engLXX	And king Solomon gave to the queen of Saba all that she desired, whatsoever she asked, besides all that he had given her by the hand of king Solomon: and she returned, and came into her own land, she and her servants.
2Ch. 9:12		And king Solomon gave to the queen of Sheba all her **desire**, whatsoever she asked, beside *that* which she had brought unto the king. So she turned, and went away to her own land, she and her servants.
	YLT	And king Solomon hath given to the queen of Sheba all her **desire** that she asked, apart from that which she had brought unto the king, and she turneth and goeth to her land, she and her servants.

THELÉMA - desire, will, wish, decree – a divergent translation with "her servants" (KJV) not rendered – the queen of Sheba was given all she wished

	LXX	*KAI HO BASILEUS SALÓMÓN EDÓKE TÉ BASILISSÉ SABA PANTA TA* ***THELÉMATA*** and the king Solomon gave the queen Saba all the desire *AUTÉS HA ÉTÉSEN EKTOS PANTÓN HÓN ÉNEGKE TÓ BASILEI SALÓMÓN KAI* of her which asked for outside of all what she brought to the king Solomon and *APESTREPSEN EIS TÉN GÉN AUTÉS* she turned back into the land of her
	engLXX	And king Solomon gave to the queen of Saba all that she requested, besides all that she brought to king Solomon: and she returned to her *own* land.
Job 21:21		For what **pleasure** *hath* he in his house after him, when the number of his months is cut off in the midst?
	YLT	For what *is* his **delight** in his house after him, and the number of his months cut off?

THELÉMA - desire, will, wish, decree – a divergent translation with no sense of a question imparted in the rendering – the wicked are in view (V.17) as Job (V.1) recounts how their will over their house, their ongoing family: is not possible, as they (themselves) are cut off in life

LXX *HOTI TO* ***THELÉMA*** *AUTOU EN OIKÓ AUTOU MET AUTOU KAI ARITHMOI MÉNÓN*
since the desire of him in house of him with him and number of months

AUTOU DIÉRETHÉSAN
of him divided

engLXX For his desire is in his house with him, and the number of his months has been suddenly cut off.

Job 22:3 *Is it* any **pleasure** to the Almighty, that thou art righteous? Or *is it* gain *to him*, that thou makest thy ways perfect?

YLT Is it a **delight** to the Mighty One that thou art righteous? Is it gain, that thou makest perfect thy ways?

MELÓ - to care – a direct translation – Eliphaz (V.1) one of Job's friends who did not speak what is right in the eyes of the Lord: "the Lord said to Eliphaz the Temanite, 'My wrath is aroused against you and your two friends, for you have not spoken of Me *what is* right, as My servant Job *has*' " (Job 42:7 NKJV): he had said: why should the Lord care, have pleasure, delight in you being good?

LXX *TI GAR* ***MELEI*** *TÓ KURIÓ EAN SU ÉSTHA TOIS ERGOIS AMEMPTOS É ÓPHELEIA*
what for concern to the Lord if you were with the works blameless or benefit

HOTI HAPLÓSEIS TÉN HODON SOU
since simplify the way of you

engLXX For what matters it to the Lord, if thou wert blameless in *thy* works? Or is it profitable that thou shouldest perfect thy way?

Job 31:16 If I have withheld the poor from *their* **desire**, or have caused the eyes of the widow to fail;

YLT If I withhold from **pleasure** the poor, and the eyes of the widow do consume,

CHREIA – need, what is necessary – a divergent translation with "If I have" (KJV) or "If I withhold" (YLT), not rendered – what the poor, the helpless (engLXX), desire: what they need

LXX *ADUNATOI DE **CHREIAN** HÉN POTE EICHON OUK APETUCHON CHÉRAS DE TON*
unable but need what at some time | not missed of widow but the

OPHTHALMON OUK EXETÉXA they had
eye not wasted

engLXX But the helpless missed not whatever need they had, and I did not cause the eye of the widow to fail.

Psa. 1:2 But his **delight** *is* in the law of the LORD; and in his law doth he meditate day and night.

THELÉMA - desire, will, wish, decree – a direct translation – the righteous (Vss 5 and 6) take pleasure in the word of God, His law

LXX *ALL É EN TÓ NOMÓ KURIOU TO **THELÉMA** AUTOU KAI EN TÓ NOMÓ AUTOU*
but is in the law of Lord the desire of him and in the law of him

MELETÉSEI HÉMERAS KAI NUKTOS
shall meditate day and night

engLXX But his pleasure is in the law of the Lord; and in his law will he meditate day and night.

Psa. 16:3 *But* to the saints that *are* in the earth, and *to* the excellent, in whom *is* all my **delight**.

YLT For the holy ones who *are* in the land, and the honourable, all my **delight** *is* in them.

THELÉMA - desire, will, wish, decree – a divergent translation with "the excellent" (KJV) or "the honourable" (YLT), not rendered – the king's delight is in the righteous in the land

LXX **15:3** *TOIS HAGIOIS TOIS EN TÉ GÉ AUTOU ETHAUMASTÓSE PANTA TA **THELÉMATA***
to the holy to the in the land of him magnified all the desire

AUTOU EN AUTOIS
of him in them

engLXX On behalf of the saints that are in his land, he has magnified all his pleasure in them.

Psa. 107:30 Then are they glad because they be quiet; so he bringeth them unto their **desired** haven.

YLT And they rejoice because they are quiet, and He leadeth them to the haven of their **desire**.

THELÉMA - desire, will, wish, decree – a direct translation – those who operate ships (V.23) after crying out to the Lord for help (V.28) and receive it as a storm is stilled (V.29) rejoice, as they are led to the safety they desire

LXX **106:30** *KAI EUPHRANTHÉSAN HOTI HÉSUCHASAN KAI HÓDÉGÉSEN AUTOUS EPI*
and made glad since | they were brought to rest and he guided them upon

LIMENA ***THELÉMATOS*** *AUTÓN*
harbour of desire of them

engLXX And they are glad, because they are quiet; and he guides them to their desired haven.

Psa. 111:2 The works of the LORD *are* great, sought out of all them that have **pleasure** therein.

YLT Great *are* the works of Jehovah, Sought out by all **desiring** them.

THELÉMA - desire, will, wish, decree – a divergent translation with "his" (engLXX) added, indicating the desire, purpose or will is God's and not "all" as per the Heb. – All who wish, desire the works of the Lord, seek them (Heb.); the Lord desires, wishes, wills to seek out all his works (Gk.)

LXX **110:2** *MEGALA TA ERGA KURIOU EXEZÉTÉMENA EIS PANTA TA* ***THELÉMATA*** *AUTOU*
great the works of Lord sought out into all the desire of him

engLXX The works of the Lord are great, sought out according to all his will.

Pro. 3:15 She *is* more precious than rubies: and all the things thou canst **desire** are not to be compared unto her.

YLT Precious she *is* above rubies, and all thy **pleasures** are not comparable to her.

AXIOS – worthy, deserving – a divergent translation with "no evil thing shall resist her" (engLXX) added – wisdom (V.13) is not to be compared to any pleasure desired (Heb.); to any precious thing in value (Gk.) [see 8:11 below]

LXX ***TIMIÓTERA DE ESTI LITHÓN POLUTELÓN OUK ANTITAXETAI AUTÉ OUDEN PONÉRON***
more valued but is of stones very costly not shall resist she neither evil

EUGNÓSTOS ESTI PASI TOIS EGGIZOUSIN AUTÉ PAN DE TIMION OUK* AXION *AUTÉS ESTI
familiar is all to the come near she every but precious not worth of her is

engLXX And she is more valuable than precious stones: no evil thing shall resist her: she is well known to all that approach her, and no precious thing is equal to her in value.

Pro. 8:11 For wisdom *is* better than rubies; and all the things that may be **desired** are not to be compared to it.

YLT For better *is* wisdom than rubies, yea, all **delights** are not comparable with it.

AXIOS - worthy, deserving – a divergent translation with "rubies" (KJV) rendered as "precious stones" (engLXX) – wisdom is not to be compared: to any desired delight (Heb.); to any precious thing in value (Gk.) [see 3:15 above]

LXX ***KREISSÓN GAR SOPHIA LITHÓN POLUTELÓN PAN DE TIMION OUK* AXION *AUTÉS ESTIN***
better for wisdom of stones very costly all but precious not worthy of her is

engLXX For wisdom is better than precious stones; and no valuable substance is of equal worth with it.

Pro. 31:13 She seeketh wool, and flax, and worketh **willingly** with her hands.

YLT She hath sought wool and flax, and with **delight** she worketh *with* her hands.

EUCHRÉSTOS - useful, serviceable – a divergent translation with an attitude or feeling of "worketh willingly" (KJV) or "with delight she worketh" (YLT), rendered as the act of transformation "makes it serviceable" (engLXX); as opposed to her attitude whilst she does – a virtuous woman (V.10 KJV) delights and thus works willingly the raw materials she obtains (Heb.); transforms them into useful things (Gk.)

LXX *MÉRUOMENÉ ERIA KAI LINON EPOIÉSEN* ***EUCHRÉSTON*** *TAIS CHERSIN AUTÉS*
gathering up wool and flax she makes useful with the hands of her

engLXX Gathering wool and flax, she makes it serviceable with her hands.

Ecc. 3:1 To every *thing there is* a season, and a time to every **purpose** under the heaven:

YLT To everything - a season, and a time to every **delight** under the heavens:

PRAGMA - deed, act, matter – a direct translation – for every thing to do, there is a proper time for it

LXX *TOIS PASIN HO CHRONOS KAI KAIROS TÓ PANTI* ***PRAGMATI*** *HUPO TON OURANON*
to the all the time and season to the every matter under the heaven

engLXX To all things there is a time, and a season for every matter under heaven.

Ecc. 3:17 I said in mine heart, God shall judge the righteous and the wicked: for *there is* a time there for every **purpose** and for every work.

YLT I said in my heart, 'The righteous and the wicked doth God judge, for a time *is* to every **matter** and for every work there.'

PRAGMA - deed, act, matter – a direct translation – every intent, purpose, delight, thing, there is a time for: but if wicked God will judge; if righteous he will discern

LXX *KAI EIPA EGÓ EN KARDIA MOU SUN TON DIKAION KAI SUN TON ASEBÉ KRINEI*
and said I in heart of me with the righteous and with the impious judge

HO THEOS HOTI KAIROS TÓ PANTI ***PRAGMATI*** *KAI EPI PANTI TÓ POIÉMATI EKEI*
the God since season to the every matter and upon every to the doing there

engLXX And I said in my heart, God will judge the righteous and the ungodly: for there is a time there for every action and for every work.

Ecc. 5:4 When thou vowest a vow unto God, defer not to pay it; for *he hath* no **pleasure** in fools: pay that which thou hast vowed.

THELÉMA - desire, will, wish, decree – a direct translation – God has no delight, no pleasure, in fools: identified here as someone who made a promise to God and whilst able, delays in fulfilling it. This is separate and different to tithing, wherein the law under which it was governed for the Jews, permitted a withholding which terminated with a later payment of it with a fifth to be added to what is owed, when the ability to repay occurs (20%): "If a man wants at all to redeem *any* of his tithes, he shall add one-fifth to it" (Lev. 27:31 NKJV)

LXX **5:3** ***KATHÓS EUXÉ EUCHÉN TÓ THEÓ MÉ CHRONISÉS TOU APODOUNAI AUTÉN***
and as vow vow to the God not time of the to render her

HOTI OUK ESTI **THELÉMA** ***EN APHROSI SU OUN HOSA EAN EUXÉ APODOS***
since not is desire in foolish you therefore | as many as if vowed render

engLXX Whenever thou shalt vow a vow to God, defer not to pay it; for *he has* no pleasure in fools: pay thou therefore whatsoever thou shalt have vowed.

Ecc. 5:8 If thou seest the oppression of the poor, and violent perverting of judgment and justice in a province, marvel not at the **matter**: for *he that is* higher than the highest regardeth; and *there be* higher than they.

YLT If oppression of the poor, and violent taking away of judgment and righteousness thou seest in a province, do not marvel at the **matter**, for a higher than the high is observing, and high ones *are* over them.

PRAGMA - deed, act, matter – a direct translation – one is not to wonder, to be too upset, at the evil desire, wish, action of a functionary as there is in place others above him (also) watching

LXX **5:7** *EAN SUKOPHANTIAN PENÉTOS KAI HARPAGÉN KRIMATOS KAI DIKAIOSUNÉS*
if oppression of needy and seizure of judgment and of judicial right

IDÉS EN CHÓRA MÉ THAUMASÉS EPI TÓ ***PRAGMATI*** *HOTI HUPSÉLOS EPANÓ*
see in land not marvel over the matter since high above

HUPSÉLOU PHULAXAI KAI HUPSÉLOI EP AUTOIS
of high shall guard and high ones over them

engLXX If thou shouldest see the oppression of the poor, and the wresting of judgment and of justice in the land, wonder not at the matter: for *there is* a high one to watch over him that is high, and high ones over them.

Ecc. 8:6 Because to every **purpose** there is time and judgment, therefore the misery of man *is* great upon him.

YLT For to every **delight** there is a time and a judgment, for the misfortune of man is great upon him.

PRAGMA - deed, act, matter – a divergent translation with "misery" (KJV) or "misfortune" (YLT), rendered as "knowledge" (engLXX): though it could be argued this is one of those interpretations of "knowing"… - every purpose, delight, matter there is a time for, but a corresponding judgment also, dependent on whether it was righteous or wicked

LXX *HOTI PANTI* ***PRAGMATI*** *ESTI KAIROS KAI KRISIS HOTI GNÓSIS TOU*
since every matter is season and judgment since knowledge of the

ANTHRÓPOU POLLÉ EP AUTON
man large unto him

engLXX For to every thing there is time and judgment; for the knowledge of a man is great to him.

Ecc. 12:1 Remember now thy Creator in the days of thy youth, while the evil days come not, nor the years draw nigh, when thou shalt say, I have no **pleasure** in them;

THELÉMA - desire, will, wish, decree – a direct translation – as one grows much older, in contrast to one's youth, the days have less pleasure, it can be said: and these, as well as evil days will be best handled or not happen, if one remains true to God throughout one's early days. Reminiscent of the promise of a long life if one honours one's parents (Ephesians 6:1-3)

LXX *KAI MNÉSTHÉTI TOU KTISANTOS SE EN HÉMERAIS NEOTÉTOS SOU*
and remember of the creating you in days of youth of you

HEÓS HOTOU MÉ ELTHÓSIN HAI HÉMERAI TÉS KAKIAS KAI PHTHASÓUSIN ETÉ
while not should come the days of the bad and should arrive years

EN HOIS EREIS OUK ESTI MOI EN AUTOIS ***THELÉMA***
in which you shall say not is to me in them desire

engLXX And remember thy Creator in the days of thy youth, before the days of evil come, and the years overtake *thee* in which thou shalt say, I have no pleasure in them.

Ecc. 12:10 The preacher sought to find out **acceptable** words: and *that which was* written *was* upright, *even* words of truth.

YLT The preacher sought to find out **pleasing** words, and, written *by* the upright, words of truth.

THELÉMA - desire, will, wish, decree – a direct translation – words that are good, correct, helpful, pleasing, desirable: all for the purpose of writing down

LXX *POLLA EZÉTÉSEN EKKLÉSIASTÉS TOU HEUREIN LOGOUS* ***THELÉMATOS*** *KAI*
much sought ecclesiastic of the to find words desirable and

GEGRAMMENON EUTHUTÉTOS LOGOUS ALÉTHEIAS
writing of uprightness words of truth

engLXX The Preacher sought diligently to find out acceptable words, and a correct writing, *even* words of truth.

Isa. 44:28 That saith of Cyrus, *He is* my shepherd, and shall perform all my **pleasure**: even saying to Jerusalem, Thou shalt be built; and to the temple, Thy foundation shall be laid.

YLT Who is saying of Cyrus, My shepherd, and all my **delight** He doth perfect, so as to say of Jerusalem, Thou art built, and of the temple, Thou art founded.

THELÉMA - desire, will, wish, decree – a divergent translation with the added of Cyrus being asked to "be wise" (engLXX) lit. Gk. to discern, be intelligent, or think [cf. *SOPHIA* = wisdom] – all that the Lord (V.24) wishes done, all he is pleased to see happen, what He delights in occurring, His will, shall be done by Cyrus: in particular context, release the Jews to return to rebuild Jerusalem and the temple

LXX

HO	*LEGÓN*	*KURÓ*	*PHRONEIN*	*KAI*	*PANTA*	*TA*	***THELÉMATA***	*MOU*	*POIÉSEI*	*HO*	*LEGÓN*
the	telling	Cyrus	to think	and	all	the	desire	of me	shall do	the	telling

HIEROUSALÉM	*OIKODOMÉTHÉSÉ*	*KAI*	*TON*	*OIKON*	*TON*	*HAGION*	*MOU*	*THEMELIÓSÓ*
Jerusalem	shall be built	and	the	house	the	holy	of me	shall found

engLXX Who bids Cyrus be wise, and he shall perform all my will: who says to Jerusalem, Thou shalt be built, and I will lay the foundation of my holy house.

Isa. 46:10 Declaring the end from the beginning, and from ancient times *the things* that are not *yet* done, saying, My counsel shall stand, and I will do all my **pleasure**:

YLT Declaring from the beginning the latter end, and from of old that which hath not been done, saying, 'My counsel doth stand, and all My **delight** I do.'

BOULEU-Ó/OMAI - take counsel, to devise – a divergent translation with "they are accomplished together" (engLXX) added and not readable in the Heb. – all that God (V.9) delights to see happen, all His pleasure, which He declares beforehand shall come to pass. This is unlike what God plans or intends to do, but does not declare beforehand (cf. 1Sa. 13:13 where the plan to have Saul's dynasty remain forever was not declared beforehand: whilst David's was, and Jesus was thereby ensured to become a "son of David" since God does, what He declares: "Indeed I have spoken *it*; I will also bring it to pass. I have purposed *it*; I will also do it." (Isa. 46:11 NKJV): in context, as per Isa. 46:10 above, God declared in advance that after 70 years he would bring the people back and to do this He raised up Cyrus to release them to go and rebuild Jerusalem

LXX *ANAGGELLÓN PROTERON TA ESCHATA PRIN GENESTHAI KAI HAMA SUNETELESTHÉ KAI*
announcing formerly the last before becoming and also completed and

EIPA PASA HÉ BOULÉ MOU STÉSETAI KAI PANTA HOSA ***BEBOULEUMAI*** *POIÉSÓ*
said all the will of me shall stand and all as much as have planned I shall do

engLXX telling beforehand the latter events before they come to pass, and they are accomplished together: and I said, all my counsel shall stand, and I will do all things that I have planned:

Isa. 48:14 All ye, assemble yourselves, and hear; which among them hath declared these *things*? The LORD hath loved him: he will do his **pleasure** on Babylon, and his arm *shall be on* the Chaldeans.

YLT Be gathered all of you, and hear, who among them did declare these things? Jehovah hath loved him, He doth His **pleasure** on Babylon, and His arm *is on* the Chaldeans.

THELÉMA - desire, will, wish, decree – a divergent translation with "his arm *shall be on* the Chaldeans" (KJV) rendered as "to abolish the seed of the Chaldeans" (engLXX) – The Lord does what He pleases upon Babylon

LXX *KAI SUNACHTHÉSONTAI PANTES KAI AKOUSONTAI TIS AUTOIS ANÉGGEILE TAUTA AGAPÓN*
and shall assemble all and shall hear who to them proclaimed these loving

SE EPOIÉSA TO ***THELÉMA*** *SOU EPI BABULÓNA TOU ARAI SPERMA CHALDAIÓN*
you did the desire of you upon Babylon of the lift away seed of Chaldeans

engLXX And all shall be gathered, and shall hear: who has told them these things? Out of love to thee I have fulfilled thy desire on Babylon, to abolish the seed of the Chaldeans.

Isa. 53:10 Yet it pleased the LORD to bruise him; he hath put *him* to grief: when thou shalt make his soul an offering for sin, he shall see *his* seed, he shall prolong *his* days, and the **pleasure** of the LORD shall prosper in his hand.

YLT And Jehovah hath delighted to bruise him, He hath made him sick, if his soul doth make an offering for guilt, He seeth seed - he prolongeth days, and the **pleasure** of Jehovah in his hand doth prosper.

NOT in LXX – a divergent translation with "and the pleasure of the LORD shall prosper in his hand." (KJV) or "and the pleasure of Jehovah in his hand doth prosper" (YLT), not translated: the very clause that contains the word

LXX *KAI KURIOS BOULETAI KATHARISAI AUTON APO TÉS PLÉGÉS EAN DÓTE PERI*
and Lord willed to clean him from the beating if should give about

HAMARTIAS HÉ PSUCHÉ HUMÓN OPSETAI SPERMA MAKROBION
sin the soul of you shall see seed long-live

engLXX The Lord also is pleased to purge him from his stroke. If ye can give an offering for sin, your soul shall see a long-lived seed:

Isa. 54:12 And I will make thy windows of agates, and thy gates of carbuncles, and all thy borders of **pleasant** stones.

YLT And have made of agate thy pinnacles, and thy gates of carbuncle stones, and all thy border of stones of **delight**,

NKJV I will make your pinnacles of rubies, your gates of crystal, and all your walls of **precious** stones.

NASB "Moreover, I will make your battlements of rubies, and your gates of crystal, and your entire wall of **precious** stones.

NIV I will make your battlements of rubies, your gates of sparkling jewels, and all your walls of **precious** stones.

NLT I will make your towers of sparkling rubies, your gates of shining gems, and your walls of **precious** stones.

EKLEKTOS – with possible exception to "jasper" (engLXX) rendered for "agates" (KJV) and, "crystal" (engLXX) rendered for "carbuncles" [a red gem] (KJV), it is otherwise a direct translation – precious stones of quality

LXX *KAI THÉSÓ TAS EPALXEIS SOU IASPIN KAI TAS PULAS SOU LITHOUS*
and will set the battlements of you jasper and the gates of you stones

KRUSTALLOU KAI TON PERIBOLON SOU LITHOUS ***EKLEKTOUS***
crystal and the enclosure of you stones choice

engLXX and I will make thy buttresses jasper, and thy gates crystal, and thy border precious stones.

Isa. 58:3 Wherefore have we fasted, *say they*, and thou seest not? *Wherefore* have we afflicted our soul, and thou takest no knowledge? Behold, in the day of your fast ye find **pleasure**, and exact all your labours.

YLT 'Why have we fasted, and Thou hast not seen? We have afflicted our soul, and Thou knowest not.' Lo, in the day of your fast ye find **pleasure**, and all your labours ye exact.

THELÉMA - desire, will, wish, decree – a divergent translation with "Behold" (KJV) or "Lo" (YLT), not rendered: given as "Nay" (engLXX) but not from the LXX – instead of really fasting, the people of Jacob (V.1) were both using their time to find pleasure and exacting upon their workers: fasting is identifying with a contrition of the soul and not just a physical deprivation of some kind, so that using the time on oneself is contradictory

LXX *LEGONTES TI HOTI ENÉSTEUSAMEN KAI OUK EIDES ETAPEINÓSAMEN TAS*
saying why since we fasted and not look we humbled the

PSUCHAS HÉMÓN KAI OUK EGNÓS EN GAR TAIS HÉMERAIS TÓN NÉSTEIÓN
souls of us and not know in for the days of the fasts

HUMÓN HEURISKETE TA ***THELÉMATA*** *HUMÓN KAI PANTAS TOUS*
you ye find the desires of you and all the

HUPOCHEIRIOUS HUMÓN HUPONUSSETE
under of you ye goad

	engLXX	saying, Why have we fasted, and thou regardest not? *Why* have we afflicted our souls, and thou didst not know it? Nay, in the days of your fasts ye find your pleasures, and all them that are under your power ye wound.
Isa. 58:13a		If thou turn away thy foot from the sabbath, *from* doing thy **pleasure** on my holy day; and call the sabbath a delight, the holy of the LORD, (. . .)
	YLT	If thou dost turn from the sabbath thy foot, doing thine own **pleasure** on My holy day, and hast cried to the sabbath, 'A delight,' to the holy of Jehovah, (. . .)

THELÉMA - desire, will, wish, decree – a divergent translation remitting "sabbath" (KJV) in the plural – if you cease what you desire to do, the normal pleasures, for a day a week to commit it to the Lord

LXX

EAN APOSTREPSÉS TON PODA SOU APO TÓN SABBATÓN TOU MÉ POIEIN TA
If turn back the feet of you from the sabbaths of the not to do the

THELÉMATA *SOU EN TÉ HÉMERA TÉ HAGIA KAI KALESEIS TA SABBATA*
desires of you in the day the holy and you shall call the sabbaths

TRUPHERA HAGIA TÓ THEÓ . . .
delightful holy to the God

	engLXX	If thou turn away thy foot from the sabbath, so as not to do thy pleasure on the holy days, and shalt call the sabbaths delightful, holy to God; (. . .)
Isa. 58:13b		. . . honourable; and shalt honour him, not doing thine own ways, nor finding thine own **pleasure**, nor speaking *thine own* words:
	YLT	. . . 'Honoured,' and hast honoured it, without doing thine own ways, without finding thine own **pleasure**, and speaking a word.

ERGON – work, deed, occupation – a divergent translation with “honourable; and shalt honour him” (KJV) or “‘Honoured,’ and hast honoured it” (YLT), not rendered – finding thine own pleasure rendered as “lift up thy foot to work” (engLXX): doing your own pleasure (Heb.) doing your own work (Gk.)

LXX . . . *OUK AREIS TON PODA SOU EP* ***ERGÓ*** *OUDE LALÉSEIS LOGON EN ORGÉ EK*
not lift the feet of you upon work nor speak word in anger out of

TOU STOMATOS SOU
the mouth of you

engLXX . . . *if* thou shalt not lift up thy foot to work, nor speak a word in anger out of thy mouth,

Jer. 22:28 *Is* this man Coniah a despised broken idol? *Is he* a vessel wherein *is* no **pleasure**? Wherefore are they cast out, he and his seed, and are cast into a land which they know not?

YLT A grief -- a despised broken thing -- is this man Coniah? A vessel in which there is no **pleasure**? Wherefore have they been cast up and down, he and his seed, Yea, they were cast on to a land that they knew not?

CHREIA - need, what is necessary – a divergent translation with “Wherefore are they cast out, he and his seed” (KJV) or “Wherefore have they been cast up and down, he and his seed” (YLT), not rendered – a vessel in which there is no pleasure, no use, no need [see 48:38 below]

LXX *ÉTIMÓTHÉ IECHONIAS HÓS SKEUOS HOU OUK ESTI* ***CHREIA*** *AUTOU HOTI*
disgraced Jechonias as vessel which not is need of it since

EXERRIPHÉ KAI EXEBLÉTHÉ EIS GÉN HÉN OUK ÉDEI
thrown out and cast forth into land which not knew

engLXX Jechonias is dishonoured as a good-for-nothing vessel; for he is thrown out and cast forth into a land which he knew not.

Jer. 48:38 — *There shall be* lamentation generally upon all the housetops of Moab, and in the streets thereof: for I have broken Moab like a vessel wherein *is* no **pleasure**, saith the LORD.

YLT — On all roofs of Moab, and in her broad-places, all of it - *is* lamentation, for I have broken Moab as a vessel in which there is no **pleasure**, an affirmation of Jehovah.

CHREIA - need, what is necessary – a divergent translation with the second Moab not rendered - a vessel in which there is no pleasure, no use, no need [see 22:28 above]

LXX **31:38** — *KAI EPI PANTÓN TÓN DÓMATÓN MÓAB KAI EPI TAIS PLATEIAIS AUTÉS HOTI*
and upon all the roofs of Moab and upon the squares of her since

SUNETRIPSA PHÉSI KURIOS HÓS AGGEION HOU OUK ESTI ***CHREIA*** *AUTOU*
I crushed completely says Lord as receptacle which not is need of it

engLXX — And on all the housetops of Moab, and in his streets *shall be mourning:* for I have broken *him*, saith the Lord, as a vessel, which is useless.

Hos. 8:8 — Israel is swallowed up: now shall they be among the Gentiles as a vessel wherein *is* no **pleasure**.

YLT — Israel hath been swallowed up, now they have been among nations, as a vessel in which is no **delight**.

ACHRÉSTOS - unprofitable, useless – a direct translation - a vessel in which there is no pleasure, no delight, no need, useless

LXX — *KATEPOTHÉ ISRAÉL NUN EGENETO EN TOIS ETHNESIN HÓS SKEUOS* ***ACHRÉSTON***
swallowed down Israel now become in the nations as vessel useless

engLXX — Israel is swallowed up: now is he become among the nations as a worthless vessel.

Mal. 1:10 — Who *is there* even among you that would shut the doors *for nought*? Neither do ye kindle *fire* on mine altar for nought. I have no **pleasure** in you, saith the LORD of hosts, neither will I accept an offering at your hand.

YLT Who *is* even among you, and he shutteth the two-leaved doors? Yea, ye do not kindle Mine altar for nought, I have no **pleasure** in you, said Jehovah of Hosts, and a present I do not accept of your hand.

THELÉMA - desire, will, wish, decree – a direct translation – the priests (V.6) and all Israel (V.1) do not honour God, and as the priests are singled out, the shutting of temple doors, perhaps a reference to lack of service being provided, and also the altar fire not maintained, so the Lord exclaims He has no pleasure in them: He has no desire in them

LXX *DIOTI KAI EN HUMIN SUGKLEISTHÉSONTAI THURAI KAI OUK ANAPSETAI TO*
because and in you shall be shut doors and not lit the

THUSIASTÉRION MOU DÓREAN OUK ESTI MOU ***THELÉMA*** *EN HUMIN LEGEI*
altar of me gratuitously not is of me desire in you says

KURIOS PANTOKRATÓR KAI THUSIAN OU PROSDEXOMAI EK TÓN CHEIRÓN HUMÓN
Lord Almighty and sacrifice not receive favourably out of the hands of you

engLXX Because even among you the doors shall be shut, and *one* will not kindle *the fire of* mine altar for nothing, I have no pleasure in you, saith the Lord Almighty, and I will not accept a sacrifice at your hands.

Mal. 3:12 And all nations shall call you blessed: for ye shall be a **delightsome** land, saith the LORD of hosts.

YLT And declared you happy have all the nations, for ye are a **delightful** land, said Jehovah of Hosts.

THELÉTOS aNT - wished for, desired – a direct translation – the land of Israel is blessed and a delight when God's blessing rests on it and the enemy is rebuked, as a direct outcome of the people being faithful in tithing (V.10)

LXX *KAI MAKARIOUSIN HUMAS PANTA TA ETHNÉ DIOTI ESESTHE HUMEIS GÉ*
and pronounce happy you all the nations because ye shall be you land

THELÉTÉ *LEGEI KURIOS PANTOKRATÓR*
wanted says Lord Almighty

engLXX And all nations shall call you blessed: for ye shall be a desirable land, saith the Lord Almighty.

13 - CHOPHESH

Translated into Greek in the LXX

EKLEKTOS	**1**	**Ezekiel 27:20**
TOTAL	1	

Translated into English - Both KJV related

Ys Conc.	Count	Ss Conc. No. H 2667	Count
precious	1	precious	1
TOTAL	1	TOTAL	1

Refs	Text quotes KJV unless otherwise stated
Eze. 27:20	Dedan *was* thy merchant in **precious** clothes for chariots.
YLT	Dedan *is* thy merchant, for clothes **of freedom** for riding.
NKJV	Dedan *was* your merchant in **saddlecloths** for riding.
NASB	Dedan traded with you in **saddlecloths** for riding.
NIV	Dedan traded in **saddle** blankets with you.
NLT	"Dedan sent merchants to trade their expensive **saddle** blankets with you.

EKLEKTOS - A divergent translation with "precious clothes" (KJV) given as "choice cattle" (engLXX) - the ongoing emphasis of high value is retained with the word: precious, choice

LXX *DAIDAN EMPOROI SOU META KTÉNÓN* ***EKLEKTÓN*** *EIS HARMATA*
Daidan merchants of you with livestock choice to chariots

engLXX *The people of* Dædan were thy merchants, with choice cattle for chariots.

14 - DEROR

Translated into Greek in the LXX

EKLEKTOS		**1**		**Exodus 30:23**
APHESIS	(release)	7		
STROUTHOS	(sparrow)	1	aNT	
TRUGÓN	(turtle-dove)	1		
TOTAL		10		

Translated into English - Both KJV related

Ys Conc.	Count	Ss Conc. No. H 1865 / H1866	Count
		1865	
liberty	7	liberty	7
pure	1	pure	1
		1866	
swallow	2	swallow	2
TOTAL	10	TOTAL	10

Refs	Text quotes KJV unless otherwise stated
Exo. 30:23	Take thou also unto thee principal spices, of **pure** myrrh five hundred *shekels*, and of sweet cinnamon half so much, *even* two hundred and fifty *shekels*, and of sweet calamus two hundred and fifty *shekels*,
YLT	And thou, take to thyself principal spices, **wild** honey five hundred *shekels*; and spice-cinnamon, the half of that, two hundred and fifty; and spice-cane two hundred and fifty;
NKJV	"Also take for yourself quality spices—five hundred *shekels* of **liquid** myrrh, half as much sweet-smelling cinnamon (two hundred and fifty *shekels*), two hundred and fifty *shekels* of sweet-smelling cane,
NASB	"Take also for yourself the finest of spices: of **flowing** myrrh five hundred *shekels*, and of fragrant cinnamon half as much, two hundred and fifty, and of fragrant cane two hundred and fifty,
NIV	'Take the following fine spices: 500 shekels of **liquid** myrrh, half as much (that is, 250 shekels) of fragrant cinnamon, 250 shekels of fragrant calamus,
NLT	"Collect choice spices—12 1⁄2 pounds of **pure** myrrh, 6 1⁄4 pounds of fragrant cinnamon, 6 1⁄4 pounds of fragrant calamus,

EKLEKTOS – a divergent translation with "flower" added – YLT has "wild honey": on page 784 of (his) Ys Concordance he has the Hebrew word understood as "*Liberty, wildness*"; but why "honey" is unclear - the idea of "pure" is conveyed by "choice" myrrh

LXX

KAI SU LABE HÉDUSMATA TO ANTHOS SMURNÉS ***EKLEKTÉS*** *PENTAKOSIOUS*
and you take spices the flower myrrh choice five hundred

SIKLOUS KAI KINNAMÓMOU EUÓDOUS TO HÉMISU TOUTOU DIAKOSIOUS
shekels and cinnamon fragrant the half of this two hundred

PENTÉKONTA KAI KALAMOU EUÓDOUS DIAKOSIOUS PENTÉKONTA
fifty and calamus fragrant two hundred fifty

engLXX Do thou also take sweet herbs, the flower of choice myrrh five hundred shekels, and the half of this two hundred and fifty shekels of sweet -smelling cinnamon, and two hundred and fifty shekels of sweet-smelling calamus,

Levi. 25:10 And ye shall hallow the fiftieth year, and proclaim **liberty** throughout *all* the land unto all the inhabitants thereof: it shall be a jubile unto you; and ye shall return every man unto his possession, and ye shall return every man unto his family.

YLT and ye have hallowed the year, the fiftieth year; and ye have proclaimed **liberty** in the land to all its inhabitants; a jubilee it is to you; and ye have turned back each unto his possession; yea, each unto his family ye do turn back.

APHESIS – release, letting go, cancellation (of debt) – a divergent translation with the added "given a year of release" (engLXX) in front of "a jubilee" – a release of debt in the year of jubilee

LXX *KAI HAGIASETE TO ETOS TON PENTÉKOSTON ENIAUTON KAI DIABOÉSETE*
and ye sanctify the year the fiftieth year and proclaim forth

APHESIN *EPI TÉS GÉS PASI TOIS KATOIKOUSIN AUTÉN ENIAUTOS APHESEÓS*
release upon the land to all the dwelling her year of release

SÉMASIA AUTÉ ESTAI HUMIN KAI APELEUSETAI EIS HEKASTOS EIS TÉN KTÉSIN
sign she shall be to you and depart into each into the | acquisition

AUTOU KAI HEKASTOS EIS TÉN PATRIAN AUTOU APELEUSESTHE
of him and each into the family of him depart

engLXX And ye shall sanctify the year, the fiftieth year, and ye shall proclaim a release upon the land to all that inhabit it; it shall be given a year of release, a jubilee for you; and each one shall depart to his possession, and ye shall go each to his family.

Psa. 84:3 Yea, the sparrow hath found an house, and the **swallow** a nest for herself, where she may lay her young, *even* thine altars, O LORD of hosts, my King, and my God.

YLT (Even a sparrow hath found a house, and a **swallow** a nest for herself, where she hath placed her brood,) thine altars, O Jehovah of Hosts, my king and my God.

TRUGÓN – turtledove – a divergent translation with a different bird "turtle-dove" (engLXX) instead of "swallow" (KJV) – Heb. swallow Gk. turtledove

LXX **83:3**
KAI GAR STROUTHION HEUREN HEAUTÓ OIKIAN KAI ***TRUGÓN*** *NOSSIAN HEAUTÉ*
and for small sparrow found for himself house and turtle-dove nestlings for herself

HOU THÉSEI TA NOSSIA HEAUTÉS TA THUSIASTÉRIA SOU KURIE TÓN
where lay the nestlings of herself the altars of you Lord of the

DUNAMEÓN HO BASILEUS MOU KAI HO THEOS MOU
powers the king of me and the God of me

engLXX Yea, the sparrow has found himself a home, and the turtle-dove a nest for herself, where she may lay her young, *even* thine altars, O Lord of hosts my King, and my God.

Pro. 26:2 As the bird by wandering, as the **swallow** by flying, so the curse causeless shall not come.

YLT As a bird by wandering, as a **swallow** by flying, so reviling without cause doth not come.

STROUTHOS aNT – sparrow, ostrich [e.g. Job 30:29 engLXX] – a divergent translation with "swallow" (KJV) given as different bird: "sparrow" (engLXX) - heb. swallow Gk. sparrow

LXX
HÓSPER ORNEA PETATAI KAI ***STROUTHOI*** *HOUTÓS ARA MATAIA OUK EPELEUSETAI OUDENI*
even as birds fly and sparrows so cursing vain not come upon not one

engLXX As birds and sparrows fly, so a curse shall not come upon any one without a cause.

Isa. 61:1 — The Spirit of the Lord GOD *is* upon me; because the LORD hath anointed me to preach good tidings unto the meek; he hath sent me to bind up the brokenhearted, to proclaim **liberty** to the captives, and the opening of the prison to *them that are* bound;

YLT — The Spirit of the Lord Jehovah *is* on me, because Jehovah did anoint me to proclaim tidings to the humble, He sent me to bind the broken of heart, to proclaim to captives **liberty**, and to bound ones an opening of bands.

APHESIS - release, letting go, cancellation (of debt) – a divergent translation with "recovery of sight to the blind" (engLXX) added – release, liberty, pronounced to the captives

LXX — *PNEUMA KURIOU EP EME HOU HEINEKEN ECHRISE ME EUAGGELISASTHAI*
Spirit of Lord upon me where for cause anoint me to proclaim

PTÓCHOIS APESTALKE ME IASASTHAI TOUS SUNTETRIMMENOUS TÉN KARDIAN
to poor sent me to heal the broken with the heart

KÉRUXAI AICHMALÓTOIS ***APHESIN*** *KAI TUPHLOIS ANABLEPSIN*
to proclaim to captives release and to blind seeing

engLXX — The Spirit of the Lord is upon me, because he has anointed me; he has sent me to preach glad tidings to the poor, to heal the broken in heart, to proclaim liberty to the captives, and recovery of sight to the blind;

Jer. 34:8 — *This is* the word that came unto Jeremiah from the LORD, after that the king Zedekiah had made a covenant with all the people which *were* at Jerusalem, to proclaim **liberty** unto them;

YLT — The word that hath been unto Jeremiah from Jehovah, after the making by the king Zedekiah of a covenant with all the people who *are* in Jerusalem, to proclaim to them **liberty**,

APHESIS - release, letting go, cancellation (of debt) – a divergent translation with "Jerusalem" not rendered – the proclaiming of release, liberty to the Hebrew manservants and maidservants (V.9)

LXX **41:8** *HO LOGOS HO GENOMENOS PROS HIEREMIAN PARA KURIOU META TO SUNTELESAI TON*
the word the came to be to Jeremiah by Lord after the complete the

BASILEA SEDEKIAN DIATHÉKÉN PROS TON LAON TOU KALESAI ***APHESIN***
king Sedekia covenant with the people of the to call release

engLXX The word that came from the Lord to Jeremias, after king Sedekias had concluded a covenant with the people, to proclaim a release;

Jer. 34:15 And ye were now turned, and had done right in my sight, in proclaiming **liberty** every man to his neighbour; and ye had made a covenant before me in the house which is called by my name:

YLT And ye turn back, ye to-day, and ye do that which is right in Mine eyes, to proclaim **liberty** each to his neighbour, and ye make a covenant before Me in the house over which My name is called.

APHESIS - release, letting go, cancellation (of debt) – a direct translation – the declaring of release, liberty, to annul debt held in servitude

LXX **41:15** *KAI EPESTREPSAN SÉMERON POIÉSAI TO EUTHES PRO OPHTHALMÓN MOU TOU KALESAI*
and turned today to do the right before eyes of me of the to call

APHESIN *HEKASTON TOU PLÉSION AUTOU KAI SUNETELESAN DIATHÉKÉN KATA PROSÓPON*
release each of the neighbour of him and complete covenant according to face

MOU EN TÓ OIKÓ HOU EPEKLÉTHÉ TO ONOMA MOU EP AUTÓ
of me in the house where called the name of me upon to it

engLXX And this day they turned to do that which was right in my sight, to proclaim every one the release of his neighbour; and they had concluded a covenant before me, in the house whereon my name is called.

Jer. 34:17a Therefore thus saith the LORD; ye have not hearkened unto me, in proclaiming **liberty**, every one to his brother, and every man to his neighbour: (. . .)

YLT 'Therefore, thus said Jehovah: Ye have not hearkened unto Me to proclaim **freedom**, each to his brother, and each to his neighbour; (. . .)

APHESIS - release, letting go, cancellation (of debt) – a divergent translation omitting to translate "every one to his brother" (KJV); only translating "every man to his neighbour" (KJV) – the declaring of release, liberty, was not carried out

LXX **41:17a**
DIATOUTO HOUTÓS EIPE KURIOS HUMEIS OUK ÉKOUSATE MOU TOU KALESAI
because of this thus says Lord you not listened of me of the to call

APHESIN *HEKASTOS PROS TON PLÉSION AUTOU . . .*
release each to the neighbour of him

engLXX Therefore thus said the Lord; ye have not hearkened to me, to proclaim a release every one to his neighbour: . . .

Jer. 34:17b . . . behold, I proclaim a **liberty** for you, saith the LORD, to the sword, to the pestilence, and to the famine; and I will make you to be removed into all the kingdoms of the earth.

YLT . . . lo, I am proclaiming to you **liberty** - an affirmation of Jehovah – unto the sword, unto the pestilence, and unto the famine, and I have given you for a trembling to all kingdoms of the earth.

APHESIS - release, letting go, cancellation (of debt) – a divergent translation omitting to translate "saith the LORD" – a release to discipline and judgment

LXX **41:17b**
. . . *IDOU EGÓ KALÓ* ***APHESIN*** *HUMIN EIS MACHAIRAN KAI EIS TON THANATON*
look I call release you into sword and into the death

KAI EIS TON LIMON KAI DÓSÓ HUMAS EIS DIASPORAN PASAIS TAIS BASILEIAIS TÉS GÉS
And into the famine and shall give you into dispersion all the kingdoms of the earth

engLXX . . . behold, I proclaim a release to you, to the sword, and to the pestilence, and to the famine; and I will give you up to dispersion *among* all the kingdoms of the earth.

Eze. 46:17 But if he give a gift of his inheritance to one of his servants, then it shall be his to the year of **liberty**; after it shall return to the prince: but his inheritance shall be his sons' for them.

YLT And when he giveth a gift out of his inheritance to one of his servants, then it hath been to him till the year of **freedom**, and it hath turned back to the prince, only the inheritance of his sons is theirs.

APHESIS - release, letting go, cancellation (of debt) – a divergent translation with "his inheritance" (KJV) omitted to be translated from the gift to the servant – the year of release, or liberty ["freedom" in YLT]

LXX *EAN DE DÓ DOMA HENI TÓN PAIDÓN AUTOU KAI ESTAI AUTÓ HEÓS TOU ETOUS*
If but give gift one of the | young servants | of him and shall be | for him | until of the year

TÉS ***APHESEÓS*** *KAI APODÓSEI TÓ APHÉGOUMENÓ PLÉN TÉS KLÉRONOMIAS*
of the release and give back to the leader except of the inheritance

TÓN HUIÓN AUTOU AUTOIS ESTAI
of the sons of him to them shall be

engLXX But if he give a gift to one of his servants, then it shall belong to him until the year of release; and *then* he shall restore *it* to the prince: but of the inheritance of his sons *the possession* shall continue to them.

15 - GELAL

Translated into Greek in the LXX

EKLEKTOS	**1**	**Ezra 5:8**
KRATAIOS (mighty, great, strong)	1	
TOTAL	2	

Translated into English - Both KJV related

Ys Conc.	Count	Ss Conc. No. H 1556	Count
great	2	great	2
TOTAL	2	TOTAL	2

Refs	**Text quotes KJV unless otherwise stated**
Ezr. 5:8	Be it known unto the king, that we went into the province of Judea, to the house of the great God, which is builded with **great** stones, and timber is laid in the walls, and this work goeth fast on, and prospereth in their hands.

YLT To Darius the king, all peace! Be it known to the king that we have gone to the province of Judah, to the great house of God, and it is built *with* **rolled** stones, and wood is placed in the walls, and this work is done speedily, and prospering in their hand.

NKJV Let it be known to the king that we went into the province of Judea, to the temple of the great God, which is being built with **heavy** stones, and timber is being laid in the walls; and this work goes on diligently and prospers in their hands.

NASB Let it be known to the king that we have gone to the province of Judah, to the house of the great God, which is being built with **huge** stones, and beams are being laid in the walls; and this work is going on with great care and is succeeding in their hands.

NIV The king should know that we went to the district of Judah, to the temple of the great God. The people are building it with **large** stones and placing the timbers in the walls. The work is being carried on with diligence and is making rapid progress under their direction.

NLT "The king should know that we went to the construction site of the Temple of the great God in the province of Judah. It is being rebuilt with **specially prepared** stones, and timber is being laid in its walls. The work is going forward with great energy and success.

EKLEKTOS – A direct translation - The "great" stones (KJB), "rolled" stones (YLT), are the mighty prepared elements of the building: quality

LXX **5:7** . . . ***DAREÓ TÓ BASILEI EIRÉNÉ PASA***
Darius to the king peace all

LXX **5:8** ***GNÓSTON ESTÓ TÓ BASILEI HOTI EPOREUTHÉMEN EIS TÉN IOUDAIAN CHÓRAN***
known be to the king since we conveyed into the Judea area

EIS OIKON TOU THEOU TOU MEGALOU KAI AUTOS OIKODOMEITAI LITHOIS
into house of the God of the Great and he built stones

EKLEKTOIS *KAI XULA ENTITHETAI EN TOIS TOICHOIS KAI TO ERGON EKEINO*
choice and timber inserted in to the walls and the work that

EPIDEXION GINETAI KAI EUODOUTAI EN TAIS CHERSIN AUTÓN
fittingly being and prospers in the hands of him

engLXX Be it known to the king, that we went into the land of Judea, to the house of the great God; and it is building with choice stones, and they are laying timbers in the walls, and that work is prospering, and goes on favourably in their hands.

Ezr. 6:4 *With* three rows of **great** stones, and a row of new timber: and let the expenses be given out of the king's house:

YLT three rows of **rolled** stones, and a row of new wood, and the outlay let be given out of the king's house.

KRATAIOS – mighty, great, strong - a divergent translation with "new" (KJV) for the timber missing - the stones are "great" (KJV), "rolled" (YLT) are the mighty principal elements of the building: quality

LXX *KAI DOMOI LITHINOI* ***KRATAIOI*** *TREIS KAI DOMOS XULINOS EIS KAI HÉ DAPANÉ*
and courses stones fortified three and course timber into and the expense

EX OIKOU TOU BASILEÓS DOTHÉSETAI
out of house of the king shall give

engLXX And *let there be* three strong layers of stone, and one layer of timber; and the expense shall be paid out of the house of the king.

16 - MANAMMIM

Translated into Greek in the LXX

EKLEKTOS	**1**	**Psalm 141:4**
TOTAL	1	

Translated into English - Both KJV related

Ys Conc.	Count	Ss Conc. No. H 4516	Count
dainties	1	dainties	1
TOTAL	1	TOTAL	1

Refs	Text quotes KJV unless otherwise stated
Psa. 141:4	Incline not my heart to *any* evil thing, to practise wicked works with men that work iniquity: and let me not eat of their **dainties**.
YLT	Incline not my heart to an evil thing, to do habitually actions in wickedness, with men working iniquity, yea, I eat not of their **pleasant** things.
NKJV	Do not incline my heart to any evil thing, to practice wicked works with men who work iniquity; and do not let me eat of their **delicacies**.

NASB Do not incline my heart to any evil thing, to practice deeds of wickedness with men who do iniquity; and do not let me eat of their **delicacies**.

NIV Do not let my heart be drawn to what is evil so that I take part in wicked deeds along with those who are evildoers; do not let me eat their **delicacies**.

NLT Don't let me drift toward evil or take part in acts of wickedness. Don't let me share in the **delicacies** of those who do wrong.

EKLEKTOS – A divergent translation with "eat" (KJV) rendered as "unite" (engLXX) - to eat with others seen as a sign of uniting with them a possible rendition: The word emphasises the chief of the things eaten or the chief persons united with

LXX **140:4**

MÉ EKKLINÉS TÉN KARDIAN MOU EIS LOGOUS PONÉRIAS TOU
not turn aside the heart of me to words evil of the

PROPHASIZESTHAI PROPHASEIS EN HAMARTIAIS SUN ANTHRÓPOIS
to allege excuse in sins with men

ERGAZOMENOIS TÉN ANOMIAN KAI OU MÉ SUNDOIASÓ META TÓN ***EKLEKTÓN*** *AUTÓN*
working the lawlessness and in no wise gather with the choice of them

engLXX Incline not my heart to evil things, to employ pretexts for sins, with men who work iniquity: and let me not unite with their choice ones.

17 - MASETH

Translated into Greek in the LXX

EKLEKTOS		**1**		**Amos 5:11**
MERIS	(part, portion)	2		
SUSSÉMON	(signal)	2		
APHORISMOS	(offering)	1	aNT	
ARSIS	(distilled, portion)	1	aNT	
DÓRON	(gift, present)	1		
EPARSIS	(rising, swelling)	1	aNT	
KRINÓ	(distinguish, judge)	1		
LAMBANÓ	(to take, receive)	1		
LÉMMA	(argument)	1	aNT	
SÉMEION	(mark, sign)	1		
NOT translated in LXX		2		
TOTAL		15		

Translated into English - Both KJV related

Ys Conc.	Count	Ss Conc. No. H 4864	Count
burden	3	burden	3
collection	2	mess	3
flame	1	collection	2
great flame	1	flame	2
gifts	1	gifts	1
lifting up	1	oblations	1
mess	3	reward	1
oblation	1	sign	1
reward	1	lifting up	1
sign of fire	1		
TOTAL	15	TOTAL	15

Refs	**Text quotes KJV unless otherwise stated**
Gen. 43:34a	And he took *and sent* **messes** unto them from before him: (. . .)
YLT	and he lifteth up **gifts** from before him unto them, (. . .)
NKJV	Then he took **servings** to them from before him, (. . .)

MERIS - part, share, portion – a divergent rendering with "he" (KJV 2nd word) given as "they" (engLXX) – portions of food

LXX *ÉRAN DE* ***MERIDAS*** *PAR AUTOU PROS HEAUTOUS . . .*
took but portions from him to themselves

engLXX And they took their portions from him to themselves; (. . .)

Gen. 43:34b . . . but Benjamin's **mess** was five times so much as any of theirs. And they drank, and were merry with him.

YLT . . . and the **gift** of Benjamin is five hands more than the gifts of all of them; and they drink, yea, they drink abundantly with him.

NKJV . . . but Benjamin's **serving** was five times as much as any of theirs. So they drank and were merry with him.

MERIS - part, share, portion – a direct translation – portions of food

LXX . . . *EMEGALUNTHÉ DE HÉ* ***MERIS*** *BENIAMIN PARA TAS MERIDAS PANTÓN*
magnified but the portion of Benjamin by the portions of all

PENTAPLASIÓS PROS TAS EKEINÓN EPION DE KAI EMETHUSTHÉSAN MET AUTOU
five-fold to the of those drank but and intoxicated with him

engLXX . . . but Benjamin's portion was five times as much as the portions of *the others*. And they drank and were filled with drink with him.

Jud. 20:38 Now there was an appointed sign between the men of Israel and the liers in wait, that they should make a great **flame** with smoke rise up out of the city.

YLT And there was the appointed sign to the men of Israel with the ambush – their causing to go up a great **volume** of smoke from the city.

SUSSÉMON – signal – a loose translation with "men of Israel" (KJV) rendered as "children of Israel" (engLXX) – a signal of smoke rising up

LXX *KAI SÉMEION ÉN TOIS HUIOS ISRAÉL META TOU ENEDROU TÉS MACHÉS*
and sign was to the sons of Israel with the ambush of the battle

ANENEGKAI AUTOUS ***SUSSÉMON*** *KAPNOU APO TÉS POLEÓS*
bring up them signal of smoke from the city

engLXX And the children of Israel had a signal of battle with the liers in wait, that they should send up a signal of smoke from the city.

Jud. 20:40 But when the **flame** began to arise up out of the city with a pillar of smoke, the Benjamites looked behind them, and, behold, the flame of the city ascended up to heaven.

YLT and the **volume** hath begun to go up from the city - a pillar of smoke – and Benjamin turneth behind, and lo, gone up hath the perfection of the city toward the heavens.

SUSSÉMON - signal – a direct translation with "perfection of the city" (YLT) i.e. understood as a completion and thereby rendered as "destruction of the city" (engLXX) – the pillar of smoke as a signal

LXX *KAI TO* ***SUSSÉMON*** *ANEBÉ EPI PLEION EPI TÉS POLEÓS HÓS STULOS KAPNOU*
and the signal arose over full upon the city as pillar of smoke

KAI EPEBLEPSE BENIAMIN OPISÓ AUTOU KAI IDOU ANEBÉ SUNTELEIA TÉS
and looked Benjamin behind him and look ascends | of the
consummation

POLEÓS HEÓS OURANOU
city unto heaven

engLXX And the signal went up increasingly over the city as a pillar of smoke; and Benjamin looked behind him, and behold the destruction of the city went up to heaven.

2Sa. 11:8 — And David said to Uriah, Go down to thy house, and wash thy feet. And Uriah departed out of the king's house, and there followed him a **mess** *of meat* from the king.

YLT — And David saith to Uriah, 'Go down to thy house, and wash thy feet;' and Uriah goeth out of the king's house, and there goeth out after him a **gift** from the king,

ARSIS aNT - distilled, portion, that which is lifted – a direct translation – a portion of food

LXX **2Ki.11:8** — ***KAI EIPE DAUID TÓ OURIA KATABÉTHI EIS TON OIKON SOU KAI NIPSAI TOUS***
and said David to the Uria go down into the house of you and wash the

PODAS SOU KAI EXÉLTHEN OURIAS EX OIKOU TOU BASILEÓS KAI EXÉLTHEN
feet of you and went Urias out of house of the king and went

OPISÓ AUTOU **ARSIS** ***TOU BASILEÓS***
after him portion of the king

engLXX — And David said to Urias, Go to thy house, and wash thy feet: and Urias departed from the house of the king, and a portion *of meat* from the king followed him.

2Ch. 24:6 — And the king called for Jehoiada the chief, and said unto him, Why hast thou not required of the Levites to bring in out of Judah and out of Jerusalem the **collection**, *according to the commandment* of Moses the servant of the LORD, and of the congregation of Israel, for the tabernacle of witness?

YLT — And the king calleth for Jehoiada the head, and saith to him, 'Wherefore hast thou not required of the Levites to bring in out of Judah and out of Jerusalem the **tribute** of Moses, servant of Jehovah, and of the assembly of Israel, for the tent of the testimony?

KRINÓ – to distinguish, judge – a divergent translation with "for the tabernacle of witness" (KJV) rendered as "at the tabernacle of witness" (engLXX): it is for that place the funds were to be gathered; not about where they were assembled when Moses gave the instruction – the decided amount to collect

LXX *KAI EKALESEN HO BASILEUS IÓAS TON IÓDAE TON ARCHONTA KAI EIPEN AUTÓ*
and called the king Joas the Jodae the chief and said to him

DIATI OUK EPESKEPSÓ PERI TÓN LEUITÓN TOU EISENEGKAI APO IOUDA KAI
why not oversee about the Levites of the to carry in from Juda and

HIEROUSALÉM TO ***KEKRIMENON*** *HUPO MÓUSÉ ANTHRÓPOU TOU THEOU HOTI*
Jerusalem the adjudged by Moses man of the God since

EXEKKLÉSIASE TON ISRAÉL EIS TÉN SKÉNÉN TOU MARTURIOU
assembled the Israel into the tent of the witness

engLXX And king Joas called Jodae the chief, and said to him, Why hast thou not looked after the Levites, so that they should bring from Juda and Jerusalem that which was prescribed by Moses the man of God, when he assembled Israel at the tabernacle of witness?

2Ch. 24:9 And they made a proclamation through Judah and Jerusalem, to bring in to the LORD the **collection** *that* Moses the servant of God *laid* upon Israel in the wilderness.

YLT and give an intimation in Judah and in Jerusalem to bring in to Jehovah the **tribute** of Moses, servant of God, *laid* on Israel in the wilderness.

NOT in LXX – a divergent translation with MASETH not rendered, but assumed in the context

LXX *KAI KÉRUXATÓSAN EN IOUDA KAI EN HIEROUSALÉM EISENEGKAI KURIÓ*
and herald in Juda and in Jerusalem to carry in to Lord

KATHÓS EIPE MÓUSÉS PAIS TOU THEOU EPI TON ISRAÉL EN TÉ ERÉMÓ
as said Moses | of the God upon the Israel in the desert
young servant

engLXX And let *men* proclaim in Juda and in Jerusalem, that *the people* should bring to the Lord, as Moses the servant of God spoke concerning Israel in the wilderness.

Est. 2:18 Then the king made a great feast unto all his princes and his servants, *even* Esther's feast; and he made a release to the provinces, and gave **gifts**, according to the state of the king.

NOT in LXX – a divergent translation: the whole clause: "and gave gifts, according to the state of the king" (KJV) is not translated

LXX *KAI EPOIÉSEN HO BASILEUS POTON PASI TOIS PHILOIS AUTOU KAI TAIS*
and made the king drinking for all the friends of him and for the

DUNAMESIN EPI HÉMERAS HEPTA KAI HUPSÓSE TOUS GAMOUS ESTHÉR KAI
powerful upon days seven and exalted the wedding of Esther and

APHESIN EPOIÉSE TOIS HUPO TÉN BASILEIAN AUTOU
release made to the under the kingdom of him

engLXX And the king made a banquet for all his friends and great men for seven days, and he highly celebrated the marriage of Esther; and he made a release to those who were under his dominion.

Psa. 141:2 Let my prayer be set forth before thee *as* incense; *and* the **lifting up** of my hands *as* the evening sacrifice.

YLT My prayer is prepared - incense before Thee, the lifting up of my hands - - the evening present.

EPARSIS aNT - rising, swelling – a direct translation – the lifting up of hands

LXX **140:2** *KATEUTHUNTHÉTÓ HÉ PROSEUCHÉ MOU HÓS THUMIAMA ENÓPION SOU*
direct the prayer of me as incense before you

EPARSIS *TÓN CHEIRÓN MOU THUSIA ESPERINÉ*
rising of the hands of me sacrifice evening

engLXX Let my prayer be set forth before thee as incense; the lifting up of my hands *as* an evening sacrifice.

Jer. 6:1 — O ye children of Benjamin, gather yourselves to flee out of the midst of Jerusalem, and blow the trumpet in Tekoa, and set up a **sign** of fire in Bethhaccerem: for evil appeareth out of the north, and great destruction.

YLT — Strengthen yourselves, sons of Benjamin, from the midst of Jerusalem, and in Tekoa blow ye a trumpet, and over Beth-Haccerem lift ye up a **flame**, for evil hath been seen from the north, and great destruction.

SÉMEION - mark, sign – a direct translation – a fire beacon given as a signal of warning

LXX — *ENISCHUSATE HUIOI BENIAMIN EK MESOU TÉS HIEROUSALÉM KAI EN THEKOUE*
strengthen ye sons of Benjamin out of midst of the Jerusalem and in Tekoa

SÉMANATE SALPIGGI KAI HUPER BAITHACHARMA ARATE ***SÉMEION*** *HOTI KAKA*
signify by trumpet and over Baithacharma set up sign since bad

EKKEKUPHEN APO BORRA KAI SUNTRIBÉ MEGALÉ GINETAI
appears out from north and crushing great is coming

engLXX — Strengthen yourselves, ye children of Benjamin, *to flee* out of the midst of Jerusalem, and sound an alarm with the trumpet in Thecue, and set up a signal over Bæthacharma: for evil threatens from the north, and a great destruction is coming.

Jer. 40:5 — Now while he was not yet gone back, *he said*, Go back also to Gedaliah the son of Ahikam the son of Shaphan, whom the king of Babylon hath made governor over the cities of Judah, and dwell with him among the people: or go wheresoever it seemeth convenient unto thee to go. So the captain of the guard gave him victuals and a **reward**, and let him go.

YLT — and while he doth not reply – 'Or turn back unto Gedaliah son of Ahikam, son of Shaphan, whom the king of Babylon hath appointed over the cities of Judah, and dwell with him in the midst of the people, or whithersoever it is right in thine eyes to go - go.' And the chief of the executioners giveth to him for the way, and a **gift**, and sendeth him away,

DÓRON – gift, present, offering – a divergent translation with "in the land of Juda" (engLXX) added to "dwell with him in the midst of the people" (YLT) – a gift to Jeremiah from the captain of the guard (V.2) not to send him on his way emptyhanded

LXX **47:5**

EI DE MÉ APOTREXE KAI ANASTREPSON PROS TON GODOLIAN HUION
if but not run from and turn back to the Godolia son

ACHEIKAM HUIOU SAPHAN HON KATESTÉSE BASILEUS BABULÓNOS EN GÉ
of Acheikam of son Saphan whom established king of Babylon in land

IOUDA KAI OIKÉSON MET AUTOU EN MESÓ TOU LAOU EN GÉ IOUDA EIS APANTA
of Juda and dwell with him in midst of the people in land of Juda into all

TA AGATHA EN OPHTHALMOIS SOU TOU POREUTHÉNAI EKEI KAI POREUOU KAI
the good in eyes of you of the to go there and go and

EDÓKEN AUTÓ HO ARCHIMAGEIROS ***DÓRA*** *KAI APESTEILEN AUTON*
gave to him the chief guard gifts and sent him

engLXX But if not, depart; return to Godolias the son of Achicam, the son of Saphan, whom the king of Babylon has appointed governor in the land of Juda, and dwell with him in the midst of the people in the land of Juda: to whatsoever places it seems good in thine eyes to go, do thou even go. And the captain of the guard made him presents, and let him go.

Lam. 2:14 Thy prophets have seen vain and foolish things for thee: and they have not discovered thine iniquity, to turn away thy captivity; but have seen for thee false **burdens** and causes of banishment.

YLT Thy prophets have seen for thee a false and insipid thing, and have not revealed concerning thine iniquity, to turn back thy captivity, and they see for thee false **burdens** and causes of expulsion.

LÉMMA aNT – argument, commission received – a divergent translation with "causes of banishment" (KJV) or "causes of expulsion" (YLT), rendered as "worthless visions" (engLXX) lit. Gk. "empty words" – the verbal burden or false argument offered up by the false prophets

LXX *NOUN PROPHÉTAI SOU EIDOSAN SOI MATAIA KAI APHROSUNÉN KAI OUK*
NOUN prophets of you seen for you vain and folly and not

APEKALUPSAN EPI TÉN ADIKIAN SOU TOU EPISTREPSAI AICHMALÓSIAN SOU
uncover into the | unrighteousness of you of the turn back captivity of you

KAI EIDOSAN SOI ***LÉMMATA*** *MATAIA KAI EXÓSMATA*
and saw for you argument vain and empty words

engLXX NUN. Thy prophets have seen for thee vanities and folly: and they have not discovered thine iniquity, to turn back thy captivity; but they have seen for thee vain burdens, and worthless visions.

Eze. 20:40 For in mine holy mountain, in the mountain of the height of Israel, saith the Lord God, there shall all the house of Israel, all of them in the land, serve me: there will I accept them, and there will I require your offerings, and the firstfruits of your **oblations**, with all your holy things.

YLT For, in My holy mountain, In the mountain of the height of Israel, an affirmation of the Lord Jehovah, There serve Me do all the house of Israel, all of it, in the land - there I accept them, and there I do seek your heave-offerings, and with the first-fruit of your **gifts**, with all your holy things.

APHORISMOS aNT – special or separate offering – a divergent translation with "all of them in the land" (KJV) not translated – the offerings which were to be made at God's holy mountain

LXX *DIOTI ETI TOU OROUS TOU HAGIOU MOU EP OROUS HUPSÉLOU LEGEI KURIOS*
for yet of the mountains of the holy of me upon mountains high says Lord

KURIOS EKEI DOULEUSOUSI MOI PAS OIKOS ISRAÉL EIS TELOS KAI EKEI
Lord there serve me all house of Israel into end and there

PROSDEXOMAI KAI EKEI EPISKEPSOMAI TAS APARCHAS HUMÓN KAI TAS
accept and there review the first fruits of you and the

APARCHAS TÓN **APHORISMÓN** *HUMÓN EN PASI TOIS HAGIASMASIN HUMÓN*
first fruits of the offerings of you in all the sanctified of you

engLXX For upon my holy mountain, on the high mountain, saith the Lord, *even* the Lord, there shall all the house of Israel serve me for ever: and there will I accept *you*, and there will I have respect to your first-fruits, and the first-fruits of your offerings, in all your holy things.

Amo. 5:11 Forasmuch therefore as your treading *is* upon the poor, and ye take from him **burdens** of wheat: ye have built houses of hewn stone, but ye shall not dwell in them; ye have planted pleasant vineyards, but ye shall not drink wine of them.

YLT Therefore, because of your trampling on the poor, and the **tribute** of corn ye take from him, houses of hewn work ye have built, and ye do not dwell in them, desirable vineyards ye have planted, and ye do not drink their wine.

NKJV Therefore, because you tread down the poor and take grain **taxes** from him, though you have built houses of hewn stone, yet you shall not dwell in them; you have planted pleasant vineyards, but you shall not drink wine from them.

NASB Therefore because you impose heavy rent on the poor and exact a **tribute** of grain from them, *though* you have built houses of well-hewn stone, yet you will not live in them;

NIV You levy a straw tax on the poor and impose a **tax** on their grain. Therefore, though you have built stone mansions, you will not live in them; though you have planted lush vineyards, you will not drink their wine.

NLT You trample the poor, stealing their grain through **taxes** and unfair rent. Therefore, though you build beautiful stone houses, you will never live in them. Though you plant lush vineyards, you will never drink wine from them.

EKLEKTOS – a loose translation with "burdens of wheat" (KJV) or "tribute of corn" (YLT) rendered as receiving "choice gifts" (engLXX); a divergent translation with "treading *is* upon the poor" (KJV) or "trampling on the poor" (YLT) rendered as "smitten the poor with their fists" (engLXX) - choice gifts taken from the poor

LXX *DIATOUTO ANTH HÓN KATEKONDULIZON PTÓCHOUS KAI DÓRA* ***EKLEKTA*** *EDEXASTHE PAR*
therefore for the sake of whom ye struck poor and gifts choice ye took from

AUTÓN OIKOUS XESTOUS ÓKODOMÉSATE KAI OU MÉ KATOIKÉSÉTE EN AUTOIS AMPELÓNAS
them houses planed ye built and in no wise ye shall dwell in them vineyards

EPITHUMÉTOUS EPHUTEUSATE KAI OU MÉ PIÉTE TON OINON AUTÓN
desirable ye shall plant and in no wise ye drink the wine of them

engLXX Therefore because they have smitten the poor with their fists, and ye have received of them choice gifts; ye have built polished houses, but ye shall not dwell in them; ye have planted desirable vineyards, but ye shall not drink the wine of them.

Zep. 3:18 I will gather *them that are* sorrowful for the solemn assembly, *who* are of thee, *to whom* the reproach of it *was* a **burden**.

YLT Mine afflicted from the appointed place I have gathered, from thee they have been, **bearing** for her sake reproach.

LAMBANÓ - to take, receive – a divergent translation with "the solemn assembly" KJV or "the appointed place" not rendered – the "bearing for her sake reproach" (YLT) given as a taking of it: the grief of the issue is taken to oneself: it was a burden

LXX *KAI SUNAXÓ TOUS SUNTETRIMMENOUS SOU OUAI TIS* ***ELABEN*** *EP AUTÉN ONEIDISMON*
and gather the crushed internally of you woe any taken upon her reproach

engLXX And I will gather thine afflicted ones. Alas! Who has taken up a reproach against her?

18 - MATSOR

Translated into Greek in the LXX

EKLEKTOS		**1**		**Jeremiah 10:17**
PERIOCHÉ	(surrounding siege)	10		
SUGKLEISMOS	(siege)	3	aNT	
THLIPSIS	(pressure, affliction)	3		
OCHUROS	(strong)	2	aNT	
SUNOCHÉ	(besiege)	2		
CHARAKÓSIS	(siege)	1	aNT	
CHARAX	(siege stake)	1		
DIÓRUX	(canal, defence trench)	1	aNT	
OCHURÓMA	(fortress)	1		
PETRA	(rock)	1		
SUGKLEIÓ	(shut, closed)	1		
SUNAGÓGÉ	(gathered together)	1		
TEICHÉRÉS	(walled in)	1	aNT	
TUROS	(Tyre)	1		
TOTAL		30		

Translated into English - Both KJV related

Ys Conc.	Count	Ss Conc. No. H 4692 + **4693**	Count
Besieged place	2	siege	13
bulwark	1	besieged	2
fortress	2	strong	2
siege	13	besieged	2
stronghold	1	bulwarks	1
tower	1	defence + **defence**	**1**+1
fenced	1	fenced	1
fortified	1	fortress + **fortress**	**1**+1
strong	1	hold	1
besieged	4[1]	tower	1
		besieged place	**2**
		fortified	**1**
TOTAL	30	TOTAL	30

1. See Ys Conc. page 90

Refs	Text quotes KJV unless otherwise stated
Deu. 20:19	When thou shalt besiege a city a long time, in making war against it to take it, thou shalt not destroy the trees thereof by forcing an axe against them: for thou mayest eat of them, and thou shalt not cut them down (for the tree of the field *is* man's *life*) to employ *them* in the **siege**:

CHARAX - siege stake, palisade, bulwark, stockade – a direct translation – offensive ramparts for a siege is not to be made from wood from fruit trees

LXX

EAN DE PERIKATHISÉS PERI POLIN MIAN HÉMERAS PLEIOUS EKPOLEMÉSAI
if but shall besiege around city one days many to war

AUTÉN EIS KATALÉPSIN AUTÉS OUK EXOLOTHREUSEIS TA DENDRA AUTÉS
her into taking of her not destroy utterly the trees of her

EPIBALEIN EP AUTA DIDÉRON ALL É AP AUTOU PHAGÉ AUTO DE OUK
to thrust upon them iron *tools* but is from it eat it but not

EKKOPSEIS MÉ ANTHRÓPOS TO XULON TO EN TÓ AGRÓ EISELTHEIN APO
cut out not man the tree the in the field to enter from

PROSÓPOU SOU EIS TON ***CHARAKA***
face of you into the stakes

engLXX: And if thou shouldest besiege a city many days to prevail against it by war to take it, thou shalt not destroy its trees, by applying an iron tool to them, but thou shalt eat of it, and shalt not cut it down: Is the tree that is in the field a man, to enter before thee into the work of the siege?

Deu. 20:20	Only the trees which thou knowest that they *be* not trees for meat, thou shalt destroy and cut them down; and thou shalt build **bulwarks** against the city that maketh war with thee, until it be subdued.
YLT	Only, the tree, which thou knowest that it *is* not a fruit-tree, it thou dost destroy, and hast cut down, and hast built a **bulwark** against the city which is making with thee war till thou hast subdued it.

CHARAKÓSIS aNT – siege, palisade, bulwark, stockade – a direct translation – the mound or bulwark using wood to build in a siege of a city

LXX *ALLA XULON HO EPISTASAI HOTI OU KARPOBRÓTON ESTI TOUTO*
but tree which know since not fruit-bearing is this

OLOTHREUSEIS KAI EKKOPSEIS KAI OIKODOMÉSEIS ***CHARAKÓSIN*** *EPI TÉN*
obliterate and cut out and build siege upon the

POLIN HÉTIS POIEI PROS SE TON POLEMON HEÓS AN PARADOTÉ
city whichever make to you the war until whenever handed over

engLXX But the tree which thou knowest to be not fruit-bearing, this thou shalt destroy and cut down; and thou shalt construct a mound against the city, which makes war against thee, until it be delivered up.

Deu. 28:53 And thou shalt eat the fruit[2] of thine own body, the flesh of thy sons and of thy daughters, which the Lord thy God hath given thee, in the **siege**, and in the straitness, wherewith thine enemies shall distress thee:

THLIPSIS - pressure, affliction, oppression – a divergent translation with "the Lord thy God" (KJV) not translated – the result of a siege, affliction or oppression: hence straitness is given by the translator [see V.55 below]

LXX *KAI PHAGÉ TA EKGONA*[2] *TÉS KOILIAS SOU KREA HUIÓN SOU KAI THUGATERÓN*
and eat the progeny of the belly of you meat of sons of you and daughters

SOU HOSA EDÓKE SOI EN TÉ STENOCHÓRIA SOU KAI EN TÉ ***THLIPSEI*** *SOU HÉ*
of you as many as gave to you in the straits of you and in the affliction of you the

THLIPSEI SE HO ECHTHROS SOU
affliction you the enemy of you

2 See PERI

engLXX And thou shalt eat the fruit of thy body, the flesh of thy sons and of thy daughters, all that he has given thee, in thy straitness and thy affliction, with which thine enemy shall afflict thee.

Deu. 28:55 So that he will not give to any of them of the flesh of his children whom he shall eat: because he hath nothing left him in the **siege**, and in the straitness, wherewith thine enemies shall distress thee in all thy gates.

THLIPSIS - pressure, affliction, oppression – Since the "siege" is the cause of the "straitness", a loose translation with the outcome of the cause rendered first - the siege is the affliction [seeV.53 above]

LXX *HÓSTE DOUNAI ENI AUTÓN APO TÓN SARKÓN TÓN TEKNÓN AUTOU HÓN AN*
so that give one of them from the flesh of the children of him whom ever

KATESTHÉ DIA TO MÉ KATALEIPHTHÉNAI AUTÓ OUDEN EN TÉ STENOCHÓRIA SOU KAI EN
should eat | the not left behind to him not one in the straits of you and in
because of

TÉ ***THLIPSEI*** *SOU HÉ AN THLIPSÓSI SE HOI ECHTHROI SOU EN PASAIS TAIS POLESI SOU*
the affliction of you which ever afflicts you the enemies of you in all the cities of you

engLXX so as *not* to give to one of them of the flesh of his children, whom he shall eat, because of his having nothing left him in thy straitness, and in thy affliction, with which thine enemies shall afflict thee in all thy cities.

Deu. 28:57 And toward her young one that cometh out from between her feet, and toward her children which she shall bear: for she shall eat them for want of all *things* secretly in the **siege** and straitness, wherewith thine enemy shall distress thee in thy gates.

YLT and against her seed which cometh out from between her feet, even against her sons whom she doth bear, for she doth eat them for the lacking of all things in secret, in the **siege** and in the straitness with which thine enemy doth straiten thee within thy gates.

THLIPSIS - pressure, affliction, oppression - Since the "siege" is the cause of the "straitness", a loose translation with the outcome of the cause rendered first - the siege is the affliction [seeV.55 above]

LXX *KAI TO KORION*[3] *AUTÉS TO EXELTHON DIA TÓN MÉRÓN AUTÉS KAI TO TEKNON AUTÉS HO*
and the afterbirth of her the coming forth through the thighs of her and the child of her which

EAN TEKÉ KATAPHAGETAI GAR AUTA DIA TÉN ENDEIAN PANTÓN KRUPHÉ EN TÉ STENOCHÓRIA
ever births shall eat for them because of the lack of all secret in the straitness

SOU KAI EN TÉ ***THLIPSEI*** *SOU HÉ THLIPSEI SE HO ECHTHROS SOU EN TAIS POLESI SOU*
of you and in the affliction of you which affliction you the enemy of you in the cities of you

engLXX and her offspring that comes out between her feet, and the child which she shall bear; for she shall eat them because of the want of all things, secretly in thy straitness, and in thy affliction, with which thine enemy shall afflict thee in thy cities.

2Ki. 19:24 I have digged and drunk strange waters, and with the sole of my feet have I dried up all the rivers of **besieged places**.

PERIOCHÉ - surrounding siege, fortified enclosure, hemming – a divergent translation with the 1st verb "to dig" (KJV) not translated – water that gathers by un-drained areas of siege mounds in view: hemming in fortifications [cf. Isa.37:25 below]

LXX **4Ki.19:24** *EGÓ EPSUXA KAI EPION HUDATA ALLOTRIA KAI EXÉRÉMÓSA TÓ ICHNEI TOU*
I cooled and drank waters alien and dry out with the sole of the

PODOS MOU PANTAS POTAMOUS ***PERIOCHÉS***
foot of me all rivers of enclosing places

engLXX I have refreshed *myself*, and have drunk strange waters, and I have dried up with the sole of my foot all the rivers of fortified places.

---

3. LXX used reads *KORION* which could be a misprint since that should be *CHORION* aNT: the Gk. *CH* is pronounded *K*, the same as in Christ

2Ki. 24:10 At that time the servants of Nebuchadnezzar king of Babylon came up against Jerusalem, and the city was **besieged**.

PERIOCHÉ - surrounding siege, fortified enclosure, hemming – a divergent translation with "the servants" not translated – the surrounding siege of Jerusalem carried out by Nebuchadnezzar

LXX *EN TÓ KAIRÓ EKEINÓ ANEBÉ NABOUCHODONOSOR BASILEUS BABULÓNOS EIS*
4Ki.24:10 in the season that rose up Nabouchodonosor king of Babylon into

HIEROUSALÉM KAI ÉLTHEN HÉ POLIS EN ***PERIOCHÉ***
Jerusalem and came the city in surrounded

engLXX At that time went up Nabuchodonosor king of Babylon to Jerusalem, and the city was besieged.

2Ki. 25:2 And the city was **besieged** unto the eleventh year of king Zedekiah.
3 and on the ninth *day* of the *fourth* month . . .

PERIOCHÉ - surrounding siege, fortified enclosure, hemming – a direct translation + a portion of next verse - the surrounding siege of Jerusalem

LXX *KAI ÉLTHEN HÉ POLIS EN* ***PERIOCHÉ*** *HEÓS TOU ENDEKATOU ETOUS TOU*
4Ki.25:2 and came the city in surrounding until the eleventh year of the

BASILEÓS SEDEKIOU ENNATÉ TOU MÉNOS
king Sedekia ninth of the month

engLXX And the city was besieged until the eleventh year of king Sedekias on the ninth day of the month.

2Ch. 8:5 Also he built Beth-horon the upper, and Beth-horon the nether, **fenced** cities, with walls, gates, and bars;

YLT And he buildeth Beth-Horon the upper, and Beth-Horon the lower – cities of **defence**, with walls, two-leaved doors, and bar -

OCHUROS aNT – strong, firm, fortified – a direct translation – the strength of cities seen in their fortifications

LXX *KAI ÓKODOMÉSE TÉN BAITHÓRÓN TÉN ANÓ KAI TÉN BAITHÓRÓN TÉN KATÓ*
and built the Baithoron the upper and the Baithoron the lower

POLEIS ***OCHURAS*** *TEICHÉ PULAI KAI MOCHLOI*
cities strong walls gates and bars

engLXX And he built Bæthoron the upper, and Bæthoron the lower, strong cities,- they had walls, gates, and bars;

2Ch. 11:5 And Rehoboam dwelt in Jerusalem, and built cities for **defence** in Judah.

YLT And Rehoboam dwelleth in Jerusalem, and buildeth cities for a **bulwark** in Judah,

TEICHÉRÉS aNT - walled in, fortified – a direct translation – the walls of defence of cities in Judah

LXX *KAI KATÓKÉSE RHOBOAM EIS HIEROUSALÉM KAI ÓKODOMÉSE POLEIS*
and dwelt Rhoboam into Jerusalem and built cities

TEICHÉREIS *EN TÉ IOUDAIA*
walled in the Judea

engLXX And Roboam dwelt in Jerusalem, and he built walled cities in Judæa.

2Ch. 32:10 Thus saith Sennacherib king of Assyria, Whereon do ye trust, that ye abide in the **siege** in Jerusalem?

YLT Thus said Sennacherib king of Asshur, On what are ye trusting and abiding in the **bulwark**, in Jerusalem?

PERIOCHÉ - surrounding siege, fortified enclosure, hemming – a direct translation – the walls of defence surrounding Jerusalem

LXX *HOUTÓS LEGEI SENNACHÉRIM BASILEUS ASSURIÓN EPI TI HUMEIS*
thus says Sennacherim king of Assyria upon whom you

		PEPOITHATE KAI KATHÉSESTHE EN TÉ PERIOCHÉ EN HIEROUSALÉM rely and remain in the siege in Jerusalem
	engLXX	Thus says Sennacherim king of the Assyrians, On what do ye trust, that ye will remain in the siege in Jerusalem?
Psa. 31:21		Blessed *be* the LORD: for he hath shewed me his marvellous kindness in a **strong** city.
	YLT	Blessed *is* Jehovah, for He hath made marvellous His kindness to me in a city of **bulwarks**.

PERIOCHÉ - surrounding siege, fortified enclosure, hemming – a divergent translation with "me" not rendered: to whom the kindness is given – the surrounding fortification of a city

	LXX **30:21**	*EULOGÉTOS KURIOS HOTI ETHAUMASTÓSE TO ELEOS AUTOU EN POLEI* ***PERIOCHÉS*** blessed Lord since caused wonders the mercy of him in city encompassed (walled)
	engLXX	Blessed be the Lord: for he has magnified his mercy in a fortified city.
Psa. 60:9		Who will bring me *into* the **strong** city? Who will lead me into Edom?
	YLT	Who doth bring me *to* a city of **bulwarks**? Who hath led me unto Edom?

PERIOCHÉ - surrounding siege, fortified enclosure, hemming – a direct translation – the surrounding fortification of a city

	LXX **59:9**	*TIS APAXEI ME EIS POLIN* ***PERIOCHÉS*** *TIS HODÉGÉSEI ME HEÓS TÉS IDOUMAIAS* who shall take me into city encompassed whom shall guide me unto the Idumea
	engLXX	Who will lead me into the fortified city? Who will guide me as far as Idumea?
Isa. 19:6		And they shall turn the rivers far away; *and* the brooks of **defence** shall be emptied and dried up: the reeds and flags shall wither.
	YLT	And they have turned away the flowings, weak and dried up have been brooks of the **bulwark**, reed and flag have withered.

DIÓRUX aNT - canal, defence trench, channel – *DIÓRUCHES* is likely a misprint of *DIÓRUGES* - a divergent translation with the defence trenches, "brooks of defence" (KJV) or "brooks of the bulwark" (YLT), rendered as "canals of the river" (engLXX), thus removing an inference of use for defence – the defence moats of a city

LXX *KAI EKLEIPSOUSIN HOI POTAMOI KAI HAI* ***DIÓRUCHES*** *TOU POTAMOU KAI*
and leave out the rivers and the canals of the river and

XÉRANTHÉSETAI PASA SUNAGÓGÉ HUDATOS KAI EN PANTI HELEI KALAMOU KAI PAPUROU
shall dry up every gathered water and in every marsh of reed and papyrus

engLXX And the streams shall fail, and the canals of the river; and every reservoir of water shall be dried up, in every marsh also of reed and papyrus.

Isa. 37:25 I have digged, and drunk water; and with the sole of my feet have I dried up all the rivers of the **besieged places**.

YLT I - I have dug and drunk waters, and I dry up with the sole of my steps all floods of a **bulwark**.

SUNAGÓGÉ - gathered together, collection, pile – a divergent translation with "I have digged, and drunk water" (KJV) rendered as "I have made a bridge" (engLXX) – the gathered water in defence moats [cf. 2Ki.19:24 above]

LXX *KAI ETHÉKA GEPHURAN KAI ÉRÉMÓSA HUDATA KAI PASAN* ***SUNAGÓGÉN*** *HUDATOS*
and made bridge and dried up waters and every gathered water

engLXX and I have made a bridge, and dried up the waters, and every pool of water.

Jer. 10:17 Gather up thy wares out of the land, O inhabitant of the **fortress**.

YLT Gather from the land thy merchandise, O dweller in the **bulwark**,

NKJV Gather up your wares from the land, O inhabitant of the **fortress**!

NASB Pick up your bundle from the ground, you who dwell under **siege**!

NIV Gather up your belongings to leave the land, you who live under **siege**.

NLT Pack your bags and prepare to leave; the **siege** is about to begin.

EKLEKTOS – the reading of the engLXX is somewhat different from the literal word for word Greek: it is a more direct translation in the lit. Gk. – the dweller in view in the last clause is not the substance (wares or merchandise) in view, and thus not a choice vessel, but a choice place to dwell in: i.e. the strong city with defence walls is best to dwell in

LXX *SUNÉGAGEN EXÓTHEN TÉN HUPOSTASIN SOU KATOIKOUSAN EN* ***EKLEKTOIS***
gather from without the substance of you dwelling in choice

engLXX He has gathered thy substance from without that lodged in choice *vessels*.

Jer. 19:9 And I will cause them to eat the flesh of their sons and the flesh of their daughters, and they shall eat every one the flesh of his friend in the **siege** and straitness, wherewith their enemies, and they that seek their lives, shall straiten them.

YLT And I have caused them to eat the flesh of their sons, and the flesh of their daughters, and each the flesh of his friend they do eat, in the **siege** and in the straitness with which straiten them do their enemies, and those seeking their life.

PERIOCHÉ - surrounding siege, fortified enclosure, hemming - a divergent translation with "I will cause them" (KJV) not rendered - the surrounding siege of Jerusalem (V.7)

LXX *KAI EDONTAI TAS SARKAS TÓN HUIÓN AUTÓN KAI TAS SARKAS TÓN THUGATERÓN*
and eat the flesh of the sons of them and the flesh of the daughters

AUTÓN KAI HEKASTOS TAS SARKAS TOU PLÉSION AUTOU EDONTAI EN TÉ ***PERIOCHÉ***
of them and each the flesh of the neighbour of him eat in the siege

KAI EN TÉ POLIORKIA HÉ POLIORKÉSOUSIN AUTOUS HOI ECHTHROI AUTÓN
and in the blockade which shall assault them the enemies of them

engLXX And they shall eat the flesh of their sons, and the flesh of their daughters; and they shall eat every one the flesh of his neighbour in the blockade, and in the siege wherewith their enemies shall besiege them.

Jer. 52:5 So the city was **besieged** unto the eleventh year of king Zedekiah.
and the city cometh into **siege** till the eleventh year of king Zedekiah.

SUNOCHÉ – besiege, siege – a direct translation - the siege of Jerusalem

LXX *KAI ÉLTHEN HÉ POLIS EIS* ***SUNOCHÉN*** *HEÓS ENDEKATOU ETOUS TÓ BASILEI SEDEKIA*
and came the city into besiege until eleventh year to the king Sedekia

engLXX So the city was besieged, until the eleventh year of king Sedekias,

---

Eze. 4:2 And lay **siege** against it, and build a fort against it, and cast a mount against it; set the camp also against it, and set *battering* rams against it round about.

YLT and hast placed against it a **siege**, and builded against it a fortification, and poured out against it a mount, and placed against it camps, yea, set thou against it battering-rams round about.

PERIOCHÉ - surrounding siege, fortified enclosure, hemming – a direct translation - the surrounding siege of Jerusalem

LXX *KAI DÓSEIS EP AUTÉN* ***PERIOCHÉN*** *KAI OIKODOMÉSEIS EP AUTÉN*
and give upon her siege and build upon her

PROMACHÓNAS KAI PERIBALEIS EP AUTÉN CHARAKA KAI DÓSEIS EP AUTÉN
battlements and put around upon her palisades and shall give upon her

PAREMBOLAS KAI TAXEIS TAS BELOSTASEIS KUKLÓ
camps and set the arrow weapons around

engLXX And thou shalt besiege it, and build works against it, and throw up a mound round about it, and pitch camps against it, and set up engines round about.

Eze. 4:3 Moreover take thou unto thee an iron pan, and set it *for* a wall of iron between thee and the city: and set thy face against it, and it shall be **besieged**, and thou shalt lay siege against it. This *shall be* a sign to the house of Israel.

SUGKLEIÓ – to shut, close, confine – a direct translation – the siege, the act of confining the tile (KJV V.1), the emblem of Jerusalem

LXX *KAI SU LABE SEAUTÓ TÉGANON SIDÉROUN KAI THÉSEIS AUTO TOICHON*
and you take to yourself pan iron and place it wall

SIDÉROUN ANAMESON SOU KAI ANAMESON TÉS POLEÓS KAI HETOIMASEIS
iron in amongst of you and in midst of the city and shall prepare

TO PROSÓPON SOU EP AUTÉN KAI ESTAI EN SUGKLEISMÓ KAI ***SUGKLEISEIS***
the face of you against her and shall be in siege and shall confine

AUTÉN SÉMEION ESTI TOUTO TOIS HUIOIS ISRAÉL
her sign is this to the sons of Israel

engLXX And take thou to thyself an iron pan, and thou shalt set it *for* an iron wall between thee and the city: and thou shalt set thy face against it, and it shall be in a siege, and thou shalt besiege it. This is a sign to the children of Israel.

Eze. 4:7 Therefore thou shalt set thy face toward the **siege** of Jerusalem, and thine arm *shall be* uncovered, and thou shalt prophesy against it.

YLT And unto the **siege** of Jerusalem thou dost prepare thy face, and thine arm *is* uncovered, and thou hast prophesied concerning it.

SUGKLEISMOS aNT – sieged, closed up, shut up place – a divergent translation: Ezekiel's arm itself in view, having *as a prophetic sign* lain on one side with one arm immobile and then, after a set time, on the other side with the released no longer covered, so that, "thine arm *shall be* uncovered" (KJV) or "thine arm *is* uncovered" (YLT) then rendered as "shalt strengthen thine arm" (engLXX) is divergent – the confined Jerusalem, its siege

LXX *KAI EIS TON* ***SUGKLEISMON*** *HIEROUSALÉM HETOIMASEIS TO PROSÓPON SOU*
and into the siege of Jerusalem shall prepare the face of you

KAI TON BRACHIONA SOU STEREÓSEIS KAI PROPHÉTEUSEIS EP AUTÉN
and the arm of you shall stiffen and prophesy upon her

engLXX So thou shalt set thy face to the siege of Jerusalem, and shalt strengthen thine arm, and shalt prophesy against it.

Eze. 4:8 And, behold, I will lay bands upon thee, and thou shalt not turn thee from one side to another, till thou hast ended the days of thy **siege**

SUGKLEISMOS aNT - sieged, closed up, shut up place – a direct translation – the "siege" of Ezekiel the prophet, i.e. his confinement in remaining in that position, was enabled him by the Lord, by the Spirit preventing him from turning, so that the sign or simile could be realised in full. He was constrained, not unlike Paul was "bound in the spirit" in Acts 20:22 to go to Jerusalem, but here more so and physically.

LXX *KAI EGÓ IDOU DEDÓKA EPI SE DESMOUS KAI MÉ STRAPHÉS APO TOU PLEUROU*
and I look gave upon you bonds and not turned from the side

SOU EPI TO PLEURON SOU HEÓS HOU SUNTELESTHÓSIN HÉMERAI TOU ***SUGKLEISMOU*** *SOU*
of you upon the side of you until of which completed days of the siege of you

engLXX And, behold, I have prepared bonds for thee, and thou mayest not turn from thy one side to the other, until the days of thy siege shall be accomplished.

Eze. 5:2 Thou shalt burn with fire a third part in the midst of the city, when the days of the **siege** are fulfilled: and thou shalt take a third part, *and* smite about it with a knife: and a third part thou shalt scatter in the wind; and I will draw out a sword after them.

YLT A third part with fire thou dost burn in the midst of the city, at the fulness of the days of the **siege**; and thou hast taken the third part, thou dost smite with a weapon round about it; and the third part thou dost scatter to the wind, and a weapon I draw out after them.

SUGKLEISMOS aNT - sieged, closed up, shut up place – a divergent translation with the 3 part judgment seemingly divided into 4 parts: "a third part" rendered as "a fourth part", but not in reality since the first two of the LXX version is the same, but repeated event: i.e. "fire in the midst of the city" (engLXX) is the same event as "burnt it up in the midst of it" (engLXX) – the confinement, the prophetic siege of Ezekiel

LXX *TO TETARTON EN PURI ANAKAUSEIS EN MESÉ TÉ POLEI KATA TÉN PLÉRÓSIN TÓN HÉMERÓN*
the fourth in fire shall burn in midst the city according to the fullness of the days

TOU ***SUGKLEISMOU*** *KAI LÉPSÉ TO TETARTON KAI KATAKAUSEIS AUTO EN MESÓ AUTÉS KAI*
of the siege and seize the fourth and incinerate It in midst of her and

TO TETARTON KATAKOPSEIS EN RHOMPHAIA KUKLÓ AUTÉS KAI TO TETARTON DIASKORPIEIS
the fourth cut in pieces in broad sword around of her and the fourth shall disperse

TÓ PNEUMATI KAI MACHAIRAN EKKENÓSÓ OPISÓ AUTÓN
to the wind and sword empty out after them

engLXX A fourth part thou shalt burn in the fire in the midst of the city, at the fulfilment of the days of the siege: and thou shalt take a fourth part, and burn it up in the midst of it: and a fourth part thou shalt cut with a sword round about it: and a fourth part thou shalt scatter to the wind; and I will draw out a sword after them.

Mic. 5:1 Now gather thyself in troops, O daughter of troops: he hath laid **siege** against us: they shall smite the judge of Israel with a rod upon the cheek.

SUNOCHÉ - besiege, siege – a divergent translation with "smite the judge of Israel" (KJV) rendered as "smite the tribes of Israel" (engLXX) – the final siege against the people of Israel (4:11-13)

LXX **5:1** *NUN EMPHRACHTHÉSETAI THUGATÉR EMPHRAGMÓ* ***SUNOCHÉN*** *ETAXEN EPH*
now obstructed daughter obstruction siege set for

HÉMAS EN RHABDÓ PATAXOUSIN EPI SIAGONA TAS PHULAS TOU ISRAÉL
us in rod shall strike upon jaw the tribes of the Israel

engLXX Now shall the daughter *of Sion* be completely hedged in: he has laid siege against us: they shall smite the tribes of Israel with a rod upon the cheek.

Mic. 7:12a *In* that day *also* he shall come even to thee from Assyria, and *from* the **fortified cities, (. . .)**

YLT That day - even unto thee it doth come in, from Asshur and the cities of the **fortress**, (. . .)

OCHUROS aNT - strong, firm, fortified - a divergent translation with "thy cities shall be levelled" (engLXX) added – the first occurrence of MATSOR in the verse is for the fortifications in the cities [See also 7:12b below]

LXX *KAI HAI POLEIS SOU ÉXOUSIN EIS HOMALISMON KAI EIS DIAMERISMON*
and the cities of you shall have into levelling and into partitioning

ASSURIÓN KAI HAI POLEIS SOU HAI ***OCHURAI*** . . .

engLXX And thy cities shall be levelled, and parted among the Assyrians; and thy strong cities . . .

Mic. 7:12b . . . and from the **fortress** even to the river, and from sea to sea, and *from* mountain to mountain.

YLT . . . and from the **fortress** even unto the river, and from sea to sea, and mount to mount.

TUROS – Tyre [the city] – a divergent translation with "the **fortress**" (KJV) rendered as "Tyre" (engLXX) - the fortified city in the far west of Israel, "even to the river" (KJV) in the far East of Israel, the LXX translator pictured "the fortress" as Tyre: however Tyre itself was destroyed by various conquests [prophesied in Ezekiel 26] whilst this word to Micah seems to be for a later end time fulfilment [See also 7:12a above]

LXX . . . *EIS DIAMERISMON APO* ***TUROU*** *HEÓS TOU POTAMOU KAI APO THALASSÉS*
into partitioning from Tyre until the river and from sea

HEÓS THALASSÉS KAI APO OROUS HEÓS TOU OROUS
until sea and from mountain until the mountain

engLXX . . . shall be parted from Tyre to the river, and from sea to sea, and from mountain to mountain.

Nah. 3:14 Draw thee waters for the **siege**, fortify thy strong holds: go into clay, and tread the morter, make strong the brickkiln.

PERIOCHÉ - surrounding siege, fortified enclosure, hemming – a loose translation with “make strong the brickkiln” (KJV) rendered as “make *the fortifications* stronger than brick” (engLXX) – the surrounding siege is in view, causing the need to make preparations

LXX *HUDÓR* ***PERIOCHÉS*** *EPISPASAI SEAUTÉ KAI KATAKRATÉSON TÓN OCHURÓMATÓN SOU*
water encompassed draw for yourself and secure of the fortresses of you

EMBÉTHI EIS PÉLON KAI SUMPATÉTHÉTI EN ACHUROIS KATAKRATÉSON HUPER PLINTHON
step into mortar and trample together in straw secure more than brick

engLXX Draw thee water for a siege, and well secure thy strong-holds: enter into the clay, and be thou trodden in the chaff, make *the fortifications* stronger than brick.

Hab. 2:1 I will stand upon my watch, and set me upon the **tower**, and will watch to see what he will say unto me, and what I shall answer when I am reproved.

YLT On my charge I stand, and I station myself on a **bulwark**, and I watch to see what He doth speak against me, and what I do reply to my reproof.

PETRA – rock – a loose translation with the word itself rendered as “rock” (engLXX) - a stronghold or other towering edifice in view

LXX *EPI TÉS PHULAKÉS MOU STÉSOMAI KAI EPIBÉSOMAI EPI* ***PETRAN*** *KAI APOSKOPEUSÓ*
upon the watch of me shall stand and shall mount upon rock and shall watch over

TOU IDEIN TI LALÉSEI EN EMOI KAI TI APOKRITHÓ EPI TON ELEGCHON MOU
the to look what | in me and what shall answer upon the reproof of me
should speak

engLXX I will stand upon my watch, and mount upon the rock, and watch to see what he will say by me, and what I shall answer when I am reproved.

Zec. 9:3 And Tyrus did build herself a **strong hold**, and heaped up silver as the dust, and fine gold as the mire of the streets.

YLT And Tyre doth build a **bulwark** to herself, and doth heap silver as dust, and gold as mire of out-places.

OCHURÓMA – fortress, stronghold – a direct translation – the fortress of Tyre

LXX *KAI ÓKODOMÉSE TUROS* ***OCHURÓMATA*** *HAUTÉ KAI ETHÉSAURISEN*
and built Tyrus fortress she and treasured up

ARGURION HÓS CHOUN KAI SUNÉGAGE CHRUSION HÓS PÉLON HODÓN
silver as dust and gathered gold as mud of ways

engLXX And Tyrus built strong-holds for herself, and heaped up silver as dust, and gathered gold as the mire of the ways.

Zec. 12:2 Behold, I will make Jerusalem a cup of trembling unto all the people round about, when they shall be in the **siege** both against Judah *and* against Jerusalem.

YLT Lo, I am making Jerusalem a cup of reeling to all the peoples round about, and also against Judah it is, in the **siege** against Jerusalem.

PERIOCHÉ - surrounding siege, fortified enclosure, hemming – a loose translation with "a cup of trembling" (KJV) or "a cup of reeling" (YLT), rendered as "trembling door-posts" (engLXX) – a surrounding siege involving both Jerusalem and Judah: centred on Jerusalem in the Gk. of the LXX and in the YLT; in the KJV, NKJV, NASB, NIV, NLT both Judah and Jerusalem are besieged

LXX *IDOU EGÓ TITHÉMI TÉN HIEROUSALÉM HÓS PROTHURA SALEUOMENA PASI TOIS*
look I appoint the Jerusalem as thresholds for shaking off all to the

LAOIS KUKLÓ KAI EN TÉ IOUDAIA ESTAI ***PERIOCHÉ*** *EPI HIEROUSALÉM*
peoples around and in the Judea shall be siege upon Jerusalem

engLXX Behold, I *will* make Jerusalem as trembling door-posts to all the nations round about, and in Judea there shall be a siege against Jerusalem.

19 - MIBCHAR

Translated into Greek in the LXX

EKLEKTOS		**7**		***EKLEKTOS*:**
EPILEKTOS	(choice)	3	aNT	**Genesis 23:6; Deuteronomy 12:11**
KALLOS	(beauty)	1	aNT	**Isaiah 22:7; Jeremiah 22:7; Jeremiah 48:15**
NOT translated in LXX		1		**Ezekiel 31:16; Daniel 11:15**
TOTAL		12		

Translated into English - Both KJV related

Ys Conc.	Count	Ss Conc. No. H 4005	Count
choice	3	choice	7
choice (adj.)	4	chosen	4
choicest	1	choicest	1
chosen	4		
TOTAL	12	TOTAL	12

Refs		Text quotes KJV unless otherwise stated
Gen. 23:6		Hear us, my lord: thou *art* a mighty prince among us: in the **choice** of our sepulchres bury thy dead of our sepulchres bury thy dead; none of us shall withhold from thee his sepulchre, but that thou mayest bury thy dead.
	YLT	Hear us, my lord; a prince of God *art* thou in our midst; in the **choice** of our burying-places bury thy dead: none of us his burying-place doth withhold from thee, from burying thy dead.'
	NKJV	"Hear us, my lord: You *are* a mighty prince among us; bury your dead in the **choicest** of our burial places. None of us will withhold from you his burial place, that you may bury your dead."
	NASB	"Hear us, my lord, you are a mighty prince among us; bury your dead in the **choicest** of our graves; none of us will refuse you his grave for burying your dead."
	NIV	'Sir, listen to us. You are a mighty prince among us. Bury your dead in the **choicest** of our tombs. None of us will refuse you his tomb for burying your dead.'
	NLT	"Listen, my lord, you are an honored prince among us. Choose the **finest** of our tombs and bury her there. No one here will refuse to help you in this way."

EKLEKTOS – a loose translation with "prince" (KJV) rendered as "king" (engLXX) – the best places for burial

LXX [5]*MÉ KURIE* [6]*AKOUSON DE HÉMÓN BASILEUS PARA THEOU SU EI EN HÉMIN EN TOIS* ***EKLEKTOIS***
not Lord hear but us king by God you are in us in the choice

MNÉMEIOIS HÉMÓN THAPSON TON NEKRON SOU OUDEIS GAR HÉMÓN OU MÉ KÓLUSEI TÓ
tombs of us entomb the dead of you not one for of us in no wise withhold for the

MNÉMEION AUTOU APO SOU TOU THAPSAI TON NEKRON SOU EKEI
tomb of him from you of the to entomb the dead of you there

engLXX but hear us; thou art in the midst of us a king from God; bury thy dead in our choice sepulchres, for not one of us will by any means withhold his sepulchre from thee, so that thou shouldest not bury thy dead there.

Exo. 15:4		Pharaoh's chariots and his host hath he cast into the sea: his **chosen** captains also are drowned in the Red sea.
	YLT	Chariots of Pharaoh and his force He hath cast into the sea; and the **choice** of his captains have sunk in the Red Sea!
	NKJV	Pharaoh's chariots and his army He has cast into the sea; his **chosen** captains also are drowned in the Red Sea.
	NASB	"Pharaoh's chariots and his army He has cast into the sea; and the **choicest** of his officers are drowned in the Red Sea.
	NIV	Pharaoh's chariots and his army he has hurled into the sea. The **best** of Pharaoh's officers are drowned in the Red Sea.
	NLT	Pharaoh's chariots and army he has hurled into the sea. The **finest** of Pharaoh's officers are drowned in the Red Sea.

EPILEKTOS aNT – a divergent translation with "mounted" (engLXX) added – the best captains in view they are seen as excellent above others [See separate chapter for *EPILEKTOS*]

LXX

HARMATA PHARAÓ KAI TÉN DUNAMIN AUTOU ERRHIPSEN EIS THALASSAN
chariots of Pharaoh and the power of him tossed into sea

EPILEKTOUS *ANABATAS TRISTATAS KATEPOTHÉSAN EN ERUTHRA THALASSÉ*
choice mounted officers sank in red sea

engLXX He has cast the chariots of Pharao and his host into the sea, the chosen mounted captains: they were swallowed up in the Red Sea.

Deu. 12:11 Then there shall be a place which the LORD your God shall choose[1] to cause his name to dwell there; thither shall ye bring all that I command you; your burnt offerings, and your sacrifices, your tithes, and the heave offering of your hand, and all your **choice** vows which ye vow unto the LORD:

YLT And it hath been, the place on which Jehovah your God doth fix to cause His name to tabernacle there, thither ye bring in all that which I am commanding you, your burnt-offerings, and your sacrifices, your tithes, and the heave-offering of your hand, and all the **choice** of your vows which ye vow to Jehovah;

NKJV then there will be the place where the LORD your God chooses to make His name abide. There you shall bring all that I command you: your burnt offerings, your sacrifices, your tithes, the heave offerings of your hand, and all your **choice** offerings which you vow to the LORD.

NASB then it shall come about that the place in which the LORD your God will choose for His name to dwell, there you shall bring all that I command you: your burnt offerings and your sacrifices, your tithes and the contribution of your hand, and all your **choice** votive offerings which you will vow to the LORD.

NIV Then to the place the LORD your God will choose as a dwelling for his Name – there you are to bring everything I command you: your burnt offerings and sacrifices, your tithes and special gifts, and all the **choice** possessions you have vowed to the LORD.

NLT you must bring everything I command you—your burnt offerings, your sacrifices, your tithes, your sacred offerings, and your offerings to fulfill a vow—to the designated place of worship, the place the LORD your God chooses for his name to be honored.

EKLEKTOS – a divergent translation with "choice vows" (KJV) rendered as "choice gift" (engLXX) – the best vows (Heb.) the best gifts (Gk.)

LXX *KAI ESTAI HO TOPOS HON AN EKLEXÉTAI*[1] *KURIOS HO THEOS SOU EPIKLÉTHÉNAI TO ONOMA*
and shall be the place which ever chose Lord the God of you called the name

AUTOU EKEI EKEI OISETE PANTA HOSA EGÓ ENTELLOMAI HUMIN SÉMERON
of him there there bring ye all as many as I charge to you today

1. See BACHAR

TA HOLOKAUTÓMATA HUMÓN KAI TA THUSIASMATA HUMÓN KAI TA EPIDEKATA HUMÓN
the whole burnt offerings of you and the sacrifices of you and the tithes of you

KAI TAS APARCHAS TÓN CHEIRÓN HUMÓN KAI PAN ***EKLEKTON*** *TÓN DÓRÓN HUMÓN*
and the first fruits of the hands of you and all choice of the gifts of you

HOSA AN EUXÉSTHE KURIÓ TÓ THEÓ HUMÓN
as many as ever ye vow to Lord the God of you

	engLXX	And there shall be a place which the Lord thy God shall choose for his name to be called there, thither shall ye bring all things that I order you to- day; your whole-burnt-offerings, and your sacrifices, and your tithes, and the first-fruits of your hands, and every choice gift of yours, whatsoever ye shall vow to the Lord your God.
Isa. 22:7		And it shall come to pass, *that* thy **choicest** valleys shall be full of chariots, and the horsemen shall set themselves in array at the gate.
	YLT	And it cometh to pass, the **choice** of thy valleys have been full of chariots, and the horsemen place themselves diligently at the gate.
	NKJV	It shall come to pass *that* your **choicest** valleys shall be full of chariots, and the horsemen shall set themselves in array at the gate.
	NASB	Then your **choicest** valleys were full of chariots, and the horsemen took up fixed positions at the gate.
	NIV	Your **choicest** valleys are full of chariots, and horsemen are posted at the city gates.
	NLT	Chariots fill your beautiful valleys, and charioteers storm your gates.

EKLEKTOS – a divergent translation with "horsemen shall set themselves in array" (KJV) or "horsemen place themselves diligently" (YLT), rendered as "horsemen shall block up" (engLXX) – the best valleys [i.e. like the valley of Megiddo with lots of room]

LXX *KAI ESONTAI HAI* ***EKLEKTAI*** *PHARAGGES SOU PLÉSTHÉSONTAI HARMATÓN HOI*
and will be the choice ravines of you filled of chariots the

DE HIPPEIS EMPHRAXOUSI TAS PULAS SOU
but horsemen block the gates of you

engLXX And it shall be *that* thy choice valleys shall be filled with chariots, and horsemen shall block up thy gates.

Isa. 37:24 By thy servants hast thou reproached the Lord, and hast said, By the multitude of my chariots am I come up to the height of the mountains, to the sides of Lebanon; and I will cut down the tall cedars thereof, *and* the **choice** fir trees thereof: and I will enter into the height of his border, *and* the forest of his Carmel.

YLT By the hand of thy servants thou hast reviled the Lord, and sayest: In the multitude of my chariots I have come up to a high place of hills, the sides of Lebanon, and I cut down the height of its cedars, the **choice** of its firs, and I enter the high place of its extremity, the forest of its Carmel.

KALLOS aNT – beauty - a loose translation with "choice fir trees" (KJV) given poetically as "beauty of his cypresses" (engLXX) – the best firs (Heb.) the beauty of cypresses (Gk.)

LXX *HOTI DI AGGELÓN ÓNEIDISAS KURION SU GAR EIPAS TÓ PLÉTHEI TÓN*
since through messengers berate Lord you for said to the many the

HARMATÓN EGÓ ANEBÉN EIS HUPSOS OREÓN KAI EIS TA ESCHATA TOU
chariots I ascend into heights | and into the ends of the
of mountains

LIBANOU KAI EKOPSA TO HUPSOS TÉS KEDROU AUTOU KAI TO ***KALLOS*** *TÉS*
Lebanon and felled the height of the cedar of it and the beauty of the

KUPARISSOU KAI EISÉLTHON EIS HUPSOS MEROUS TOU DRUMOU
cypress and enter into high regions of the forest

engLXX For thou hast reproached the Lord by messengers; for thou hast said, With the multitude of chariots have I ascended to the height of mountains, and to the sides of Libanus; and I have cropped the height of his cedars and the beauty of his cypresses; and I entered into the height of the forest region:

Jer. 22:7 And I will prepare destroyers against thee, every one with his weapons: and they shall cut down thy **choice** cedars, and cast *them* into the fire.

YLT And I have separated for thee destroyers, each with his weapons, and they have cut down the **choice** of thy cedars, and have cast them on the fire.

NKJV I will prepare destroyers against you, everyone with his weapons; they shall cut down your **choice** cedars and cast *them* into the fire.

NASB "For I will set apart destroyers against you, each with his weapons; and they will cut down your **choicest** cedars and throw *them* on the fire.

NIV I will send destroyers against you, each man with his weapons, and they will cut up your **fine** cedar beams and throw them into the fire.

NLT I will call for wreckers, who will bring out their tools to dismantle you. They will tear out all your **fine** cedar beams and throw them on the fire.

EKLEKTOS – a divergent translation with "destroyers" (KJV) given as "a destroying man" (engLXX) and associated: "his weapons" (KJV) given as "his axe" (engLXX) – the best cedars

LXX *KAI EPAXÓ EPI SE OLOTHREUONTA ANDRA KAI TON PELEKUN AUTOU KAI*
and bring upon you annihilating man and the axe of him and

EKKOPSOUSI TAS ***EKLEKTAS*** *KEDROUS SOU EMBALOUSIN EIS TO PUR*
cut down the choice cedars of you put into the fire

	engLXX	and I will bring upon thee a destroying man, and his axe: and they shall cut down thy choice cedars, and cast *them* into the fire.
Jer. 48:15		Moab is spoiled, and gone up *out of* her cities, and his **chosen** young men[2] are gone down to the slaughter, saith the King, whose name *is* the LORD of hosts.
	YLT	Spoiled is Moab, and her cities hath one gone up, and the **choice** of its young men have gone down to slaughter, an affirmation of the King, Jehovah of Hosts *is* His name.
	NKJV	Moab is plundered and gone up *from* her cities; her **chosen** young men have gone down to the slaughter," says the King, whose name *is* the LORD of hosts.
	NASB	"Moab has been destroyed and men have gone up to his cities; his **choicest** young men have also gone down to the slaughter," Declares the King, whose name is the LORD of hosts.
	NIV	Moab will be destroyed and her towns invaded; her **finest** young men will go down in the slaughter,' declares the King, whose name is the LORD Almighty.
	NLT	But now Moab and his towns will be destroyed. His **most promising** youth are doomed to slaughter," says the King, whose name is the LORD of Heaven's Armies.

EKLEKTOS – a divergent translation with "saith the King, whose name is the LORD of hosts" (KJV) not translated – the best young men

	LXX **31:15**	*ÓLETO MÓAB POLIS AUTOU KAI* ***EKLEKTOI*** *NEANISKOI*[2] *AUTOU KATEBÉSAN EIS SPHAGÉN* destroyed Moab cities of it and choice young men of him went down to slaughter
	engLXX	Moab is ruined, *even* his city, and his choice young men have gone down to slaughter.
Eze. 23:7		Thus she committed her whoredoms with them, with all them *that were* the **chosen** men of Assyria, and with all on whom she doted: with all their idols she defiled herself.

2 See BACHUR for "young men"

YLT And she giveth her whoredoms on them, the **choice** of the sons of Asshur, all of them - even all on whom she doted, by all their idols she hath been defiled.

NKJV Thus she committed her harlotry with them, all of them **choice** men of Assyria; and with all for whom she lusted, with all their idols, she defiled herself.

NASB She bestowed her harlotries on them, all of whom *were* the **choicest** men of Assyria; and with all whom she lusted after, with all their idols she defiled herself.

NIV She gave herself as a prostitute to all the **elite** of the Assyrians and defiled herself with all the idols of everyone she lusted after.

NLT And so she prostituted herself with the **most desirable** men of Assyria, worshiping their idols and defiling herself.

EPILEKTOS aNT – a divergent translation with "idols" (KJV) rendered as "thoughts" (LXX-inter) or "devices" (engLXX) – the best sons (YLT) of Assyria [See separate chapter for *EPILEKTOS*]

LXX *KAI EDÓKE TÉN PORNEIAN AUTÉS EP AUTOUS* ***EPILEKTOI*** *HUIOI ASSURIÓN PANTES KAI*
LXX-inter and gave the whoredoms of her upon them choice sons of Assyrians all and

EPI PANTAS HOUS EPETHETO EN PASI TOIS ENTHUMÉMASIN AUTOIS EMIAINETO
upon all whom doted in all the thoughts to them defile

engLXX And she bestowed her fornication upon them; all were choice sons of the Assyrians: and on whomsoever she doted herself, with them she defiled herself in all *their* devices.

Eze. 24:4 Gather the pieces thereof into it, *even* every good piece, the thigh, and the shoulder; fill *it* with the **choice** bones.

YLT To gather its pieces unto it, every good piece, thigh and shoulder, the **choice** of the bones to fill in.

NOT in LXX – a divergent translation: the bones are mentioned, but not their quality: the word is not translated: perhaps the LXX thought not to repeat the mention of quality which is then mentioned in the next verse [See Eze. 24:5 below]

LXX *KAI EMBALE EIS AUTON TA DICHOTOMÉMATA PAN DICHOTOMÉMA KALON*
and put into him the pieces every piece good

SKELOS KAI ÓMON EKSESARKISMENA APO TÓN OSTÓN
leg and shoulder flesh removed from the bones

engLXX and put the pieces into it, every prime piece, the leg and shoulder taken off from the bones,

Eze. 24:5 Take the **choice** of the flock, and burn also the bones under it, *and* make it boil well, and let them seethe the bones of it therein.

YLT The **choice** of the flock to take, and also to pile of the bones under it, boil it thoroughly, yea, cook its bones in its midst.

NKJV Take the **choice** of the flock. Also pile *fuel* bones under it, make it boil well, and let the cuts simmer in it."

NASB "Take the **choicest** of the flock, and also pile wood under the pot. Make it boil vigorously. Also seethe its bones in it."

NIV take **the pick** of the flock. Pile wood beneath it for the bones; bring it to the boil and cook the bones in it.

NLT Use only the **best** sheep from the flock, and heap fuel on the fire beneath the pot. Bring the pot to a boil, and cook the bones along with the meat.

EPILEKTOS aNT – a divergent translation with "well" (KJV) or "thoroughly" (YLT) not rendered – the best of the "flock" (Heb.) - "herd" (Gk.) [See separate chapter for *EPILEKTOS*]

LXX *EX* ***EPILEKTÓN*** *KTÉNÓN EILÉMMENÓN KAI HUPOKAIE TA OSTA HUPOKATÓ*
out of choice cattle take and burn the bones under

AUTÓN EZESE KAI HÉPSÉTAI TA OSTA AUTÉS EN MESÓ AUTÉS
of them boil and cook the bones of her in midst of her

	engLXX	*which are* taken from choice cattle, and burn the bones under them: her bones are boiled and cooked in the midst of her.
Eze. 31:16		I made the nations to shake at the sound of his fall, when I cast him down to hell with them that descend into the pit: and all the trees of Eden, the **choice** and best of Lebanon, all that drink water, shall be comforted in the nether parts of the earth.
	YLT	From the sound of his fall I have caused nations to shake, in My causing him to go down to sheol, with those going down to the pit, and comforted in the earth - the lower part, are all trees of Eden, the **choice** and the good of Lebanon, all drinking waters.
	NKJV	I made the nations shake at the sound of its fall, when I cast it down to hell together with those who descend into the Pit; and all the trees of Eden, the **choice** and best of Lebanon, all that drink water, were comforted in the depths of the earth.
	NASB	I made the nations quake at the sound of its fall when I made it go down to Sheol with those who go down to the pit; and all the well-watered trees of Eden, the **choicest** and best of Lebanon, were comforted in the earth beneath.
	NIV	I made the nations tremble at the sound of its fall when I brought it down to the realm of the dead to be with those who go down to the pit. Then all the trees of Eden, the **choicest** and best of Lebanon, the well-watered trees, were consoled in the earth below.
	NLT	I made the nations shake with fear at the sound of its fall, for I sent it down to the grave with all the others who descend to the pit. And all the other proud trees of Eden, the **most beautiful** and the best of Lebanon, the ones whose roots went deep into the water, took comfort to find it there with them in the depths of the earth.

EKLEKTOS – a divergent translation with "trees of Eden" (KJV) rendered as "trees of Delight" (engLXX) – the best trees of Lebanon

LXX *APO TÉS PHÓNÉS TÉS PTÓSEÓS AUTOU ESEISTHÉSAN TA ETHNÉ HOTE KATEBIBAZON AUTON*
from the sound of the fall of him shook the nations when brought down him

EIS HADOU META TÓN KATABAINONTÓN EIS LAKKON KAI PAREKALOUN AUTON EN GÉ[3] *PANTA*
into Hades with the going down into pit and comfort him in earth and

TA XULA TÉS TRUPHÉS KAI TA ***EKLEKTA*** *TOU LIBANOU PANTA TA PINONTA HUDÓR*
the trees of the luxuries and the choice of the Lebanon all the drinking water

engLXX At the sound of his fall the nations quaked, when I brought him down to Hades with them that go down to the pit: and all the trees of Delight comforted him in the heart[2], and the choice *plants* of Libanus, all that drink water.

Dan. 11:15 So the king of the north shall come, and cast up a mount, and take the most fenced cities: and the arms of the south shall not withstand, neither his **chosen** people, neither *shall there be any* strength to withstand.

YLT And the king of the north cometh in, and poureth out a mount, and hath captured fenced cities; and the arms of the south do not stand, nor the people of his **choice**, yea, there is no power to stand.

NKJV "So the king of the North shall come and build a siege mound, and take a fortified city; and the forces of the South shall not withstand *him*. Even his **choice** troops *shall have* no strength to resist.

NASB Then the king of the North will come, cast up a siege ramp and capture a well-fortified city; and the forces of the South will not stand *their ground*, not even their **choicest** troops, for there will be no strength to make a stand.

3. Perhaps a misreading or mistake by the physical typesetter (as in the printing process of the day): *GÉ* = earth, land – and is in the LXX source: the translated section copied here verbatim: "earth" seen as "heart" with the "h" in the beginning of the word instead of the end

NIV Then the king of the North will come and build up siege ramps and will capture a fortified city. The forces of the South will be powerless to resist; even their **best** troops will not have the strength to stand.

NLT Then the king of the north will come and lay siege to a fortified city and capture it. The **best** troops of the south will not be able to stand in the face of the onslaught.

EKLEKTOS – a divergent translation with the second "the arms of the south shall not withstand" (KJV) rendered as "the arms of the king of the south shall withstand" (engLXX): the exact opposite action and the word "king" added – the best people, troops

LXX *KAI EISELEUSETAI BASILEUS TOU BORRA KAI EKCHEEI PROSCHÓMA KAI SULLÉPSETAI*
and enter king of the north and pour out mounds and seize

POLEIS OCHURAS KAI HOI BRACHIONES TOU BASILEÓS TOU NOTOU STÉSONTAI KAI
cities strong and the arms of the king of the south stand and

ANASTÉSONTAI HOI ***EKLEKTOI*** *AUTOU KAI OUK ESTAI ISCHUS TOU STÉNAI*
arise the choice of him and not shall be strength of the to stand

engLXX And the king of the north shall come in, and cast up a mound, and take strong cities: and the arms of the king of the south shall withstand, and his chosen ones shall rise up, but there shall be no strength to stand.

20 - MIBCHOR

Translated into Greek in the LXX

EKLEKTOS		**1**		**2 Kings 19:23**
OCHUROS	(secure, strong)	1	aNT	
TOTAL		2		

Translated into English - Both KJV related

Ys Conc.	Count	Ss Conc. No. H 4004	Count
choice	2	choice	2
TOTAL	2	TOTAL	2

Refs	**Text quotes KJV unless otherwise stated**
2Ki. 3:19	And ye shall smite every fenced city, and every **choice** city, and shall fell every good tree, and stop all wells of water, and mar every good piece of land with stones.

OCHUROS aNT – A divergent translation with the first "city": "every fenced city" (KJV) not translated - Perhaps a combination of the idea of being "fenced" (KJV) and "choice" (KJV) is conveyed in "strong" (engLXX): firm, secure.

LXX **4Ki.3:19** *KAI PATAXETE PASAN POLIN* ***OCHURAN*** *KAI PAN XULON AGATHON KATABALEITE KAI*
and ye shall strike every city strong and every tree good ye shall throw down and

PASAS PÉGAS HUDATOS EMPHRAXESTHE KAI PASAN MERIDA AGATHÉN ACHREIÓSETE EN LITHOIS
every well of water obstruct and every portion good spoil in stones

engLXX And ye shall smite every strong city, and ye shall cut down every good tree, and ye shall stop all wells of water, and spoil every good piece *of land* with stones.

2Ki. 19:23 By thy messengers thou hast reproached the Lord, and hast said, With the multitude of my chariots I am come up to the height of the mountains, to the sides of Lebanon, and will cut down the tall cedar trees thereof, *and* the **choice** fir trees thereof: and I will enter into the lodgings of his borders, *and into* the forest of his Carmel.

YLT By the hand of thy messengers thou hast reproached the Lord, and sayest: In the multitude of my chariots I have come up to a high place of mountains - The sides of Lebanon, and I cut down the height of its cedars, the **choice** of its firs, and I enter the lodging of its extremity, the forest of its Carmel.

NKJV By your messengers you have reproached the Lord, and said: "By the multitude of my chariots I have come up to the height of the mountains, to the limits of Lebanon; I will cut down its tall cedars *and* its **choice** cypress trees; I will enter the extremity of its borders, *to* its fruitful forest.

NASB 'Through your messengers you have reproached the Lord, and you have said, "With my many chariots I came up to the heights of the mountains, to the remotest parts of Lebanon; and I cut down its tall cedars and its **choice** cypresses. And I entered its farthest lodging place, its thickest forest.

NIV By your messengers you have ridiculed the Lord. And you have said, "With my many chariots I have ascended the heights of the mountains, the utmost heights of Lebanon. I have cut down its tallest cedars, the **choicest** of its junipers. I have reached its remotest parts, the finest of its forests.

NLT By your messengers you have defied the Lord. You have said, 'With my many chariots I have conquered the highest mountains— yes, the remotest peaks of Lebanon. I have cut down its tallest cedars and its **finest** cypress trees. I have reached its farthest corners and explored its deepest forests.

EKLEKTOS – A divergent translation with the "borders" (KJV) or "its extremity" (YLT) not rendered - The best "fir trees" (KJV) given as "cypresses" (engLXX) are "choice" (engLXX).

LXX *EN CHEIRI AGGELÓN SOU ÓNEIDISAS KURION KAI EIPAS EN TÓ PLÉTHEI TÓN*
4Ki.19:23 In hand | of you reproach Lord and said in the multitude of the
of messengers

HARMATÓN MOU EGÓ ANABÉSOMAI EIS HUPSOS OREÓN MÉROUS TOU
chariots of me I ascend into height of mountains sides of the

LIBANOU KAI EKOPSA TO MEGETHOS TÉS KEDROU AUTOU TA ***EKLEKTA***
Lebanon and cut the great of the cedar of him the choice

KUPARISSÓN AUTOU KAI ÉLTHON EIS MESON DRUMOU KAI KARMÉLOU
cypresses of him and come into midst of wood and of Carmel

engLXX By thy messengers thou has reproached the Lord, and hast said, I will go up with the multitude of my chariots, to the height of the mountains, to the sides of Libanus, and I have cut down the height of his cedar, *and* his choice cypresses; and I have come into the midst of the forest and of Carmel.

21 - NESHEQ

Translated into Greek in the LXX

EKLEKTOS		**1**	**Isaiah 22:8**
HOPLON	(arm, weapon)	3	
ISCHUS	(strength)	1	
POLEMOS	(war, battle)	1	
PURGOS	(tower)	1	
SIDÉROS	(iron)	1	
NOT in LXX		2	
TOTAL		10	

Translated into English - Both KJV related

Ys Conc.	Count	Ss Conc. No. H 5402	Count
armed men	1	armour	3
armour	3	weapons	3
armoury	1	battle	1
battle	1	armed	1
harness	1	harness	1
weapon	3	armoury	1
TOTAL	10	TOTAL	10

Refs	Text quotes KJV unless otherwise stated
1Ki. 10:25	And they brought every man his present, vessels of silver, and vessels of gold, and garments, and **armour**, and spices, horses, and mules, a rate year by year.

NOT in LXX – A divergent translation with the clause "and armour" (KJV) not translated

LXX *KAI AUTOI EPHERON HEKASTOS TA DÓRA SKEUÉ CHRUSA KAI HIMATISMON*
3Ki.10:25 and they brought each the gifts vessels of gold and raiment

STAKTÉN KAI HÉDUSMATA KAI HIPPOUS KAI HÉMIONOUS TO KAT ENIAUTON ENIAUTÓ
stacte and spices and horses and mules the | according to year by year

engLXX And they brought every one their gifts, vessels of gold, and raiment, and stacte, and spices, and horses, and mules, a rate year by year.

2Ki. 10:2 Now as soon as this letter cometh to you, seeing your master's sons *are* with you, and *there are* with you chariots and horses, a fenced city also, and **armour**;

HOPLON – arm, weapon - a direct translation - the arms, armour of the place

LXX
4Ki.10:2

KAI NUN HÓS AN ELTHÉ TO BIBLION TOUTO PROS HUMAS KAI METH HUMÓN HOI
and now as soon as comes the book this to you and with you the

HUIOI TOU KURIOU HUMÓN KAI METH HUMÓN TO HARMA KAI HOI HIPPOI KAI
sons of the lord of you and with you the chariot and the horses and

POLEIS OCHURAI KAI TA ***HOPLA***
cities strong and the arms

engLXX Now then, as soon as this letter shall have reached you, whereas *there are* with you the sons of your master, and with you chariots and horses, and strong cities, and arms,

---

2Ch. 9:24 And they brought every man his present, vessels of silver, and vessels of gold, and raiment, **harness**, and spices, horses, and mules, a rate year by year.

NOT in LXX – A divergent translation with "harness" (KJV) rendered as "stacte" (LXX-inter) or "myrrh" (engLXX): i.e. not translated.

LXX
LXX-inter

KAI AUTOI EPHERON HEKASTOS TA DÓRA AUTOU SKEUÉ ARGURA KAI SKEUÉ
and they brought each the gifts of him vessels of silver and vessels

CHRUSA KAI HIMATISMON STAKTÉN KAI HÉDUSMATA HIPPOUS KAI HÉMIONOUS
of gold and raiment stacte and spices horses and mules

TO KAT ENIAUTON ENIAUTON
the | (according to) year year

engLXX And they brought every one his gifts, silver vessels and golden vessels, and raiment, myrrh and spices, horses and mules, a rate every year.

Neh. 3:19 And next to him repaired Ezer the son of Jeshua, the ruler of Mizpah, another piece over against the going up to the **armoury** at the turning *of the wall.*

PURGOS - tower - a divergent translation with "second" (LXX-inter) or "another" (engLXX) added - the word for "armoury" (KJV) is paraphrased as "tower" (engLXX) e.g. corner building where arms are generally kept

LXX *KAI EKRATÉSAN EPI CHEIRA AUTOU AZOUR HUIOS IÉSOU ARCHÓN TOU*
LXX-inter and repaired upon hand of him Azur son of Jesus chief of the

MASPHAI METRON DEUTERON ***PURGOU*** *ANABASEÓS TÉS SUNAPTOUSÉS TÉS GÓNIAS*
Masphai measured second tower of ascent of the join together of the corner

engLXX And next to him repaired Azur the son of Joshua, ruler of Masphai, another portion of the tower of ascent, where it meets the corner.

Job 20:24 He shall flee from the iron **weapon**, *and* the bow of steel shall strike him through.

YLT He fleeth from an iron **weapon**, pass through him doth a bow of brass.

SIDÉROS – iron - a loose translation with the phrase "iron weapon" (KJV) understood in just the words "of iron" (LXX-inter) and thus given as "sword" (engLXX)

LXX *KAI OU MÉ SÓTHÉ EK CHEIROS* ***SIDÉROU*** *TRÓSAI AUTON TOXON CHALKEION*
LXX-inter and in no wise saved out of hand of iron pierce him bow brass

engLXX And he shall by no means escape from the power of the sword; let the brazen bow wound him.

Job 39:21 He paweth in the valley, and rejoiceth in *his* strength: he goeth on to meet the **armed men**.

YLT They dig in a valley, and he rejoiceth in power, he goeth forth to meet the **armour**.

ISCHUS – strength - a divergent translation with "rejoicing in *his* strength" (KJV) or "he rejoiceth in power" (YLT) not rendered - the phrase "armed men" (KJV) or "armour" (YLT) gone forth to be met, re-arranged to read "goes forth in strength into the plain" (engLXX)

LXX *ANORUSSÓN EN PEDIÓ GAURIA EKPOREUETAI DE EIS PEDION EN* ***ISCHUI***
digging up in plain prances goes forth and into plain in strength

engLXX He paws exulting in the plain, and goes forth in strength into the plain.

Psa. 140:7 O God the Lord, the strength of my salvation, thou hast covered my head in the day of **battle**.

POLEMOS – war, battle - a direct translation - the Lord proclaimed as shield or helmet in the day of fighting: the day of needing armour

LXX **139:7** *KURIE KURIE DUNAMIS TÉS SÓTÉRIAS MOU EPESKIASAS EPI TÉN KEPHALÉN*
Lord Lord power of the salvation of me shadowed upon the head

MOU EN HÉMERA ***POLEMOU***
of me in day of war

engLXX O Lord God, the strength of my salvation; thou hast screened my head in the day of battle.

Isa. 22:8 And he discovered the covering of Judah, and thou didst look in that day to the **armour** of the house of the forest.

YLT And one removeth the covering of Judah, and thou lookest in that day unto the **armour** of the house of the forest,

NKJV He removed the protection of Judah. You looked in that day to the **armor** of the House of the Forest;

NASB And He removed the defense of Judah. In that day you depended on the **weapons** of the house of the forest,

NIV The Lord stripped away the defences of Judah, and you looked in that day to the **weapons** in the Palace of the Forest.

NLT Judah's defenses have been stripped away. You run to the **armory** for your weapons.

EKLEKTOS – A divergent translation with the "armour of the house" (KJV) rendered as "choice houses" (engLXX) - the flow of thought in the LXX can be seen in the following words of the next verse "secret places" (V.9) [of the "houses of the city" (V.8)] then being "uncovered" (V.9); whilst the Heb. translated refers to "breaches of the city" (V.9 KJV): i.e. the defensive walls needing repair. The high value of "armour" retained in the "choice" adjective, but in the divergent rendering points to the best houses

LXX *KAI ANAKALUPSOUSI TAS PULAS IOUDA KAI EMBLEPSONTAI TÉ HÉMERA*
and shall uncover the gates of Juda and shall look in the day

EKEINÉ EIS TOUS ***EKLEKTOUS*** *OIKOUS TÉS POLEÓS*
that into the choice houses of the city

engLXX And they shall uncover the gates of Juda, and they shall look in that day on the choice houses of the city.

Eze. 39:9 And they that dwell in the cities of Israel shall go forth, and shall set on fire and burn the **weapons**, both the shields and the bucklers, the bows and the arrows, and the handstaves, and the spears, and they shall burn them with fire seven years:

HOPLON – arm, weapon - a direct translation - the weapons of this eventual battle or war will be made of burnable material.

LXX *KAI EXELEUSONTAI HOI KATOIKOUNTES TAS POLEIS ISRAÉL KAI KAUSOUSIN EN*
and shall come forth the dwelling the cities of Israel and set aflame in

TOIS ***HOPLOIS*** *PELTAIS KAI KONTOIS KAI TOXOIS KAI TOXEUMASI KA*
the arms shields and spears and bows and arrows and

RHABDOIS CHEIRÓN KAI LOGCHAIS KAI KAUSOUSIN EN AUTOIS PUR HEPTA ETÉ
staves of hands and lances and set aflame in to them fire seven years

engLXX And they that inhabit the cities of Israel shall come forth, and make a fire with the arms, the shields and spears, and bows and arrows, and hand-staves, and lances, and they shall keep fire burning with them for seven years:

Eze. 39:10 So that they shall take no wood out of the field, neither cut down *any* out of the forests; for they shall burn the **weapons** with fire: and they shall spoil those that spoiled them, and rob those that robbed them, saith the Lord GOD.

HOPLON – arm, weapon - a direct translation - the arms made of combustible material will be so many that no local natural resource will be required for fuel for seven years.

LXX *KAI OU MÉ LABÓSI XULA EK TOU PEDIOU OUDE MÉ KOPSÓSIN EK TÓN DRUMÓN*
and in no wise take trees out of the plain neither not fell out of the groves

ALL É TA ***HOPLA*** *KATAKAUSOUSI PURI KAI PRONOMEUSOUSI TOUS PRONOMEUSANTAS*
but only the arms shall incinerate with fire and shall plunder the plundering

AUTOUS KAI SKULEUSOUSI TOUS SKULEUSANTAS AUTOUS LEGEI KURIOS
them and shall despoil the despoiling them says Lord

engLXX and they shall not take any wood out of the field, neither shall they cut any out of the forests, but they shall burn the weapons with fire: and they shall plunder those that plundered them, and spoil those that spoiled them, saith the Lord.

22 - PERI

Translated into Greek in the LXX

EKLEKTOS		**2**		***EKLEKTOS*:**
KARPOS	(fruit)	82		**Ezekiel 19:12; Ezekiel 19:14**
GENNÉMA	(produce)	10		
EKGONOS	(born of)	10		
EKPHORION	(increase of land)	2	aNT	
KARPOPHOROS	(fruitful)	2		
BOUKOLION	(herd)	1	aNT	
EULOGIA	(blessing)	1		
KARPIZ-Ó/-OMAI	(enjoy fruit of)`	1	aNT	
KARPIMOS	(fruit bearing)	1	aNT	
SPERMA	(seed)	1		
TEKNON	(child)	1		
NOT in LXX		5		
TOTAL		119		

Translated into English - Both KJV related

	Ys Conc.	Count	Ss Conc. No. H 6529	Count
	bough	1	fruit	113
See Ys Conc. P.377[1]	fruit	13+1	fruitful	2
	reward for	1	boughs	1
Counted as 1	fruitful	2	firstfruits [with7225]	1
	[+firstfruit	1[2]]	reward	1
			fruit thereof	1
	TOTAL	119	TOTAL	119

Refs **Text quotes KJV unless otherwise stated**

Gen. 1:11a And God said, Let the earth bring forth grass, the herb yielding seed, *and* the **fruit** tree . . .

KARPIMOS aNT – fruit bearing - a divergent translation with added clause "according to likeness" (engLXX) [cf. 1:12 below] - a fruit bearing tree

LXX *KAI EIPEN HO THEOS BLASTÉSATÓ HÉ GÉ BOTANÉN CHORTOU SPEIRON*
and said the God let bring forth the earth herb of grass sowing

1. Jer. 29:5 & 29:28
2 See Ys Conc. P.352 Deu.26:10 with RESHITH

SPERMA KATA GENOS KAI KATH HOMOIOTÉTA KAI XULON ***KARPIMON*** . . .
seed according to kind and according to likeness and tree fruitful

engLXX And God said, Let the earth bring forth the herb of grass bearing seed according to its kind and according to its likeness, and the fruit-tree . . .

Gen. 1:11b . . . yielding **fruit** after his kind, whose seed *is* in itself, upon the earth: and it was so.

KARPOS – fruit - a direct translation – fruit from a tree

LXX . . . *POIOUN* ***KARPON*** *HOU TO SPERMA AUTOU EN AUTÓ KATA GENOS EPI TÉS*
making fruit where the seed of it in it | kind upon the

GÉS KAI EGENETO HOUTÓS according to
earth and became this

engLXX . . . bearing fruit whose seed is in it, according to its kind on the earth, and it was so.

Gen. 1:12 And the earth brought forth grass, *and* herb yielding seed after his kind, and the tree yielding **fruit**, whose seed *was* in itself, after his kind: and God saw that *it was* good.

KARPOS – fruit - a divergent translation with the first "after his kind" (KJV) rendered as "according to its kind and according to its likeness" (engLXX) in contrast to the second "after his kind" (KJV) rendered "according to its kind" (engLXX) – fruit from fruit tree

LXX *KAI EXÉNEGKEN HÉ GÉ BOTANÉN CHORTOU SPEIRON SPERMA KATA GENOS*
and brought forth the earth pasturage of grass sowing seed according to kind

KAI KATH HOMIOTÉTA KAI XULON KARPIMON POIOUN ***KARPON*** *HOU TO*
and according to likeness and tree fruit making fruit which the

SPERMA AUTOU EN AUTÓ KATA GENOS EPI TÉS GÉS KAI EIDEN HO THEOS HOTI KALON
seed of it in it according to kind upon the earth and saw the God that good

engLXX And the earth brought forth the herb of grass bearing seed according to its kind and according to its likeness, and the fruit tree bearing fruit whose seed is in it, according to its kind on the earth, and God saw that it was good.

Gen. 1:29 And God said, Behold, I have given you every herb bearing seed, which *is* upon the face of all the earth, and every tree, in the which *is* the **fruit** of a tree yielding seed; to you it shall be for meat.

KARPOS – fruit - a direct translation – fruit of fruit tree producing seed

LXX *KAI EIPEN HO THEOS IDOU DEDÓKA HUMIN PANTA CHORTON SPORIMON*
and said the God look gave to you every grass seeding

SPEIRON SPERMA HO ESTIN EPANÓ PASÉS TÉS GÉS KAI PAN XULON HO ECHEI
sowing seed which is above all the earth and every tree which has

EN HEAUTÓ ***KARPON*** *SPERMATOS SPORIMOU HUMIN ESTAI EIS BRÓSIN*
in itself fruit seed seeding to you shall be into food

engLXX And God said, Behold I have given to you every seed-bearing herb sowing seed which is upon all the earth, and every tree which has in itself the fruit of seed that is sown, to you it shall be for food.

Gen. 3:2 And the woman said unto the serpent, We may eat of the **fruit** of the trees of the garden:

KARPOS – fruit - a direct translation – fruit from tree

LXX *KAI EIPEN HÉ GUNÉ TÓ OPHEI APO* ***KARPOU*** *TOU XULOU TOU PARADEISOU PHAGOUMETHA*
3:3 and said the woman to the serpent from fruit of the tree of the garden we eat

engLXX And the woman said to the serpent, We may eat of the fruit of the trees of the garden,

---

Gen. 3:3 But of the **fruit** of the tree which *is* in the midst of the garden, God hath said, Ye shall not eat of it, neither shall ye touch it, lest ye die.

KARPOS – fruit - a direct translation – fruit of the tree

LXX **3:4** *APO DE TOU* ***KARPOU*** *TOU XULOU HO ESTIN EN MESÓ TOU PARADEISOU EIPEN HO THEOS*
from but of the fruit of the tree which is in midst of the garden said the God

OU PHAGESTHE AP AUTOU OUDE MÉ APSÉSTHE AUTOU HINA MÉ APOTHANÉTE
not ye eat from of it neither not touch ye of it | in order that not ye should die

engLXX but of the fruit of the tree which is in the midst of the garden, God said, Ye shall not eat of it, neither shall ye touch it, lest ye die.

Gen. 3:6 And when the woman saw that the tree *was* good for food, and that it *was* pleasant to the eyes, and a tree to be desired to make *one* wise, she took of the **fruit thereof**, and did eat, and gave also unto her husband with her; and he did eat.

KARPOS – fruit - a divergent translation with "to make *one* wise" (KJV) not rendered – fruit of tree

LXX **3:7** *KAI EIDEN HÉ GUNÉ HOTI KALON TO XULON EIS BRÓSIN KAI HOTI ARESTON TOIS*
and saw the woman since good the tree into food and since pleasing to the

OPHTHALMOIS IDEIN KAI HÓRAION ESTI TOU KATANOÉSAI KAI LABOUSA APO TOU ***KARPOU***
eyes to look and seasonable is of the to observe and take from the fruit

AUTOU EPHAGE KAI EDÓKE KAI TÓ ANDRI AUTÉS MET AUTÉS KAI EPHAGON
of it ate and gave and to the husband of her with her and they ate

engLXX And the woman saw that the tree was good for food, and that it was pleasant to the eyes to look upon and beautiful to contemplate, and having taken of its fruit she ate, and she gave to her husband also with her, and they ate.

Gen. 4:3 And in process of time it came to pass, that Cain brought of the **fruit** of the ground an offering unto the LORD.

KARPOS – fruit - a direct translation – fruit of the earth

LXX *KAI EGENETO METH HÉMERAS ÉNEGKE KAIN APO TÓN* ***KARPÓN*** *TÉS GÉS THUSIAN TÓ KURIÓ*
and came to be after days brought Cain from the fruits of the earth offering to the Lord

engLXX And it was so after some time that Cain brought of the fruits of the earth a sacrifice to the Lord.

Gen. 30:2 And Jacob's anger was kindled against Rachel: and he said, *Am* I in God's stead, who hath withheld from thee the **fruit** of the womb?

KARPOS – fruit - a direct translation – fruit of womb

LXX *THUMÓTHEIS DE IAKÓB TÉ RACHÉL EIPEN AUTÉ MÉ ANTI THEOU EGÓ EIMI HOS*
enraged but Jacob with the Rachel said she not as good as of God I am who

ESTERÉSE SE ***KARPON*** *KOILIAS*
deprived you fruit of womb

engLXX And Jacob was angry with Rachel, and said to her, Am I in the place of God, who has deprived thee of the fruit of the womb?

Exo. 10:15 For they covered the face of the whole earth, so that the land was darkened; and they did eat every herb of the land, and all the **fruit** of the trees which the hail had left: and there remained not any green thing in the trees, or in the herbs of the field, through all the land of Egypt.

KARPOS – fruit - a divergent translation with "the land was darkened" (KJV) rendered as "the land was wasted" (engLXX) – fruit of the trees

LXX *KAI EKALUPSE TÉN OPSIN TÉS GÉS KAI EPHTHARÉ HÉ GÉ KAI KATEPHAGE*
and covered the appearance of the land and spoiled the land and ate

PASAN BOTANÉN TÉS GÉS KAI PANTA TON ***KARPON*** *TÓN XULÓN HOS*
all pasturage of the land and all the fruit of the trees which

HUPELEIPHTHÉ APO TÉS CHALAZÉS OUCH HUPELEIPHTHÉ CHLÓRON OUDEN
left behind from the hail not left behind green neither

EN TOIS XULOIS KAI EN PASÉ BOTANÉ TOU PEDIOU EN PASÉ GÉ AIGUPTOU
in the trees and in every pasture of the field in all land of Egypt

engLXX And they covered the face of the earth, and the land was wasted, and they devoured all the herbage of the land, and all the fruit of the trees, which was left by the hail: there was no green thing left on the trees, nor on all the herbage of the field, in all the land of Egypt.

Lev. 19:23 And when ye shall come into the land, and shall have planted all manner of trees for food, then ye shall count the **fruit** thereof as uncircumcised: three years shall it be as uncircumcised unto you: it shall not be eaten of.

KARPOS – fruit - a divergent translation with "which the Lord your God gives you" (engLXX) added – fruit of tree planted not to be eaten for 3 years

LXX *HOTAN DE EISELTHÉTE EIS TÉN GÉN HÉN KURIOS HO THEOS HUMÓN DIDÓSIN HUMIN KAI*
when but ye enter into the land which Lord the God of you gives you and

KATAPHUTEUSETE PAN XULON BRÓSIMON KAI PERIKATHARIEITE TÉN AKATHARSIAN AUTOU
should plant every tree eatable and shall purge away the uncleanness of it

*HO **KARPOS** AUTOU TRIA ETÉ ESTAI HUMIN APERIKATHARTOS OU BRÓTHÉSETAI*
the fruit of it three years shall be to you impure not be eaten

engLXX And whenever ye shall enter into the land which the Lord your God gives you, and shall plant any fruit-tree, then shall ye purge away its uncleanness; its fruit shall be three years uncleansed to you, it shall not be eaten.

Lev. 19:24 But in the fourth year all the **fruit** thereof shall be holy to praise the LORD *withal.*

KARPOS – fruit - a direct translation – fruit of tree in 4th year as per NLT "consecrated to the Lord as a celebration of praise"

LXX *KAI TÓ ETEI TÓ TETARTÓ ESTAI PAS HO* ***KARPOS*** *AUTOU HAGIOS AINETOS TÓ KURIÓ*
and with the year the fourth shall be all the fruit of it holy praiseworthy | Lord
to the

engLXX And in the fourth year all its fruit shall be holy, a subject of praise to the Lord.

Lev. 19:25 And in the fifth year shall ye eat of the **fruit** thereof, that it may yield unto you the increase thereof: I *am* the LORD your God.

KARPOS – fruit - a direct translation – fruit of tree to be eaten in 5th year

LXX *EN DE TÓ ETEI TÓ PEMPTÓ PHAGESTHE TON* ***KARPON*** *PROSTHEMA HUMIN TA*
in but the year the fifth shall eat the fruit increase to you the

GENNÉMATA AUTOU EGÓ EIMI KURIOS HO THEOS HUMÓN
produce of it I am Lord the God of you

engLXX And in the fifth year ye shall eat the fruit, its produce is an increase to you. I am the Lord your God.

Lev. 23:40 And ye shall take you on the first day the **boughs** of goodly trees, branches of palm trees, and the boughs of thick trees, and willows of the brook; and ye shall rejoice before the LORD your God seven days.

YLT and ye have taken to yourselves on the first day the **fruit** of beautiful trees, branches of palms, and boughs of thick trees, and willows of a brook, and have rejoiced before Jehovah your God seven days.

KARPOS – fruit - a divergent translation with "branches of osiers" (engLXX) added – fruit of tree

LXX *KAI LÉPSESTHE TÉ HÉMERA TÉ PRÓTÉ* ***KARPON*** *XULOU HÓRAION KAI*
and shall receive the day the first fruit of tree seasonable and

KALLUNTHRA PHOINIKÓN KAI KLADOUS XULOU DASEIS KAI ITEAS KAI AGNOU
palm branches of palm trees and | of tree bushy and willows and |
tender branches of chaste tree

KLADOUS EK CHEIMARROU EUPHRANTHÉNAI ENANTI KURIOU TOU THEOU
tender branches out of rushing stream shall be glad before Lord the God

HUMÓN HEPTA HÉMERAS TOU ENIAUTOU
of you seven days of the year

engLXX And on the first day ye shall take goodly fruit of trees, and branches of palm trees, and thick boughs of trees, and willows, and branches of osiers from the brook, to rejoice before the Lord your God seven days in the year.

Lev. 25:19 And the land shall yield her **fruit**, and ye shall eat your fill, and dwell therein in safety.

YLT and the land hath given its **fruit**, and ye have eaten to satiety, and have dwelt confidently on it.

EKPHORION aNT – increase of land - a direct translation – "fruit" (KJV) of land rendered as "increase" (LXX-inter) of land

LXX *KAI DÓSEI HÉ GÉ TA* ***EKPHORIA*** *AUTÉS KAI PHAGESTHE EIS PLÉSMONÉN KAI*
LXX-inter and shall give the land the increase of her and shall eat into fullness and

KATOIKÉSETE PEPOITHOTES EP AUTÉS
shall dwell confident upon her

engLXX And the land shall yield her increase, and ye shall eat to fullness, and shall dwell securely in it.

Lev. 26:4 Then I will give you rain in due season, and the land shall yield her increase, and the trees of the field shall yield their **fruit**.

KARPOS – fruit - a direct translation – fruit of the trees of the field

LXX *KAI DÓSÓ TON HUETON HUMIN EN KAIRÓ AUTOU KAI HÉ GÉ DÓSEI TA*
and shall give the rain to you in season of it and the earth shall give the

GENÉMATA AUTÉS KAI TA XULA TÓN PEDIÓN APODÓSEI TON ***KARPON*** *AUTÓN*
produce of her and the trees of the fields shall yield the fruit of them

engLXX then will I give you the rain in its season, and the land shall produce its fruits, and the trees of the field shall yield their fruit.

Lev. 26:20 And your strength shall be spent in vain: for your land shall not yield her increase, neither shall the trees of the land yield their **fruits**.

KARPOS – fruit - a loose translation with "trees of the land" (KJV) given as "of the field" (engLXX) and "increase" (KJV) given as "sowing" (engLXX: ability to sow by providing seed): fruit of trees

LXX *KAI ESTAI EIS KENON HÉ ISCHUS HUMÓN KAI OU DÓSEI HÉ GÉ HUMÓN TON*
and shall be into vain the strength of you and not shall give the land of you the

SPORON AUTÉS KAI TO XULON TOU AGROU HUMÓN OU DÓSEI TON ***KARPON*** *AUTOU*
sowing of her and the tree of the field of you not shall give the fruit of it

engLXX And your strength shall be in vain; and your land shall not yield its seed, and the tree of your field shall not yield its fruit.

Lev. 27:30 And all the tithe of the land, *whether* of the seed of the land, *or* of the **fruit** of the tree, *is* the LORD's: *it is* holy unto the LORD.

KARPOS – fruit - a direct translation – fruit of the tree

LXX *PASA DEKATÉ TÉS GÉS APO TOU SPERMATOS TÉS GÉS KAI TOU* ***KARPOU*** *TOU*
every tenth of the land from the seed of the land and of the fruit of the

XULINOU TÓ KURIÓ ESTIN HAGION TÓ KURIÓ
wood to the Lord is holy to the Lord

engLXX Every tithe of the land, both of the seed of the land, and of the fruit of trees, is the Lord's, holy to the Lord.

Num. 13:20 And what the land *is*, whether it *be* fat or lean, whether there be wood therein, or not. And be ye of good courage, and bring of the **fruit** of the land. Now the time *was* the time of the firstripe grapes.

KARPOS – fruit - a direct translation – fruit of the land to be taken from Canaan by the spies (V.17)

LXX **13:21**
KAI TIS HÉ GÉ É PIÓN É PAREIMENÉ EI ESTIN EN AUTÉ DENDRA É OU KAI
and what the land is plentiful or neglected if is in she trees or not and

PROSKARTERÉSANTES LÉPSESTHE APO TÓN ***KARPÓN*** *TÉS GÉS KAI HAI*
adhere firmly take from the fruits of the land and the

HÉMERAI HÉMERAI EAROS PRODROMOI STAPHULÉS
days days of spring forerunners of grape

engLXX And what the land is, whether rich or poor; whether there are trees in it or no: and ye shall persevere and take of the fruits of the land: and the days *were* the days of spring, the forerunners of the grape.

Num. 13:26 And they went and came to Moses, and to Aaron, and to all the congregation of the children of Israel, unto the wilderness of Paran, to Kadesh; and brought back word unto them, and unto all the congregation, and shewed them the **fruit** of the land.

YLT And they go and come in unto Moses, and unto Aaron, and unto all the company of the sons of Israel, unto the wilderness of Paran, to Kadesh; and they bring them and all the company back word, and shew them the **fruit** of the land.

KARPOS – fruit - a direct translation – fruit of the land spied out (V.25)

LXX **13:27**
KAI POREUTHENTES ÉLTHON PROS MÓUSÉN KAI AARÓN KAI PROS PASAN SUNAGÓGÉN
and having gone they came to Moses and Aaron and to all assembly

HUIÓN ISRAÉL EIS TÉN ERÉMON PHARAN KADÉS KAI APEKRITHÉSAN AUTOIS RHÉMA
of sons of Israel into the desert of Pharan Cades and answered to them word

KAI PASÉ SUNAGÓGÉ KAI EDEIXAN TON ***KARPON*** *TÉS GÉS*
and all assembly and showed the fruit of the land

engLXX And they proceeded and came to Moses and Aaron and all the congregation of the children of Israel, to the wilderness of Pharan Cades; and they brought word to them and to all the congregation, and they shewed the fruit of the land:

Num. 13:27 And they told him, and said, We came unto the land whither thou sentest us, and surely it floweth with milk and honey; and this *is* the **fruit** of it.

KARPOS – fruit - a direct translation – fruit of the land

LXX *KAI DIÉGÉSANTO AUTÓ KAI EIPAN ÉLTHAMEN EIS TÉN GÉN EIS HÉN*
13:28 and described to him and said we came into the land into which

APESTEILAS HÉMAS GÉN RHEOUSAN GALA KAI MELI KAI HOUTOS HO ***KARPOS*** *AUTÉS*
sent us land flowing milk and honey and this the fruit of her

engLXX and they reported to him, and said, We came into the land into which thou sentest us, a land flowing with milk and honey; and this is the fruit of it.

Deu. 1:25 And they took of the **fruit** of the land in their hands, and brought *it* down unto us, and brought us word again, and said, *It is* a good land which the Lord our God doth give us.

KARPOS – fruit - a direct translation – fruit of the land

LXX *KAI ELABOSAN EN TAIS CHERSIN AUTÓN APO TOU* ***KARPOU*** *TÉS GÉS KAI*
and took in the hands of them from the fruit of the land and

KATÉNEGKAN PROS HUMAS KAI ELEGON AGATHÉ HÉ GÉ HÉN KURIOS HO
carried to you and said good the land which Lord the

THEOS HÉMÓN DIDÓSIN HÉMIN
God of us gives us

engLXX And they took in their hands of the fruit of the land, and brought it to you, and said, The land is good which the Lord our God gives us.

Deu. 7:13a And he will love thee, and bless thee, and multiply thee: he will also bless the **fruit** of thy womb, (. . .)

EKGONOS - born of - a direct translation - offspring from your [own] body

LXX *KAI AGAPÉSEI SE KAI EULOGÉSEI SE KAI PLÉTHUNEI SE KAI EULOGÉSEI TA*
and shall love you and bless you and shall multiply you and will bless the

EGGONA[3] *TÉS KOILAS SOU . . .*
offspring of the body of you

engLXX And he will love thee, and bless thee, and multiply thee; and he will bless the off-spring of thy body, (. . .)

Deu. 7:13b . . . and the **fruit** of thy land, thy corn, and thy wine, and thine oil, the increase of thy kine, and the flocks of thy sheep, in the land which he sware unto thy fathers to give thee.

KARPOS – fruit - a direct translation – fruit of the land

LXX . . . *KAI TON* ***KARPON*** *TÉS GÉS SOU TON SITON SOU KAI TON OINON SOU KAI*
and the fruit of the land of you the grain of you and the wine of you and

---

3. spelling as per source; likely a misspelling; or a misprint due to print method: Shown as *EKGONOS* in LXX Conc. at that ref. [cf. Deu. 28:51a below]

TO ELAION SOU TA BOUKOLIA TÓN BOÓN SOU KAI TA POIMNIA TÓN PROBATÓN
the oil of you the herds of the oxen of you and the flocks of the sheep

SOU EPI TÉS GÉS HÉS ÓMOSE KURIOS TOIS PATRASI SOU DOUNAI SOI
of you upon the land which swore Lord to the fathers of you to give to you

engLXX . . . and the fruit of thy land, thy corn, and thy wine, and thine oil, the herds of thine oxen, and the flocks of thy sheep, on the land which the Lord sware to thy fathers to give to thee.

Deu. 26:2 That thou shalt take of the first of all the **fruit** of the earth, which thou shalt bring of thy land that the LORD thy God giveth thee, and shalt put *it* in a basket, and shalt go unto the place which the LORD thy God shall choose to place his name there.

KARPOS – fruit - a divergent translation with "the fruit of the earth, which thou shalt bring of thy land" (KJV) rendered as "the fruits of thy land" (engLXX) earth and land reduced to just "land" - fruit of the land

LXX *KAI LÉPSÉ APO TÉS APARCHÉS TÓN* ***KARPÓN*** *TÉS GÉS SOU HÉS KURIOS HO*
and shall take from the firs(-fruit) of the fruits of the land of you which Lord the

THEOS SOU DIDÓSI SOI KAI EMBALEIS EIS KARTALLON KAI POREUSÉ EIS TON
God of you gives to you and shall put into basket and shall go into the

TOPON HON AN EKLEXÉTAI KURIOS HO THEOS SOU EPIKLÉTHÉNAI TO ONOMA AUTOU EKEI
place which ever shall choose Lord the God of you to call upon the name of him there

engLXX that thou shalt take of the first of the fruits of thy land, which the Lord thy God gives thee, and thou shalt put them into a basket, and thou shalt go to the place which the Lord thy God shall choose to have his name called there.

Deu. 26:10 And now, behold, I have brought the **firstfruits** of the land, which thou, O LORD, hast given me. And thou shalt set it before the LORD thy God, and worship before the LORD thy God:

YLT And now, lo, I have brought in the first of the **fruits** of the ground which thou hast given to me, O Jehovah; - and thou hast placed it before Jehovah thy God, and bowed thyself before Jehovah thy God,

GENNÉMA – produce - a divergent translation with the added "flowing with milk and honey" (engLXX) – produce of the land

LXX *KAI NUN IDOU ENÉNOCHA TÉN APARCHÉN TÓN* ***GENNÉMATÓN*** *TÉS GÉS HÉS*
and now look I have brought the first(-fruit) of the produce of the land which

EDÓKAS MOI KURIE GÉN RHEOUSAN GALA KAI MELI KAI APHÉSEIS AUTO
gave to me Lord land flowing milk and honey and shall leave it

APENANTI KURIOU TOU THEOU SOU KAI PROSKUNÉSEIS ENANTI KURIOU TOU THEOU SOU
before Lord the God of you and shall worship before Lord the God of you

engLXX And now, behold, I have brought the first of the fruits of the land, which thou gavest me, O Lord, a land flowing with milk and honey: and thou shalt leave it before the Lord thy God, and thou shalt worship before the Lord thy God;

Deu. 28:4a Blessed *shall be* the **fruit** of thy body, (. . .)

EKGONOS – born of - a direct translation – fruit of the body: children

LXX *EULOGÉMENA TA* ***EKGONA*** *TÉS KOILIAS SOU . . .*
will be blessed the offspring of the body of you

engLXX Blessed shall be the offspring of thy body, (. . .)

Deu. 28:4b . . . and the **fruit** of thy ground, (. . .)

GENNÉMA – produce - a direct translation – produce of the ground

LXX . . . *KAI TA **GENNÉMATA** TÉS GÉS SOU* . . .
and the produce of the ground of you

engLXX . . . and the fruits of thy land, (. . .)

Deu. 28:4c . . . and the **fruit** of thy cattle, the increase of thy kine, and the flocks of thy sheep.

BOUKOLION aNT – herd - a divergent translation with "the increase of thy kine" (KJV) omitted - the "herds" (engLXX) being the fruit of the thy cattle paraphrased

LXX . . . *KAI TA **BOUKOLIA** TÓN BOÓN SOU KAI TA POIMNIA TÓN PROBATÓN SOU*
and the herds of the oxen of you and the flocks of the sheep of you

engLXX . . . and the herds of thy oxen, and the flocks of thy sheep.

Deu. 28:11a And the Lord shall make thee plenteous in goods, in the **fruit** of thy body, (. . .)
YLT `And Jehovah hath made thee abundant in good, in the **fruit** of thy womb, (. . .)

EKGONOS – born of - a direct translation – offspring of the body

LXX *KAI PLÉTHUNEI SE KURIOS HO THEOS SOU EIS AGATHA EN TOIS **EKGONOIS***
and shall multiply you Lord the God of you into good in the offspring

TÉS KOILIAS SOU . . .
of the body of you

engLXX And the Lord thy God shall multiply thee for good in the offspring of thy body, (. . .)

Deu. 28:11b . . . and in the **fruit** of thy cattle, (. . .)
YLT . . . and in the **fruit** of thy cattle, (. . .)

EKGONOS – born of - a direct translation – offspring of the cattle

LXX . . . ***KAI EPI TOIS*** ***EKGONOIS*** ***TÓN KTÉNÓN SOU*** . . .
and upon the offspring of the cattle of you

engLXX . . . and in the offspring of thy cattle, (. . .)

Deu. 28:11c . . . and in the **fruit** of thy ground, in the land which the LORD sware unto thy fathers to give thee.

YLT . . . and in the **fruit** of thy ground, on the ground which Jehovah hath sworn to thy fathers to give to thee.

GENNÉMA – produce - a divergent translation with the 2nd "thy" in "thy land" added – produce of the land

LXX ***KAI EPI TOIS*** ***GENNÉMASI*** ***TÉS GÉS SOU EPI TÉS GÉS SOU HÉS ÓMOSE KURIOS***
and upon the produce of the land of you upon the land of you which sware Lord

TOIS PATRASI SOU DOUNAI SOI
to the fathers of you to give to you

engLXX . . . and in the fruits of thy land, on thy land which the Lord sware to thy fathers to give to thee.

Deu. 28:18a Cursed *shall be* the **fruit** of thy body, (. . .)

EKGONOS – born of - a direct translation – offspring of the body

LXX ***EPIKATARATA TA*** ***EKGONA*** ***TÉS KOILIAS SOU*** . . .
cursed the offspring of the body of you

engLXX Cursed shall be the offspring of thy body, (. . .)

Deu. 28:18b . . . and the **fruit** of thy land, the increase of thy kine, and the flocks of thy sheep.

GENNÉMA – produce - a direct translation – produce of the land

LXX ***KAI TA*** ***GENNÉMATA*** ***TÉS GÉS SOU TA BOUKOLIA TÓN BOÓN SOU KAI TA***
and the produce of the land of you the herds of the oxen of you and the

POIMNIA TÓN PROBATÓN SOU
flocks of the sheep of you

engLXX . . . and the fruits of thy land, the herds of thine oxen, and the flocks of thy sheep.

Deu. 28:33 The **fruit** of thy land, and all thy labours, shall a nation which thou knowest not eat up; and thou shalt be only oppressed and crushed alway:

EKPHORION aNT – increase of land - a direct translation - the produce of the land

LXX *TA* ***EKPHORIA*** *TÉS GÉS SOU KAI PANTAS TOUS PONOUS SOU PHAGETAI ETHNOS HO OUK*
the output of the land of you and all the labour of you shall eat nation which not

EPISTASAI KAI ESÉ ADIKOUMENOS KAI TETHRAUSMENOS PASAS TAS HÉMERAS
know and will be injured and devastated all the days

engLXX A nation which thou knowest not shall eat the produce of thy land, and all thy labours; and thou shalt be injured and crushed always.

Deu. 28:42 All thy trees and **fruit** of thy land shall the locust consume.

GENNÉMA – produce - a loose to divergent translation with "locust" (KJV) rendered as "blight" (engLXX) – produce of the land

LXX *PANTA TA XULINA SOU KAI TA* ***GENNÉMATA*** *TÉS GÉS SOU EXANALÓSEI HÉ ERISUBÉ*
all the woods of you and the produce of the land of you shall consume the blight

engLXX All thy trees and the fruits of thy land shall the blight consume.

Deu. 28:51a And he shall eat the **fruit** of thy cattle, (. . .)

EKGONOS - born of - a direct translation - offspring of cattle

LXX *KAI KATEDETAI TA* ***EGKONA***[4] *TÓN KTÉNÓN SOU* . . .
and shall devour the offspring of the cattle of you

engLXX And it shall eat up the young of thy cattle, (. . .)

Deu. 28:51b . . . and the **fruit** of thy land, until thou be destroyed: which *also* shall not leave thee *either* corn, wine, or oil, *or* the increase of thy kine, or flocks of thy sheep, until he have destroyed thee.

GENNÉMA – produce - a divergent translation with the first mention of "until thou be destroyed" (KJV) not translated – produce of the land

LXX . . . *KAI TA* ***GENNÉMATA*** *TÉS GÉS SOU HÓSTE MÉ KATALIPEIN SOI SITON OINON*
and the produce of the land of you | in so much that | not leave behind for you grain wine

ELAION TA BOUKOLIA TÓN BOÓN SOU KAI TA POIMNIA TÓN PROBATÓN SOU
oil the herds of the oxen of you and the flocks of the sheep of you

HEÓS AN APOLESÉ SE
until whenever shall destroy you

engLXX . . . and the fruits of thy land, so as not to leave to thee corn, wine, oil, the herds of thine oxen, and the flocks of thy sheep, until it shall have destroyed thee;

Deu. 28:53 And thou shalt eat the **fruit** of thine own body, the flesh of thy sons and of thy daughters, which the LORD thy God hath given thee, in the siege[5], and in the straitness, wherewith thine enemies shall distress thee:

4. spelling as per source; likely a misspelling; or a misprint due to print method: Shown as *EKGONOS* in LXX Conc. at that ref. [cf. Deu. 7:13a above]
5. See MATSOR

EKGONOS – born of - a divergent translation with "the LORD thy God" (KJV) not rendered – offspring of the body

LXX *KAI PHAGÉ TA* ***EKGONA*** *TÉS KOILIAS SOU KREA HUIÓN SOU KAI THUGATERÓN*
and eat the offspring of the body of you meat of sons of you and of daughters

SOU HOSA EDÓKE SOI EN TÉ STENOCHÓRIA SOU KAI EN TÉ THLIPSEI[4]
of you | as many as gave to you in the straitness of you and in the affliction

SOU HÉ THLIPSEI SE HO ECHTHROS SOU
of you which afflict you the enemy of you

engLXX And thou shalt eat the fruit of thy body, the flesh of thy sons and of thy daughters, all that he has given thee, in thy straitness and thy affliction, with which thine enemy shall afflict thee.

Deu. 30:9a And the LORD thy God will make thee plenteous in every work of thine hand, in the **fruit** of thy body, (. . .)

EKGONOS – born of - a direct translation – offspring of the body

LXX *KAI EULOGÉSEI SE KURIOS HO THEOS SOU EN PANTI ERGÓ TÓN CHEIRÓN*
andshall take much care you Lord the God of you in all work of the hands

SOU, EN TOIS ***EKGONOIS*** *TÉS KOILIAS SOU . . .*
of you in the offspring of the body of you

engLXX And the Lord thy God shall bless thee in every work of thine hands, in the offspring of thy body, (. . .)

Deu. 30:9b . . . and in the **fruit** of thy cattle, (. . .)

EKGONOS – born of - a direct translation – offspring of the cattle

LXX *. . . KAI EN TOIS* ***EKGONOIS*** *TÓN KTÉNÓN SOU . . .*
and in the offspring of the cattle of you

engLXX . . . and in the offspring of thy cattle, (. . .)

Deu. 30:9c . . . and in the **fruit** of thy land, for good: for the Lord will again rejoice over thee for good, as he rejoiced over thy fathers:

GENNÉMA – produce - a divergent translation with the first mention of "for good" not rendered – produce of the land

LXX . . . ***KAI EN TOIS* GENNÉMASI *TÉS GÉS SOU HOTI EPISTREPSEI KURIOS HO THEOS***
and in the produce of the ground of you since shall turn Lord the God

SOU EUPHRANTHÉNAI EPI SOI EIS AGATHA KATHOTI EUPHRANTHÉ EPI TOIS PATRASI SOU
of you to be glad over you into good as was glad over the fathers of you

engLXX . . . and in the fruits of thy land, because the Lord thy God will again rejoice over thee for good, as he rejoiced over thy fathers:

2Kin. 19:29 And this *shall be* a sign unto thee, Ye shall eat this year such things as grow of themselves, and in the second year that which springeth of the same; and in the third year sow ye, and reap, and plant vineyards, and eat the **fruits** thereof.

KARPOS – fruit - a direct translation – fruit of land and vineyards

LXX ***KAI TOUTON SOI TO SÉMEION PHAGE TOUTON TON ENIAUTON AUTOMATA KAI***
4Ki.19:29 and this to you the sign eat this the year by themselves and

TÓ ETEI TÓ DEUTERÓ TA ANATELLONTA KAI ETEI TRITÓ SPORA KAI AMÉTOS
with the year the second the rising up and year third sowing and reaping

KAI PHUTEIA AMPELÓNÓN KAI PHAGESTHE TON* KARPON *AUTÓN
and plant vineyards and ye eat the fruit of them

engLXX And this shall be a sign to thee; eat this year the things that grow of themselves, and in the second year the things which spring up: and in the third year *let there be* sowing, and reaping, and planting of vineyards, and eat ye the fruit of them.

2Kin. 19:30 And the remnant that is escaped of the house of Judah shall yet again take root downward, and bear **fruit** upward.

KARPOS – fruit - a direct translation – fruit as a simile of children of the survivors of Judah

LXX **4Ki.19:30**
KAI PROSTHÉSEI TON DIASESÓSMENON OIKOU IOUDA TO HUPOLEIPHTHEN
and shall add the being preserved of house of Juda the being left behind

RHIZAN KATÓ KAI POIÉSEI ***KARPON*** *ANÓ*
root down and shall make fruit above

engLXX And he shall increase him that has escaped of the house of Juda: and the remnant *shall strike* root beneath, and it shall produce fruit above.

Neh. 9:36 Behold, we *are* servants this day, and *for* the land that thou gavest unto our fathers to eat the **fruit** thereof and the good thereof, behold, we *are* servants in it:

KARPOS – fruit - a direct translation – fruit of the land

LXX
IDOU SÉMERON ESMEN DOULOI KAI HÉ GÉ HÉN EDÓKAS TOIS PATRASIN HÉMÓN PHAGEIN
look today we are servants and the land which gave to the fathers of us to eat

TON ***KARPON*** *AUTÉS KAI TA AGATHA AUTÉS IDOU ESMEN DOULOI EP AUTÉS*
the fruit of her and the good of her look we are servants upon her

engLXX Behold, we are servants this day, and *as for* the land which thou gavest to our fathers to eat the fruit of it and the good things of it, behold, we are servants upon it:

Neh. 10:35 And to bring the firstfruits of our ground, and the firstfruits of all **fruit** of all trees, year by year, unto the house of the LORD:

KARPOS – fruit - a direct translation – fruit of trees

LXX
KAI ENEGKAI TA PRÓTOGENNÉMATA TÉS GÉS HÉMÓN KAI PRÓTOGENNÉMATA
and to bring the first produce of the land of us and first produce

	***KARPOU** PANTOS XULOU ENIAUTON KAT ENIAUTON EIS OIKON KURIOU* of fruit of every tree year(-ly) according to year into house of Lord
engLXX	and to bring the first-fruits of our land, and the first-fruits of the fruit of every tree, year by year, into the house of the Lord:
Neh. 10:37	And *that* we should bring the firstfruits of our dough, and our offerings, and the **fruit** of all manner of trees, of wine and of oil, unto the priests, to the chambers of the house of our God; and the tithes of our ground unto the Levites, that the same Levites might have the tithes in all the cities of our tillage.
YLT	And the beginning of our dough, and our heave-offerings, and the **fruit** of every tree, of new wine, and of oil, we bring in to the priests, unto the chambers of the house of our God, and the tithe of our ground to the Levites; and they - the Levites - have the tithes in all the cities of our tillage;

KARPOS – fruit - a divergent translation with "and our offerings" (KJV) or "and our heave-offerings" (YLT) omitted – fruit of trees

LXX	*KAI TÉN APARCHÉN SITÓN HÉMÓN KAI TON **KARPON** PANTOS XULOU OINOU* and the first-fruit of corn of us and the fruit of every tree of wine *KAI ELAIOU OISOMEN TOIS HIEREUSIN EIS TO GAZOPHULAKION OIKOU TOU* and of oil we shall bring to the priests into the treasuries of house of the *THEOU KAI DEKATÉN GÉS HÉMÓN TOIS LEUITAIS KAI AUTOI HOI LEUITAI* God and tenth of land of us to the Levites and they the Levites *DEKATOUNTES EN PASAIS POLESI DOULEIAS HÉMÓN* tenth in all cities of service of us
engLXX	And the first-fruits of our corn, and the fruit of every tree, of wine, and of oil, will we bring to the priests to the treasury of the house of God; and a tithe of our land to the Levites: for the Levites themselves shall receive tithes in all the cities of the land we cultivate.

Psa. 1:3 And he shall be like a tree planted by the rivers of water, that bringeth forth his **fruit** in his season; his leaf also shall not wither; and whatsoever he doeth shall prosper.

KARPOS – fruit - a direct translation – fruit of life of person (Vss. 1-2) likened to of a tree

LXX *KAI ESTAI HÓS TO XULON TO PEPHUTEUMENON PARA TAS DIEXODOUS TÓN*
and shall be as the tree the planted by the outlet of the

HUDATÓN HO TON ***KARPON*** *AUTOU DÓSEI EN KAIRÓ AUTOU KAI TO PHULLON*
waters which the fruit of it shall give in season of it and the leaf

AUTOU OUK APORRUÉSETAI KAI PANTA HOSA AN POIÉ KATEUODÓTHÉSETAI
of it not drop down and all as whatsoever do shall succeed

engLXX And he shall be as a tree planted by the brooks of waters, which shall yield its fruit in its season, and its leaf shall not fall off; and whatsoever he shall do shall be prospered.

Psa. 21:10 Their **fruit** shalt thou destroy from the earth, and their seed from among the children of men.

KARPOS – fruit - a direct translation – fruit of enemies (V.8); fruit of God haters

LXX **20:10** *TON* ***KARPON*** *AUTÓN APO GÉS APOLEIS KAI TO SPERMA AUTÓN APO HUIÓN ANTHRÓPÓN*
the fruit of them from earth destroy and the seed of them from sons of men

engLXX Thou shalt destroy their fruit from the earth, and their seed from *among* the sons of men.

Psa. 58:11 So that a man shall say, Verily *there is* a **reward** for the righteous: verily he is a God that judgeth in the earth.

YLT And man saith: 'Surely **fruit** *is* for the righteous: surely there is a God judging in the earth!'

KARPOS – fruit - a loose translation with the addition of "them" (engLXX) which is a reference to the context since the whole psalm is about the wicked in the earth and in the end their judgment is in view – the fruit of the righteous is as per the preceding verse "The righteous shall rejoice when he sees the vengeance" (Psa. 58:10 NKJV)

LXX **57:11** *KAI EREI ANTHRÓPOS EI ARA ESTI* ***KARPOS*** *TÓ DIKAIÓ ARA ESTIN HO THEOS*
and shall say man if then is fruit for the righteous then is the God

KRINÓN AUTOUS EN TÉ GÉ
judging them in the earth

engLXX And a man shall say, Verily then there is a reward for the righteous: verily there is a God that judges them in the earth.

Psa. 72:16 There shall be an handful of corn in the earth upon the top of the mountains; the **fruit** thereof shall shake like Lebanon: and *they* of the city shall flourish like grass of the earth.

YLT There is a handful of corn in the earth, on the top of mountains, shake like Lebanon doth its **fruit**, and they flourish out of the city as the herb of the earth.

KARPOS – fruit - a divergent translation since, the first clause with, "a handful of corn" (KJV) rendered as "an establishment" (engLXX) – the corn like seeds of wheat growing up on long stalks – i.e. its fruit - is poetically and prophetically portrayed as "shaking" like waving in the wind

LXX **71:16** *ESTAI STÉRIGMA EN TÉ GÉ EP AKRÓN TÓN OREÓN HUPERARTHÉSETAI HUPER TON LIBANON*
shall be foundation in the earth upon top of the mountains shall be exalted above the Lebanon

HO ***KARPOS*** *AUTOU KAI EXANTHÉSOUSIN EK POLEÓS HÓSEI CHORTOS TÉS GÉS*
the fruit of it and shall blossom out of city as grass of the earth

engLXX There shall be an establishment on the earth on the tops of the mountains: the fruit thereof shall be exalted above Libanus, and they of the city shall flourish as grass of the earth.

Psa. 104:13 He watereth the hills from his chambers: the earth is satisfied with the **fruit** of thy works.

KARPOS – fruit - a direct translation – fruit of God's (V.1) works: specifically His supply of water through having created the means for the earth to be refreshed with it

LXX **103:13** *POTIZÓN ORÉ EK TÓN HUPERÓÓN AUTOU APO* ***KARPOU*** *TÓN ERGÓN SOU*
watering mountain out of the upper rooms of him from fruit of the works of you

CHORTASTHÉSETAI HÉ GÉ
shall satisfy the earth

engLXX He waters the mountains from his chambers: the earth shall be satisfied with the fruit of thy works.

Psa. 105:35 And did eat up all the herbs in their land, and devoured the **fruit** of their ground.

KARPOS – fruit - a direct translation – fruit of the land: all that was eaten by the locusts (V.34) in the plague Egypt suffered for Pharaoh refusing to let the people go

LXX **104:35** *KAI KATEPHAGE PANTA TON CHORTON EN TÉ GÉ AUTÓN KAI KATEPHAGE TON*
and eat all the grass in the land of them and eat the

KARPON *TÉS GÉS AUTÓN*
fruit of the land of them

engLXX and devoured all the grass in their land, and devoured the fruit of their ground.

Psa. 107:34 A **fruitful** land into barrenness, for the wickedness of them that dwell therein.

KARPOPHOROS – fruitful - a direct translation – fruitful land

LXX **106:34** *GÉN* ***KARPOPHORON*** *EIS HALMÉN APO KAKIAS TÓN KATOIKOUNTÓN EN AUTÉ*
land fruitful into salty from evil of the dwellers in it

engLXX a fruitful land into saltness, for the wickedness of them that dwell in it.

Psa. 107:37 And sow the fields, and plant vineyards, which may yield **fruits** of increase.

KARPOS – fruit - a direct translation – fruit of produce

LXX **106:37** *KAI ESPEIRAN AGROUS KAI EPHUTEUSAN AMPELÓNAS KAI EPOIÉSAN* ***KARPON*** *GENNÉMATOS*
and sow fields and plant vineyards and make fruit of produce

engLXX And they sow fields, and plant vineyards, and they yield fruit of increase.

Psa. 127:3 Lo, children *are* an heritage of the LORD: *and* the **fruit** of the womb *is his* reward.

KARPOS – fruit - a divergent translation with "children" (KJV) given as "sons" (LXX-inter) – fruit of the womb

LXX **126:3** ***IDOU HÉ KLÉRONOMIA KURIOU HUIOI HO MISTHOS TOU KARPOU TÉS GASTROS***
LXX-inter look the inheritance of Lord sons the reward of the fruit of the womb

engLXX Behold, the inheritance of the Lord, children, the reward of the fruit of the womb.

Psa. 132:11 The LORD hath sworn *in* truth unto David; he will not turn from it; Of the **fruit** of thy body will I set upon thy throne.

KARPOS – fruit - a direct translation – fruit of the body: offspring of David will be made king

LXX **131:11** ***ÓMOSE KURIOS TÓ DAUID ALÉTHEIAN KAI OU MÉ ATHETÉSEI AUTÉN EK***
swore Lord to the David truth and in no wise shall annul her out of

KARPOU TÉS KOILIAS SOU THÉSOMAI EPI TOU THRONOU SOU
fruit of the body of you will I place upon the throne of you

engLXX The Lord sware *in* truth to David, and he will not annul it, *saying*, Of the fruit of thy body will I set *a king* upon thy throne.

Psa. 148:9 Mountains, and all hills; **fruitful** trees, and all cedars

KARPOPHOROS – fruitful - a direct translation – fruitbearing trees

LXX ***TA ORÉ KAI PANTES BOUNOI XULA KARPOPHORA KAI PASAI KEDROI***
the mountains and all hills trees fruitful and all cedars

engLXX Mountains, and all hills; fruitful trees, and all cedars:

Pro. 1:31 Therefore shall they eat of the **fruit** of their own way, and be filled with their own devices.

KARPOS – fruit - a direct translation – fruit of one's life, here: results of wickedness

LXX *TOIGAROUN EDONTAI TÉS HEAUTÓN HODOU TOUS* ***KARPOUS*** *KAI TÉS*
wherefore they eat the of themselves way the fruits and of the

EAUTÓN[6] *ASEBEIAS PLÉSTHÉSONTAI*
of themselves impiety shall be filled

engLXX Therefore shall they eat the fruits of their own way, and shall be filled with their own ungodliness.

Pro. 8:19 My **fruit** *is* better than gold, yea, than fine gold; and my revenue than choice silver.

KARPIZ-Ó/-OMAI aNT – enjoy fruit of - a divergent translation with "fine gold" (KJV) given as "precious stones" (engLXX) – verb: the gathering of fruit, here: the gathering of fruit of wisdom

LXX *BELTION EME* ***KARPIZESTHAI*** *HUPER CHRUSION*[7] *KAI LITHON TIMION TA DE*
best my enjoy fruit over gold and stones precious the but

EMA GENNÉMATA KREISSÓ ARGURIOU EKLEKTOU[8]
my produce better of silver of choice

engLXX *It is* better to have my fruit than *to have* gold and precious stones; and my produce is better than choice silver.

Pro. 11:30 The **fruit** of the righteous *is* a tree of life; and he that winneth souls *is* wise

KARPOS – fruit - a divergent translation with "winning" and "wise" (KJV) not rendered, but replaced by the wicked as "cut off before their time" (engLXX) – fruit of righteousness

6. Likely printer error as accent is as per text: should be as per 6 words words earlier
7. See CHARUTS
8. See BACHAR

LXX *EK* ***KARPOU*** *DIKAIOSUNÉS PHUETAI DENDRON ZÓÉS APHAIROUNTAI DE AÓROI*
out of fruit of righteousness bring forth tree of life take away from but | untimely

PSUCHAI PARANOMÓN
lives of lawbreakers

engLXX Out of the fruit of righteousness grows a tree of life; but the souls of transgressors are cut off before their time.

Pro. 12:14 A man shall be satisfied with good by the **fruit** of *his* mouth: and the recompence of a man's hands shall be rendered unto him.

KARPOS – fruit - a divergent translation with the recompence "of a man's hands" (KJV) replaced by "of his lips" (engLXX) – fruit of mouth

LXX *APO* ***KARPÓN*** *STOMATOS PSUCHÉ ANDROS PLÉSTHÉSETAI AGATHÓN*
from fruit of mouth soul of a man shall be filled of good

ANTAPODOMA DE CHEILEÓN AUTOU DOTHÉSETAI AUTÓ
recompense but of lips of him shall be given to him

engLXX The soul of a man shall be filled with good from the fruits of his mouth; and the recompence of his lips shall be given to him.

Pro. 13:2 A man shall eat good by the **fruit** of *his* mouth: but the soul of the transgressors *shall eat* violence.

YLT From the **fruit** of the mouth a man eateth good, and the soul of the treacherous - violence.

KARPOS – fruit - a divergent translation with the added time factor to the expectation of the wicked "before their time" (engLXX) – fruit of mouth includes implication that it is good fruit: i.e. righteous words

LXX *APO* ***KARPÓN*** *DIKAIOSUNÉS PHAGETAI AGATHOS PSUCHAI DE PARANOMÓN*
from fruit of righteousness shall eat good lives but of lawbreakers

OLOUNTAI AÓROI
shall be destroyed untimely

engLXX A good *man* shall eat of the fruits of righteousness: but the lives of transgressors shall perish before their time.

Pro. 18:20 A man's belly shall be satisfied with the **fruit** of his mouth; *and* with the increase of his lips shall he be filled.

YLT From the **fruit** of a man's mouth is his belly satisfied, *from the* increase of his lips he is satisfied.

KARPOS - fruit - a direct translation – fruit of mouth

LXX *APO* ***KARPÓN*** *STOMATOS ANÉR PIMPLÉSI KOILIAN AUTOU APO DE KARPÓN*
from fruit of mouth man shall fill body of him from but fruits

CHEILEÓN AUTOU EMPLÉSTHÉSETAI
of lips of him shall be filled full

engLXX A man fills his belly with the fruits of his mouth; and he shall be satisfied with the fruits of his lips.

Pro. 18:21 Death and life *are* in the power of the tongue: and they that love it shall eat the **fruit** thereof.

YLT Death and life *are* in the power of the tongue, and those loving it eat its **fruit**.

KARPOS – fruit - a loose translation with "they that love it" (KJV) rendered as "they that rule it" (engLXX) – fruit of the tongue: the result of what one says

LXX *THANATOS KAI ZÓÉ EN CHEIRI GLÓSSÉS HOI DE KRATOUNTES AUTES EDONTAI*
death and life in hands of tongue the but power of it shall eat

TOUS ***KARPOUS*** *AUTÉS*
the fruits of her

engLXX Life and death are in the power of the tongue; and they that rule it shall eat the fruits thereof.

Pro. 27:18 Whoso keepeth the fig tree shall eat the **fruit** thereof: so he that waiteth on his master shall be honoured.

KARPOS – fruit - a divergent translation with "keepeth the fig tree" (KJV) given as "plants a fig tree" (engLXX) – fruits of fig tree

LXX *HOS PHUTEUEI SUKÉN PHAGETAI TOUS* ***KARPOUS*** *AUTÉS HOS DE PHULASSEI*
who plants fig-tree shall eat the fruits of her who but guards

TON HEAUTOU KURION TIMÉTHÉSETAI
the his own lord shall be honoured

engLXX He that plants a fig-tree shall eat the fruits of it: so he that waits on his own master shall be honoured.

Pro. 31:16 She considereth a field, and buyeth it: with the **fruit** of her hands she planteth a vineyard.

KARPOS – fruit - a divergent translation with "planteth a vineyard" (KJV) given as "plants a possession" (engLXX) – fruits of hands: results of hard work

LXX *THEÓRÉSASA GEÓRGION EPRIATO APO DE* ***KARPÓN*** *CHEIRÓN AUTÉS*
considers field buys from and of fruits of hands of her

KATEPHUTEUSE KTÉMA
she plants a possession

engLXX She views a farm, and buys it: and with the fruit of her hands she plants a possession.

Pro. 31:31 Give her of the **fruit** of her hands; and let her own works praise her in the gates.

YLT Give ye to her of the **fruit** of her hands, and her works do praise her in the gates!

KARPOS – fruit - a divergent translation with "her own works" (KJV) or "her works" (YLT) praising her in the gates, rendered as "her husband" praised in the gates (engLXX): the engLXX differs somewhat from the LXX i.e. "hands" (LXX) given as "lips" (engLXX) - fruits of hands: results of hard work

LXX *DOTE AUTÉ APO* ***KARPÓN*** *CHEILEÓN AUTÉS KAI AINEISTHÓ EN PULAIS HO ANÉR AUTÉS*
give her from fruits of hands of her and shall praise in gates the husband of her

engLXX Give her of the fruits of her lips; and let her husband be praised in the gates.

Ecc. 2:5 I made me gardens and orchards, and I planted trees in them of all *kind of* **fruits**:

KARPOS - fruit - a divergent translation limiting the type of fruit to those from the "fruit-tree" (engLXX) – fruit of fruit trees (Gk.)

LXX *EPOIÉSA MOI KÉPOUS KAI PARADEISOUS KAI EPHUTEUSA EN AUTOIS XULON PAN* ***KARPOU***
made for me orchards and gardens and planted in them tree every of fruit

engLXX I made me gardens and orchards, and planted in them every kind of fruit-tree.

Sng. 2:3 As the apple tree among the trees of the wood, so *is* my beloved among the sons. I sat down under his shadow with great delight, and his **fruit** *was* sweet to my taste.

KARPOS – fruit - a direct translation – fruit of beloved: fruit of the man

LXX *HÓS MÉLON EN TOIS XULOIS TOU DRUMOU HOUTÓS ADELPHIDOS MOU*
as apple in the trees of the wood so beloved of me

ANAMESON TÓN HUIÓN EN TÉ SKIA AUTOU EPETHUMÉSA KAI EKATHISA KAI
in the midst of the sons in the shadow of him I desired and I sat and

KARPOS *AUTOU GLUKUS EN LARUGGI MOU*
fruit of him sweet in (taste) larynx of me

engLXX As the apple among the trees of the wood, so is my kinsman among the sons. I desired his shadow, and sat down, and his fruit was sweet in my throat.

Sng. 4:13 Thy plants *are* an orchard of pomegranates, with pleasant **fruits**; camphire, with spikenard,

YLT Thy shoots a paradise of pomegranates, with precious **fruits**, 14cypresses with nard . . .

KARPOS – fruit - a divergent translation with "pleasant" (KJV) or "precious" (YLT) replaced with "of fruit trees" (LXX-inter) – fruit of orchard

LXX *APOSTOLAI SOU PARADEISOS RHOÓN META* ***KARPOU*** *AKRODRUÓN KUPROI META NARDÓN*
LXX-inter shoots of you garden of pomegranates with fruit of fruit-trees camphor with spikenard

engLXX Thy shoots are a garden of pomegranates, with the fruit of choice berries; camphor, with spikenard:

Sng. 4:16 Awake, O north wind; and come, thou south; blow upon my garden, *that* the spices thereof may flow out. Let my beloved come into his garden, and eat his pleasant **fruits**.

KARPOS – fruit - a divergent translation with "pleasant" (KJV) given as "of fruit trees" (LXX-inter) – fruit of fruit trees (Gk.)

LXX**4:16-5:1** *EXEGERTHÉTI BORRA KAI ERCHOU NOTE KAI DIAPNEUSON KÉPON MOU KAI*
LXX-inter awake north and come south and refresh garden of me and

RHEUSATÓSAN ARÓMATA MOU 5:1*KATABÉTÓ ADELPHIDOS MOU EIS KÉPON*
let flow spices of me let go down beloved of me into garden

AUTOU KAI PHAGETÓ ***KARPON*** *AKRODRUÓN AUTOU . . .*
of him and eat fruit of fruit-trees of him

engLXX Awake, O north wind; and come, O south; and blow through my garden, and let my spices flow out; Let my kinsman come down into his garden, and eat the fruit of his choice berries. . .

Sng. 8:11 Solomon had a vineyard at Baalhamon; he let out the vineyard unto keepers; every one for the **fruit** thereof was to bring a thousand *pieces* of silver.

KARPOS – fruit - a direct translation – fruit of vineyard

LXX *AMPELÓN EGENÉTHÉ TÓ SALÓMÓN EN BEELAMÓN EDÓKE TON AMPELÓNA*
vineyards were there to the Solomon in Beelamon gave the vineyard

AUTOU TOIS TÉROUSIN ANÉR OISEI EN ***KARPÓ*** *AUTOU CHILIOUS ARGURIOU*
of him to the keeping man to bring in fruit of it thousands of silver

engLXX Solomon had a vineyard in Beelamon; he let his vineyard to keepers; every one was to bring for its fruit a thousand *pieces* of silver.

Sng. 8:12 My vineyard, which *is* mine, *is* before me: thou, O Solomon, *must have* a thousand, and those that keep the **fruit** thereof two hundred.

KARPOS – fruit - a direct translation – fruit of vineyard

LXX *AMPELÓN MOU EMOS ENÓPION MOU HOI CHILIOI SALÓMÓN KAI HOI DIAKOSIOI*
vineyards of me mine before me the thousands Solomon and the | two hundred

TOIS TÉROUSI TON ***KARPON*** *AUTOU*
to the keepers the fruit of it

engLXX My vineyard, even mine, is before me; Solomon *shall have* a thousand, and they that keep its fruit two hundred.

Isa. 3:10 Say ye to the righteous, that *it shall be* well *with him*: for they shall eat the **fruit** of their doings.

YLT Say ye to the righteous, that *it is* good, because the **fruit** of their doings they eat.

GENNÉMA – produce - a divergent translation with saying to the righteous "that *it shall be* well" (KJV) or "That *it is* good" (YLT) replaced by "Let us bind the just, for he is burdensome to us" (engLXX) – result or produce of doing wrong

N.B. "Woe to their soul, for they have devised an evil counsel against themselves" of the engLXX is from V.9 of LXX

LXX *EIPONTES DÉSÓMEN TON DIKAION HOTI DUSCHRÉSTOS HÉMIN ESTI TOINUN TA*
saying we should bind the righteous since inconvenient to us he is | the therefore

GENNÉMATA *TÓN ERGÓN AUTÓN PHAGONTAI*
produce of the works of them shall they eat

engLXX Woe to their soul, for they have devised an evil counsel against themselves, saying against themselves, Let us bind the just, for he is burdensome to us: therefore shall they eat the fruits of their works.

Isa. 4:2 In that day shall the branch of the Lord be beautiful and glorious, and the **fruit** of the earth *shall be* excellent and comely for them that are escaped of Israel.

YLT In that day is the Shoot of Jehovah for desire and for honour, and the **fruit** of the earth for excellence and for beauty to the escaped of Israel.

NOT in LXX - a divergent translation with "the branch" (KJV) of the Lord or "the Shoot" (YLT) of Jehovah not translated - "the fruit" is not translated

LXX ***TÉ DE HÉMERA EKEINÉ EPILAMPSEI HO THEOS EN BOULÉ META DOXÉS EPI***
the and day that shall shine the God in will with glory upon

TÉS GÉS TOU HUPSÓSAI KAI DOXASAI TO KATALEIPHTHEN TOU ISRAÉL
the earth of the lifted high and to glorify the remnant of the Israel

engLXX And in that day God shall shine gloriously in counsel on the earth, to exalt and glorify the remnant of Israel.

Isa. 10:12 Wherefore it shall come to pass, *that* when the Lord hath performed his whole work upon mount Zion and on Jerusalem, I will punish the **fruit** of the stout heart of the king of Assyria, and the glory of his high looks.

YLT And it hath come to pass, when the Lord doth fulfil all His work in mount Zion and in Jerusalem, I see concerning the **fruit** of the greatness of the heart of the king of Asshur. And concerning the glory of the height of his eyes.

NOT in LXX – a divergent translation with "the fruit" not rendered

LXX ***KAI ESTAI HOTAN SUNTELESÉ KURIOS PANTA POIÓN EN TÓ OREI SIÓN KAI EN***
and shall be when shall finish Lord all works in the mount Zion and in

HIEROUSALÉM EPISKEPSOMAI EPI TON NOUN TON MEGAN EPI TON ARCHONTA
Jerusalem I will bring upon the mind/heart the great upon the ruler

TÓN ASSURIÓN KAI EPI TO HUPSOS TÉS DOXÉS TÓN OPHTHALMÓN AUTOU
of the Assyrians and upon the height of the glory of the eyes of him

engLXX And it shall come to pass, when the Lord shall have finished doing all things on Mount Sion and Jerusalem, *that* I will visit upon the proud heart, *even* upon the ruler of the Assyrians, and upon the boastful haughtiness of his eyes.

Isa. 13:18 *Their* bows also shall dash the young men to pieces; and they shall have no pity on the **fruit** of the womb; their eye shall not spare children.

YLT And bows dash young men to pieces, and the **fruit** of the womb they pity not, on sons their eye hath no pity.

TEKNON – child - a divergent translation with "dash the young men to pieces" (KJV) given as "break the bows of the young men" (engLXX) – fruit of the body: children

LXX ***TOXEUMATA NEANISKÓN SUNTRIPSOUSI KAI TA*** **TEKNA** ***HUMÓN OU MÉ***
bow of young men shall break and the children of you in no wise

ELEÉSÓSIN OUDE EPI TOIS TEKNOIS SOU PHEISONTAI HOI OPHTHALMOI AUTÓN
shall havemercy neither upon the children of you spare the eyes of them

engLXX They shall break the bows of the young men; and they shall have no mercy on your children; nor shall their eyes spare thy children.

Isa. 14:29 Rejoice not thou, whole Palestina, because the rod of him that smote thee is broken: for out of the serpent's root shall come forth a cockatrice, and his **fruit** *shall be* a fiery flying serpent.

YLT Rejoice not thou, Philistia, all of thee, that broken hath been the rod of thy smiter, for from the root of a serpent cometh out a viper, and its **fruit** *is* a flying saraph.

EKGONOS – born of - a divergent translation with "serpent" (KJV) rendered as "serpents" (engLXX) – fruit of serpent: flying serpent

LXX *MÉ EUPHRANTHEIÉTE HOI ALLOPHULOI PANTES SUNETRIBÉ GAR HO ZUGOS*
not rejoice ye the Philistines all shattered for the yoke

TOU PAIONTOS HUMAS EK GAR SPERMATOS OPHEÓS EXELEUSETAI EKGONA
of the striking you out of for seed of serpent shall come forth offspring

ASPIDÓN KAI TA ***EKGONA*** *AUTÓN EXELEUSONTAI OPHEIS PETAMENOI*
of asps and the young of them shall come out serpents flying

engLXX Rejoice not, all ye Philistines, because the yoke of him that smote you is broken: for out of the seed of the serpent shall come forth the young of asps, and their young shall come forth flying serpents,

---

Isa. 27:9 By this therefore shall the iniquity of Jacob be purged; and this *is* all the **fruit** to take away his sin; when he maketh all the stones of the altar as chalkstones that are beaten in sunder, the groves and images shall not stand up.

YLT Therefore by this is the iniquity of Jacob covered, and this *is* all the **fruit** – to take away his sin, in His setting all the stones of an altar, as chalkstones beaten in pieces, they rise not - shrines and images.

EULOGIA – blessing - a divergent translation with "as a thicket afar off" (engLXX) added – the fruit of giving up sin: the blessing of doing so: the verse is about how

LXX *DIATOUTO APHAIRETHÉSETAI ANOMIA IAKÓB KAI TOUTO ESTIN HÉ*
on account of this shall be removed lawlessness Jacob and this is the

EULOGIA *AUTOU HOTAN APHELÓMAI TÉN HAMARTIAN AUTOU HOTAN THÓSI*
blessing of him when remove the sin of him when furnish

PANTAS TOUS LITHOUS TÓN BÓMÓN KATAKEKOMMENOUS HÓS KONIAN
all the stones of the shrines cut down as powder

LEPTÉN KAI OU MÉ MEINÉ TA DENDRA AUTÓN KAI TA EIDÓLA AUTÓN
fine and in no wise remain the trees of them and the idols of them

EKKEKOMMENA HÓSPER DRUMOS MAKRAN
cut down as forest far off

engLXX Therefore shall the iniquity of Jacob be taken away; and this is his blessing, when I shall have taken away his sin; when they shall have broken to pieces all the stones of the altars as fine dust, and their trees shall not remain, and their idols shall be cut off, as a thicket afar off.

Isa. 37:30 And this *shall be* a sign unto thee, Ye shall eat *this* year such as groweth of itself; and the second year that which springeth of the same: and in the third year sow ye, and reap, and plant vineyards, and eat the **fruit** thereof.

YLT - And this to thee *is* the sign, Food of the year *is* self-sown grain, and in the second year the spontaneous growth, and in the third year, sow ye and reap, and plant vineyards, and eat their **fruit**.

KARPOS – fruit - a divergent translation with "eat *this* year such as groweth of itself" (KJV) or "Food of the year *is* self-sown grain" (YLT), rendered as "Eat this year what thou hast sown" (engLXX): the sowing occurs on the 3rd year in the Heb. translated, so not the 1st year as per LXX – fruit of vineyards

LXX *TOUTO DE SOI TO SÉMEION PHAGE TOUTON TON ENIAUTON HA ESPARKAS TÓ*
this but to you the sign eat this the year the sown to the

DE ENIAUTÓ TÓ DEUTERÓ TÓ KATALEIMMA TÓ DE TRITÓ SPEIRANTES
but year the second to the remnant to the but third sow

AMÉSATE KAI PHUTEUSATE AMPELÓNAS KAI PHAGESTHE TON ***KARPON*** *AUTÓN*
reap and plant ye vineyards and ye eat the fruit of them

engLXX And this shall be a sign to thee, Eat this year what thou hast sown; and the second year that which is left: and the third year sow, and reap, and plant vineyards, and eat the fruit of them.

Isa. 37:31 And the remnant that is escaped of the house of Judah shall again take root downward, and bear **fruit** upward:

SPERMA – seed - a direct translation – fruit of womb: sperm or seed: offspring

LXX *KAI ESONTAI HOI KATALELEIMMENOI EN TÉ IOUDAIA PHUÉSOUSI RHIZAN KATÓ*
and shall be the remnant in the Judea shall germinate root down

KAI POIÉSOUSI ***SPERMA*** *ANÓ*
and shall make seed above

engLXX And they that are left in Judea shall take root downward, and bear fruit upward:

Isa. 65:21 And they shall build houses, and inhabit *them*; and they shall plant vineyards, and eat the **fruit** of them.

GENNÉMA – produce - a direct translation – the produce of vineyards

LXX *KAI OIKODOMÉSOUSIN OIKIAS KAI AUTOI ENOIKÉSOUSI KAI KATAPHUTEUSOUSIN*
and shall build houses and they shall dwell and shall plant

AMPELÓNAS KAI AUTOI PHAGONTAI TA ***GENNÉMATA*** *AUTÓN*
vineyards and they shall eat the produce of them

engLXX and they shall build houses, and themselves shall dwell in *them*; and they shall plant vineyards, and themselves shall eat the fruit thereof.

Jer. 2:7 And I brought you into a plentiful country, to eat the **fruit** thereof and the goodness thereof; but when ye entered, ye defiled my land, and made mine heritage an abomination.

YLT Yea, I bring you in to a land of fruitful fields, to eat its **fruit** and its goodness, and ye come in and defile My land, and Mine inheritance have made an abomination.

KARPOS – fruit - KARMEL in Heb. means "garden-land", so in that sense, a direct translation; otherwise loose, as the text is about all the land and not just the 1 place within it which is named "Carmel" – fruits of the land

LXX *KAI ÉGAGON HUMAS EIS TON KARMÉLON TOU PHAGEIN HUMAS TOUS*
and led you into the Carmel of the to eat you the

KARPOUS *AUTOU KAI TA AGATHA AUTOU KAI EISÉLTHETE KAI EMIANATE TÉN*
fruits of it and the good of it and ye entered and defiled the

GÉN MOU KAI TÉN KLÉRONOMIAN MOU ETHESTHE EIS BDELUGMA
land of me and the inheritance of me ye made into abomination

engLXX And I brought you to Carmel, that ye should eat the fruits thereof, and the good thereof; and ye went in, and defiled my land, and made mine heritage an abomination.

Jer. 6:19 Hear, O earth: behold, I will bring evil upon this people, *even* the **fruit** of their thoughts, because they have not hearkened unto my words, nor to my law, but rejected it.

YLT Hear, O earth, lo, I am bringing evil on this people, the **fruit** of their devices, for to My words they gave no attention, and My law - they kick against it.

KARPOS – fruit - a direct translation – fruit of rebellions/thoughts

LXX *AKOUE GÉ IDOU EGÓ EPAGÓ EPI TON LAON TOUTON KAKA TON* ***KARPON***
hear earth see I will bring upon the people this evil the fruit

APOSTROPHÉS AUTÓN HOTI TÓN LOGÓN MOU OU PROSESCHON KAI TON
of turnings of them since of the words of me not heeded and the

NOMON MOU APÓSANTO
law of me thrust away

engLXX Hear, O earth: behold, I will bring evils upon this people, *even* the fruit of their rebellions; for they have not heeded my words, and they have rejected my law.

Jer. 7:20 Therefore thus saith the Lord God; Behold, mine anger and my fury shall be poured out upon this place, upon man, and upon beast, and upon the trees of the field, and upon the **fruit** of the ground; and it shall burn, and shall not be quenched.

GENNÉMA – produce - a direct translation – produce of the land

LXX ***DIATOUTO TADE LEGEI KURIOS IDOU ORGÉ KAI THUMOS MOU XEITAI EPI TON***
therefore thus says Lord look anger and wrath of me poured upon the

TOPON TOUTON KAI EPI TOUS ANTHRÓPOUS KAI EPI TA KTÉNÉ KAI EPI PAN
place this and upon the men and upon the cattle and upon | every

XULON TOU AGROU AUTÓN KAI EPI TA **GENNÉMATA** ***TÉS GÉS KAI***
tree of the field of them and upon the produce of the earth and

KAUTHÉSETAI KAI OU SBESTHÉSETAI
shall be kindled and not extinguished

engLXX Therefore thus saith the Lord; Behold, my anger and wrath shall be poured out upon this place, and upon the men, and upon the cattle, and upon every tree of their field, and upon the fruits of the land; and it shall burn, and not be quenched.

Jer. 11:16 The Lord called thy name, A green olive tree, fair, *and* of goodly **fruit**: with the noise of a great tumult he hath kindled fire upon it, and the branches of it are broken.

YLT 'An olive, green, fair, of goodly **fruit**,' hath Jehovah called thy name, at the noise of a great tumult He hath kindled fire against it, and broken have been its thin branches.

NOT in LXX – a divergent translation with "goodly fruit" (KJV) not rendered – the word is not translated

LXX ***ELAIAN HÓRAIAN EUSKION TÓ EIDEI EKALESE KURIOS TO ONOMA SOU EIS***
olive tree | shadowy the appearance called Lord the name of you into
at 1st appearance/in season/i.e. green

PHÓNÉN PERITOMÉS AUTÉS ANÉPHTHÉ PUR EP AUTÉN MEGALÉ HÉ THLIPSIS
sound of circular incision of her lit fire upon her great the affliction

EPI SE ÉCHREIÓTHÉSAN HOI KLADOI AUTÉS
upon you spoiled the branches of her

engLXX The Lord called thy name a fair olive tree, of a goodly shade in appearance, at the noise of its being lopped, fire was kindled against it; great is the affliction *coming* upon thee: her branches are become good for nothing.

Jer. 12:2 Thou hast planted them, yea, they have taken root: they grow, yea, they bring forth **fruit**: thou *art* near in their mouth, and far from their reins.

YLT Thou hast planted them, yea, they have taken root, they go on, yea, they have made **fruit**, near *art* Thou in their mouth, and far off from their reins.

KARPOS – fruit - a divergent translation with "they have begotten children" added – fruit of life of the wicked in Heb. in context Vss 1-3, LXX renders as fruit of the womb: children

LXX *EPHUTEUSAS AUTOUS KAI ERRHIZÓTHÉSAN ETEKNOPOIÉSANTO KAI EPOIÉSAN* ***KARPON***
planted them and took root made children and they made fruit

EGGUS EI SU TOU STOMATOS AUTÓN KAI PORRHÓ APO TÓN NEPHRÓN AUTÓN
near are you of the mouth of them and distance from the kidneys of them

engLXX Thou hast planted them, and they have taken root; they have begotten children, and become fruitful; thou art near to their mouth, and far from their reins.

Jer. 17:8 For he shall be as a tree planted by the waters, and *that* spreadeth out her roots by the river, and shall not see when heat cometh, but her leaf shall be green; and shall not be careful in the year of drought, neither shall cease from yielding **fruit**.

YLT — And hath been as a tree planted by waters, and by a rivulet he sendeth forth his roots, and he doth not see when heat cometh, and his leaf hath been green, and in a year of dearth he is not sorrowful, nor doth he cease from making **fruit**.

KARPOS – fruit - a loose translation with "her leaf shall be green" (KJV) or "his leaf hath been green" (YLT), given as "shall be upon him shady branches" (engLXX) – fruit of tree

LXX — *KAI ESTAI HÓS XULON EUTHÉNOUN PAR HUDATA KAI EPI IKMADA BALEI RHIZAN AUTOU*
and shall be as tree prospering by water and upon moist cast root of him

OU PHOBÉTHÉSETAI HOTAN ELTHÉ KAUMA KAI ESTAI EP AUTÓ STELECHÉ ALSÓDÉ EN
not fear when comes burning heat and shall be upon him trunks of woods in

ENIAUTÓ ABROCHIAS OU PHOBÉTHÉSETAI KAI OU DIALEIPSEI POIÓN ***KARPON***
year of drought not fear and not cease to make fruit

engLXX — And he shall be as a thriving tree by the waters, and he shall cast forth his root toward a moist place: he shall not fear when heat comes, and there shall be upon him shady branches: he shall not fear in a year of drought, and he shall not fail to bear fruit.

Jer. 17:10 — I the LORD search the heart, *I* try the reins, even to give every man according to his ways, *and* according to the **fruit** of his doings.

YLT — I Jehovah do search the heart, try the reins, even to give to each according to his way, according to the **fruit** of his doings.

KARPOS – fruit - a direct translation – fruit of doings/life practices

LXX — *EGÓ KURIOS ETAZÓN KARDIAS KAI DOKIMAZÓN NEPHROUS*[9] *TOU DOUNAI*
I Lord examine hearts and test kidneys of the to give

9. the Heb. word KELAIOTH is translated in the KJV: "reins" (13); "kidneys" (18)

HEKASTÓ KATA TAS HODOUS AUTOU KAI KATA TOUS ***KARPOUS*** *TÓN*
each according to the ways of him and according to the fruits of the

EPITÉDEUMATÓN AUTOU
practices of him

engLXX I the Lord try the hearts, and prove the reins, to give to every one according to his ways, and according to the fruits of his devices.

Jer. 21:14 But I will punish you according to the **fruit** of your doings, saith the LORD: and I will kindle a fire in the forest thereof, and it shall devour all things round about it.

YLT And I have laid a charge against you, according to the **fruit** of your doings, an affirmation of Jehovah, and I have kindled a fire in its forest, and it hath consumed - all its suburbs!

NOT in LXX – "But I will punish you according to the fruit of your doings, saith the LORD" (KJV) is not rendered – clause containing word is not translated

LXX *KAI ANAPSÓ PUR EN TÓ DRUMÓ AUTÉS KAI EDETAI PANTA TA KUKLÓ AUTÉS*
and alight fire in the forest of her and devour all the round about of her

engLXX And I will kindle a fire in the forest thereof, and it shall devour all things round about it.

Jer. 29:5 Build ye houses, and dwell *in them*; and plant gardens, and eat the **fruit** of them;

KARPOS – fruit - a direct translation – fruit of gardens

LXX **36:5** *OIKODOMÉSATE OIKOUS KAI KATOIKÉSATE KAI PHUTEUSATE PARADEISOUS*
ye build houses and ye dwell and ye plant gardens

KAI PHAGETE TOUS ***KARPOUS*** *AUTÓN*
and ye eat the fruits of them

engLXX Build ye houses, and inhabit *them*; and plant gardens, and eat the fruits thereof;

Jer. 29:28 For therefore he sent unto us *in* Babylon, saying, This *captivity* is long: build ye houses, and dwell *in them*; and plant gardens, and eat the **fruit** of them.

YLT Because that he hath sent unto us to Babylon, saying, It *is* long, build ye houses, and abide; and plant ye gardens, and eat their **fruit**.'

KARPOS – fruit - a divergent translation with "in the course of the month" (engLXX) added – fruit of gardens

LXX **36:28**
OU DIATOUTO APESTEILEN HOTI DIA TOU MÉNOS TOUTOU APESTEILE PROS
not therefore sent since through the month this sent to

HUMAS EIS BABULÓNA LEGÓN MAKRAN ESTIN OIKODOMÉSATE OIKIAS KAI
you into Babylon saying far is build ye houses and

KATOIKÉSATE KAI PHUTEUSATE KÉPOUS KAI PHAGESTHE TON ***KARPON*** *AUTÓN*
dwell ye and plant ye gardens and eat ye the fruit of them

engLXX Did he not send for this purpose? For in the course of this month he sent to you to Babylon, saying, It is far off: build ye houses, and inhabit *them*; and plant gardens, and eat the fruit of them.

Jer. 32:19 Great in counsel, and mighty in work: for thine eyes *are* open upon all the ways of the sons of men: to give every one according to his ways, and according to the **fruit** of his doings:

YLT Great in counsel, and mighty in act, in that Thine eyes are open on all the ways of the sons of Adam, to give to each according to his ways, and according to the **fruit** of his doings:

NOT in LXX - a divergent translation with "the great Almighty God, and Lord of great name" (engLXX) added, though this is likely a rendering of the end of the preceding verse "the Great, the Mighty God, whose name is the LORD of hosts" (Jer. 32:18 NKJV) - the last clause "according to the **fruit** of his doings" not translated

LXX **39:19**
KURIOS MEGALÉS BOULÉS KAI DUNATOS TOIS ERGOIS HO THEOS HO MEGAS
Lord great counsel and strong with the works the God the great

HO PANTOKRATÓR KAI MEGALÓNUMOS KURIOS HOI OPHTHALMOI SOU EIS TAS
the almighty and great-name Lord the eyes of you are the

HODOUS TÓN HUIÓN TÓN ANTHRÓPÓN DOUNAI EKASTÓ KATA TÉN ***HODON*** *AUTOU*
ways of the sons of the men to give each | according to the way of him

engLXX the Lord of great counsel, and mighty in deeds, the great Almighty God, and Lord of great name: thine eyes are upon the ways of the children of men, to give to every one according to his way:

Lam. 2:20 Behold, O Lord, and consider to whom thou hast done this. Shall the women eat their **fruit**, *and* children of a span long? Shall the priest and the prophet be slain in the sanctuary of the Lord?

YLT See, O Jehovah, and look attentively, to whom Thou hast acted thus, do women eat their **fruit**, infants of a handbreadth? Slain in the sanctuary of the Lord are priest and prophet?

KARPOS – fruit - a divergent translation with "the cook has made a gathering" (engLXX) added – fruit of body: offspring

LXX *RHCHS IDE KURIE KAI EPIBLEPSON TINI EPEPHULLISAS HOUTÓS EI*
RHCHS look Lord and see what gleaned thus shall

PHAGONTAI GUNAIKES ***KARPON*** *KOILIAS AUTÓN EPIPHULLIDA EPOIÉSE*
eat women fruit of body of them gleaning made

MAGEIROS PHONEUTHÉSONTAI NÉPIA THÉLAZONTA MASTOUS APOKTENEIS EN
cook shall be murdered infants nursing breasts kill in

HAGIASMATI KURIOU HIEREA KAI PROPHÉTÉN
sanctuary of Lord priest and prophet

engLXX RHECHS. Behold, O Lord, and see for whom thou has gathered thus. Shall the women eat the fruit of their womb? The cook has made a gathering: shall the infants sucking at the breasts be slain? Wilt thou slay the priest and prophet in the sanctuary of the Lord?

Eze. 17:8 It was planted in a good soil by great waters, that it might bring forth branches, and that it might bear **fruit**, that it might be a goodly vine.

KARPOS – fruit - a direct translation – fruit of vine

LXX *EIS PEDION KALON EPH HUDATI POLLÓ AUTÉ PIAINETAI TOU POIEIN BLASTOUS*
into field good upon water much she fattened of the produce buds

KAI PHEREIN ***KARPON*** *TOU EINAI EIS AMPELON MEGALÉN*
and to bear fruit of the to be into vineyard great

engLXX She thrives in a fair field by much water, to produce shoots and bear fruit, that she might become a great vine.

Eze. 17:9 Say thou, Thus saith the Lord God; Shall it prosper? Shall he not pull up the roots thereof, and cut off the **fruit** thereof, that it wither? It shall wither in all the leaves of her spring, even without great power or many people to pluck it up by the roots thereof.

YLT Say: Thus said the Lord Jehovah: It prospereth - its roots doth he not draw out, and its **fruit** cut off, and it is withered? *In* all the leaves of its springing it withereth, and not by great strength, and by a numerous people, to lift it up by its roots.

KARPOS – fruit - a direct translation – fruit of vine (See V.8)

LXX *DIATOUTO EIPON TADE LEGEI KURIOS EI KATEUTHUNEI OUCHI HAI RHIZAI TÉS*
therefore say thus says Lord shall prosper not the roots of the

HAPALOTÉTOS AUTÉS KAI HO ***KARPOS*** *SAPÉSETAI KAI XÉRANTHÉSETAI*
tenderness of her and the fruit rot and shall be dried up

PANTA TA PROANATELLONTA AUTÉS KAI OUK EN BRACHIONI MEGALÓ OUDE
all the shooting up early of her and not in arm great neither

EN LAÓ POLLÓ TOU EKSPASAI AUTÉN EK RHIZÓN AUTÉS
in people many of the to pull out her out of roots of her

engLXX Therefore say, Thus saith the Lord; Shall it prosper? Shall not the roots of her tender stem and her fruit be blighted? Yea, all her early shoots shall be dried up, and *that* not by a mighty arm, nor by many people, to tear her up from her roots.

Eze. 17:23 In the mountain of the height of Israel will I plant it: and it shall bring forth boughs, and bear **fruit**, and be a goodly cedar: and under it shall dwell all fowl of every wing; in the shadow of the branches thereof shall they dwell.

YLT In a mountain - the high place of Israel, I plant it, and it hath borne boughs, and yielded **fruit**, and become a goodly cedar, and dwelt under it have all birds of every wing, in the shade of its thin shoots they dwell.

KARPOS – fruit - a direct translation – fruit of cedar

LXX *KAI KREMASÓ AUTON EN OREI METEÓRÓ ISRAÉL KAI KATAPHUTEUSÓ KAI*
and shall hang it in mountain elevated Israel and shall plant and

EXOISEI BLASTON KAI POIÉSEI ***KARPON*** *KAI ESTAI EIS KEDRON MEGALÉN KAI*
bring out bud and make fruit and shall be into cedar great and

ANAPAUSETAI HUPOKATÓ AUTOU PAN ORNEON KAI PAN PETEINON HUPO TÉN
shall rest underneath of it every bird and every winged under the

SKIAN AUTOU ANAPAUSETAI TA KLÉMATA AUTOU APOKATASTATHÉSETAI
shadow of it shall rest the branches of it shall be restored

engLXX and I will hang it on a lofty mountain of Israel: yea, I will plant it, and it shall put forth shoots, and shall bear fruit, and it shall be a great cedar: and every bird shall rest beneath it, even every fowl shall rest under its shadow: its branches shall be restored.

Eze. 19:12 But she was plucked up in fury, she was cast down to the ground, and the east wind dried up her **fruit**: her strong rods were broken and withered; the fire consumed them.

YLT And it is plucked up in fury, to the earth it hath been cast, and the east wind hath dried up its **fruit**, broken and withered hath been the rod of its strength, fire hath consumed it.

NKJV But she was plucked up in fury, she was cast down to the ground, and the east wind dried her **fruit**. Her strong branches were broken and withered; the fire consumed them.

NASB 'But it was plucked up in fury; it was cast down to the ground; and the east wind dried up its **fruit**. Its strong branch was torn off so that it withered; the fire consumed it.

NIV But it was uprooted in fury and thrown to the ground. The east wind made it shrivel, it was stripped of its **fruit**; its strong branches withered and fire consumed them.

NLT But the vine was uprooted in fury and thrown down to the ground. The desert wind dried up its **fruit** and tore off its strong branches, so that it withered and was destroyed by fire.

EKLEKTOS – a direct translation – the context gives appreciation of what **fruit** refers:

"10 Thy mother *is* like a vine in thy blood, planted by the waters: she was fruitful and full of branches by reason of many waters. 11 And she had strong rods for the sceptres of them that bare rule, and her stature was exalted among the thick branches, and she appeared in her height with the multitude of her branches."

The "strong rods" of the vine are those that bear rule – princes – sceptre holders. As such they are seen as the best of the people: choice [cf 19:14 below]

LXX *KAI KATEKLASTHÉ EN THUMÓ EPI GÉN ERRHIPHÉ KAI ANEMOS HO KAUSÓN*
and broken down in rage upon ground tossed and wind the hot

EXÉRANE TA ***EKLEKTA*** *AUTÉS EXEDIKÉTHÉSAN KAI EXÉRANTHÉ HÉ RHABDOS*
dried up the choice of her were punished and were dried the rods

	ISCHUOS AUTÉS PUR ANÉLÓSEN AUTÉN of strength of her fire consumed her
engLXX	But she was broken down in wrath, she was cast upon the ground, and the east wind dried up her choice *branches*: vengeance came upon them, and the rod of her strength was withered; fire consumed it.
Eze. 19:14	And fire is gone out of a rod of her branches, *which* hath devoured her **fruit**, so that she hath no strong rod *to be* a sceptre to rule. This *is* a lamentation, and shall be for a lamentation.
YLT	And go forth doth fire from a rod of its boughs, its **fruit** it hath devoured, and it hath no rod of strength - a sceptre to rule, Lamentation it *is* – and it is for a lamentation!
NKJV	Fire has come out from a rod of her branches *and* devoured her **fruit**, so that she has no strong branch— a scepter for ruling.'" This *is* a lamentation, and has become a lamentation.
NASB	'And fire has gone out from *its* branch; it has consumed its shoots *and* **fruit**, so that there is not in it a strong branch, a scepter to rule.'" This is a lamentation, and has become a lamentation.
NIV	Fire spread from one of its main branches and consumed its **fruit**. No strong branch is left on it fit for a ruler's sceptre." 'This is a lament and is to be used as a lament.'
NLT	A fire has burst out from its branches and devoured its **fruit**. Its remaining limbs are not strong enough to be a ruler's scepter. "This is a funeral song, and it will be used in a funeral."

EKLEKTOS – a divergent translation with the fire "devoured her **fruit**" (KJV) rendered as "has devoured her" (engLXX) – as per Eze.19:12 (above) the context and the words within "sceptre to rule" the "fruit" are the rulers: the choice

LXX	*KAI EXÉLTHE PUR EK RHABDOU* ***EKLEKTÓN*** *AUTÉS KAI KATEPHAGEN AUTÉN* and ye come out fire out of rod choice of her and eat up her
	KAI OUK ÉN EN AUTÉ RHABDOS ISCHUOS PHULÉ EIS PARABOLÉN THRÉNOU and not was in she rod strong kindred into parable of lament

ESTI KAI ESTAI EIS THRÉNON
is and shall be into lamentation

engLXX And fire is gone out of a rod of her choice *boughs*, and has devoured her; and there was no rod of strength in her. Her race is become a parable of lamentation, and it shall be for a lamentation.

Eze. 25:4 Behold, therefore I will deliver thee to the men of the east for a possession, and they shall set their palaces in thee, and make their dwellings in thee: they shall eat thy **fruit**, and they shall drink thy milk.

YLT Therefore, lo, I am giving thee to sons of the east for a possession, and they set their towers in thee, and have placed in thee their tabernacles. They eat thy **fruit**, and they drink thy milk,

KARPOS – fruit - a divergent translation with "men of the east" (KJV) replaced by "children of Kedem" (engLXX) – fruit of the land

LXX *DIATOUTO IDOU EGÓ PARADIDÓMI HUMAS TOIS HUIOIS KEDEM EIS*
therefore look I deliver up you to the sons of Kedem into

KLÉRONOMIAN KAI KATASKÉNÓSOUSIN EN TÉ APARTIA AUTÓN EN SOI KAI
inheritance and they shall encamp in the utensils of them in you and

DÓSOUSIN EN SOI TA SKÉNÓMATA AUTÓN AUTOI PHAGONTAI TOUS ***KARPOUS***
assign in you the tents of them they eat the fruits

SOU KAI AUTOI PIONTAI TÉN PIOTÉTA SOU
of you and they drink the fatness of you

engLXX therefore, behold, I *will* deliver you to the children of Kedem for an inheritance, and they shall lodge in thee with their stuff, and they shall pitch their tents in thee: they shall eat thy fruits, and they shall drink thy milk.

Eze. 34:27 — And the tree of the field shall yield her **fruit**, and the earth shall yield her increase, and they shall be safe in their land, and shall know that I *am* the LORD, when I have broken the bands of their yoke, and delivered them out of the hand of those that served themselves of them.

YLT — And given hath the tree of the field its **fruit**, and the land doth give her increase, and they have been on their land confident, and they have known that I *am* Jehovah, in My breaking the bands of their yoke, and I have delivered them from the hand of those laying service on them.

KARPOS – fruit - a direct translation – fruit of the field

LXX

KAI TA XULA TA EN TÓ PEDIÓ DÓSEI TON ***KARPON*** *AUTÓN KAI HÉ GÉ DÓSEI*
and the trees the in the plain shall give the fruit of them and the earth shall give

TÉN ISCHUN AUTÉS KAI KATOIKÉSOUSIN EPI TÉS GÉS AUTÓN EN ELPIDI EIRÉNÉS
the strength of her and dwell upon the land of them in hope of peace

KAI GNÓSONTAI HOTI EGÓ EIMI KURIOS EN TÓ SUNTRIPSAI ME TON ZUGON AUTÓN KAI
and shall know since I am Lord in the breaking me the yoke of them and

EXELOUMAI AUTOUS EK CHEIROS TÓN KATADOULÓSAMENÓN AUTOUS
shall rescue them out of hands of the enslaving them

engLXX — And the trees that are in the field shall yield their fruit, and the earth shall yield her strength, and they shall dwell in the confidence of peace on their land, and they shall know that I am the Lord, when I have broken their yoke; and I will deliver them out of the hand of those that enslaved them.

Eze. 36:8 — But ye, O mountains of Israel, ye shall shoot forth your branches, and yield your **fruit** to my people of Israel; for they are at hand to come.

YLT — And ye, O mountains of Israel, your branch ye give out, and your **fruits** ye bear for My people Israel, for they have drawn near to come.

KARPOS – fruit - a divergent translation with "ye shall shoot forth your branches" (KJV) rendered as "your grapes" (engLXX) – fruit of land

LXX *HUMÓN DE ORÉ ISRAÉL TÉN STAPHULÉN KAI TON* ***KARPON*** *HUMÓN*
of you but mountains of Israel the grapes and the fruit of you

KATAPHAGETAI HO LAOS MOU HOTI ELPIZOUSI TOU ELTHEIN
shall eat the people of me since hoping of the to come

engLXX But your grapes and your fruits, O mountains of Israel, shall my people eat; for they are hoping to come.

Eze. 36:30 And I will multiply the **fruit** of the tree, and the increase of the field, that ye shall receive no more reproach of famine among the heathen.

KARPOS – fruit - a direct translation – fruit of trees

LXX *KAI PLÉTHUNÓ TON* ***KARPON*** *TOU XULOU KAI TA GENNÉMATA TOU AGROU*
and shall multiply the fruit of the trees and the produce of the field

HOPÓS AN MÉ LABÉTE ONEIDISMON LIMOU EN TOIS ETHNESI
so that ever not ye take scorn of famine in the nations

engLXX And I will multiply the fruit of the trees, and the produce of the field, that ye may not bear the reproach of famine among the nations.

Eze. 47:12a And by the river upon the bank thereof, on this side and on that side, shall grow all trees for meat, whose leaf shall not fade, neither shall the **fruit** thereof be consumed: (. . .)

KARPOS – fruit - a direct translation – fruit of trees by the river

LXX *KAI EPI TOU POTAMOU ANABÉSETAI EPI TOU CHEILOUS AUTOU ENTHEN KAI ENTHEN PAN*
and on the river shall arise on the edges of it side and side every

XULON BRÓSIMON OU MÉ PALAIÓTHÉ EP AUTOU OUDE MÉ EKLEIPÉ HO ***KARPOS*** *AUTOU . . .*
tree meat in no wise shall decay upon it nor not fail the fruit of it

engLXX And every fruit tree shall grow by the river, *even* on the bank of it on this side and on that side: they shall not decay upon it, neither shall their fruit fail: (. . .)

Eze. 47:12b . . . it shall bring forth new fruit according to his months, because their waters they issued out of the sanctuary: and the **fruit** thereof shall be for meat, and the leaf thereof for medicine.

KARPOS – fruit - a divergent translation with "according to his months" (KJV) not translated – fruit of trees by the water

LXX . . . *TÉS KAINOTÉTOS AUTOU PRÓTOBOLÉSEI HOTI TA HUDATA AUTÓN EK TÓN*
of the newness of it shall put forth first since the waters of it out of the

HAGIÓN TAUTA EKPOREUETAI KAI ESTAI HO ***KARPOS*** *AUTÓN EIS BRÓSIN*
holy these go forth and shall be the fruit of them into food

KAI ANABASIS AUTÓN EIS HUGIEIAN
and ascending of them into health

engLXX . . . they shall bring forth the first-fruit of their early crop, for these their waters come forth of the sanctuary: and their fruit shall be for meat, and their foliage for health.

Hos. 9:16 Ephraim is smitten, their root is dried up, they shall bear no **fruit**: yea, though they bring forth, yet will I slay *even* the beloved *fruit* of their womb.

KARPOS – fruit - a direct translation – fruit of Ephraim: offspring

LXX *EPONESEN EPHRAIM TAS RHIZAS AUTOU EXÉRANTHÉ* ***KARPON*** *OUK ETI MÉ*
afflicted Ephraim the roots of him dried up fruit not any more

ENEGKÉ DIOTI KAI EAN GENNÉSÓSIN APOKTENÓ TA EPITHUMÉMATA KOILIAS AUTÓN
should bear therefore and if they should be I shall kill the desired of womb of them

engLXX Ephraim is sick, he is dried up at his roots, he shall in no wise any more bear fruit: wherefore even if they should beget *children*, I will kill the desired *fruit* of their womb.

Hos. 10:1a Israel *is* an empty vine, he bringeth forth **fruit** unto himself: (. . .)

YLT An empty vine *is* Israel, **fruit** he maketh like to himself, (. . .)

KARPOS – fruit - a divergent translation with "empty vine" (KJV) given as "vine with goodly branches" (engLXX) – fruit of vine

LXX *AMPELOS EUKLÉMATOUSA ISRAÉL HO* ***KARPOS*** *EUTHÉNÓN AUTÉS*
vineyard having good vine branches Israel the fruit prospering of her

engLXX Israel is a vine with goodly branches, her fruit is abundant: (. . .)

Hos. 10:1b . . . according to the multitude of his **fruit** he hath increased the altars; according to the goodness of his land they have made goodly images.

YLT . . . according to the abundance of his **fruit**, he hath multiplied for the altars, according to the goodness of his land, they have made goodly standing-pillars.

KARPOS – fruit - a direct translation – fruit of vine

LXX . . . *KATA TO PLÉTHOS TÓN* ***KARPÓN*** *AUTÉS EPLÉTHUNE TA THUSIASTÉRIA*
according to the multitude of the fruits of her multiplied the altars

KATA TA AGATHA TÉS GÉS AUTOU ÓKODOMÉSE STÉLAS
according to the good of the land of him built monuments

engLXX . . . according to the multitude of her fruits she has multiplied *her* altars; according to the wealth of his land, he has set up pillars.

Hos. 10:13 Ye have plowed wickedness, ye have reaped iniquity; ye have eaten the **fruit** of lies: because thou didst trust in thy way, in the multitude of thy mighty men.

KARPOS – fruit - a divergent translation with "Ye have plowed wickedness" (KJV) rendered as "Wherefore have ye passed over ungodliness in silence" (engLXX) – fruit of lies

LXX *HINATI PARESIÓPÉSATE ASEBEIAN KAI TAS ADIKIAS AUTÉS ETRUGÉSATE EPHAGETE* ***KARPON***
why pass over in silence impious and the unrighteous of her gathered ye ate fruit

PSEUDÉ HOTI ÉLPISAS EN TOIS HAMARTÉMASI SOU EN PLÉTHEI DUNAMEÓS SOU
false since hoped in the sins of you in abundance of power of you

engLXX Wherefore have ye passed over ungodliness in silence, and reaped the sins of it? Ye have eaten false fruit; for thou has trusted in thy sins, in the abundance of thy power.

Hos. 14:8 Ephraim *shall say*, What have I to do any more with idols? I have heard *him*, and observed him: I *am* like a green fir tree. From me is thy **fruit** found.

YLT O Ephraim, what to Me any more with idols? I - I afflicted, and I cause him to sing: 'I *am* as a green fir-tree,' from Me is thy **fruit** found.

KARPOS – fruit - a direct translation – the fruit of your life

LXX **14:9** [8]*TÓ EPHRAIM* [9]*TI AUTÓ ETI KAI EIDÓLOIS EGÓ ETAPEINÓSA AUTON KAI KATISCHUSÓ AUTON*
to the Ephraim what to him yet and to idols I humbled him and shall strengthen him

EGÓ HÓS ARKEUTHOS PUKAZOUSA EX EMOU HO ***KARPOS*** *SOU HEURÉTAI*
I as juniper made dense out of me the fruit of you found

engLXX What *has* he to do any more with idols? I have afflicted him, and I will strengthen him: I am as a leafy juniper tree. From me is thy fruit found.

Joe. 2:22 Be not afraid, ye beasts of the field: for the pastures of the wilderness do spring, for the tree beareth her **fruit**, the fig tree and the vine do yield their strength.

KARPOS – fruit - a direct translarion – fruit of tree

LXX *THARSEITE KTÉNÉ TOU PEDIOU HOTI BEBLASTÉKE TA PEDIA TÉS ERÉMOU HOTI XULON*
be of good cheer cattle of the plain since have burst forth the plains of the desert since tree

*ÉNEGKE TON **KARPON** AUTOU SUKÉ KAI AMPELOS EDÓKAN TÉN ISCHUN AUTÓN*
bears the fruit of it fig and vineyard give the strength of them

engLXX Be of good courage, ye beasts of the plain, for the plains of the wilderness have budded, for the trees have borne their fruit, the fig tree and the vine have yielded their strength.

Amo. 2:9 Yet destroyed I the Amorite before them, whose height *was* like the height of the cedars, and he *was* strong as the oaks; yet I destroyed his **fruit** from above, and his roots from beneath.

KARPOS – fruit - a direct translation – fruit of the Amorite

LXX *EGÓ DE EXÉRA TON AMORRHAION EK PROSÓPOU AUTÓN HOU ÉN KATHÓS HUPSOS KEDROU*
I but lifted away the Amorite out of face of them where was as height of cedar

*TO HUPSOS AUTOU KAI ISCHUROS ÉN HÓS DRUS KAI EXÉRANA TON **KARPON** AUTOU*
the height of him and strength was as oak and take out the fruit of him

EPANÓTHEN KAI TAS RHIZAS AUTOU HUPOKATÓTHEN
from above and the roots of him from beneath

engLXX Nevertheless I cut off the Amorite from before them, whose height was as the height of a cedar, and he was strong as an oak; and I dried up his fruit from above, and his roots from beneath.

Amo. 6:12 Shall horses run upon the rock? Will *one* plow *there* with oxen? For ye have turned judgment into gall, and the **fruit** of righteousness into hemlock:

YLT Do horses run on a rock? Doth one plough *it* with oxen? For ye have turned to gall judgment, and the fruit of righteousness to wormwood.

KARPOS – fruit - a divergent translation with "Will *one* plow *there* with oxen?" (KJV) replaced with "Will they refrain from neighing at mares" (engLXX) – fruit of righteousness

LXX **6:13** *EI DIÓXONTAI EN PETRAIS HIPPOI EI PARASIÓPÉSONTAI EN THÉLEIAIS HOTI*
shall pursue in rocks horses shall they remain silent in females since

EXESTREPSATE EIS THUMON KRIMA KAI ***KARPON*** *DIKAIOSUNÉS EIS PIKRIAN*
ye turned out into wrath judgment and fruit of righteousness into bitterness

engLXX Will horses run upon rocks? Will they refrain from neighing at mares? For ye have turned judgment into poison, and the fruit of righteousness into bitterness:

Amo. 9:14 And I will bring again the captivity of my people of Israel, and they shall build the waste cities, and inhabit *them*; and they shall plant vineyards, and drink the wine thereof; they shall also make gardens, and eat the **fruit** of them.

KARPOS – fruit - a direct translation – fruit of gardens

LXX *KAI EPISTREPSÓ TÉN AICHMALÓSIAN TOU LAOU MOU ISRAÉL KAI OIKODOMÉSOUSI POLEIS*
and shall turn the captivity of the people of me Israel and shall build cities

TAS ÉPHANISMENAS KAI KATOIKÉSOUSI KAI PHUTEUSOUSIN AMPELÓNAS KAI PIONTAI
the destroyed and shall dwell and shall plant vineyards and drink

TON OINON AUTÓN KAI POIÉSOUSI KÉPOUS KAI PHAGONTAI TON ***KARPON*** *AUTÓN*
the wine of them and shall make gardens and eat the fruit of them

engLXX And I will turn the captivity of my people Israel, and they shall rebuild the ruined cities, and shall inhabit *them*; and they shall plant vineyards, and shall drink the wine from them; and they shall form gardens, and eat the fruit of them.

Mic. 6:7 Will the Lord be pleased with thousands of rams, *or* with ten thousands of rivers of oil? shall I give my firstborn *for* my transgression, the **fruit** of my body *for* the sin of my soul? sin of my soul?

YLT Is Jehovah pleased with thousands of rams? With myriads of streams of oil? Do I give my first-born *for* my transgression? The **fruit** of my body *for* the sin of my soul?

KARPOS – fruit - a divergent translation with "ten thousands of rivers of oil" (KJV) replaced by "ten thousands of fat goats" (engLXX) – fruit of body: offspring, in particular firstborn

LXX *EI PROSDEXETAI KURIOS EN CHILIASI KRIÓN É EN MURIASI CHIMARÓN PIONÓN*
shall accept Lord in thousands of rams or in myriads of goats fat

EI DÓ PRÓTOTOKA MOU HUPER ASEBEIAS ***KARPON*** *KOILIAS MOU HUPER*
shall give firstborn of me for ungodliness fruit of body of me for

HAMARTIAS PSUCHÉS MOU
sins of soul of me

engLXX Will the Lord accept thousands of rams, or ten thousands of fat goats? should I give my first-born for ungodliness, the fruit of my body for the sin of my soul?

Mic. 7:13 Notwithstanding the land shall be desolate because of them that dwell therein, for the **fruit** of their doings.

YLT And the land hath been for a desolation, because of its inhabitants, because of the **fruit** of their doings.

KARPOS – fruit - a divergent translation with "because of them" (KJV) rendered as "with them" (engLXX) – fruit of doings

LXX *KAI ESTAI HÉ GÉ EIS APHANISMON SUN TOIS KATOIKOUSIN AUTÉN APO*
and shall be the land into vanish away with the dwellers her from

KARPÓN *EPITÉDEUMATÓN AUTÓN*
fruits practices of them

engLXX And the land shall be utterly desolate together with them that inhabit it, because of the fruit of their doings.

Zec. 8:12 For the seed *shall be* prosperous; the vine shall give her **fruit**, and the ground shall give her increase, and the heavens shall give their dew; and I will cause the remnant of this people to possess all these *things*.

YLT Because of the sowing of peace, the vine doth give her **fruit**, and the earth doth give her increase, and the heavens do give their dew, and I have caused the remnant of this people to inherit all these.

KARPOS – fruit - a direct translation – fruit of vineyard

LXX *ALL É DEIXÓ EIRÉNÉN HÉ AMPELOS DÓSEI TON* ***KARPON*** *AUTÉS KAI HÉ GÉ*
but shall show peace the vineyard shall give the fruit of her and the land

DÓSEI TA GENNÉMATA AUTÉS KAI HO OURANOS DÓSEI TÉN DROSON AUTOU
shall give the produce of her and the heaven shall give the dew of it

KAI KATAKLÉRONOMÉSÓ TOIS KATALOIPOIS TOU LAOU MOU TOUTOU TAUTA PANTA
and shall allot to the remnants of the people of me of this these all

engLXX But I will shew peace: the vine shall yield her fruit, and the land shall yield her produce, and the heaven shall give its dew: and I will give as an inheritance all these things to the remnant of my people.

Mal. 3:11 And I will rebuke the devourer for your sakes, and he shall not destroy the **fruits** of your ground; neither shall your vine cast her fruit before the time in the field, saith the LORD of hosts.

KARPOS – fruit - a divergent translation with "the devourer" (KJV) omitted – fruit of the land

LXX *KAI DIASTELÓ HUMIN EIS BRÓSIN KAI OU MÉ DIAPHTHEIRÓ HUMÓN TON*
and will give command to you into food and in no wise will destroy of you the

KARPON *TÉS GÉS KAI OU MÉ ASTHENÉSÉ HUMÓN HÉ AMPELOS HÉ EN TÓ*
fruit of the land and in no wise shall fail of you the vineyard the in the

AGRÓ LEGEI KURIOS PANTOKRATÓR
field says Lord Almighty

engLXX And I will appoint food for you, and I will not destroy the fruit of your land; and your vine in the field shall not fail, saith the Lord Almighty.

23 - TSAMMERETH

Translated into Greek in the LXX

EKLEKTOS		**1**		**Ezekiel 17:22**
ARCHÉ	(top, first)	3		
EPILEKTOS		1	aNT	
TOTAL		5		

Translated into English - Both KJV related

Ys Conc.	Count	Ss Conc. No. H 6788	Count
highest branch	2	highest branch	2
top	3	top	3
TOTAL	5	TOTAL	5

Refs		Text quotes KJV unless otherwise stated
Eze. 17:3		And say, Thus saith the Lord GOD; A great eagle with great wings, longwinged, full of feathers, which had divers colours, came unto Lebanon, and took the **highest branch** of the cedar:
	YLT	and thou hast said: Thus said the Lord Jehovah: the great eagle, great-winged, long-pinioned, full of feathers, that hath diverse colours, hath come in unto Lebanon, and it taketh the **foliage** of the cedar,
	NKJV	and say, 'Thus says the Lord GOD: "A great eagle with large wings and long pinions, full of feathers of various colors, came to Lebanon and took from the cedar the **highest branch**.
	NASB	saying, 'Thus says the Lord GOD, "A great eagle with great wings, long pinions and a full plumage of many colors came to Lebanon and took away the **top** of the cedar.
	NIV	Say to them, "This is what the Sovereign LORD says: a great eagle with powerful wings, long feathers and full plumage of varied colours came to Lebanon. Taking hold of the **top** of a cedar,
	NLT	Give them this message from the Sovereign Lord: "A great eagle with broad wings and long feathers, covered with many-colored plumage, came to Lebanon. He seized the **top** of a cedar tree

EPILEKTOS aNT – a divergent translation with "divers colours" (KJV) not translated - the highest branch is the overlooking uppermost branch *EPILEKTOS* is in the same family as *EKLEKTOS* with much the same meaning: here to represent the best of the cedar taken by the "eagle" of the Lord's riddle or parable/simile (17:2): i.e. "highest branch" (KJV) or "foliage" (YLT). See separate chapter on *EPILEKTOS*.

LXX

KAI EREIS TADE LEGEI KURIOS AETOS HO MEGAS HO MEGALOPTERUGOS
and shall say thus says Lord eagle the great the large winged

HO MAKROS TÉ EKTASEI PLÉRÉS ONUCHÓN HOS ECHEI TO HÉGÉMA
the long the stretching full of claws which he has the purposing

EISELTHEIN EIS TON LIBANON KAI ELABE TA ***EPILEKTA*** *TÉS KEDROU*
to enter into the Lebanon and took the choice of the cedar

engLXX and thou shalt say, Thus saith the Lord; A great eagle with large wings, spreading them out very far, with many claws, which has the design of entering into Libanus-- and he took the choice *branches* of the cedar:

Eze. 17:22 Thus saith the Lord God; I will also take of the **highest branch** of the high cedar, and will set *it*; I will crop off from the top of his young twigs a tender one, and will plant *it* upon an high mountain and eminent:

YLT Thus said the Lord Jehovah: I have taken of the foliage of the **high** cedar, and I have set *it*, from the top of its tender shoots a tender one I crop, and I - I have planted *it* on a mountain high and lofty.

NKJV Thus says the Lord God: "I will take also *one* of the **highest branches** of the high cedar and set *it* out. I will crop off from the topmost of its young twigs a tender one, and will plant *it* on a high and prominent mountain.

NASB Thus says the Lord God, "I will also take a *sprig* from the **lofty top** of the cedar and set *it* out; I will pluck from the topmost of its young twigs a tender one and I will plant *it* on a high and lofty mountain.

NIV '"This is what the Sovereign Lord says: I myself will take a shoot from the **very top** of a cedar and plant it; I will break off a tender sprig from its topmost shoots and plant it on a high and lofty mountain.

NLT "This is what the Sovereign Lord says: I will take a branch from the **top** of a tall cedar, and I will plant it on the top of Israel's highest mountain.

EKLEKTOS – a divergent translation with "I will crop off from the top of his young twigs a tender one" (KJV) rendered as "I will crop off their hearts" (engLXX) - the highest or best of the cedar described by the word: the highest, the top

LXX *DIOTI TADE LEGEI KURIOS KAI LÉPSOMAI EGÓ EK TÓN* ***EKLEKTÓN*** *TÉS KEDROU EK*
since thus says Lord and take I out of the choice of the cedar out of

KORUPHÉS KARDIAS AUTÓN APOKNIÓ KAI KATAPHUTEUSÓ EGÓ EP OROS HUPSÉLON
crown of hearts of them pluck and plant I upon mountain high

engLXX For thus saith the Lord; I will even take of the choice *branches* of the cedar from the top *thereof*, I will crop off their hearts, and I will plant it on a high mountain:

Eze. 31:3 Behold, the Assyrian *was* a cedar in Lebanon with fair branches, and with a shadowing shroud, and of an high stature; and his **top** was among the thick boughs.

YLT Lo, Asshur, a cedar in Lebanon, fair in branch, and shading bough, and high in stature, and between thickets hath its **foliage** been.

ARCHÉ – A divergent translation with "and with a shadowing shroud" (KJV) not rendered - the chief, first or top element of the cedar is given by the word

LXX *IDOU ASSOUR KUPARISSOS EN TÓ LIBANÓ KAI KALOS TAIS PARAPHUASI KAI*
look Assyria cypress in the Lebanon and good the shoots and

HUPSÉLOS TÓ MEGETHEI EIS MESON NEPHELÓN EGENETO HÉ ***ARCHÉ*** *AUTOU*
high with the stature into midst of clouds came to be the top of it

engLXX Behold, the Assyrian was a cypress in Libanus, and was fair in shoots, and high in stature: his top reached to the midst of the clouds.

Eze. 31:10 Therefore thus saith the Lord God; because thou hast lifted up thyself in height, and he hath shot up his **top** among the thick boughs, and his heart is lifted up in his height;

YLT Therefore, thus said the Lord Jehovah: Because that thou hast been high in stature, and he yieldeth his **foliage** between thickets, and high is his heart in his haughtiness,

ARCHÉ – a divergent translation with "among the thick boughs" (KJV) or "between thickets" (YLT), rendered as "in the midst of the clouds" (engLXX) - the chief element of the cedar in height or lush foliage is seen by the word [cf. 31:14 below]

LXX *DIATOUTO TADE LEGEI KURIOS ANTH HÓN EGENOU MEGAS TÓ MEGETHEI KAI EDÓKAS*
therefore thus says Lord | for the sake of who became great with the stature and gave

TÉN ***ARCHÉN*** *SOU EIS MESON NEPHELÓN KAI EIDON EN TÓ HUPSÓTHÉNAI AUTON*
the top of you into midst of clouds and saw in the lift high him

engLXX Therefore thus saith the Lord; Because thou art grown great, and hast set thy top in the midst of the clouds, and I saw when he was exalted;

Eze. 31:14 To the end that none of all the trees by the waters exalt themselves for their height, neither shoot up their **top** among the thick boughs, neither their trees stand up in their height, all that drink water: for they are all delivered unto death, to the nether parts of the earth, in the midst of the children of men, with them that go down to the pit.

YLT In order that none of the trees of the waters may become haughty because of their stature, nor give their **foliage** between thickets, nor any drinking waters stand up unto them in their haughtiness, for all of them are given up to death, unto the earth -- the lower part, in the midst of the sons of men, unto those going down to the pit.

ARCHÉ – a divergent translation with “among the thick boughs” (KJV) or “between thickets” (YLT), rendered as “in the midst of the clouds” (engLXX) - the top or lush part of the tree is highlighted by the word. [cf. 31:10 above]

LXX *HOPÓS MÉ HUPSÓTHÓSIN EN TÓ MEGETHEI AUTÓN PANTA TA XULA TA EN TÓ HUDATI KAI*
so that not exalted in the stature of them all the trees the in the water and

EDÓKAN TÉN ***ARCHÉN*** *AUTÓN EIS MESON NEPHELÓN KAI OUK ESTÉSAN EN TÓ HUPSEI*
gave the top of them into midst of clouds and not stand in the height

AUTÓN PROS AUTA PANTES HOI PINONTES HUDÓR PANTES EDOTHÉSAN EIS THANATON
of them to them all the drinking water all given into death

EIS GÉS BATHOS EN MESÓ HUIÓN ANTHRÓPÓN PROS KATABAINONTAS EIS BOTHRON
into earth depth in midst sons of men to go down into pit

engLXX in order that none of the trees by the water should exalt themselves by reason of their size: whereas they set their top in the midst of the clouds, yet they continued not in their high state in their place, all that drank water, all were consigned to death, to the depth of the earth, in the midst of the children of men, with them that go down to the pit.

24 - TSEBI

Translated into Greek in the LXX

EKLEKTOS		**2**		**Ezekiel 7:20; Ezekiel 25:9**
DORKAS	(doe, type of deer)	10	aNT	
DUNAMIS	(power, might)	3		
DOXA	(glory)	2		
ELPIS	(hope, expectation)	2		
ENDOXOS	(honoured, gloried)	2		
KÉRION	(honeycomb)	2		
DORKADION	(fawn, little gazelle)	1	aNT	
DORKÓN	(roe, buck)	1	aNT	
EPILAMPÓ	(to shine upon)	1	aNT	
STÉLOÓ	(stand still, set up stone)	1	aNT	
SABAEIM	(beauty, glory)	1	aNT	
SABAEIN	(beauty, glory)	1	aNT	
SABEI	(beauty, glory)	1	aNT	
NOT in LXX		2		
TOTAL		32		

Translated into English - Both KJV related

Ys Conc.	Count	Ss Conc. No. H 6643	Count
beauty	2	roe	9
glory	8	roebuck	5
beautiful	1	glory	8
glorious	5	glorious	6
goodly	1	beautiful	1
pleasant	1	beauty	1
roe	9	goodly	1
roebuck	5	pleasant	1
TOTAL	32	TOTAL	32

Refs	**Text quotes KJV unless otherwise stated**
Deu. 12:15	Notwithstanding thou mayest kill and eat flesh in all thy gates, whatsoever thy soul lusteth after, according to the blessing of the LORD thy God which he hath given thee: the unclean and the clean may eat thereof, as of the **roebuck**, and as of the hart.
YLT	Only, with all the desire of thy soul thou dost sacrifice, and hast eaten flesh according to the blessing of Jehovah thy God which He hath given to thee, in all thy gates; the unclean and the clean do eat it, as of the **roe**, and as of the hart.

DORKAS aNT - doe, type of deer – a direct translation – a female deer

LXX *ALL É EN PASÉ EPITHUMIA SOU THUSEIS KAI PHAGÉ KREA KATA TÉN EULOGIAN*
but be in all desirable of you sacrifice and eat meats | the blessing
according to

KURIOU TOU THEOU SOU HÉN EDÓKE SOI EN PASÉ POLEI HO AKATHARTOS EN
of Lord of the God of you which given to you in every city the unclean in

SOI KAI HO KATHAROS EPI TO AUTO PHAGETAI AUTO HÓS ***DORKADA*** *É ELAPHON*
you and the clean upon the it to eat it as doe or stag

engLXX But thou shalt kill according to all thy desire, and shalt eat flesh according to the blessing of the Lord thy God, which he has given thee in every city; the unclean that is within thee and the clean shall eat it on equal terms, as the doe or the stag.

Deu. 12:22 Even as the **roebuck** and the hart is eaten, so thou shalt eat them: the unclean and the clean shall eat *of* them alike.

DORKAS aNT - doe, type of deer – a direct translation – a female deer

LXX *HÓS ESTHETAI HÉ* ***DORKAS*** *KAI HÉ ELAPHOS HOUTÓ PHAGÉ AUTO HO*
as eat the doe and the stag even so eat it the

AKATHARTOS EN SOI KAI HO KATHAROS HÓSAUTÓS EDETAI
unclean in you and the clean just so shall eat

engLXX As the doe and the stag are eaten, so shalt thou eat it; the unclean in thee and the clean shall eat it in like manner.

Deu. 14:5 The hart, and the **roebuck**, and the fallow deer, and the wild goat, and the pygarg, and the wild ox, and the chamois.

DORKAS aNT - doe, type of deer – a divergent translation with 7 different animals rendered into 5; two are not rendered – a female deer

LXX *ELAPHON KAI* ***DORKADA*** *KAI PUGARGON ORUGA KAI KAMÉLOPARDALIN*
stag and doe and roebuck antelope and camelopard

engLXX the stag, and doe, and pygarg, and wild goat, and camelopard.

Deu. 15:22 Thou shalt eat it within thy gates: the unclean and the clean *person shall eat it* alike, as the **roebuck**, and as the hart.

DORKAS aNT - doe, type of deer – a direct translation – a female deer

LXX *EN TAIS POLESI SOU PHAGÉ AUTO HO AKATHARTOS EN SOI KAI HO KATHAROS*
in the cities of you eat it the unclean in you and the clean

HÓSAUTÓS EDETAI HÓS ***DORKADA*** *É ELAPHON*
Just so shall eat as doe or stag

engLXX Thou shalt eat it in thy cities; the unclean in thee and the clean shall eat it in like manner, as the doe or the stag.

2Sa. 1:19 The **beauty** of Israel is slain upon thy high places: how are the mighty fallen!

YLT The **Roebuck**, O Israel, on thy high places *is* wounded; how have the mighty fallen!

STÉLOÓ aNT - stand still, set up stone, pillar – a divergent translation with "the beauty" (KJV) or "the Roebuck" (YLT) given as "Set up a pillar" (engLXX) - the best of Israel, like a standing male deer seen in the mountains silhouetted against the sky, so also the young men of Israel: a poetic reference to Saul and Jonathan (V.12) who lost their lives in battle – Erected stone (Gk.); male deer (Heb.)

LXX ***STÉLÓSON*** *ISRAÉL HUPER TÓN TETHNÉKOTÓN EPI TA HUPSÉ SOU*
2Ki.1:19 set up stone Israel for the dead upon the heights of you

		TRAUMATIÓN PÓS EPESAN DUNATOI wounded how fallen mighty
	engLXX	Set up a pillar, O Israel, for the slain that died upon thy high places: how are the mighty fallen!
2Sa. 2:18		And there were three sons of Zeruiah there, Joab, and Abishai, and Asahel: and Asahel *was as* light of foot as a wild **roe**.
	YLT	And there are there three sons of Zeruiah, Joab, and Abishai, and Asahel, and Asahel *is* light on his feet, as one of the **roes** which *are* in the field,

DORKAS aNT - doe, type of deer – a direct translation – a female deer

	LXX **2Ki.2:18**	*KAI EGENONTO EKEI TREIS HUIOI SAROUIA IÓAB KAI ABESSA KAI ASAÉL KAI* and be there three sons of sarouia Joab and Abessa and Asael and *ASAÉL KOUPHOS TOIS POSIN AUTOU HÓSEI MIA* ***DORKAS*** *EN AGRÓ* Asael light with the feet of him as one doe in field
	engLXX	And there were there the three sons of Saruia, Joab, and Abessa, and Asael: and Asael was swift in his feet as a roe in the field.
1Ki. 4:23		Ten fat oxen, and twenty oxen out of the pastures, and an hundred sheep, beside harts, and **roebucks**, and fallowdeer, and fatted fowl.
	YLT	ten fat oxen, and twenty feeding oxen, and a hundred sheep, apart from hart, and **roe**, and fallow-deer, and fatted beasts of the stalls,
	NKJV	ten **fatted** oxen, twenty oxen from the pastures, and one hundred sheep, besides deer, gazelles, roebucks, and fatted fowl.
	NASB	ten **fat** oxen, twenty pasture-fed oxen, a hundred sheep besides deer, gazelles, roebucks, and fattened fowl.

NIV ten head of **stall-fed** cattle, twenty of pasture-fed cattle and a hundred sheep and goats, as well as deer, gazelles, roebucks and choice fowl.

NLT also 10 oxen from the **fattening** pens, 20 pasture-fed cattle, 100 sheep or goats, as well as deer, gazelles, roe deer, and choice poultry.

DORKAS aNT - doe, type of deer - a divergent translation with "harts, and roebucks, and fallowdeer, and fatted fowl" (KJV) or "hart, and roe, and fallow-deer, and fatted beasts of the stalls" (YLT), rendered much shorter by "stags, and choice fatted does" (engLXX) – a female deer

LXX **3Ki.4:23**

KAI	*DEKA*	*MOSCHOI*	*EKLEKTOI*[1]	*KAI*	*EIKOSI*	*BOES*	*NOMADES*	*KAI*	*HEKATON*
and	ten	calves	choice	and	twenty	oxen	grazing	and	hundred

PROBATA	*EKTOS*	*ELAPHÓN*	*KAI*	***DORKADÓN***	*EKLEKTÓN*[2]	*SITEUTA*
sheep	outside	of stags	and	does	choice	fatted

engLXX and ten choice calves, and twenty pastured oxen, and a hundred sheep, besides stags, and choice fatted does.

1Ch. 12:8 And of the Gadites there separated themselves unto David into the hold to the wilderness men of might, *and* men of war *fit* for the battle, that could handle shield and buckler, whose faces *were like* the faces of lions, and *were as* swift as the **roes** upon the mountains;

YLT And of the Gadite there have been separated unto David, to the fortress, to the wilderness, mighty of valour, men of the host for battle, setting in array target and buckler, and their faces the face of the lion, and as **roes** on the mountains for speed:

DORKAS aNT - doe, type of deer – a divergent translation with "buckler" (KJV - a type of shield) rendered as "spears" (engLXX) – a female deer

1. See BARI
2. See the a*EKLEKTOS* chapter

LXX
12:9

KAI APO TOU GADDI ECHÓRISTHÉSAN PROS DAUID APO TÉS ERÉMOU ISCHUROI DUNATOI
and from the Gad separated to David from the desert strong mighty

ANDRES PARATAXEÓS POLEMOU AIRONTES THUREOUS KAI DORATA KAI PROSÓPON LEONTOS
men paraded of war raise shields and spears and face of lion

TA PROSÓPA AUTÓN KAI KOUPHOI HÓS ***DORKADES*** *EPI TÓN OREÓN TÓ TAXEI*
the faces of them and light as does upon the mountains with the speed

engLXX And from Gad these separated themselves to David from the wilderness, strong mighty men of war, bearing shields and spears, and their faces *were as* the face of a lion, and they were nimble as roes upon the mountains in speed.

Pro. 6:5 Deliver thyself as a **roe** from the hand *of the hunter*, and as a bird from the hand of the fowler.

YLT Be delivered as a **roe** from the hand, and as a bird from the hand of a fowler.

DORKAS aNT - doe, type of deer – a divergent translation with "hand" (KJV) twice involving a person, rendered with "toils" and "snares" (engLXX): removing any person in view and just mentioning the tools employed instead: the means of capture or retention rather than the type of person holding on – a female deer

LXX *HINA SÓZÉ HÓSPER* ***DORKAS*** *EK BROCHÓN KAI HÓSPER ORNEON EK PAGIDOS*
| save so as doe out of nooses and even as bird out of trap
in order that

engLXX that thou mayest deliver thyself as a doe out of the toils, and as a bird out of a snare.

Sng. 2:7 I charge you, O ye daughters of Jerusalem, by the **roes**, and by the hinds of the field, that ye stir not up, nor awake *my* love, till he please.

YLT I have adjured you, daughters of Jerusalem, by the **roes** or by the hinds of the field, stir not up nor wake the love till she please!

DUNAMIS - power, might, strength – a divergent translation with "roes" and "hinds" (KJV), given as "powers" and "virtues" (engLXX): just as deer grazing in the field are easily spooked, so the pleading not to disturb is pictured: this is then rendered as "by the powers and by the virtues of the field" (engLXX), as if the appeal was to some other natural appreciation – a natural powers [= Sng 3:5 below]

LXX *HÓRKISA HUMAS THUGATERES HIEROUSALÉM EN* ***DUNAMESI*** *KAI EN*
charged you daughters of Jerusalem in powers and in

ISCHUSESI TOU AGROU EAN EGEIRÉTE KAI EXEGEIRÉTE TÉN AGAPÉN HEÓS HOU THELÉSÉ
strengths of the field if arise and awake the love until of which will

engLXX I have charged you, ye daughters of Jerusalem, by the powers and by the virtues of the field, that ye do not rouse or wake *my* love, until he please.

Sng. 2:9 My beloved is like a **roe** or a young hart: behold, he standeth behind our wall, he looketh forth at the windows, shewing himself through the lattice.

DORKAS aNT - doe, type of deer – a divergent translation with "the mountains of Bæthel" (engLXX) added – a female deer

LXX *HOMOIOS ESTIN ADELPHIDOS MOU TÉ* ***DORKADI*** *É NEBRÓ ELAPHÓN EPI TA*
alike is beloved of me the doe or fawn of hinds upon the

ORÉ BAITHÉL IDOU HOUTOS OPISÓ TOU TOICHOU HÉMÓN PARAKUPTÓN DIA
mountains of Baithel look he behind the wall of us lean over through

TÓN THURIDÓN EKKUPTÓN DIA TÓN DIKTUÓN
the windows looking out through the lattices

engLXX My kinsman is like a roe or a young hart on the mountains of Bæthel: behold, he is behind our wall, looking through the windows, peeping through the lattices.

Sng. 2:17 Until the day break, and the shadows flee away, turn, my beloved, and be thou like a **roe** or a young hart upon the mountains of Bether.

YLT Till the day doth break forth, and the shadows have fled away, turn, be like, my beloved, to a **roe**, or to a young one of the harts, on the mountains of separation!

DORKÓN aNT - roe, buck – a direct translation ["beloved" (KJV) though rendered as "kinsman" in the engLXX is nevertheless accurate in the Gk.] – a deer

LXX *HEÓS HOU DIAPNEUSÉ HÉ HÉMERA KAI KINÉTHÓSIN HAI SKIAI APOSTREPSON*
until of which refresh the day and move the shadows turn

HOMOIÓTHÉTI SU ADELPHIDE MOU TÓ ***DORKÓNI*** *É NEBRÓ ELAPHÓN EPI ORÉ*
be like you beloved of me to the buck or fawn of hinds upon | mountains

KOILÓMATÓN
of ravines

engLXX Until the day dawn, and the shadows depart, turn, my kinsman, be thou like to a roe or young hart on the mountains of the ravines.

Sng. 3:5 I charge you, O ye daughters of Jerusalem, by the **roes**, and by the hinds of the field, that ye stir not up, nor awake *my* love, till he please.

YLT I have adjured you, daughters of Jerusalem, By the **roes** or by the hinds of the field, Stir not up nor wake the love till she please!

DUNAMIS - power, might, strength – a divergent translation with "roes" and "hinds" (KJV), given as "powers" and "virtues" (engLXX): just as deer grazing in the field are easily spooked, so the pleading not to disturb is pictured: this is then rendered as "by the powers and by the virtues of the field" (engLXX), as if the appeal was to some other natural appreciation – a natural powers [= Sng 2:7 above]

LXX *HÓRKISA HUMAS THUGATERES HIEROUSALÉM EN TAIS* ***DUNAMESI*** *KAI EN TAIS*
charge you daughters of Jerusalem in the powers and in the

ISCHUSESI TOU AGROU EAN EGEIRÉTE KAI EXEGEIRÉTE TÉN AGAPÉN HEÓS AN THELÉSÉ
strengths of the field if arise and awake the love until whenever will

engLXX I have charged you, O daughters of Jerusalem, by the powers and by the virtues of the field, that ye rouse not nor awake *my* love, until he please.

Sng. 8:14 Make haste, my beloved, and be thou like to a **roe** or to a young hart upon the mountains of spices.

YLT **8:13-14** 13 Flee, my beloved, and be like to a **roe**, 14 or to a young one of the harts on mountains of spices!

DORKAS aNT - doe, type of deer – a direct translation ["beloved" (KJV) rendered as "kinsman" in the engLXX is nevertheless accurate in the Gk.] – a female deer

LXX *PHUGE ADELPHIDE MOU KAI HOMOIÓTHÉTI TÉ* ***DORKADI*** *É TÓ NEBRÓ TÓN*
flee beloved of me and be like the doe or the fawn of the

ELAPHÓN EPI ORÉ TÓN ARÓMATÓN
hinds upon mountains of the fragrant

engLXX Away, my kinsman, and be like a doe or a fawn on the mountains of spices.

Isa. 4:2 In that day shall the branch of the LORD be **beautiful** and glorious, and the fruit of the earth *shall be* excellent and comely for them that are escaped of Israel.

YLT In that day is the Shoot of Jehovah for **desire** and for honour, and the fruit of the earth for excellence and for beauty to the escaped of Israel.

EPILAMPÓ aNT - to shine upon – a divergent translation with "the branch of the LORD" (KJV) or "the Shoot of Jehovah" (YLT), given as "God" (engLXX) - the Hebrew word's 2nd meaning comes to "light" here: its core of splendour, glory, or beauty is seen in the movement and appreciation of a graceful deer, hence most of the above uses of the word as the name in Heb. for the animal i.e. like calling a doe "a glory" by name: here the glory itself is in view: God shall shine Gk.

LXX *TÉ DE HÉMERA EKEINÉ* ***EPILAMPSEI*** *HO THEOS EN BOULÉ META DOXÉS EPI*
the but day that shall shine the God in will with glory upon

TÉS GÉS TOU HUPSÓSAI KAI DOXASAI TO KATALEIPHTHEN TOU ISRAÉL
the earth of the to exalt and to glorify the left behind of the Israel

engLXX And in that day God shall shine gloriously in counsel on the earth, to exalt and glorify the remnant of Israel.

Isa. 13:14 And it shall be as the chased **roe**, and as a sheep that no man taketh up: they shall every man turn to his own people, and flee every one into his own land.

YLT And it hath been, as a **roe** driven away, and as a flock that hath no gatherer, each unto his people - they turn, and each unto his land – they flee.

DORKADION aNT - fawn, little gazelle – a divergent translation with "they that are left" (engLXX) added – a young female deer

LXX *KAI ESONTAI HOI KATALELEIMMENOI HÓS* ***DORKADION*** *PHEUGON KAI HÓS PROBATÓN*
and shall be the left behind as fawn fleeing and as sheep

PLANÓMENON KAI OUK ESTAI HO SUNAGÓN HÓSTE ANTHRÓPON EIS TON LAON AUTOU
wandering and not shall be the gather so as man into the people of him

APOSTRAPHÉNAI KAI ANTHRÓPOS EIS TÉN CHÓRAN HEAUTOU DIÓXETAI
turn and man into the region himself shall flee

engLXX And they that are left shall be as a fleeing fawn, and as a stray sheep, and there shall be none to gather *them*: so that a man shall turn back to his people, and a man shall flee to his own land.

Isa. 13:19 — And Babylon, the **glory** of kingdoms, the beauty of the Chaldees' excellency, shall be as when God overthrew Sodom and Gomorrah.

YLT — And Babylon, the **beauty** of kingdoms, the glory, the excellency of the Chaldeans, hath been as overthrown by God, with Sodom and with Gomorrah.

ENDOXOS - honoured, gloried, esteemed – a divergent translation with "excellency" (KJV) not rendered – the 2nd meaning of the Heb. word [cf. Isa 4:2 above]: glory of Babylon

LXX — *KAI ESTAI BABULÓN HÉ KALEITAI* ***ENDOXOS*** *APO BASILEÓS CHALDAIÓN HON*
and shall be Babylon the called glorious by king of Chaldeans in which

TROPON KATESTREPSEN HO THEOS SODOMA KAI GOMORRHA
manner eradicated the God Sodom and Gomorrha

engLXX — And Babylon, which is called glorious by the king of the Chaldeans, shall be as *when* God overthrew Sodoma, and Gomorrha.

Isa. 23:9 — The LORD of hosts hath purposed it, to stain the pride of all **glory**, *and* to bring into contempt all the honourable of the earth.

YLT — Jehovah of Hosts hath counselled it, to pollute the excellency of all **beauty**, to make light all the honoured of earth.

ENDOXOS - honoured, gloried, esteemed – a divergent translation with "glory" (KJV) or "beauty" (YLT), personified as "glorious ones" – the 2nd meaning of the Heb. word [cf. Isa 4:2 above]: the gloried

LXX — *KURIOS SABAÓTH EBOULEUSATO PARALUSAI PASAN TÉN HUBRIN TÓN*
Lord of Hosts purposed to detach all the insolence of the

ENDOXÓN *KAI ATIMASAI PAN ENDOXON EPI TÉS GÉS*
glorious ones and dishonour every glorious upon the earth

	engLXX	The Lord of hosts has purposed to bring down all the pride of the glorious ones, and to disgrace every glorious thing on the earth.
Isa. 24:16		15. . . the name of the LORD God of Israel in the isles of the sea. 16From the uttermost part of the earth have we heard songs, *even* **glory** to the righteous. But I said, My leanness, my leanness, woe unto me! The treacherous dealers have dealt treacherously; yea, the treacherous dealers have dealt very treacherously.
	YLT	15. . . Jehovah, God of Israel. 16From the skirt of the earth we heard songs, the **desire** of the righteous. And I say, 'Leanness *is* to me, Leanness *is* to me, wo *is* to me.' Treacherous dealers dealt treacherously, yea, treachery, treacherous dealers dealt treacherously.

ELPIS - hope, expectation – a divergent translation with "glory" (KJV) or "desire" (YLT), rendered as "hope" (engLXX) – since this is a report of something heard in song that was glorious and thereby desired, it gives hope – hope to the pious Gk. [cf. Isa. 28:5 below]

LXX *KURIE HO THEOS ISRAÉL APO TÓN PTERUGÓN TÉS GÉS TERATA ÉKOUSAMEN* ***ELPIS*** *TÓ*
Lord the God of Israel from the wings of the earth miracles we heard hope to the

EUSEBEI KAI EROUSIN OUAI TOIS ATHETOUSIN HOI ATHETOUNTES TON NOMON
pious and shall say Woe to the rejecters the reject the law

	engLXX	O Lord God of Israel, from the ends of the earth we have heard wonderful things, *and there is* hope to the godly: but they shall say, Woe to the despisers, that despise the law.
Isa. 28:1		Woe to the crown of pride, to the drunkards of Ephraim, whose **glorious** beauty *is* a fading flower, which *are* on the head of the fat valleys of them that are overcome with wine!
	YLT	Wo *to* the proud crown of the drunkards of Ephraim. And the fading flower of the **beauty** of his glory, that *is* on the head of the fat valley of the broken down of wine.

DOXA – glory, honour, magnificence – a divergent translation with "drunkards" (KJV) given as "hirelings" (engLXX) – the overall passage gives a contrast between the "crown" of Ephraim to the later "crown" of the Lord himself (V.5 see below): the 2nd meaning of the Heb. word [cf. Isa 4:2 above]: the glory of Ephraim

LXX ***OUAI TÓ STEPHANÓ TÉS HUBREÓS HOI MISTHÓTOI EPHRAIM TO ANTHOS TO***
woe to the crown of the injurious the rejecters of Ephraim the flower the

EKPESON EK TÉS **DOXÉS** ***EPI TÉS KORUPHÉS TOU OROUS TOU PACHEOS HOI***
fallen out of the glory upon the top of the mountains of the thick the

METHUONTES ANEU OINOU
drunken without wine

engLXX Woe to the crown of pride, the hirelings of Ephraim, the flower that has fallen from the glory of the top of the fertile mountain, they that are drunken without wine.

Isa. 28:4 And the **glorious** beauty, which *is* on the head of the fat valley, shall be a fading flower, *and* as the hasty fruit before the summer; which *when* he that looketh upon it seeth, while it is yet in his hand he eateth it up.

YLT And the fading flower of the **beauty** of his glory that *is* on the head of the fat valley, hath been as its first-fruit before summer, that its beholder seeth, while it *is* yet in his hand he swalloweth it.

DOXA - glory, honour, magnificence – a divergent translation with "head of the fat valley" (KJV) rendered as "top of the high mountain" (engLXX) - the overall passage gives a contrast between the "crown" of Ephraim (V.1) to the later "crown" of the Lord himself (V.5 see below) - the 2nd meaning of the Heb. word [cf. Isa 4:2 above]: the glory on top of Ephraim

LXX ***KAI ESTAI TO ANTHOS TO EKPESON TÉS ELPIDOS TÉS*** **DOXÉS** ***EP AKROU TOU***
and shall be the flower the fallen of the hope of the glory upon tip of the

OROUS TOU HUPSÉLOU HÓS PRODROMOS SUKOU HO IDÓN AUTO PRIN É EIS
mountains of the high as forerunner of fig the seeing it before be into

TÉN CHEIRA AUTOU LABEIN AUTO THELÉSEI AUTO KATAPIEIN
the hand of him to take it shall will it to swallow

engLXX And the fading flower of the glorious hope on the top of the high mountain shall be as the early fig; he that sees it, before he takes it into his hand, will desire to swallow it down.

Isa. 28:5 In that day shall the LORD of hosts be for a crown of **glory**, and for a diadem of beauty, unto the residue of his people,

YLT In that day is Jehovah of Hosts for a crown of **beauty**, and for a diadem of glory, to the remnant of His people.

ELPIS - hope, expectation – a divergent translation with "glory" (KJV) or "beauty" (YLT), rendered as "hope" (engLXX) – the hope offered, by the contrast of what the Lord will be, to the "crowning" in the preceding verses: hope in that day Gk. [cf. Isa. 24:16 above]

LXX *TÉ HÉMERA EKEINÉ ESTAI KURIOS SABAÓTH HO STEPHANOS TÉS* ***ELPIDOS*** *HO*
with the day that shall be Lord of hosts the crown of the hope the

PLEKEIS TÉS DOXÉS TÓ KATALEIPHTHENTI TOU LAOU
plated of the glory to the remaining of the people

engLXX In that day the Lord of hosts shall be the crown of hope, the woven *crown* of glory, to the remnant of the people.

Jer. 3:19 But I said, How shall I put thee among the children, and give thee a pleasant[3] land, a **goodly** heritage of the hosts of nations? and I said, Thou shalt call me, My father; and shalt not turn away from me.

YLT And I have said, How do I put thee among the sons, and give to thee a desirable[3] land, a **beauteous** inheritance of the hosts of nations, and I say, My father - ye do call to Me, and from after Me ye do not turn back.

3. See CHEMDAH/CHAMUDOTH

NOT in LXX - a divergent translation with the question of "how shall I" (KJV) rendered as "So be it, Lord" (engLXX) – the land being *EKLEKTOS* is given its adjective, but "inheritance" stands without an adjective: word not translated

LXX *KAI EGÓ EIPA GENOITO KURIE HOTI TAXÓ SE EIS TEKNA KAI DÓSÓ SOI GÉN*
and I said be Lord since set you into children and give to you land

EKLEKTÉN[3] *KLÉRONOMIAN THEOU PANTOKRATOROS ETHNÓN KAI EIPA*
choice inheritance of God Almighty of nations and said

PATERA KALESETE ME KAI AP EMOU OUK APOSTRAPHÉSESTHE
Father call me and from me not turn

engLXX And I said, So be it, Lord, for *thou saidst* I will set thee among children, and will give thee a choice land, the inheritance of the Almighty God of the Gentiles: and I said, Ye shall call me Father; and ye shall not turn away from me.

Eze. 7:20 As for the **beauty** of his ornament, he set it in majesty: but they made the images of their abominations *and* of their detestable things therein: therefore have I set it far from them.

YLT As to the **beauty** of his ornament, for excellency He set it, and the images of their abominations, their detestable things -- they made in it, therefore I have given it to them for impurity,

NKJV 'As for the **beauty** of his ornaments, He set it in majesty; but they made from it the images of their abominations *and* their detestable things; therefore I have made it like refuse to them.

NASB They transformed the **beauty** of His ornaments into pride, and they made the images of their abominations *and* their detestable things with it; therefore I will make it an abhorrent thing to them.

NIV They took proud in their **beautiful** jewellery and used it to make their detestable idols. They made it into vile images; therefore I will make it a thing unclean for them.

NLT They were proud of their **beautiful** jewelry and used it to make detestable idols and vile images. Therefore, I will make all their wealth disgusting to them.

EKLEKTOS – a loose to divergent translation with "he set it in majesty" (KJV) or "for excellency He set it" (YLT), rendered as "they employed them for pride" (engLXX) - beautiful decoration or ornament [ornament, another meaning of the Gk. *KOSMOS*]

LXX ***EKLEKTA*** *KOSMOU EIS HUPERÉPHANIAN ETHENTO AUTA KAI EIKONAS TÓN BDELUGMATÓN*
choice decoration into arrogance set them and images of the abominations

AUTÓN EPOIÉSAN EX AUTÓN HENEKEN TOUTOU DEDÓKA AUTA AUTOIS EIS AKATHARSIAN
of them made out of them on account of this gave them to them into uncleanness

engLXX *As for* their choice ornaments, they employed them for pride, and they made of them images of their abominations: therefore have I made them uncleanness to them.

Eze. 20:6 In the day *that* I lifted up mine hand unto them, to bring them forth of the land of Egypt into a land that I had espied for them, flowing with milk and honey, which *is* the **glory** of all lands:

YLT In that day I did lift up My hand to them, to bring them forth from the land of Egypt, unto a land that I spied out for them, flowing with milk and honey, a **beauty** it *is* to all the lands,

KÉRION - honeycomb – a divergent translation with "I lifted up mine hand" (KJV) or "I did lift up My hand" (YLT), rendered as "I helped them with my hand" (engLXX): the preceding verse informs us "I lift up My hand to them, saying, I *am* Jehovah your God." (Eze. 20:5 YLT) indicating the purpose of lifting up the hand was to announce arrival and presence, before any act of ongoing help – honey and milk in abundance is reflected in the presence of cells, honeycombs everywhere: a glorious sight, a beautiful sight: honeycombs [cf. V.15 below]

LXX *EN EKEINÉ TÉ HÉMERA ANTELABOMÉN TÉ CHEIRI MOU AUTÓN TOU EXAGAGEIN*
in that the day took hold with the hand of me of them of the to lead

AUTOUS EK GÉS AIGUPTOU EIS TÉN GÉN HÉN HÉTOIMASA AUTOIS GÉN
them out of land of Egypt into the land which prepared for them land

RHEOUSAN GALA KAI MELI ***KÉRION*** *ESTI PARA PASAN TÉN GÉN*
flowing milk and honey honeycomb is by every the land

engLXX in that day I helped them with my hand, to bring them out of the land of Egypt into the land which I prepared for them, a land flowing with milk and honey, it is abundant beyond every land.

Eze. 20:15 Yet also I lifted up my hand unto them in the wilderness, that I would not bring them into the land which I had given *them*, flowing with milk and honey, which *is* the **glory** of all lands;

YLT And also, I, I have lifted up My hand to them in the wilderness, not to bring them in to the land that I had given, flowing with milk and honey, a **beauty** it *is* to all the lands,

KÉRION – honeycomb – a contrasting purpose for lifting up of the hand in announcement of presence V.5 is here used instead in proclaiming a stop and a prevention: the unbelieving being refused entry into the promised land - a loose translation with honey and milk in abundance reflected in the presence of cells, honeycombs everywhere - a glorious sight, a beautiful sight: honeycombs [cf. V.6 above]

LXX *KAI EGÓ EXÉRA TÉN CHEIRA MOU EP AUTOUS EN TÉ ERÉMÓ TO PARAPAN TOU*
and I lifted the hand of me over them in the desert the altogether of the

MÉ EISAGAGEIN AUTOUS EIS TÉN GÉN HÉN EDÓKA AUTOIS GÉN RHEOUSAN
not to bring them into the land which gave to them land flowing

GALA KAI MELI ***KÉRION*** *ESTI PARA PASAN TÉN GÉN*
milk and honey honeycomb is by every the land

engLXX But I lifted up my hand against them in the wilderness once for all, that I would not bring them into the land which I gave them, a land flowing with milk and honey, it is sweeter than all lands:

Eze. 25:9 Therefore, behold, I will open the side of Moab from the cities, from his cities *which are* on his frontiers, the **glory** of the country, Bethjeshimoth, Baalmeon, and Kiriathaim,

YLT Therefore, lo, I am opening the shoulder of Moab - from the cities – from his cities - from his frontier, the **beauty** of the land, Beth-Jeshimoth, Baal- Meon, and Kiriathaim,

NKJV therefore, behold, I will clear the territory of Moab of cities, of the cities on its frontier, the **glory** of the country, Beth Jeshimoth, Baal Meon, and Kirjathaim.

NASB therefore, behold, I am going to [b]deprive the flank of Moab of *its* cities, of its cities which are on its frontiers, the **glory** of the land, Beth-jeshimoth, Baal-meon and Kiriathaim,

NIV therefore I will expose the flank of Moab, beginning at its frontier towns – Beth Jeshimoth, Baal Meon and Kiriathaim – the **glory** of that land.

NLT I will open up their eastern flank and wipe out their **glorious** frontier towns—Beth-jeshimoth, Baal-meon, and Kiriathaim.

EKLEKTOS – a divergent translation with the addition of "above the fountain" (engLXX) – three cities are named as the best in the land of Moab

LXX *DIATOUTO IDOU EGÓ PARALUÓ TON ÓMON MÓAB APO POLEÓN AKRÓTÉRIÓN AUTOU*
therefore look I disable the shoulder of Moab from cities of borders of him

EKLEKTÉN *GÉN OIKON BETHASIMOUTH EPANÓ PÉGÉS POLEÓS PARATHALASSIAS*
choice land house of Bethasimuth above spring of city by sea

engLXX Therefore, behold, I will weaken the shoulder of Moab from his frontier cities, *even* the choice land, the house of Bethasimuth above the fountain of the city, by the sea-side.

Eze. 26:20 When I shall bring thee down with them that descend into the pit, with the people of old time, and shall set thee in the low parts of the earth, in places desolate of old, with them that go down to the pit, that thou be not inhabited; and I shall set **glory** in the land of the living;

YLT And I have caused thee to go down, with those going down to the pit, unto the people of old, and I have caused thee to dwell in the land, the lower parts - in wastes of old, with those going down to the pit, so that thou art not inhabited, and I have given **beauty** in the land of the living.

NOT in LXX – a divergent translation with "I shall set glory in the land of the living" (KJV) or "I have given beauty in the land of the living" (YLT), rendered as "nor stand upon the land of life" (engLXX) – word not translated

LXX *KAI KATABIBASÓ SE PROS TOUS KATABAINONTAS EIS BOTHRON PROS LAON AIÓNOS KAI*
and bring down you to the gone down into pit to people of age and

KATOIKIÓ SE EIS BATHÉ TÉS GÉS HÓS ERÉMON AIÓNION META KATABAINONTÓN EIS
dwell you into depth of the earth as desert everlasting with gone down into

BOTHRON HOPÓS MÉ KATOIKÉTHÉS MÉDE ANASTÉS EPI GÉS ZÓÉS
pit even so not dwell neither arise upon land of life

engLXX and I shall bring thee down to them that go down to the pit, to the people of old time, and shall cause thee to dwell in the depths of the earth, as in everlasting desolation, with them that go down to the pit, that thou mayest not be inhabited, nor stand upon the land of life;

Dan. 8:9 And out of one of them came forth a little horn, which waxed exceeding great, toward the south, and toward the east, and toward the **pleasant** *land*.

YLT And from the one of them come forth hath a little horn, and it exerteth itself greatly toward the south, and toward the east, and toward the **beauteous** *land*;

DUNAMIS - power, might, strength – a divergent translation with "a little horn" (KJV) given as "one strong horn" (engLXX) – the pleasant land, the beauteous land, Israel [understood] is the Lord's home: the Lord of hosts

LXX *KAI EK TOU ENOS AUTÓN EXÉLTHE KERAS HEN ISCHURON KAI EMEGALUNTHÉ*
and out of the one of them came forth horn one strong and magnified

PERISSÓS PROS TON NOTON KAI PROS TÉN ***DUNAMIN***
extremely to the south and to the mighty

engLXX And out of one of them came forth one strong horn, and it grew very great toward the south, and toward the host:

Dan. 11:16 But he that cometh against him shall do according to his own will, and none shall stand before him: and he shall stand in the **glorious** land, which by his hand shall be consumed.

YLT And he who is coming unto him doth according to his will, and there is none standing before him; and he standeth in the **desirable** land, and *it is* wholly in his hand.

SABEI aNT - beauty, glory – a direct translation – the 2nd meaning of the Heb. word [cf. Isa 4:2 above]: the glorious land

LXX *KAI POIÉSEI HO EISPOREUOMENOS PROS AUTON KATA TO THELÉMA AUTOU*
and shall do the entering to him according to the will of him

KAI OUK ESTIN HESTÓS KATA PROSÓPON AUTOU KAI STÉSETAI EN TÉ GÉ TOU
and not is stand according to face of him and shall stand in the land of the

SABEI *KAI TELESTHÉSETAI EN TÉ CHEIRI AUTOU*
glory and complete in the hand of him

engLXX And he that comes in against him shall do according to his will, and there is no one to stand before him: and he shall stand in the land of beauty, and it shall be consumed by his hand

---

Dan. 11:41 He shall enter also into the **glorious** land, and many *countries* shall be overthrown: but these shall escape out of his hand, *even* Edom, and Moab, and the chief of the children of Ammon.

YLT and hath come into the **desirable** land, and many do stumble, and these escape from his hand: Edom, and Moab, and the chief of the sons of Ammon.

SABAEIM aNT - beauty, glory – a direct translation – the 2nd meaning of the Heb. word [cf. Isa 4:2 above]: the beautiful land

LXX *KAI EISELEUSETAI EIS TÉN GÉN TOU* ***SABAEIM*** *KAI POLLOI ASTHENÉSOUSI KAI HOUTOI*
and shall enter into the land of the glory and many shall weaken and these

DIASÓTHÉSONTAI EK CHEIROS AUTOU EDÓM KAI MÓAB KAI ARCHÉ HUIÓN AMMÓN
shall deliver out of hand of him Edom and Moab and chief sons of Ammon

engLXX and he shall enter into the land of beauty, and many shall fail: but these shall escape out of his hand, Edom, and Moab, and the chief of the children of Ammon.

Dan. 11:45 And he shall plant the tabernacles of his palace between the seas in the **glorious** holy mountain; yet he shall come to his end, and none shall help him.

YLT and he planteth the tents of his palace between the seas and the holy **desirable** mountain, and hath come unto his end, and there is no helper to him.

SABAEIN aNT - beauty, glory – a direct translation – the 2nd meaning of the Heb. word [cf. Isa 4:2 above]: the glorious mountain

LXX *KAI PÉXEI TÉN SKÉNÉN AUTOU EPHADANÓ ANAMESON TÓN THALASSÓN EIS OROS* ***SABAEIN***
and | the tent of him royal pavilion between the seas into mountain glory
shall put together

HAGION HÉXEI HEÓS MEROUS AUTOU KAI OUK ESTIN HO RHUOMENOS AUTON
holy shall come unto regions of him and not is the rescue him

engLXX And he shall pitch the tabernacle of his palace between the seas in the holy mountain of beauty: *but* he shall come to his portion, and there is none to deliver him.

EKLEKTOS IN LXX FROM NO HEBREW

There are 10 places where the LXX uses *EKLEKTOS* with no corresponding Hebrew words in the OT Scripture.

The format below, except for one example (1Ki. 4:23), is as per the main exhaustive look at every passage of the 24 Hebrew words rendered by *EKLEKTOS*, but without the commentary section. The exception for 1 Kings 4:23 (3 Kings 4:23 LXX) is needful as there is 1 *EKLEKTOS* translating the Hebrew word BARI and 1 that does not translate from a Heb. word.

The ten places are:

2Sa. 8:8 (LXX 2Ki8:8); **2X:** 1Ki. 2:46 (LXX 3Ki3:46); 1Ki. 4:23 (LXX 3Ki.4:23); 1Ch. 18:8; Job 37:11; Pro. 17:3; Isa. 40:30; Jer. 31:39 (LXX 38:39); Jer. 46:15 (LXX 26:15)

2Sa. 8:8		And from Betah, and from Berothai, cities of Hadadezer, king David took exceeding much brass.
	YLT	and from Betah, and from Berothai, cities of Hadadezer, hath king David taken very much brass.
	LXX **2Ki8:8**	***KAI EK TÉS METEBAK KAI EK TÓN*** **EKLEKTÓN** ***POLEÓN TOU ADRAAZAR ELABEN HO*** and out of the Metebac and out of the choice cities of the Adraazar took the ***BASILEUS DAUID CHALKON POLUN SPHODRA EN AUTÓ EPOIÉSE SALÓMÓN TÉN THALASSAN*** king David copper much exceedingly in it made Solomon the sea ***TÉN CHALKÉN KAI TOUS STULOUS KAI TOUS LOUTÉRAS KAI PANTA TA SKEUÉ*** the bronze and the pillars and the wash-tubs and all the vessels
	engLXX	And king David took from Metebac, and from the choice cities of Adraazar, very much brass: with that Solomon made the brazen sea, and the pillars, and the lavers, and all the furniture.

1Ki. 2:46 So the king commanded Benaiah the son of Jehoiada; which went out, and fell upon him, that he died. And the kingdom was established in the hand of Solomon.

YLT And the king chargeth Benaiah son of Jehoiada, and he goeth out and falleth on him, and he dieth, and the kingdom is established in the hand of Solomon.

LXX **3Ki3:46**

KAI ENETEILATO HO BASILEUS SALÓMÓN TÓ BANAIA HUIÓ IÓDAE KAI EXÉLTHE KAI
and gave charge the king Solomon to the Benaiah son of Jehoiada and came forth and

ANEILEN AUTON KAI ÉN HO BASILEUS SALÓMÓN PHRONIMOS SPHODRA KAI SOPHOS KAI
executed him and was the king Solomon sagacity exceedingly and wisdom and

IOUDA KAI ISRAÉL POLLOI SPHODRA HÓS HÉ AMMOS HÉ EPI TÉS THALASSÉS EIS PLÉTHOS
Juda and Israel many exceedingly as the sand the upon the sea into multitude

ESTHIONTES KAI PINONTES KAI CHAIRONTES KAI SALÓMÓN ÉN ARCHÓN EN PASAIS TAIS
eating and drinking and rejoicing and Solomon was chief in all the

BASILEIAIS KAI ÉSAN PROSPHERONTES DÓRA KAI EDOULEUON TÓ SALÓMÓN PASAS TAS
kingdoms and they were bringing gifts and served the Solomon all the

HÉMERAS TÉS ZÓÉS AUTOU KAI SALÓMÓN ÉRXATO ANOIGEIN TA DUNASTEUMATA TOU LIBANOU
days of the life of him and Solomon began to open the domains of the Lebanon

KAI AUTOS ÓKODOMÉSE TÉN THERMAI EN TÉ ERÉMÓ KAI TOUTO TO ARISTON TÓ SALÓMÓN
and he built the Thermae in the desert and this the daily provision to the Solomon

TRIAKONTA KOROI SEMIDALEÓS KAI EXÉKONTA KOROI ALEUROU KEKOPANISMENOU DEKA
thirty measures of fine flour and sixty measures of wheat meal pounded ten

MOSCHOI ***EKLEKTOI*** *KAI EIKOSI BOES NOMADES KAI HEKATON PROBATA EKTOS ELAPHÓN*
calves choice and twenty oxen nomadic and hundred sheep outside stags

KAI DORKADÓN KAI ORNITHÓN ***EKLEKTÓN*** *NOMADÓN HOTI ÉN ARCHÓN EN PANTI PERAN*
and does and birds choice nomadic since was ruler in all region

TOU POTAMOU APO RHAPHI HEÓS GAZÉS EN PASI TOIS BASILEUSI PERAN TOU POTAMOU KAI
of the river from Raphi unto Gaza in all the kingdoms region of the river and

ÉN AUTÓ EIRÉNÉ EK PANTÓN TÓN MERÓN AUTOU KUKLOTHEN KAI KATÓKEI IOUDA KAI
was it peace out of all the sides of it all around and dwelt Juda and

ISRAÉL PEPOITHOTES HEKASTOS HUPO TÉN AMPELON AUTOU KAI HUPO TÉN SUKÉN AUTOU
Israel persuaded each under the vine of him and under the fig of him

ESTHIONTES KAI PINONTES KAI HEORTAZONTES APO DAN KAI HEÓS BÉRSABEE PASAS TAS
eating and drinking and feasting from Dan and unto Beersheba all the

HÉMERAS SALÓMÓN KAI HOUTOI HOI ARCHONTES TOU SALÓMÓN AZARIOU HUIOS SADÓK
days of Solomon and these the rulers of the Solomon Azariu son of Sadoc

TOU HIEREÓS KAI ORNIOU HUIOS NATHAN ARCHÓN TÓN EPHESTÉKOTÓN KAI EDRAMEN
the priest and Orniu son of Nathan chief of the commanders and accomplished

EPI TON OIKON AUTOU KAI SOUBA GRAMMATEUS KAI BASA HUIOS ACHITHALAM
over the house of him and Suba scribe and Basa son of Achitalam

ANAMINMNÉSKÓN KAI ABI HUIOS IÓAB ARCHISTRATÉGOS KAI ACHIRE HUIOS EDRAI EPI TAS
recorder and Abi son of Joab chief commander and Achire son of Edrai over the

ARSEIS KAI BANAIAS HUIOS IÓDAE EPI TÉS AULARCHIAS KAI EPI TOU PLINTHIOU KAI
taxing and Banaias son of Jodae over the temple and over the brickwork and

KACHOUR HUIOS NATHAN HO SUMBOULOS KAI ÉSAN TÓ SALÓMÓN TESSARAKONTA CHILIADES
Cachur son of Nathan the counseller and were for the Solomon forty thousand

TOKADES HIPPOI EIS HARMATA KAI DÓDEKA CHILIADES HIPPÓN KAI ÉN ARCHÓN EN PASI
breeding horses into chariots and twelve thousand horses and was ruler in all

TOIS BASILEUSIN APO TOU POTAMOU KAI HEÓS GÉS ALLOPHULÓN KAI HEÓS HORIÓN
the kingdoms from the river and unto land of Phillistines and unto borders

AIGUPTOU KAI SALÓMÓN HUIOS DAUID EBASILEUSEN EPI ISRAÉL KAI IOUDA EN HIEROUSALÉM
of Egypt and Solomon son of David reigned over Israel and Juda in Jerusalem

engLXX And Solomon commanded Banæas the son of Jodae, and he went forth and slew him. And king Solomon was very prudent and wise: and Juda and Israel *were* very many, as the sand which is by the sea for multitude, eating, and drinking, and rejoicing: and Solomon was chief in all the kingdoms, and they brought gifts, and served Solomon all the days of his life. And Solomon began to open the domains of Libanus, and he built Thermæ in the wilderness. And this was the daily provision of Solomon, thirty measures of fine flour, and sixty measures of ground meal, ten choice calves, and twenty oxen from the pastures, and a hundred sheep, besides stags, and does, and choice fed birds. For he ruled in all the country on this side the river, from Raphi unto Gaza, over all the kings on this side the river: and he was at peace on all sides round about; and Juda and Israel dwelt safely, every one under his vine and under his fig tree, eating and drinking and feasting, from Dan even to Bersabee, all the days of Solomon.

And these *were* the princes of Solomon; Azariu son of Sadoc the priest, and Orniu son of Nathan chief of the officers, and he went to his house; and Suba the scribe, and Basa son of Achithalam recorder, and Abi son of Joab commander-in-chief, and Achire son of Edrai *was* over the levies, and Banæas son of Jodae over the household and over the brickwork, and Cachur the son of Nathan *was* counsellor.

And Solomon had forty thousand brood mares for his chariots, and twelve thousand horses. And he reigned over all the kings from the river and to the land of the Philistines, and to the borders of Egypt: so Solomon the son of David reigned over Israel and Juda in Jerusalem.

1Ki. 4:23 Ten fat oxen, and twenty oxen out of the pastures, and an hundred sheep, beside harts, and roebucks, and fallowdeer, and fatted fowl.

YLT ten fat oxen, and twenty feeding oxen, and a hundred sheep, apart from hart, and roe, and fallow-deer, and fatted beasts of the stalls,

EKLEKTOS – a divergent translation with "harts, and roebucks, and fallowdeer, and fatted fowl" (KJV) or "hart, and roe, and fallow-deer, and fatted beasts of the stalls" (YLT), rendered much shorter by "stags, and choice fatted does" (engLXX) – There are two places in this passage with *EKLEKTOS*: the first translates BARI and the second has no corresponding Hebrew word, but is seen as part of a range of quality animals provided for the palace: I incorrectly attributed the word *EKLEKTOS* here to "fatted" in *SERIOUS*.

LXX **3Ki.4:23**

KAI DEKA MOSCHOI EKLEKTOI[1] *KAI EIKOSI BOES NOMADES KAI HEKATON*
and ten calves choice and twenty oxen grazing and hundred

PROBATA EKTOS ELAPHÓN KAI DORKADÓN[2] ***EKLEKTÓN*** *SITEUTA*
sheep outside of stags and does choice fatted

engLXX and ten choice calves, and twenty pastured oxen, and a hundred sheep, besides stags, and choice fatted does.

1Ch. 18:8 Likewise from Tibhath, and from Chun, cities of Hadarezer, brought David very much brass, wherewith Solomon made the brasen sea, and the pillars, and the vessels of brass.

YLT and from Tibhath, and from Chun, cities of Hadarezer, hath David taken very much brass; with it hath Solomon made the brazen sea, and the pillars, and the vessels of brass.

LXX

KAI EK TÉS MATABÉTH KAI EK TÓN ***EKLEKTÓN*** *POLEÓN TÓN ADRAAZAR*
and out of the Matabeth and out of the choice cities of the Adraazar

ELABE DAUID CHALKON POLUN SPHODRA EX AUTOU EPOIÉSE SALÓMÓN TÉN
took David copper much exceeding out of it made Solomon the

THALASSAN TÉN CHALKÉN KAI TOUS STULOUS KAI TA SKEUÉ TA CHALKA
sea the brazen and the pillars and the vessels the brazen

---

1. See BARI
2. See TSEBI

	engLXX	And David took out of Matabeth, and out of the chief cities of Adraazar very much brass: of this Solomon made the brazen sea, and the pillars, and the brazen vessels.
Job 37:11		Also by watering he wearieth the thick cloud: he scattereth his bright cloud:
	YLT	Yea, by filling He doth press out a cloud, scatter a cloud doth His light.
	LXX	*KAI* ***EKLEKTON*** *KATAPLASSEI NEPHELÉ DIASKORPIEI NEPHOS PHÓS AUTOU* and choice covers cloud disperses cloud light of him
	engLXX	And *if* a cloud obscures *what is* precious *to him*, his light will disperse the cloud.
Pro. 17:3		The fining pot *is* for silver, and the furnace for gold: but the LORD trieth the hearts.
	YLT	A refining pot *is* for silver, and a furnace for gold, And the trier of hearts *is* Jehovah.
	LXX	*HÓSPER DOKIMAZETAI EN KAMINÓ ARGUROS KAI CHRUSOS HOUTÓS* as tested in furnace silver and gold also ***EKLEKTAI*** *KARDIAI PARA KURIÓ* choice hearts by Lord
	engLXX	As silver and gold are tried in a furnace, so are choice hearts with the Lord.
Isa. 40:30		Even the youths shall faint and be weary, and the young men[3] shall utterly fall:
	YLT	Even youths are wearied and fatigued, and young men utterly stumble,
	LXX	*PEINASOUSI GAR NEÓTEROI KAI KOPIASOUSI NEANISKOI*[3] *KAI* ***EKLEKTOI*** hungered for youth and wearied young men and choice *ANISCHUES ESONTAI* without strength shall be

3. See BACHUR

	engLXX	For the young *men* shall hunger, and the youths shall be weary, and the choice *men* shall be powerless:
Jer. 31:39		And the measuring line shall yet go forth over against it upon the hill Gareb, and shall compass about to Goath.
	YLT	And gone out again hath the measuring line over-against it, unto the height of Gareb, and it hath compassed to Goah.
	LXX **38:39**	*KAI EXELEUSETAI HÉ DIAMETRÉSIS AUTÉS APENANTI AUTÓN HEÓS BOUNÓN* and shall go the measurement of her opposite of them until hills *GARÉB KAI PERIKUKLÓTHÉSETAI KUKLÓ EX* ***EKLEKTÓN*** *LITHÓN* of Gareb and encompass with circle out of choice stones
	engLXX	And the measurement of it shall proceed in front of them as far as the hills of Gareb, and it shall be compassed with a circular wall of choice stones.
Jer. 46:15		Why are thy valiant *men* swept away? They stood not, because the LORD did drive them.
	YLT	Wherefore hath thy bull been swept away? He hath not stood, because Jehovah thrust him away.
	LXX **26:15**	*DIATI EPHUGEN APO SOU HO APIS HO MOSCHOS HO* ***EKLEKTOS*** *SOU OUK* why fled from you the Apix the calf the choice of you not *EMEINEN HOTI KURIOS PARELUSEN AUTON* remain since Lord disabled him
	engLXX	Wherefore has Apis fled from thee? Thy choice calf has not remained; for the Lord has utterly weakened him.

a*EKLEKTOS*

Places where *EKLEKTOS* is not present in the LXX used

The Concordance of the LXX by George Morrish (1814-1911) mentions "**As the modern** [written late 19th century] **printed editions of the Septuagint are not quite uniform, and vary a great deal in marking the chapters and verses, it was necessary to follow some *one* Edition: that of Tischendorf (in two vols. 8vo. Leipsic) has been adopted. The Sixth Edition, 1880, has been used.**" Tischendorf (1815-1874) did a lot of work on textual criticism: the study of source texts. His version of the LXX differs in arrangement from the version translated by Sir Lancelot in 6 places. This latter version is the commonly available edition from the British Library and publishers like Hendrickson (Samuel Baxter) and is the one used in this work for quoting and reference.

The 6 places below do not contain *EKLEKTOS* as per Morrish's Conc. Note the refs in the headlines are those of the LXX as per Morrish; the refs quoted as per Lancelot's related version

The 6 a*EKLEKTOS*: 1Ki. 4:23; 2Ki. 3:19; Psa. 88:4; Jer. 32:20; Eze. 27:22; Hag. 2:22
I highlight in bold each ref. prior to each quoted section

1Ki. 4:23; 2Ki. 3:19; Psa. 88:4; Jer. 32:20; Eze. 27:22; Hag. 2:22

1Ki. 4:23 Ten fat oxen, and twenty oxen out of the pastures, and an hundred sheep, beside harts, and roebucks, and fallowdeer, and fatted fowl.

YLT ten fat oxen, and twenty feeding oxen, and a hundred sheep, apart from hart, and roe, and fallow-deer, and fatted beasts of the stalls,

NKJV ten **fatted** oxen, twenty oxen from the pastures, and one hundred sheep, besides deer, gazelles, roebucks, and fatted fowl.

NASB	ten **fat** oxen, twenty pasture-fed oxen, a hundred sheep besides deer, gazelles, roebucks, and fattened fowl.
NIV	ten head of **stall-fed** cattle, twenty of pasture-fed cattle and a hundred sheep and goats, as well as deer, gazelles, roebucks and choice fowl.
NLT	also 10 oxen from the **fattening** pens, 20 pasture-fed cattle, 100 sheep or goats, as well as deer, gazelles, roe deer, and choice poultry.

a*EKLEKTOS* – a divergent translation with "harts, and roebucks, and fallowdeer, and fatted fowl" (KJV) or "hart, and roe, and fallow-deer, and fatted beasts of the stalls" (YLT), rendered much shorter by "stags, and choice fatted does" (engLXX) – There are two places in this passage with *EKLEKTOS*: the first translates BARI and the second has no corresponding Hebrew word, but is seen as part of a range of quality animals provided for the palace: I incorrectly attributed the word *EKLEKTOS* here to "fatted" in *SERIOUS*.

LXX
3Ki.4:23

KAI DEKA MOSCHOI EKLEKTOI[1] *KAI EIKOSI BOES NOMADES KAI EKATON*
and ten calves choice and twenty oxen grazing and hundred

PROBATA EKTOS ELAPHÓN KAI DORKADÓN[2] *EKLEKTÓN KAI SITEUTA*
sheep outside of stags and does choice and fatted

engLXX and ten choice calves, and twenty pastured oxen, and a hundred sheep, besides stags, and choice fatted does.

1Ki. 4:23; **2Ki. 3:19**; Psa. 88:4; Jer. 32:20; Eze. 27:22; Hag. 2:22

2Ki. 3:19 And ye shall smite every fenced city, and every choice city, and shall fell every good tree, and stop all wells of water, and mar every good piece of land with stones.

1. See BARI
2. See TSEBI

A divergent translation with "and every choice city" (KJV) not translated

LXX **4Ki.3:19** ***KAI PATAXETE PASAN POLIN OCHURAN KAI PAN XULON AGATHON KATABALEITE KAI***
and ye shall strike every city strong and every tree good ye shall throw down and

PASAS PÉGAS HUDATOS EMPHRAXESTHE KAI PASAN MERIDA AGATHÉN ACHREIÓSETE EN LITHOIS
every well of water obstruct and every portion good spoil in stones

engLXX And ye shall smite every strong city, and ye shall cut down every good tree, and ye shall stop all wells of water, and spoil every good piece *of land* with stones.

1Ki. 4:23; 2Ki. 3:19; **Psa. 88:4**; Jer. 32:20; Eze. 27:22; Hag. 2:22

Psa. 89:3 I have made a covenant with my chosen, I have sworn unto David my servant,

YLT I have made a covenant for My chosen, I have sworn to David My servant:

LXX **88:3** ***DIETHEMÉN DIATHÉKÉN TOIS EKLEKTOIS[3] MOU ÓMOSA DAUID TÓ DOULÓ MOU***
ordained covenant with the choice of me sworn David the servant of me

engLXX I made a covenant with my chosen ones, I sware unto David my servant.

Psa. 89:4 Thy seed will I establish for ever, and build thy throne to all generations. Selah.

YLT 'Even to the age do I establish thy seed, and have built to generation and generation thy throne. Selah.

LXX **88:4** ***HEÓS TOU AIÓNOS HETOIMASÓ TO SPERMA SOU KAI OIKODOMÉSÓ EIS***
unto the age prepare the seed of you and build into

GENEAN KAI GENEAN TON THRONON SOU DIAPSALMA
generation and generation the throne of you pause

3. The BACHIR rendering occurs once. Morrish's Conc. of the LXX suggests a 2nd *EKLEKTOS* is present [Note the LXX ref of quote is that of the proofing text] - a divergent translation making the singular into the plural: "chosen ones" (engLXX) instead of "chosen" (KJV) when only David is in view Vss 3-4

engLXX I will establish thy seed for ever, and build up thy throne to all generations. Pause.

1Ki. 4:23; 2Ki. 3:19; Psa. 88:4; **Jer. 32:20**; Eze. 27:22; Hag. 2:22

Jer. 25:20 And all the mingled people, and all the kings of the land of Uz, and all the kings of the land of the Philistines, and Ashkelon, and Azzah, and Ekron, and the remnant of Ashdod,

LXX *KAI PANTAS TOUS SUMMIKTOUS KAI PANTAS TOUS BASILEIS ALLOPHULÓN*

32:20 and all the mixed and all the kings of Philistines

KAI TÉN ASKALÓNA KAI TÉN GAZAN KAI TÉN AKKARÓN KAI TO EPILOIPON AZÓTOU

and the Ashkelon and the Gaza and the Ekron and the remnant of Azotus

engLXX and all the mingled *people*, and all the kings of the Philistines, and Ascalon, and Gaza, and Accaron, and the remnant of Azotus,

1Ki. 4:23; 2Ki. 3:19; Psa. 88:4; Jer. 32:20; **Eze. 27:22**; Hag. 2:22

Eze. 27:22 The merchants of Sheba and Raamah, they *were* thy merchants: they occupied in thy fairs with chief of all spices, and with all precious stones, and gold.

LXX *EMPOROI SABBA KAI RHAMMA HOUTOI EMPOROI SOU META PRÓTÓN HÉDUSMATÓN*

merchants of Sabba and Rhamma these merchants of you with chief of spices

KAI LITHÓN CHRÉSTÓN KAI CHRUSON EDÓKAN TÉN AGORAN SOU

and stones precious and gold they gave the market of you

engLXX The merchants of Sabba and Ramma, these were thy merchants, with choice spices, and precious stones: and they brought gold to thy market.

1Ki. 4:23; 2Ki. 3:19; Psa. 88:4; Jer. 32:20; Eze. 27:22; **Hag. 2:22**

Hag. 2:22 And I will overthrow the throne of kingdoms, and I will destroy the strength of the kingdoms of the heathen; and I will overthrow the chariots, and those that ride in them; and the horses and their riders shall come down, every one by the sword of his brother.

LXX **2:23**
KAI KATASTREPSÓ THRONOUS BASILEÓN KAI OLOTHREUSÓ DUNAMIN BASILEÓN TÓN
and shall overthrow thrones of kings and shall destroy power of kings of the

ETHNÓN KAI KATASTREPSÓ HARMATA KAI ANABATAS KAI KATABÉSONTAI HIPPOI KAI
nations and shall overthrow chariots and riders and shall come down horses and

ANABATAI AUTÓN HEKASTOS EN RHOMPHAIA PROS TON ADELPHON AUTOU
riders of them each in sword to the brother of him

engLXX and I will overthrow the thrones of kings, and I will destroy the power of the kings of the nations; and I will overthrow chariots and riders; and the horses and their riders shall come down, every one by the sword striving against his brother.

Hag. 2:21 Speak to Zerubbabel, governor of Judah , saying, I will shake the heavens and the earth;

LXX **2:22**
EIPON PROS ZOROBABEL TON TOU SALATHIÉL EK PHULÉS IOUDA LEGÓN EGÓ
say to Zerubbabel the of the Salathiel out of tribe of Judah saying I

SEIÓ TON OURANON KAI TÉN GÉN KAI TÉN THALASSAN KAI TÉN XÉRAN
shake the heaven and the earth and the sea and the dry

engLXX Speak to Zorobabel the son of Salathiel, of the tribe of Juda, saying, I shake the heaven, and the earth, and the sea, and the dry *land*;

EPILEKTOS **aNT**

EPIKLEKTOS is a Greek word in the same family as *EKLEKTOS*.

EK is the preposition for "from" or "out of"

EPI is the preposition for "on" or "upon"

The root of *EPILEKTOS* and *EKLEKTOS* is "*-LEKTOS*" and differs from another family of words which also uses the same two prepositions which shows thereby that they not related: *EKLEGÓ* and *EPILEGÓ* [See BACHAR].

The flavour of *EPI* as in higher or, over or, highest, is well seen in the examples below.

List of word From Morrish's LXX Conc.	From Heb. Word:	Meaning (KJV)
Exo. 15:4	MIBCHAR	choice (3; 4 adj.) chosen (4) choicest (1)
Exo. 24:11	ATSILIM	chief men (1) nobles (1)
Jos. 17:16	NOT From Heb.	N/A
Jos. 17:18	NOT From Heb.	N/A
Eze. 17:3	TSAMMERETH	highest branch (2) top (1)
Eze. 17:22	This is *EKLEKTOS* see below	
Eze. 23:6	CHEMED	Ys desirable (3) pleasant (2) [CHEMER red wine 1 pure 1] Ss Desirable 3 Pleasant 2 [of red wine 1]

Eze. 23:7	MIBCHAR	= Exo. 15:4
Eze. 23:12	CHEMED	= Eze. 23:6
Eze. 23:23	CHEMED	= Eze. 23:6
Eze. 24:5	MIBCHAR	= Exo. 15:4
Joe. 3:5	MACHMAD	pleasant thing (4) desire (3) beloved fruit (1) pleasant place (1) goodly (1) lovely (1) pleasant (1)

Refs		**Text quotes KJV unless otherwise stated**
Exo. 15:4		Pharaoh's chariots and his host hath he cast into the sea: **his chosen** captains also are drowned in the Red sea.
	YLT	Chariots of Pharaoh and his force He hath cast into the sea; and **the choice of his** captains Have sunk in the Red Sea!
	NKJV	Pharaoh's chariots and his army He has cast into the sea; his **chosen** captains also are drowned in the Red Sea.
	NASB	"Pharaoh's chariots and his army He has cast into the sea; and the **choicest** of his officers are drowned in the Red Sea.
	NIV	Pharaoh's chariots and his army he has hurled into the sea. The **best** of Pharaoh's officers are drowned in the Red Sea.
	NLT	Pharaoh's chariots and army he has hurled into the sea. The **finest** of Pharaoh's officers are drowned in the Red Sea.

From Heb. MIBCHAR – choice (3; 4 adj.) chosen (4) choicest (1) - a divergent translation with "mounted" (engLXX) added – the best captains in view they are seen as excellent above others

LXX *HARMATA PHARAÓ KAI TÉN DUNAMIN AUTOU ERRHIPSEN EIS THALASSAN*
chariots of Pharaoh and the power of him tossed into sea

EPILEKTOUS *ANABATAS TRISTATAS KATEPOTHÉSAN EN ERUTHRA THALASSÉ*
choice mounted officers sank in red sea

engLXX He has cast the chariots of Pharao and his host into the sea, the chosen mounted captains: they were swallowed up in the Red Sea.

Exo. 24:11 And upon the **nobles** of the children of Israel he laid not his hand: also they saw God, and did eat and drink.

YLT and unto those of the sons of Israel who are near He hath not put forth His hand, and they see God, and eat and drink.

NKJV But on the **nobles** of the children of Israel He did not lay His hand. So They saw God, and they ate and drank.

NASB Yet He did not stretch out His hand against the **nobles** of the sons of Israel; and they saw God, and they ate and drank.

NIV But God did not raise his hand against these **leaders** of the Israelites; they saw God, and they ate and drank.

NLT And though these **nobles** of Israel gazed upon God, he did not destroy them. In fact, they ate a covenant meal, eating and drinking in his presence!

From Heb. ATSILIM - chief men (1) nobles (1) - a divergent translation since "they saw God" (KJV) is rendered as "they appeared in the place of God" (engLXX): could be read as, "they were there in God's presence" - The nobles are seen as the overseers and upper echelon of the people: the excellent over all

LXX *KAI TÓN* ***EPILEKTÓN*** *TOU ISRAÉL OU DIEPHÓNÉSEN OUDE EIS KAI ÓPHTHÉSAN*
and of the choice of the Israel not dissented neither one and appeared

	EN TÓ TOPÓ TOU THEOU KAI EPHAGON KAI EPION in the place of the God and ate and drank
engLXX	And of the chosen ones of Israel there was not even one missing, and they appeared in the place of God, and did eat and drink.
Jos. 17:16	And the children of Joseph said, the hill is not enough for us: and all the Canaanites that dwell in the land of the valley have chariots of iron, *both they* who *are* of Bethshean and her towns, and *they* who *are* of the valley of Jezreel.
YLT	And the sons of Joseph say, 'The hill is not found to us, and a chariot of iron *is* with every Canaanite who is dwelling in the land of the valley – to him who *is* in Beth-Shean and its towns, and to him who *is* in the valley of Jezreel.'
NKJV	But the children of Joseph said, "The mountain country is not enough for us; and all the Canaanites who dwell in the land of the valley have chariots of iron, *both those* who *are* of Beth Shean and its towns and *those* who *are* of the Valley of Jezreel."
NASB	The sons of Joseph said, "The hill country is not enough for us, and all the Canaanites who live in the valley land have chariots of iron, both those who are in Beth-shean and its towns and those who are in the valley of Jezreel."
NIV	The people of Joseph replied, 'The hill country is not enough for us, and all the Canaanites who live in the plain have chariots fitted with iron, both those in Beth Shan and its settlements and those in the Valley of Jezreel.'
NLT	The descendants of Joseph responded, "It's true that the hill country is not large enough for us. But all the Canaanites in the lowlands have iron chariots, both those in Beth-shan and its surrounding settlements and those in the valley of Jezreel. They are too strong for us."

NOT From Heb. - a divergent translation with "chariots" (KJV) rendered as "choice cavalry" (engLXX) – lit. "choice horse" is given

LXX *KAI EIPAN OUK ARESKEI HÉMIN TO OROS TO EPHRAIM KAI HIPPOS **EPILEKTOS***
and said not please us the mount the Ephraim and horse choice

KAI SIDÉROS TÓ CHANANAIÓ TÓ KATOIKOUNTI EN AUTÓ EN BAITHSAN KAI EN
and iron the cananite the dwelling in it in Bethshan and in

TAIS KÓMAIS AUTÉS EN TÉ KOILADI IESRAÉL
the towns of her in the valley of Jezrael

engLXX And they said, the mount of Ephraim does not please us, and the Chananite dwelling in it in Bæthsan, and in its villages, *and* in the valley of Jezrael, has choice cavalry and iron.

Jos. 17:18 But the mountain shall be thine; for it *is* a wood, and thou shalt cut it down: and the outgoings of it shall be thine: for thou shalt drive out the Canaanites, though they have iron chariots, *and* though they *be* strong.

YLT because the mountain is thine; because it *is* a forest - thou hast prepared it, and its outgoings have been thine; because thou dost dispossess the Canaanite, though it hath chariots of iron - though it *is* strong.'

NKJV but the mountain country shall be yours. Although it *is* wooded, you shall cut it down, and its farthest extent shall be yours; for you shall drive out the Canaanites, though they have iron chariots *and* are strong."

NASB but the hill country shall be yours. For though it is a forest, you shall clear it, and to its farthest borders it shall be yours; for you shall drive out the Canaanites, even though they have chariots of iron *and* though they are strong."

NIV but the forested hill country as well. Clear it, and its farthest limits will be yours; though the Canaanites have chariots fitted with iron and though they are strong, you can drive them out."

NLT The forests of the hill country will be yours as well. Clear as much of the land as you wish, and take possession of its farthest corners. And you will drive out the Canaanites from the valleys, too, even though they are strong and have iron chariots."

NOT From Heb. - a divergent translation with "iron chariots" (KJV) not translated and instead "chosen cavalry" (engLXX) rendered – lit. Gk. "choice horse" is given

LXX	***HO GAR DRUMOS ESTAI SOI HOTI DRUMOS ESTI KAI EKKATHARIEIS AUTON KAI*** the for wood shall be to you since wood is and clear away it and *ESTAI SOI KAI HOTAN EXOLOTHREUSÉS TON CHANANAION HOTI HIPPOS* shall be to you and when shall destroy utterly the chanaan since horse ***EPILEKTOS*** *AUTÓ ESTI SU GAR HUPERISCHUEIS AUTOU* choice to it is you for super strong of him
engLXX	For thou shalt have the wood, for there is a wood, and thou shalt clear it, and *the land* shall be thine; even when thou shalt have utterly destroyed the Chananite, for he has chosen cavalry; yet thou art stronger than he.

Eze. 17:3	And say, Thus saith the Lord GOD; A great eagle with great wings, longwinged, full of feathers, which had divers colours, came unto Lebanon, and took the **highest** branch of the cedar:
YLT	and thou hast said: Thus said the Lord Jehovah: the great eagle, great-winged, long-pinioned, full of feathers, that hath diverse colours, hath come in unto Lebanon, and it taketh the **foliage** of the cedar,
NKJV	and say, 'Thus says the Lord GOD: "A great eagle with large wings and long pinions, full of feathers of various colors, came to Lebanon and took from the cedar the **highest branch**.
NASB	saying, 'Thus says the Lord GOD, "A great eagle with great wings, long pinions and a full plumage of many colors came to Lebanon and took away the **top** of the cedar.
NIV	Say to them, "This is what the Sovereign LORD says: a great eagle with powerful wings, long feathers and full plumage of varied colours came to Lebanon. Taking hold of the **top** of a cedar,
NLT	Give them this message from the Sovereign Lord: "A great eagle with broad wings and long feathers, covered with many-colored plumage, came to Lebanon. He seized the **top** of a cedar tree

From Heb. TSAMMERETH – highest branch (2) top (1) - a divergent translation with "the diverse colours" (KJV) not translated – the highest branch is the overlooking uppermost branch

LXX *KAI EREIS TADE LEGEI KURIOS AETOS HO MEGAS HO MEGALOPTERUGOS*
and shall say thus says Lord eagle the great the large winged

HO MAKROS TÉ EKTASEI PLÉRÉS ONUCHÓN HOS ECHEI TO HÉGÉMA
the long the stretching full of claws which he has the purposing

EISELTHEIN EIS TON LIBANON KAI ELABE TA ***EPILEKTA*** *TÉS KEDROU*
to enter into the Lebanon and took the choice of the cedar

engLXX and thou shalt say, Thus saith the Lord; A great eagle with large wings, spreading them out very far, with many claws, which has the design of entering into Libanus- and he took the choice *branches* of the cedar:

Eze. 17:22 Thus saith the Lord GOD; I will also take of the **highest branch** of the high cedar, and will set *it*; I will crop off from the top of his young twigs a tender one, and will plant *it* upon an high mountain and eminent:

EKLEKTOS; NOT *EPILEKTOS* - From Heb. TSAMMERETH - highest branch (2) top (1) - comment from TSAMMERETH: ***EKLEKTOS*** – a direct like translation with all the elements meaning the same - the highest or best of the cedar described by the word: the highest, the top.

LXX *DIOTI TADE LEGEI KURIOS KAI LÉPSOMAI EGÓ EK TÓN* ***EKLEKTÓN*** *TÉS KEDROU EK*
since thus says Lord and take I out of the choice of the cedar out of

KORUPHÉS KARDIAS AUTÓN APOKNIÓ KAI KATAPHUTEUSÓ EGÓ EP OROS HUPSÉLON
crown of hearts of them pluck and plant I upon mountain high

engLXX For thus saith the Lord; I will even take of the choice *branches* of the cedar from the top *thereof*, I will crop off their hearts, and I will plant it on a high mountain:

Eze. 23:6 *Which were* clothed with blue, captains and rulers, all of them **desirable** young men, horsemen riding upon horses.

YLT Clothed with blue - governors and prefects, **desirable** young men all of them, horsemen, riding on horses,

NKJV *Who were* clothed in purple, captains and rulers, all of them **desirable** young men, horsemen riding on horses.

NASB who were clothed in purple, governors and officials, all of them **desirable** young men, horsemen riding on horses.

NIV clothed in blue, governors and commanders, all of them **handsome** young men, and mounted horsemen.

NLT They were all **attractive** young men, captains and commanders dressed in handsome blue, charioteers driving their horses.

From Heb. CHEMED – Ys desirable (3) pleasant (2) [CHEMER red wine (1) pure (1)]; Ss Desirable (3) Pleasant (2) [of red wine (1)] – a direct translation – with the adjectives of colour, stature, importance, all preceding, there is no surprise to the build up to these men being desirable, handsome and attractive: then just as "excellent" as per *EKLEKTOS*, the young men were deemed "highly" desirable and thus *EPILEKTOS* was used

LXX *ENDEDUKOTAS HUAKINTHINA HÉGOUMENOUS KAI STRATÉGOUS NEANISKOI*
clothed with blue leaders and officers young men

KAI ***EPILEKTOI*** *PANTES HIPPEIS HIPPAZOMENOI EPH HIPPÓN*
and choice all horse riders upon horses

engLXX clothed with purple, princes and captains; *they were* young men and choice, all horsemen riding on horses.

Eze. 23:7 Thus she committed her whoredoms with them, with all them *that were* the **chosen** men of Assyria, and with all on whom she doted: with all their idols she defiled herself.

YLT And she giveth her whoredoms on them, the **choice** of the sons of Asshur, all of them - even all on whom she doted, by all their idols she hath been defiled.

NKJV Thus she committed her harlotry with them, all of them **choice** men of Assyria; and with all for whom she lusted, with all their idols, she defiled herself.

NASB She bestowed her harlotries on them, all of whom *were* the **choicest** men of Assyria; and with all whom she lusted after, with all their idols she defiled herself.

NIV She gave herself as a prostitute to all the **elite** of the Assyrians and defiled herself with all the idols of everyone she lusted after.

NLT And so she prostituted herself with the **most desirable** men of Assyria, worshiping their idols and defiling herself.

From Heb. MIBCHAR - choice (3; 4 adj.) chosen (4) choicest (1) – a divergent translation with "idols" (KJV) rendered as "thoughts" (LXX-inter) or "devices" (engLXX) – the best of the men, the most desirable young men, understood as those whom Samariah (V.4) lusted after

LXX *KAI EDÓKE TÉN PORNEIAN AUTÉS EP AUTOUS* ***EPILEKTOI*** *HUIOI ASSURIÓN PANTES KAI EPI*
LXX-inter and gave the whoredoms of her upon them choice sons Assyrians all and upon

PANTAS HOUS EPETHETO EN PASI TOIS ENTHUMÉMASIN AUTOIS EMIAINETO
all whom doted in all the thoughts to them defile

engLXX And she bestowed her fornication upon them; all were choice sons of the Assyrians: and on whomsoever she doted herself, with them she defiled herself in all *their* devices.

Eze. 23:12 She doted upon the Assyrians *her* neighbours, captains and rulers clothed most gorgeously, horsemen riding upon horses, all of them **desirable** young men[1].

YLT On sons of Asshur she hath doted, governors and prefects, neighbouring ones - clothed in perfection, horsemen, riding on horses, **desirable** young men all of them.

NKJV “She lusted for the neighboring Assyrians, captains and rulers, clothed most gorgeously, horsemen riding on horses, all of them **desirable** young men.

NASB She lusted after the Assyrians, governors and officials, the ones near, magnificently dressed, horsemen riding on horses, all of them **desirable** young men.

NIV She too lusted after the Assyrians – governors and commanders, warriors in full dress, mounted horsemen, all **handsome** young men.

NLT She fawned over all the Assyrian officers—those captains and commanders in handsome uniforms, those charioteers driving their horses—all of them **attractive** young men.

From Heb. CHEMED - Ys desirable (3) pleasant (2) [CHEMER red wine (1) pure (1)]; Ss Desirable (3) Pleasant (2) [of red wine (1)] – a direct translation – the fact that they were young men [from BACHUR alone] is not enough emphasis and the Heb. also has CHEMED to over emphasise the desirability of who was lusted after: overly desirable young men [cf. Eze. 23:23 below]

LXX *EPI TOUS HUIOUS TÓN ASSURIÓN EPETHETO HÉGOUMENOUS KAI*
upon the sons of the Assyrian set on leaders and

STRATÉGOUS TOUS EGGUS AUTÉS ENDEDUKOTAS EUPARUPHA HIPPEIS
officers the near of her clothed fine garments horse

HIPPAZOMENOUS EPH HIPPÓN NEANISKOI[1] ***EPILEKTOI*** *PANTES*
riders upon horses young men choice all

engLXX She doted upon the sons of the Assyrians, princes and captains, her neighbours, clothed with fine linen, horsemen riding on horses; *they were* all choice young men.

Eze. 23:23 The Babylonians, and all the Chaldeans, Pekod, and Shoa, and Koa, *and* all the Assyrians with them: all of them **desirable** young men[2], captains and rulers, great lords and renowned, all of them riding upon horses.

1. See BACHUR

YLT Sons of Babylon, and of all Chaldea, Pekod, and Shoa, and Koa, all the sons of Asshur with them, **desirable** young men, governors and prefects, all of them - rulers and proclaimed ones, riding on horses, all of them.

NKJV The Babylonians, all the Chaldeans, Pekod, Shoa, Koa, all the Assyrians with them, all of them **desirable** young men, governors and rulers, captains and men of renown, all of them riding on horses.

NASB the Babylonians and all the Chaldeans, Pekod and Shoa and Koa, *and* all the Assyrians with them; **desirable** young men, governors and officials all of them, officers and men of renown, all of them riding on horses.

NIV the Babylonians and all the Chaldeans, the men of Pekod and Shoa and Koa, and all the Assyrians with them, **handsome** young men, all of them governors and commanders, chariot officers and men of high rank, all mounted on horses.

NLT For the Babylonians will come with all the Chaldeans from Pekod and Shoa and Koa. And all the Assyrians will come with them—**handsome** young captains, commanders, chariot officers, and other high-ranking officers, all riding their horses.

From Heb. CHEMED - Ys desirable (3) pleasant (2) [CHEMER red wine 1 pure 1]; Ss Desirable 3 Pleasant 2 [of red wine 1] – a direct translation - the fact that they were young men [from BACHUR alone] is not enough emphasis and the Heb. also has CHEMED to over emphasise the desirability of who was lusted after: overly desirable young men [cf. Eze. 23:12 above]

LXX *HUIOUS BABULÓNOS KAI PANTAS TOUS CHALDAIOUS PHAKOUK KAI SOUE KAI HUCHOUE KAI*
sons of Babylon and all the Chaldeans Phakoud and Soue and Huchoue and

PANTAS HUIOUS ASSURIÓN MET AUTÓN NEANISKOUS[2] ***EPILEKTOUS*** *HÉGEMONAS KAI*
all sons of Assyria with them young men choice leaders and

STRATÉGOUS PANTAS TRISSOUS KAI ONOMASTOUS HIPPEUONTAS EPH HIPPÓN
commanders all tribunes and renowned riding upon horses

2. See BACHUR

engLXX the children of Babylon, and all the Chaldeans, Phacuc, and Sue, and Hychue, and all the sons of the Assyrians with them; choice young men, governors and captains, all princes and renowned, riding on horses.

Eze. 24:5 Take the **choice** of the flock, and burn also the bones under it, *and* make it boil well, and let them seethe the bones of it therein.

YLT The **choice** of the flock to take, and also to pile of the bones under it, boil it thoroughly, yea, cook its bones in its midst.

NKJV Take the **choice** of the flock. Also pile *fuel* bones under it, make it boil well, and let the cuts simmer in it."

NASB "Take the **choicest** of the flock, and also pile wood under the pot. Make it boil vigorously. Also seethe its bones in it."

NIV take **the pick** of the flock. Pile wood beneath it for the bones; bring it to the boil and cook the bones in it.

NLT Use only the **best** sheep from the flock, and heap fuel on the fire beneath the pot. Bring the pot to a boil, and cook the bones along with the meat.

From Heb. MIBCHAR - choice (3; 4 adj.) chosen (4) choicest (1) – a divergent translation with "well" (KJV) or "thoroughly" (YLT) not rendered – the best of the flock: no discernible difference here from *EKLEKTOS*

LXX *EX* ***EPILEKTON*** *KTÉNÓN EILÉMMENÓN KAI HUPOKAIE TA OSTA HUPOKATÓ*
out of choice cattle take and burn the bones under

AUTÓN EZESE KAI HÉPSÉTAI TA OSTA AUTÉS EN MESÓ AUTÉS
of them boil and cook the bones of her in midst of her

engLXX *which are* taken from choice cattle, and burn the bones under them: her bones are boiled and cooked in the midst of her.

Joe. 3:5 Because ye have taken my silver and my gold, and have carried into your temples my goodly **pleasant** things:

YLT In that My silver and My gold ye took, and My **desirable** things that are good, ye have brought in to your temples.

NKJV Because you have taken My silver and My gold, and have carried into your temples My **prized** possessions.

NASB Since you have taken My silver and My gold, brought My **precious** treasures to your temples,

NIV For you took my silver and my gold and carried off my **finest** treasures to your temples.

NLT You have taken my silver and gold and all my precious treasures, and have carried them off to your pagan temples.

From Heb. MACHMAD - pleasant thing (4) desire (3) beloved fruit (1) pleasant place (1) goodly (1) lovely (1) pleasant (1) – a direct translation – the desirable, the pleasant things of the temple in Jerusalem – this is no different to how *EKLEKTOS* is used to translate CHEPHETS or indeed *EPILEKTOS* (above) from CHEMED: desirable, pleasant things seen as best, over and above others: overly desirable

LXX 4:5 *ANTH HÓN TO ARGURION MOU KAI TO CHRUSION MOU ELABETE KAI TA*
because the silver of me and the gold of me ye took and the

EPILEKTA *MOU TA KALA EISÉNEGKATE EIS TOUS NAOUS HUMÓN*
choice of me the good ye brought into the temples of you

engLXX because ye have taken my silver and my gold, and ye have brought my choice ornaments into your temples;

TABLE SHEWING THE ORDER OF SEVERAL CHAPTERS AND VERSES IN JEREMIAH, AS THEY APPEAR IN THE HEBREW AND SEPTUAGINT RESPECTIVELY.

Hebrew, Vulgate, & English. CHAPTER	*Septuagint.* CHAPTER	*Hebrew, Vulgate, & English.* CHAPTER	*Septuagint.* CHAPTER
25 to v. 14	25 to v. 14.	39 from v. 3 to 14	wanting.
„ from v. 14 to the end	32.	40	47.
26	33.	41	48.
27 to v. 19	34.	42	49.
„ from v. 19 to the end	wanting.	43	50.
28	35.	44	51 to v. 31.
29	36.	45	„ from v. 31 to the end.
30	37.	46	26.
31	38.	47	29 first 7 verses.
32	39.	48 to v. 45	31.
33 to v. 14	40.	„ from v. 45 to the end	wanting.
„ from v. 14 to the end	wanting.	49 first 5 verses	30 first 5 verses.
34	41.	„ from v. 7 to 23	29 from v. 7 to the end.
35	42.	„ from v. 23 to 28	30 5 last verses.
36	43.	„ from v. 28 to 34	„ the 6 vv. following v. 5.
37	44.	„ from v. 34 to the end	25 from v. 13 to the end.
38	45.	50	27.
39 the 3 first verses, and 5 last.	46.	51	28.
		52	52.

β Gr. face. γ Or, cut his hair; not in *Alex.* ε *Alex.* + 'the thrones of'

Chart of Jeremiah changes of chapters and verses between Heb. and LXX

As reproduced by Samuel Bagster
N.B. Jeremiah 33:24 is not to be found in the LXX = "wanting"

ἐκλεκτός.

Gen. 23: 6	Pro. 17: 3[a]
41: 2, 4, 5	Cant. 5:15
7, 18	6: 8, 9
20	Isa. 22: 7, 8
Exo. 14: 7	28:16
30:23	40:30
Nu. 11:28	42: 1
Deu. 12:11	43:20
Jud. 20:15, 34	45: 4
1 Sa. 24: 3	49: 2
26: 2	54:12
2 Sa. 8: 8	65: 9, 15
21: 6	23
22:27, 27	Jer. 3:19
1 Ki. (3) *p46bis*	10:17
4:23	22: 7
23+A	26:15
23	31:15
2 Ki. 3:19+A	32:20
8:12	38:39
19:23	Lam. 1:15
1 Ch. 7:40	5:13, 14
9:22	Eze. 7:20
16:13	17: 3 A[b]
18: 8	22[c]
Ezra 5: 8	19:12, 14
Neh. 5:18	25: 9
Job 37:10	27:20
Psa. 17:27, 27	22 A[d]
77:31	24
88: 4	31:16
4+S[1]	Dan. 11:15
20	Amos 5:11
104: 6, 43	Hab. 1:16
105: 5, 23	Hag. 2: 7
140: 4	22+A
Pro. 8:19	Zec. 7:14
12:24	11:16

[a] S[1] ἐκλέγω. [b] *pro* ἐπίλεκτος.
[c] A ἐπίλεκτος. [d] *pro* χρηστός.

ἐπίλεκτος.

Exo. 15: 4	Eze. 23: 6,7,12
24:11	23
Jos. 17:16, 18	24: 5
Eze. 17: 3[a]	Joel 3: 5
22 A[b]	

[a] A ἐκλεκτός. [b] *pro* ἐκλεκτός.

Portion of pages of George Morrish's Concordance of Greek words in the LXX containing *EKLEKTOS* and *EPILEKTOS*

KEY to abbreviations
Separate list (repeated) for bible book Refs
Separate list of Gk. letters and their Anglicised representation

Adj.	Adjective	Gen.	Genesis
a*EKLEKTOS*	The word *EKLEKTOS* not present	Gk.	Greek
Amo.	Amos	Heb.	Hebrew
aNT	Word not used in the NT	Hos.	Hosea
C	Clement	i.e.	That is to say
cf.	Compare	Isa.	Isaiah
Ch.	Chronicles	Jer.	Jeremiah
Conc.	Concordance	Joe.	Joel
Dan.	Daniel	Jos.	Joshua
Deu.	Deuteronomy	Jud.	Judges
e.g.	For example	Ki.	Kings
Eng.	English	KJV	King James Version
engLXX	Full English translated section of LXX	Lam.	Lamentations
Est.	Esther	Lat.	Latin
Exo.	Exodus	*LDM*	*Leadership is Male?* published by Jarom Books ISBN 9781898158202 paperback 288 pages available as eBook
Eze.	Ezekiel		
Ezr.	Ezra		

Lev.	Leviticus
lit.	Literally
LXX	Septuagint
LXX-inter	Interlinear rendering of LXX
Mal.	Malachi
Mic.	Micah
N/A	Not Applicable
NASB	New American Standard Bible
N.B.	Lat. Nota Bene: note well; take note
Neh.	Nehemiah
NIV	New International Version
NKJV	New King James Version
NLT	New Living Translation
NT	New Testament
Num.	Numbers
OT	Old Testament
P.	Page
Pro.	Proverbs
Psa.	Psalm/s
Ref. or ref.	Reference (usually of a bible Ref.)
RT	Received Text
Rut.	Ruth
Sa.	Samuel
SERIOUS	*Serious Mistranslations of the bible* published by Jarom Books
	ISBN 9781898158219 paperback 352 pages available as eBook
Sng.	Song of Solomon
Ss	Strong's – James Strong Head of the team that produced Conc.
V.	Verse
Vo.	Verso
Vs.	Verses
YLT	Young's Literal Translation
Ys	Robert Young Author of Analytical Conc. & YLT
Zec.	Zechariah

For O.T. books in the regular bible order

Genesis	- Gen.	Ezra	- Ezr.	Daniel	- Dan.
Exodus	- Exo.	Nehemiah	- Neh.	Hosea	- Hos.
Leviticus	- Lev.	Esther	- Est.	Joel	- Joe.
Numbers	- Num.	Psalm	- Psa.	Amos	- Amo.
Deuteronomy	- Deu.	Proverbs	- Pro.	Micah	- Mic
Joshua	- Jos.	Ecclesiastes	- Ecc.	Nahum	- Nah.
Judges	- Jud.	Song of Sol.	- Sng.	Habakkuk	- Hab.
Ruth	- Rut.	Isaiah	- Isa.	Zephaniah	- Zep.
Samuel	- Sa.	Jeremiah	- Jer.	Haggai	- Hag.
Kings	- Ki.	Lamentations	- Lam.	Zechariah	- Zec.
Chronicles	- Ch.	Ezekiel	- Eze.	Malachi	- Mal.

Anglicised Greek letter Chart

A	Α-α	Alpha	TH	Θ-θ	Thēta	O	Ο-ο	Omīcron	CH	Χ-χ	Chī
B	Β-β	Bēta	I	Ι-ι	Iōta	P	Π-ϖ	Pī	PS	Ψ-ψ	Psī
G	Γ-γ	Gamma	K	Κ-κ	Kappa	R	Ρ-ρ	Rhō	Ó	Ω-ω	Ōmega
D	Δ-δ	Delta	L	Λ-λ	Lambda	S	Σ-ς,σ	Sigma	H	Refers to grave accent (`) present over an initial vowel/s of a word in the Gk.	
E	Ε-ε	Epsīlon	M	Μ-μ	Mu	T	Τ-τ	Tau			
Z	Ζ-ζ	Zēta	N	Ν-ν	Nu	U	Υ-υ	Upsīlon			
É	Η-η	Ēta	X	Ξ-ξ	Xī	PH	Φ-φ	Phī			

List of bible passages